BACK FROM THE BRINK

PETER SNOWDON

Back from the Brink

The Inside Story of the Tory Resurrection

Harper
Press

To Julia, with all my heart

HarperPress
An imprint of HarperCollins*Publishers*
77–85 Fulham Palace Road,
Hammersmith, London W6 8JB
www.harpercollins.co.uk

Published by HarperPress in 2010

A catalogue record for this book is available from the British Library

ISBN 13 978-0-00-730725-8
ISBN 10 0-00-730725-X

Set in Minion by Palimpsest Book Production Limited,
Grangemouth, Stirlingshire

Printed and bound in Great Britain by Clays Ltd, St Ives plc

CONTENTS

Introduction

'We will be tested. I will be tested. I'm ready for that . . . So yes, there is a steep climb ahead. But I tell you this: the view from the summit will be worth it.' David Cameron could not have chosen a more apt metaphor to describe the journey his party has to complete if it is to return to power. The scale of the task is formidable. Thirteen years ago, the British people ejected the Conservative Party from office in a landslide. So modest has the Conservative electoral recovery been since 1997 that the party Cameron leads into this year's election is barely halfway up the mountain.

In order to win the general election with an overall majority of one, his party has to achieve something quite historic: it would have to win 117 seats, and a swing from Labour of 6.9 per cent. Not since 1931 has the party managed to make up so much ground in one election. The greatest swing the Tories have achieved since the Second World War is 5.2 per cent, in the election that brought Margaret Thatcher to power in 1979. Then, the Conservatives went into the election with 277 seats. Now the party has just under two hundred. David Cameron will have to emulate the success Tony Blair accomplished in 1997, transforming the electoral landscape of Britain in just one night. It is a very tall order, but for all the difficulties they face, under Cameron the Conservatives stand a far better chance of success than at any time since 1992 – the last time the party won a general election.

The thirteen years since Tony Blair's 1997 landslide victory have been a chastening experience for a party that had become used to power. Before 1997, the Conservative Party's dominance was such that the twentieth century became known as the 'Conservative century'.[1] The party was in office, either with a working majority or as the lead partner of a coalition, for two-thirds of the century. By contrast, Labour won power with a majority above single figures on just three occasions: 1945, 1966 and 1997. In most cases Labour governments were swiftly expelled from office by a resurgent Tory opposition. The party's extraordinary success in recovering and holding on to power was due to its ability to adapt its policies and its appeal. More often than not, the Conservatives used their time in opposition wisely. The clearest example is after Labour's landslide in 1945. Within six years the Conservatives were returned to office, having revitalised their organisation and conducted a wide-ranging review of policy. Although Winston Churchill retained his standing as a popular war leader, his party had become deeply unpopular and out of touch by the end of the Second World War. By learning the lessons of defeat after 1945, the party was able to move on and forge a new direction.

The defeat in 1997 left the Tories with fifty or so fewer seats than after the Labour landslide of 1945, but the subsequent period in the wilderness would be far less propitious. The roots of the party's recent difficulties can be found in the Thatcher revolution. Mrs Thatcher and her government transformed British politics. The Conservatives' electoral success in the 1980s was due in large part to her forceful and determined leadership. But when she began to lose touch with the country after her third successive election victory, it would not be long before many in the party turned on her. The Tories' appeal to voters narrowed. They had become identified with the free market and individual freedom, but were perceived as being indifferent to social problems.

The bitterness that stemmed from the trauma of Mrs Thatcher's downfall and the divisions that underpinned it would sap the party's appetite for power in the 1990s. New Labour was born out of the rise and fall of Mrs Thatcher. Only by adapting to the Thatcher revolution did Labour find a way of becoming electable again. After eighteen long years in opposition it was desperate to win office, and as a result it embraced the formula that had sustained the Tories in government for so much of the twentieth century: adaptability and a hunger for power. The Conservative Party lost these qualities long before 1 May 1997.

In failing to adapt to the realities of the new political scene, the Conservatives dug themselves into an even deeper hole after the Labour landslide in 1997. Ignoring the public mood, they retreated to the margins of political debate, choosing a succession of unelect-able leaders through a combination of bitter enmity and ideological fixation. So grave was the malaise that had taken hold of the party, and so weak was its leadership, that in the autumn of 2003 it teetered on the brink. The prospect of a third consecutive electoral defeat devastating the party was very real.

In their own peculiar ways, each of the three leaders between 1997 and 2005 – William Hague, Iain Duncan Smith and Michael Howard – attempted to broaden the party's appeal in opposition. Why and how they failed forms the story of the first half of this book. While Howard was unable to attract greater support among the electorate, the party began to regain a sense of discipline and purpose after years of infighting and recrimination. But the personal feuds and ideological differences that had beset the parliamentary party since the early 1990s threatened to return with a vengeance after the defeat in May 2005. Annihilation had been averted, but the Tories had recovered little ground.

The emergence of a new generation of modernising Conservative politicians, led by David Cameron and George Osborne, untainted by the dying days of the last Tory government, is pivotal to this story. If the Conservative Party's decline was shaped by the legacy of Margaret Thatcher, the twists and turns in its resurrection have been influenced by the other commanding figure in British politics of recent times: Tony Blair. By learning the lessons from New Labour's electoral success under Blair, this new generation of modernising Tories have succeeded where their predecessors so visibly failed.

In December 2005, David Cameron achieved something few before him had ever accomplished. In just four and a half years he had gone from novice backbencher to Leader of the Opposition. He would have the same amount of time to pull the party back to the centre of British politics and reinvigorate it to the point of being a credible alternative government. It would be an audacious undertaking for a thirty-nine-year-old politician. The second half of *Back from the Brink* tells the story of how Cameron has sought to change his party. In essence, he has tried to heal old wounds and restore a sense of balance to Conservatism by reviving a concern for social reform.

Cameron's project to modernise the party has given it a new lease of life, yet at times it has seemed perilously close to falling apart. There have been three moments when his leadership was under severe pressure: after Gordon Brown became Prime Minister in June 2007; in the immediate aftermath of the financial crisis in October 2008; and during the expenses crisis in May 2009. On each occasion, the Conservative Party's recovery was at stake, as was Cameron's authority as leader. The fact that the Cameron project was in peril on each occasion exposes the flaws in the party's strategic direction, but at the same time it throws light on the tactical agility of its leadership in bouncing back.

David Cameron's mission to revive the fortunes of the Conservative Party has encountered reversals, yet it remains intact. Whether voters believe that he and his party are ready to take on the responsibility of governing the country is still to be seen. In Gordon Brown, the Conservatives face a battle-hardened Prime Minister who has been at or near the summit of British politics for the best part of two decades, both in opposition and in government. Brown is a great survivor: he has seen off two plots from within his Cabinet to remove him in the last two years. For the man Cameron describes as 'a steamroller who just keeps going', the general election will be a hard-fought battle to the end.

Much is at stake for both the old warhorse and the young pretender of British politics. For Brown, leading Labour into a fourth term would represent the most impressive recovery by an incumbent government in modern history. For Cameron, forming a government would end the longest uninterrupted period in opposition his party has endured since 1832. A fourth successive election defeat, however narrow, would represent a massive failure for everything Cameron has sought to achieve in the past four years, and would reduce the party to a state of acrimony and division. If the Conservatives cannot win amidst the economic gloom that pervades the country in 2010, when can they?

Based on more than 120 interviews with figures from across the Conservative Party – from successive leaders to representatives of the grassroots – this book tells the story of how a once formidable fighting force in British politics stared into the abyss before making its way back to be in contention for power. By talking to a wide range of party insiders, both on and off the record, I hope to have built up a candid and unvarnished account that sheds new light on a dramatic tale of decline and renaissance.

The Conservative Party may have come back from the brink of disaster, but rediscovering its winning formula has been far from easy. As David Cameron and his party prepare for their steep climb to the summit in the months ahead, it would probably be best if they did not look down. Theirs has been a long, harsh and often painful journey. I hope that readers will find it a compelling one.

Peter Snowdon
December 2009

ONE

The Makings of a Landslide

As the sun rose on a fine spring day, an exuberant Tony Blair left a rally on the South Bank of the River Thames and headed for his Islington home to catch a few hours' sleep. Blair had spent much of the early morning soaking up the adulation of friends, colleagues and supporters. 'A new dawn has broken, has it not?' he exclaimed to a party that had not won a general election for twenty-three years. On 1 May 1997 the country had placed its faith in Labour after the party had spent almost two decades in the wilderness. Friday, 2 May would usher in a new regime in Downing Street and a new era for British politics.

There was not much left of the old regime. It had been swept from office in a landslide. 'I remember driving back to London from Cornwall at 5 a.m. and realising that there were great swathes of the West Country that no longer had a Conservative MP. I didn't drive through a single Conservative seat until Wiltshire.'[1] Sebastian Coe, the former double Olympic gold medallist, was one of 178 Tory MPs who lost their seats. From Lands End to John o'Groats, voters had purged themselves of a party that once dominated Britain's electoral landscape. Half the parliamentary party had been wiped out overnight: only 165 were left standing by the morning. The party had polled just 31 per cent of the vote, its lowest showing since 1832, the year of the Great Reform Act. Middle England had deserted the party in droves. Leafy Birmingham Edgbaston, true blue since the Second World War, was the first of many seats to fall to New Labour's advance as Tony Blair led his party to victory with an overall majority of 179, a post-war record. Not one Conservative MP was returned to Westminster from Scotland or Wales. The surviving rump represented the outskirts of London, the Home Counties and a retinue of rural shires and market towns. The Liberal Democrats, recording the best result for a third party since 1929, sliced into Tory heartlands, picking up votes that had been cast tactically to ensure total defeat of John Major's government.

Seven Cabinet ministers lost their seats, including the Foreign Secretary, Malcolm Rifkind, and the charismatic Defence Secretary, Michael Portillo. Portillo's defeat in Enfield Southgate, a plush suburban district of north London, was the biggest scalp of the night. His should have been a safe seat. Iain Duncan Smith, a backbench MP in nearby Chingford and Woodford Green, had realised that he and Portillo were in trouble. 'Labour was all over seats like mine and Portillo's. We spent the final week of the campaign working my seat as if it was a marginal. I held on but everywhere around me went.'[2]

For some time before the votes were cast, Michael Portillo had been contemplating life in opposition. Halfway through the campaign he summoned Andrew Cooper and Michael Simmonds, two bright young aides from Central Office, to his home, and gave them a piece of paper on which he had sketched out the themes for a leadership campaign in the aftermath of a Conservative defeat, asking them to finish it off.[3] Portillo had passed up what might have been his best opportunity to lead the party only two years previously. When Major threw down the gauntlet in June 1995 by putting himself forward for re-election as party leader after three years of backbiting, the 'darling of the Right' refused to stand against him. It soon emerged that he was in fact planning to challenge Major if the contest went into a second round, after engineers were spotted installing telephone lines outside what was to be his campaign headquarters. 'I appeared happy to wound but afraid to strike: a dishonourable position,' he later confessed.[4] Two years on, Portillo's hopes of making a second attempt began to slip away when an opinion poll in the *Observer* just days before the election suggested that Enfield Southgate was too close to call. 'Tell me why this is wrong,' he asked Cooper, who oversaw the party's private polling.[5] Cooper was unable to reassure an increasingly worried Portillo, and from that moment onwards he began to come to terms with the possibility of defeat. This may explain his dignified reaction on the night, in contrast to the sourness of others who could not believe that the electorate could be so ungrateful.

As the campaign wore on, many Conservative MPs did however foresee the fate awaiting them. 'I was seduced in the first week into thinking that this was much easier than last time,' Seb Coe recalls. 'But then I realised that people were actually being polite and just wanted us off their doorsteps.'[6] It was the same for the legions of aspiring Conservative candidates hoping to make it to Westminster. Among them was David Cameron, a fresh-faced thirty-year-old corporate communications executive who was standing in the Midlands seat of Stafford. On paper, it was a seat that the Conservatives hoped to hold, despite recent boundary changes making it less secure. Initially he thought he would have a 50:50 chance, but as polling day neared his optimism drained away. Cameron was struck that during the last few days of the campaign many voters refused to look him in the eye, and braced himself for the worst.

Back at Conservative Central Office in Westminster's Smith Square, a bunker atmosphere prevailed. Morale had been quite high in the early stages of the campaign, but the more seasoned party officials knew the game was up. 'We were defending seats that were simply unwinnable. It might have been marginally better if we had fought a more defensive campaign,' says one. 'Everything was thrown into the campaign,' recalls Archie Norman, the former boss of the supermarket chain Asda and one of the few new Tory MPs elected that night. 'It was the most money ever spent in any election campaign in Britain, but also the least effective money that was ever spent.'[7]

The Prime Minister's aides were encouraged by his confidence at the beginning of the campaign. The famous soapbox, which he had used during the election five years earlier to such good effect, was dusted off. But deep down, Major knew the cause was lost. For two years he had been coming to terms with the probability of defeat. 'You can never be certain in politics, so you have to go on fighting,' he says. 'But we had been in government too long. Splits over Europe had made us unelectable. If the Tory Party had been composed of 330 Archangel Gabriels, we would have still come second.'[8] The opinion polls spoke for themselves. Labour's average rating had rarely dropped below 50 per cent since mid-1994, while the Conservatives had consistently languished at 30 per cent or below.[9]

Major hoped that a long six-week campaign would allow New Labour's 'hollowness' to be exposed under the pressure of scrutiny. Yet the reverse happened. The Tory campaign unravelled when it emerged that many candidates, including David Cameron, wrote in their personal election addresses that they would not countenance Britain joining the European single currency. This contravened the government's official policy, which was that neither the time nor the circumstances were right for entry, which the press labelled 'wait and see'. 'Like me or loathe me, do not bind my hands when I am nego- tiating on behalf of the British nation,' Major appealed to his own party in one of the most surreal moments of the campaign. Britain's uncertain relationship with Europe had plagued his premiership and was now engulfing the party's campaign in the full glare of the public. 'The destruction of John Major's government was suicidal – it was manic,' says Ken Clarke, Major's Chancellor, who was one of the most pro-European ministers in the Cabinet. 'There was an underlying assumption that because we won elections anyway people could behave in this extraordinary fashion, and with any luck we would be returned to office by getting rid of all the pro-Europeans and re-electing the Eurosceptics. The idea that we were all about to be buried in a self-inflicted landslide never crossed their minds.'[10]

The early indications at 5 p.m. on Thursday, 1 May were that the election result would be far worse than the Conservatives had imagined. Major had hoped that he could confine Labour's majority to forty or fifty. Indeed, only a few days earlier party officials had predicted that the Conservatives might win 240 seats. Late in the afternoon Major, who had returned to his Huntingdon constituency in Cambridgeshire braced for defeat, received a phone call from Central Office confirming that the party was heading for catastrophe. As the evening wore one, his closest aides thought he looked as if he had been in a car crash.[11] At 10 p.m., the BBC and ITN broadcast exit polls predicting a Labour majority of between 160 and 180. By midnight, two hours after the polls had closed, the first results showed a massive 10 per cent swing right across the country. When Labour's tally reached a hundred seats, the Conservatives had barely moved into double figures. By 2 a.m. the extent of the rout was becoming clear. Stafford was one of countless Tory seats to fall to Labour's unrelenting advance. A defeated David Cameron and his wife, Samantha, left the count down but not out. He rang Michael Green, his boss at Carlton Communications, to ask for his job back as director of communications. As the result sank in they collapsed onto a sofa together, exhausted. Cameron thought to himself that he had better get on with life for a few more years, but knew that he would give politics another go. Although this was his first taste of defeat, being on the losing side was something that he was going to have to get used to for years to come.

In Conservative Central Office, a large downstairs meeting room had been prepared for a drinks party ahead of Major's return to London. But the bottles were unopened and the shellfish lay untouched. 'Everyone was just holding themselves together. It was utterly bleak,' a senior party official recalls. William Hague, the thirty-six-year-old Welsh Secretary, cut a lonely figure as one of the few ministers on duty in party headquarters overnight. He would have the unenviable task of greeting defeated Cabinet colleagues as they returned to Central Office in the early hours. As dawn approached, a bank of camera lights lit the elegant and imposing façade of the building. Just as Tony Blair took to the stage across the river, a crowd of people including jubilant Labour supporters gathered in Smith Square. 'Tories, Tories, Tories . . . Out, out, out!' they chanted at full volume. 'This was their night,' said one official besieged in the building. 'You really did feel as if the helicopters were coming to take us off the roof.' By the early hours of Friday, 2 May, the Conservatives had well and truly been airlifted from government and dropped into the wilderness of opposition. It was far from clear how long it would take them to return, if indeed they would return at all.

From High-Water Mark to Downfall

Rewind the clock by a decade, and the scene in Smith Square could not have been more different. From a window in Central Office, a victorious Mrs Thatcher, her husband Denis and Party Chairman Norman Tebbit waved to supporters and party workers below in the early hours of Friday, 12 June 1987. It was a scene of jubilation. Mrs Thatcher had led the Conservative Party to its third successive victory since coming to power in 1979. No other Prime Minister had achieved such a feat in the twentieth century. A majority of 101 would ensure her a third full term in office.

Mrs Thatcher was at the apex of her powers as she embarked on her third term as Prime Minister, but she would be gone within three and a half years. Although an admiring party lay at her feet, all was not well at the heart of government. Her assertive style of leadership had already knocked noses out of joint, including that of Michael Heseltine. Ever since the flamboyant Defence Secretary resigned in 1986, at the height of the Westland Affair, there had been a king across the water. Heseltine would prime himself as a potential successor, around whom dissent could coalesce. Although he had served in her Cabinet and Shadow Cabinet, Heseltine was not 'one of us', as Mrs Thatcher liked to term her allies. He was from the 'One Nation' mould of Conservative politicians, who had dominated the party since the Second World War. They were more consensual and not so steadfastly wedded to the free-market principles that informed much of the Thatcher revolution. After the 1987 general election Heseltine had to bide his time on the backbenches. In the meantime, the 'Iron Lady' seemed unstoppable.

' "Can't be done" has given way to "What's to stop us!"' she declared to the party faithful at their annual conference after the election. If her second term had laid the foundations by curbing the power of trade unions and introducing a wave of privatisations, her third would extend the Thatcher revolution to the inner cities, which lay depressed amid industrial decline, and the unreformed public sector, particularly the National Health Service and education. The remaining dragons of 'state socialism' had to be slain with the help of market

6

forces. It was an ambitious and bold programme that inspired a whole new generation of Conservatives. One of them was an impressionable David Cameron, who in 1987 was in his final year at Oxford University studying Politics, Philosophy and Economics. 'David was a total fan of Mrs T but feels that a mythology has grown up around her that is not connected to reality,' a friend recalls. 'He understands that she was fortunate in having a divided and weak opposition, but that she was also quite tactical and smart in knowing when to withdraw. To him, she was a canny politician who knew how to duck and dive when she had to.'

By the beginning of 1988, however, she had become a command-and-control Prime Minister. With many of her internal critics dispatched, including Heseltine, she began to take her Cabinet for granted. William Whitelaw had been the rock of that Cabinet since 1979. He was a dependable deputy who tirelessly worked the corridors of power to ensure that the Prime Minister was kept out of danger and in touch with the party mood. 'Every Prime Minister needs a Willie,' she famously proclaimed. His retirement as Deputy Prime Minister in January 1988 meant that he was no longer around to act as 'the one-person fire brigade for collective restraint', as the Whitehall chronicler Peter Hennessy described him.[12] The powers of Mrs Thatcher's well-honed political antennae, which encouraged caution when necessary, were beginning to diminish just as she became convinced of her own invincibility. 'She lost her touch, and her feel for colleagues, which had been good, left her,' recalls Ken Clarke, who sat in her Cabinet.[13] This was never more apparent than in her deteriorating relations with her two principal lieutenants, Sir Geoffrey Howe and Nigel Lawson.

Howe, her Chancellor and then Foreign Secretary, and Lawson, his successor as Chancellor in 1983, believed that the government had to conquer inflation, the scourge of Britain's post-war economy. The rising cost of living had been a dead weight on the British economy for years, particularly during the recessions of the 1970s and early 1980s, when inflation rarely fell below double figures. Although taming inflation had been central to the Thatcher revolution from its inception, it had yet to be achieved. Her lieutenants urged her to consider a Europe-wide solution. The European Exchange Rate Mechanism (ERM) could provide stable exchange rates with other European currencies, helping to bring domestic inflation under control. This was not to Mrs Thatcher's liking: she believed that it could be mastered by controlling the domestic money supply. But her Chancellor, emboldened by his tax-cutting budget in 1988 and a booming economy, pressed her to consider joining.

European solutions were not exactly to the Prime Minister's tastes by 1988. Ever since she signed the Single European Act in 1986, which heralded closer cooperation within the European Community on a large range of policy areas, she had had her doubts. She had fought hard to win a rebate from Britain's contribution to the EC budget earlier in her premiership, but had not taken much interest in the Community's affairs since. 'Europe hadn't been on the political agenda much before the Single European Act. Ironically she was the architect for the EC's revival [as a federalist project],' Iain Duncan Smith reflects. 'It was sold to her as a market mechanism, and because she was so adamant about markets, she agreed.'[14] For the Prime Minister, a properly functioning common market did not mean 'ever closer' political and monetary union across the EC. 'We have not successfully rolled back the frontiers of the state in Britain only to see them re-imposed at a European level,' she declared to an audience in the Belgian town of Bruges on 20 September 1988. She called for cooperation between 'independent sovereign states', rather than integration which sought to create 'some sort of identikit Euro-personality'. It was a warning shot fired straight across the bows of other European capitals, and indeed some of her most senior ministers at home. The British Prime Minister had declared that she was firmly on the 'Eurosceptic' side of the argument. It was for others to decide whether to be with her or to stand against her.

Four days after Mrs Thatcher delivered her landmark speech in Bruges, a twenty-year-old David Cameron walked through the doors of Central Office to join the Conservative Research Department. The CRD was a traditional recruiting ground for ambitious graduates eager to begin their political careers, and in many cases had been the first step on the ladder to high office: Michael Portillo was but one of its alumni. As the engine room of Central Office, it pumped out high-quality research briefings for senior Tory politicians. Cameron was handed the Trade and Industry, Energy and Privatisation brief with which to cut his political teeth.

More importantly, he would befriend a group of young men and women who would become his closest aides and colleagues for years to come. Among them were Rachel Whetstone, Edward Llewellyn and Ed Vaizey, all of whom became future political allies. The 'Smith Square set' joined the party when Thatcherism was at its high-water mark. 'We were all convinced that we were on the right side of the argument in politics,' says one. 'We were pro-enterprise and hated state bureaucracy.' The head of the CRD, Robin Harris, was a disciple of the Iron Lady. 'Robin was a great Thatcherite footsoldier, so he wouldn't have let anybody through the door who wasn't committed to the revolution,' says Guy Black, who was head of the Political Section. 'We came to be known as the "brat pack" in the press – there was nothing other than loyalty to Mrs T.'[15] For them, Mrs Thatcher was known simply as 'Mother'.

Some noticed that while Cameron admired the Prime Minister as much as the others, he did not see everything in black and white ultra-Thatcherite terms. 'I remember conversations with him when I would say that we should scrap child benefit, and he said, "You can't just take away people's benefits, because it creates huge problems," ' recalls one of his closest friends from the time, Rachel Whetstone. 'He was much more thoughtful about things than I was.' Indeed, within a year of meeting him she felt that although Cameron could be 'unbelievably pompous', he had what it took to go a long way in politics. 'People used to say, "What's your dream job?" And I said, "It is to be Political Secretary to the Prime Minister, who will be David Cameron." It wasn't because he had a burning ambition,' she adds, 'it was because he had a charisma which was quite compelling.'[16]

As the new CRD recruits fawned over their seemingly invincible leader, senior ministers became increasingly worried about the direction of her government. Foreign Secretary Geoffrey Howe had been at her side from the beginning. Thoughtful and patient, he was one of her most loyal allies. Yet Howe's pro-European views, which were shared by many Tories of his generation, were at odds with the Prime Minister's deepening scepticism. He was deeply dismayed with the way in which she had seized control of foreign policy. According to Nigel Lawson, she treated Howe as 'a cross between a doormat and a punchbag'.[17]

Matters came to a head when Howe and Lawson confronted the Prime Minister on the eve of an important EC summit in Madrid in June 1989. They urged her to make a commitment to join the ERM by the end of 1992 as the best way of influencing the future direction of the EC. Their advice, once again, was met with resistance. In what she regarded as an 'ambush', Howe threatened to resign if she refused to accede to their demands. 'You should know, Prime Minister, that if Geoffrey goes, I must go too,' Lawson warned her.[18] In July she retaliated by demoting Howe from the Foreign Office to the Leadership of the House of Commons and Deputy Prime Minister, a nominal title in which he would take little consolation.

But Lawson would be the first to go. In October he resigned as Chancellor in protest at the growing influence of Mrs Thatcher's economic adviser Alan Walters, who shared her hostility to the ERM. Lawson's departure fatally weakened her grip on power, to the extent that the Cabinet presented her with little choice but to join the ERM the following year. 'The truth is that she was in a tiny minority in the government always in opposing joining the ERM, and she fought off attempt after attempt to do it,' her respected foreign affairs adviser, Charles Powell, pointed out.[19]

For Mrs Thatcher's new Chancellor, John Major, membership of the ERM was a means to an end. 'Like Nigel Lawson, I never saw it as a stepping stone to a single currency,' he says. 'Inflation for me was a week in which the week lasted longer than the money, as had been my life experience, and I knew that was the experience of many people. It wasn't an abstract political theory, I hated it – and I saw the ERM as the only available way of bringing inflation down. We had tried everything else and it failed.'[20]

By early 1990, the tension at the heart of government had begun to affect party morale from top to bottom. Mrs Thatcher had survived a leadership challenge from Sir Anthony Meyer, a stalking horse on the left of the parliamentary party, but speculation only intensified about Heseltine's intentions. Shortly after winning her third victory, she angered some by promising to 'go on and on' when asked by an interviewer about when she might stand down. Aside from Europe, a major aspect of domestic policy had become a serious bone of contention. Hailed as one of the flagship policies of the third term, the Community Charge, or 'poll tax', was intended to make local councils more accountable for the services they provided, but it became instantly unpopular in the country. Mrs Thatcher was determined to push ahead with the plan to replace the local rates, despite warnings that it would be a political disaster. 'How could a leader who was wise make thirteen million people pay a tax that they had never paid before? It showed she was no longer thinking in a rational way, and really created controversies where it was unnecessary,' recalls one of her ministers, David Mellor.[21] The costs of implementing the poll tax were spiralling, and when it was piloted in Scotland before being introduced in England, thousands refused to pay. Anger would soon spill out onto the streets, when a large demonstration in central London turned into a riot on 31 March 1990.

For the party's footsoldiers in local government there would be a heavy price to pay in town hall elections later that spring. But it was the Prime Minister who had become the real electoral liability. By April 1990 Mrs Thatcher's 'satisfaction rating' had fallen to 23 per cent, a post-war low, and many Tory MPs began to conclude that unless she stood down their seats would be in jeopardy. A series of disastrous European and by-election results in the summer reinforced their fears. 'My trouble was that the believers had fallen away,' she regretted in 1993.[22] She could not believe that her troops had lost the fire in their bellies. However, after eleven years in office, the party was exhausted and desperate for a change of leadership style, if not a change in policy direction. 'One of the mistakes that some ultra-Thatcherites made was that [they believed] you could have radicalism forever – a permanent revolution,' says another former minister, Norman Lamont. 'I don't think the public would have ever accepted that and I think there's always been this argument between those who wanted radicalism for ever and those who wanted to go back to a more traditional Conservative Party.'[23]

'Ten more years! Ten more years!' was the evangelical chant from the party faithful during what was to be Mrs Thatcher's last conference speech as leader in October 1990. The country, though, had lost its appetite for the Iron Lady's revolutionary fervour. True, Britain was no longer considered the sick man of Europe after years of economic decline and industrial unrest, but the harsh edges of Thatcherism had begun to grate on the electorate. For every admirer there seemed to be a sworn enemy. Not only had the Prime Minister become dangerously estranged from most of her Cabinet and many Conservative MPs, she had polarised public opinion to such an extent that something would have to give.

The fatal blow came from her long-suffering ally Geoffrey Howe. 'No! No! No!' was how she reported her reaction to plans for a single European currency, Social Chapter and federal Europe when she returned from an EC summit in Rome on 28 October. For Howe, her open hostility to Europe was the final straw. On 1 November he resigned. Thirteen days later a packed House of Commons listened to his resignation statement in silence. Speaking from the backbenches for the first time in fifteen years, he delivered a withering critique of Mrs Thatcher's increasingly abrasive style of leadership and ever more strident position on Europe. As he went on, the faces around him (including that of Lawson, who sat beside him) turned to ash. Uncharacteristically savage for a politician whom a Labour opponent once described as a 'half-dead sheep', Howe tore into the Prime Minister. He derided her 'casual' dismissal of the idea of a single currency, which he argued had undermined ministerial dealings in Europe. 'It is rather like sending your opening batsmen to the crease only for them to find, the moment the first balls are bowled, that their bats have been broken before the game by the team captain,' he declared to ecstatic laughter from the opposition benches. The Prime Minister sat on the frontbench visibly trying to restrain her anger. Proclaiming loyalty to the Prime Minister he had served for eleven and a half years in office, and as party leader for fifteen years, was no longer possible for Howe. 'The time has come for others to consider their own response to the tragic conflict of loyalties with which I have myself wrestled for perhaps too long.'[24]

In one of the most dramatic scenes in the House of Commons for years, the Prime Minister's longest-serving minister had fired the starting gun for a leadership election. Heseltine now declared his hand, arguing that he could take the party to a fourth term in office. As Mrs Thatcher left for an international conference in Paris with her entourage just before the first ballot, she was not even contemplating defeat. While she could hardly bring herself to court MPs in the Commons tearoom, her lacklustre campaign team led by her complacent Parliamentary Private Secretary Peter Morrison assumed it was in the bag.

Mrs Thatcher won the first ballot on 20 November, with 204 votes to Heseltine's 152, but under the rules of the contest she fell short of outright victory by an agonising four votes. Her authority was shattered. Yet on hearing the result in Paris, Mrs Thatcher resolved to fight on. The BBC's political correspondent John Sergeant was talking live on camera when the Prime Minister strode out of the British Embassy to address reporters. As Bernard Ingham, her press secretary, brushed Sergeant aside, she vowed to put her name forward for the second round of voting. The chaotic scene, watched by millions on television at home, caused widespread dismay among Tory MPs. On her return to London Mrs Thatcher held individual interviews with members of the Cabinet. Almost all of them warned that she would not win in a second ballot, despite pledging their support. 'It was treachery,' she said later, 'with a smile on its face.'[25] The following morning, Thursday, 22 November, she tearfully told the Cabinet that she had decided to resign, and urged ministers to unite behind the figure most likely to defeat Michael Heseltine. 'It's a funny old world,' she told them.

For the young team of researchers in Central Office, the defenestration of their idolised leader was an act of total betrayal. How could their political masters have done such a thing? Cameron feels that Mrs Thatcher had every right to be aggrieved, and friends remember his sadness on the day she fell. 'We were all as upset and horrified as anybody else was about her departure. But we soon adapted to the new regime,' Guy Black recalls.[26] Life had to go on: a new Prime Minister had to be found midway through the Parliament.

In the three-horse race that ensued in the week after Mrs Thatcher's announcement, John Major, the Chancellor, emerged as the winner. The outgoing Prime Minister had worked tirelessly to advance his interests, phoning newspaper editors and friends to tell them that the revolution would be more secure with him than with the other two candidates, Michael Heseltine and the Foreign Secretary, Douglas Hurd. Yet Major was hardly in need of her assistance: he already had 160 Tory MPs signed up on the day he declared his intention to stand. Heseltine admitted that 'He who wields the knife rarely wears the crown,' while the affable Douglas Hurd was considered to be too much of a patrician to have widespread appeal in the country. In the second ballot on 27 November, Major won 185 votes to Heseltine's 131 and Hurd's fifty-seven. Heseltine and Hurd graciously conceded, handing the leadership and the premiership to Major. The following morning a tearful Mrs Thatcher and her husband Denis left Downing Street after eleven and half years.

The rise of John Major was meteoric. His father, Tom, had a burgeoning career as a variety performer, including a brief spell as a trapeze artist, before settling down with his second wife, Gwen (Major's mother), in Worcester Park, south-west London. Born in 1943, during the Second World War, Major rose from humble origins in Brixton to scale the heights of the Conservative Party. He left school at sixteen, with few qualifications, because his family needed the money he could earn, but continued to study at home first thing in the morning and late at night. After periods of temporary unemployment he eventually found his feet as a banker with Standard Chartered Bank. He also became an active member of Brixton Young Conservatives. Inspired to enter political life, he was elected as a local councillor in Lambeth and eventually as MP for Huntingdon 1979, after a long search for a safe seat. Mrs Thatcher thought highly of Major as an able and loyal minister, promoting him to Chief Secretary to the Treasury in 1987.

To his surprise he replaced Geoffrey Howe as Foreign Secretary in July 1989, and succeeded Lawson as Chancellor three months later. On 28 November 1990 the forty-seven-year-old from Brixton entered 10 Downing Street as Prime Minister.

Major Tonic

'I want to see us build a country that is at ease with itself,' Major declared on the steps of Number 10. It was a sentiment that resonated throughout the country, after over a decade of Thatcherite medicine. Major's disarming smile and emollient manner were the antidote to troubled times. He had made few enemies in the party; a huge political asset that others like Heseltine could not claim. He appointed a 'Cabinet of friends', welcoming back Heseltine from the cold to become Environment Secretary, as well as promoting his campaign manager, Norman Lamont, to the Chancellorship and appointing Chris Patten as Party Chairman. Major's consensual approach to decision-making endeared him to Cabinet colleagues, who felt bruised and battered by Mrs Thatcher's handbag. A party that had been reduced to despair in the dying days before her downfall, and guilt-ridden shock in the immediate aftermath, soon recovered its poise. Major reassured her supporters by being the anointed heir, and enthused her detractors by offering an inclusive style of leadership.

Most importantly for the party, John Major's incredible rise led to a dramatic reversal in public opinion. A fortnight before Mrs Thatcher resigned, Labour enjoyed a 16 per cent lead in the opinion polls. Within days of her leaving Downing Street, the Conservatives had leapt to a 12 per cent lead.[27] Focusing the minds of Tory MPs was the reality that they would have to go to the country within eighteen months. They believed that Major represented their best hope of uniting the party after the trauma of deposing the Iron Lady. Even after more than eleven years in office, and despite the ever-widening differences of opinion on Europe, the hunger for power was still there.

The new Prime Minister's in-tray was distinctly uninviting. He had to deal with the unpopular Community Charge, complex European negotiations and a conflict in the Middle East. But by far the hardest situation facing the country was the deteriorating state of the economy. Major inherited a dire political and economic situation. 'Interest rates were at 14 per cent, inflation was going up to double figures, growth had fallen through the floor and the recession had started with a vengeance and was going to take unemployment up very high indeed.'[28] Within twelve months the Community Charge had been replaced, British troops had played a key role in expelling Iraqi forces from Kuwait, and public spending was increased to assuage concerns that the party would desert the public services during the downturn.

The future shape of the EC was one of the most immediate concerns for Major. European leaders were about to negotiate a treaty that would strengthen the institutional bonds of the European project, forging closer cooperation in a wide range of policy areas that had hitherto been the domain of individual nation states. The Single European Act, which Mrs Thatcher had signed (and then regretted) in 1986, paved the way for further integration, particularly on the creation of a single European currency and social policy (known as the Social Chapter) which the former Prime Minister had railed against since her Bruges Speech. Major headed for the Dutch town of Maastricht in December 1991 with the intention of securing 'opt-outs' from both the single currency and the Social Chapter. Unlike his predecessor, he consulted the parliamentary party and the Cabinet widely before and during the negotiations. Yet his hand was weakened when his European counterparts reminded him that Mrs Thatcher had signed up to an 'ever closer union' in Europe.

The fact that the majority of the 376-strong parliamentary party were largely pragmatic towards Europe, if not pro-European, should have been in Major's favour. Many were from a generation that came of age after the war and believed strongly that peace and prosperity would endure through closer cooperation (which involved pooling sovereignty) with Britain's Continental neighbours. However, a significant minority of Tory MPs had become deeply suspicious of what they saw as a perpetual loss of British sovereignty as unelected European institutions accrued more powers. Major feared that a growing rift at the heart of the party could very easily turn into something more dangerous. 'I was very conscious of the two historic precedents – the Corn Laws and Tariff Reform,' he recalls. 'The danger of the party splitting in November 1990 seemed to me to be very real. The proximity of an election eighteen months later actually quite helped us in the short term, because people tend to pull together, but I felt the party was near to splitting – even then.'[29]

Following some deft negotiations at Maastricht, Major returned to Westminster having secured the opt-outs from the European Social Chapter and the single currency. In the Commons, Tory MPs waved their order papers in appreciation of his achievement. He had considered ratifying the new treaty by taking it through the Commons as soon as he returned to London, but the impending general election, which was planned for the following spring, curtailed the parliamentary timetable. It was a decision he would soon come to regret.

Despite his renewed confidence after Maastricht, Major was acutely aware that his predecessor was watching his every move. His appointment of Heseltine and scrapping of the poll tax, and the government's position on Europe, particularly alarmed Mrs Thatcher, who remained in the Commons on the backbenches until the election. Soon after leaving office she had promised to be a 'good back-seat driver', words which infuriated Major. He had scrupulously consulted his predecessor in the months after her departure, but that was now becoming increasingly difficult. 'The Labour Party were very keen to play on the fact, "Oh well, she's still running the government, yet she wouldn't have won the election," ' said one senior figure within the government. 'It wasn't a credible position. Had she not said that, we could have consulted her and brought her in much more than we did.'

The former Prime Minister struggled to come to terms with the loss of power after being in office so long, particularly during the conclusion of the Gulf War, that began just before she left Number 10. Her court of former aides and advisers let it be known to a number of Tory MPs and sympathisers in the press that she was disappointed with Major's performance and questioned his judgement. She gave him her support in public, particularly as the general election approached, but as one of his aides remarked, 'The evil was in the drip feed, the constant gnawing away at him.'[30] One of the senior figures in the party still sympathetic to her admits, 'She had become her own worst enemy by blocking off anyone who could replace her – Major was the only person in Cabinet who could claim to be her heir.'

Major himself was exasperated by the influence she still commanded in the party. A low point in their relationship came in June 1991 when the press reported comments allegedly from her that he was a 'grey man' who had 'no ideas'. She had also delivered a speech in New York in which she made an implicit attack on the government's ERM policy. According to one of his closest advisers in Number 10, Judith Chaplin, the Prime Minister was exasperated, labelling Mrs Thatcher's behaviour 'emotional' and her views 'loopy'. Chaplin, who later became a Tory MP before her untimely death in 1993, recorded Major's frustration in her diaries. 'I want her isolated,' Chaplin recorded Major saying. 'I want her destroyed.'[31] Major's supporters deny that he ever said this, but Chaplin's account reveals how difficult things had become for the new Prime Minister.

Despite the bitterness and resentment behind the scenes, in March 1992 the Conservative Party went into the general election campaign with steady determination. Major's allies believed that his down-to-earth style would contrast favourably with the Labour leader, Neil Kinnock. Kinnock had led the party since its landslide defeat in 1983, when the party gained a mere 27 per cent of the vote. Originally from the left of the party, he had toiled to overturn Labour's divided image, shedding some of its most unpopular policies such as uni-lateral nuclear disarmament, withdrawal from the European Community and nationalisation of the high street banks. He had dealt with the militant tendency on the left of the party and helped to heal wounds after a breakaway group of MPs formed the Social Democratic Party (SDP) as a rival on the centre-left, in 1981. Kinnock's hope was that a deepening recession in 1991 and early 1992 would ruin the Conservatives' chances of a fourth election victory. He also hoped to capitalise on the Tories' huge unpopularity leading up to Mrs Thatcher's downfall. Yet he had a credibility problem: many voters regarded him as a Welsh windbag, and not a Prime Minister-in-waiting. The contrast with Major could not have been starker as the election drew closer. The Prime Minister noticed as he toured the country that the eyes of voters were not sliding away, and that people wanted to talk to him rather than walk away. The connection was still there, just.

The battle lines of the 1992 general election were shaped well before Major decided to go to the country in March. Even before he became Prime Minister the Conservative strategy had been to ruthlessly exploit Labour's weaknesses, particularly on tax and spending. The young guns at the CRD had prepared an offensive which culminated in the 'Labour's Tax Bombshell' poster campaign in January 1992. David Cameron now headed the department's Political Section, where he had been responsible for devising the earlier 'Summer Heat on Labour' campaign against the opposition's tax plans. Cameron's briefings were now being regularly fed into Major's preparations for Prime Minister's Questions. 'He was an extraordinarily able and bright young man,' recalls Major. 'I didn't know him well, but I was impressed with him – his coolness and his capacity to think under pressure.'[32]

As Cameron made an impression on the Prime Minister, he was making friends with someone who would become an important influence on his career. Steve Hilton had taken over Cameron's Trade and Industry brief the previous year. The son of Hungarian parents who moved to Britain in the mid-1960s to pursue their education, Hilton was not a conventional CRD recruit. Although he and Cameron shared a public school education (Hilton at Christ's Hospital and Cameron at Eton) and both went to Oxford (where they did not meet), their upbringing could not have been more different. After Hilton's parents' marriage broke down, his mother and stepfather, a builder, raised him in modest circumstances in Brighton. Cameron was the son of a stockbroker and a justice of the peace, brought up in the comfortable surroundings of an old rectory in the Berkshire village of Peasemore. Hilton's hatred of

Communism deeply informed his politics, and he found a soulmate in Cameron, who had travelled to East Germany shortly after the fall of the Berlin Wall. 'Steve had clear views about the Cold War and freedom, as did David, whose trip had left a big impression on him,' recalls a mutual friend. Learning their trade together at the CRD, they formed an enduring friendship and a shared political outlook.

They were handed a gift when Kinnock and his Shadow Chancellor, John Smith, unveiled their 'shadow budget' on 17 March, just six days after the start of the election campaign. Laid out in detail, Labour's tax and spend plans became a hostage to fortune which the CRD ruthlessly exploited. The CRD, under the direction of Andrew Lansley, primed the media with briefings about how Labour's tax increases would hit the average voter by an extra £1,000 a year. For Lansley's protégés, the 1992 campaign would leave an indelible mark. 'We could not afford to make mistakes,' recalls Lansley. 'It was a learning experience for all of them. David, in particular, learnt that an election campaign is relentless and based on rigorous research.'[33] When the party launched a highly effective poster campaign, which featured a boxer under the slogan 'Labour's Double Whammy', his gloves labelled '1. More Taxes' and '2. Higher Prices', it was clear that this was going to be a hard-hitting campaign. Designed by the party's advertising agency, Saatchi & Saatchi, it was one of the most successful political advertisements in modern times, and would haunt Labour for years to come. However, 1992 would be the last general election campaign for many years in which the Tory electoral machine would outshine its opponents'. On 1 April, eight days before the election date, with Labour seeming to hold a decisive lead in the polls as Major criss-crossed the country with his soapbox, Neil Kinnock took the stage at a glitzy rally in Sheffield. 'We're all right!' he shouted three times, overcome by emotion. His party assumed victory; the voters had not.

The Pyrrhic Victory

In the last few days of the campaign most pundits predicted either a hung Parliament or a narrow Labour victory, but on 9 April 1992 the country returned the Conservative Party to office for an unprecedented fourth term. It was a remarkable turnaround in fortunes since November 1990. Over fourteen million people had voted Tory, the largest popular vote for any party before or since. Many Conservative MPs were surprised and relieved to have held on to their seats. Major's overall majority of twenty-one was a modest reward for the 8 per cent lead his party achieved over Labour in the share of the vote. If the small swing to Labour had been uniform across the country, the Conservatives would have won a majority of seventy-one, and the history of the next five years would have been very different indeed.

The next day Major consoled one of his closest political friends, Chris Patten. The voters of Bath had ousted the Party Chairman who had masterminded the Conservative victory. 'He would have had a much bigger job had he been elected,' regrets Major. 'We sat together in the White Room of Downing Street. We were very conscious that we had won four elections in a row, which was unprecedented in modern politics, and that winning a fifth would require the Labour Party to continue to implode, or us to have a remarkable run of success.'[34] Although not impossible, they knew this would be extraordinarily difficult, especially with such a shrunken majority. Major rewarded Patten with the last governorship of Hong Kong. As he left for the Far East, Patten knew the omens for his party were not good. 'The electorate didn't really want us to win,' he recalls. 'We won by default, but they didn't really think we deserved it. From the moment we won, the press and people at large were looking for things to criticise us for: we gave them plenty of opportunity to do just that.'[35]

The 1992 general election had delivered the Conservative Party a Pyrrhic victory. Within five months, on Wednesday, 16 September, Britain's ejection from the ERM dealt a devastating blow to the party's reputation for economic competence. On 'Black Wednesday' the cornerstone of the government's economic policy was knocked out of place as interest rates soared by 5 per cent within a matter of hours. At one point they reached 15 per cent, before falling to 12 per cent. For a Prime Minister who regarded ERM entry as one of his finest achievements as Chancellor, it was particularly damaging. In fact Major had been seeking an exit point for months beforehand, aware that the government faced the prospect of a sudden hike in interest rates during a recession, and a falling exchange rate which would have rekindled inflation.

As a reserve currency in the mechanism, the pound could not be sustained at the rate at which it had originally entered, principally because of the demands of a re-unified Germany, whose domestic economic concerns had begun to dictate the whole system. Sterling became easy prey for speculators on the currency markets, while the Bank of England spent several billion pounds of its reserves trying to prop it up. The markets went into turmoil, and as the Bank of England tried and failed to stabilise the currency that morning, Major agreed with Lamont to raise interest rates to stem the run on the pound.[36] He called an emergency meeting of senior ministers at Admiralty House on Whitehall, where he had decamped because of refurbishments to Number 10.

Lamont was aghast to find that Heseltine, Hurd and Clarke had been invited to discuss the crisis – in his collegial style, Major was anxious that they should be bound into the decision-making process – and was furious when they urged Major to intervene further to keep sterling in the ERM. 'They all sat around umming and hawing and saying, "Should we put interest rates up?" ' he recalls. 'Well, of course it offended me hugely, because I felt it was my decision and the recommendation of the Governor of the Bank of England was that our membership of the ERM was over and we should recognise it.'[37] At 7.30 p.m. Lamont made a brief statement in the central court-yard of the Treasury. 'Today has been an extremely difficult and turbulent day . . . The government has concluded that Britain's best interests can be served by suspending our membership of the exchange rate mechanism.'

Lamont had lost confidence in Major. 'I don't know why the Prime Minister didn't attempt to defend himself more,' he says. 'We never attempted to get across to people that this was a crisis that began in Germany and spread to every country in Europe. In the same week that we spent nearly all our reserves, every other European central bank did the same. They all devalued, like us.'[38] Major concedes that not enough emphasis was given to the presentation of the government's position. His terse exchanges with the German Chancellor, Helmut Kohl, were lost in the reports of the events, but this does not excuse the fact that Major failed to make his case sufficiently. The government did not look as if it was in control of events. The damage to the Conservatives' credibility in managing the economy was immense, but the political ramifications were even greater. Black Wednesday had a shattering effect on John Major's confidence, and the confidence of the party in him.

The crisis had been highly instructive for the new special adviser at the Treasury. After the election, Cameron had left the CRD to help write speeches for the second most senior minister in the government. As Lamont made his brief statement outside the Treasury that evening, Cameron looked on in the full glare of the cameras. He had witnessed the day's chaotic events from a front-row seat. 'He would be conscious of how rough politics can get, but he would have also seen what the opportunities are that are sometimes thrown up by great setbacks,' recalls Lamont. 'We had a great political setback, but it presented us with an economic opportunity; I think he understood that very well.'[39] Indeed, Cameron did not believe that that day spelled the end of the government. 'He didn't think at the time, "Well that's it, the Tories would be out of power for twelve years – it's all over," ' recalls a friend. Instead he came away with a heightened awareness of the dangers of a fixed rate mechanism and all that that would entail for a single European currency. Black Wednesday was a formative day for the future Conservative leader, not least in shaping a sceptical outlook towards closer European integration.

Major did not ask for Lamont's resignation as Chancellor, but he did come very close to tendering his own in the week that followed. 'I was ready to resign,' he says. 'I had written a resignation letter and a broadcast, and I thought that it was probably right to resign.'[40] He told Ken Clarke, his preferred successor, to prepare for an imminent leadership election. Only after a senior Downing Street official,

Stephen Wall, spent two hours talking him out of it did he resolve to carry on.[41] 'I thought it was my mess, I ought to clear it up,' Major recalls. Neil Kinnock had resigned after the election, and Labour's new leader, John Smith, accused Major of being 'a devalued Prime Minister of a devalued government'. The government would never apologise for the ERM débâcle, believing that it had been right to enter it in 1990, as all political parties had agreed at the time (with the exception of Mrs Thatcher and her closest advisers).

Despite the myth that the Conservatives' opinion poll ratings dropped overnight on Black Wednesday, it took a while for the public to register their full dissatisfaction with the government. The party's average rating fell by a mere two percentage points, from 38 to 36, between September and October 1992.[42] It was the following year that was in fact the *annus horribilis*. The public finances were in a parlous state, as the budget deficit grew. The Conservatives had promised during the election that they would 'continue to reduce taxes as fast as we prudently can', and had promised specifically that there were 'no plans and no need for an extension of VAT'.[43] But now Major and Lamont realised that they would have to raise taxes and cut spending. In March 1993 Lamont's budget included tax rises, including the imposition of VAT on fuel. It pushed public support for the government over the edge. By May the party's average poll rating dropped below 30 per cent, and it would stubbornly remain there for the next four years.[44] Major's personal ratings as Prime Minister went into even steeper decline than the popularity of his party.

Lamont's 1993 budget came to be seen as a necessary evil, restoring confidence in the City by placing the country's finances on a more even keel without endangering the recovery. However, there would be a price to pay for the broken promises. A string of by-election defeats, beginning with Newbury in May 1993, began to erode the government's perilously small majority. During the Newbury campaign, Lamont uttered the infamous words '*Je ne regrette rien*' when asked by a reporter whether he regretted making comments about 'green shoots' of economic recovery. Having taken account of the views of the City and other senior ministers, Major realised that he had to appoint a new Chancellor, and on 27 May Lamont resigned from the government, after having been offered the position of Environment Secretary. Embittered, he felt that he had been made the fall guy. Yet it was Major who carried the responsibility for holding on to his Chancellor for too long after Black Wednesday.

The Poison Begins to Flow

As the public's confidence in the Major government declined, the unity and discipline of the parliamentary party began to fragment. Inside the precincts of Westminster, the party became transfixed by Britain's relationship with Europe. Having soured relations within the higher ranks of the Thatcher administration, the European question infiltrated the veins of the parliamentary party like poison. The Maastricht Treaty, which Major had signed three months before the election, now had to be ratified by Parliament, and a growing number of Conservative MPs were implacably opposed to the Treaty, despite the negotiated opt-outs on the Social Chapter and the single currency. A battle royal was in the making.

The 1992 general election had vastly changed the complexion of the Conservative parliamentary party, which had shifted in a more Eurosceptic direction. There were fifty-four newly elected Tory MPs, many of whom could be described as 'Thatcher's Children' rather than 'Major's Friends'. Some of his closest allies, such as Chris Patten, had lost their seats, and Major now had to contend with a new generation of MPs who had come into politics inspired by the Euroscepticism of Mrs Thatcher's Bruges Speech. For them, opposing a federal Europe was just as important as, if not more important than, party unity. The newly ennobled Baroness Thatcher gave them succour, as did a number of other former ministers now residing on the backbenches. No sooner had the first Queen's Speech of the new Parliament been delivered, containing a Bill to ratify Maastricht, than the former Prime Minister gave her most important speech since leaving office. Speaking in The Hague, she set out her vision for a radically different Europe from that envisaged by Major's government, calling for powers to be removed from Brussels and returned to nation states.

For senior ministers who represented an earlier generation of pro-European thinking, like Douglas Hurd, the Foreign Secretary, and Ken Clarke, who succeeded Lamont as Chancellor, the omens were not good. The question of Europe had now become inextricably linked with Mrs Thatcher's downfall. 'It stemmed from the bitterness after Margaret's removal from office,' says Ken Clarke. 'She became very bitter when she lost power, and her immediate entourage persuaded her that there had been a plot and revenge had to be taken. She lurched to the right and became even more Eurosceptic than she had been in government. This was all taken up by faithful young acolytes who hadn't served in her government but took up bizarre views which they thought were Thatcherite.'[45] To Thatcher's loyal supporters, Clarke was one of those who had betrayed her in November 1990 by telling her that she had no hope of winning in the second ballot. The resentment would flow both ways.

The Eurosceptics opposing the Maastricht Bill were emboldened by the result of a referendum in Denmark in June 1992, when a narrow majority voted against ratifying the Treaty. Rebellion had become respectable, and as the Bill made its way through the Commons the rebels grew in number and confidence, encouraged by the tacit support of senior figures from the heyday of the Thatcher revolution. Iain Duncan Smith, one of the leading Eurosceptics elected in 1992, recalls: 'I think the Whips got used to thundering things through because they could beat rebellions with large majorities. They believed they could ram Maastricht through, but they couldn't. It was the key to the whole thing unravelling.'[46] Major could not escape the fact that the 'fundamental unreconstructed anti-Europeans' outnumbered the government's diminishing majority. 'We were a minority government from the start,' he asserts. He was incensed by the behaviour of the Maastricht rebels. 'They wanted me to renege on a treaty I had negotiated on behalf of the British people. Worse, they wanted me to renege on a deal on which I had absolutely cast-iron parliamentary approval before I negotiated. If I had done that, no one would ever have trusted a British Prime Minister in negotiating in Europe today. The same people who talk about honour and sanction were the people that were asking me to break our word. That was why I was prepared, if necessary, to take it to the country.'[47] On 22 July 1993 the Bill failed to pass one of its last parliamentary hurdles (three Cabinet meetings having been held in one day in an attempt to carry the government), and the next day the government held a vote of confidence, which it won by thirty-eight votes.

Hours after the government survived, an exhausted Prime Minister sat down to be interviewed by Michael Brunson, ITN's political editor. Believing he was having a private conversation while the cameras were not rolling, he vented his frustration. 'The real problem is one of a tiny majority. Don't overlook that. I could have done all these clever, decisive things which people wanted me to do but I would have split the Conservative Party into smithereens. And you would have said I had acted like a ham-fisted leader . . . Just think it through from my perspective. You are the Prime Minister, with a majority of eighteen, a party that is still harking back to a golden age that never was, and is now invented. You have three right-wing members of the Cabinet who actually resign. What happens in the parliamentary party?' Brunson suggested he could easily find replacements. Major replied: 'I could bring in other people. But where do you think most of this poison is coming from? From the dispossessed and the never-possessed. You can think of ex-ministers who are going around causing all sorts of trouble. We don't want another three more of the bastards out there.' The tape of the conversation was leaked to the *Observer*.

Major's remark about 'bastards' was taken to refer to Michael Portillo, the Defence Secretary, Peter Lilley, the Social Security Secretary, and John Redwood, the Welsh Secretary, all prominent Eurosceptics, although he insists he did not have anyone in particular in mind. But his words brought into full public view the animosity that was absorbing the highest reaches of government. The fact that commentators swiftly identified the three Cabinet members in question revealed how much briefing was occurring.

'Tory MPs asked themselves what they were in power for during the Maastricht debates, while John Major struggled to keep discipline,' says one former aide. 'It reinforced an impression of division in the public's eyes. Here was a party that had become dogmatically obsessed, like a bickering, neurotic couple on a train – everyone just wanted them to shut up.'

There was a genuine ideological rift occurring within the Conservative Party in the early 1990s. Closer European integration created a powerful tension between a belief in the nation and the desire to spread commerce and trade. The struggle to reconcile these forces was tearing the party apart, from the Cabinet table to the grassroots in the country. The party's presence in local government had shrunk since 1979, when it had over twelve thousand councillors, to a point where it controlled just thirteen councils in 1995. Party membership had also been in decline since the 1970s, and that decline became even sharper in the 1990s.[48] 'Our associations on the ground were left with the more politically interested members, and they attracted too many zealots,' one Cabinet minister observed. The increasingly polarised views of activists and members reinforced the divisions in Westminster.

What turned the crisis into a deeper malaise was the fact that the bitterness associated with Mrs Thatcher's departure had become entangled with the disputes about Maastricht. Eurosceptics disappointed with Major's premiership after Black Wednesday despaired that, as they saw it, a great leader had been unceremoniously dumped and her inheritance was being betrayed. By the end of 1993, the trauma of the events of November 1990 had come to haunt the party. To the most ardent Thatcherite MPs, turning the tide of European integration was far more important than loyalty to the Prime Minister, who they believed was weak and indecisive, while Thatcherism had never suffered an electoral failure. Every day the Whips' Office battled to keep the government afloat, as the party's overall majority dwindled after successive by-election defeats. The malcontents had to be kept on board. 'It always irritated me, because people said Mrs Thatcher was much stronger than John Major, but he had a majority of twenty-one, which was reduced by two every time we lost a by-election, all the way down to zero at the end,' says one former whip, Andrew MacKay. 'It's easy to be strong with a big majority, but it's very difficult to be strong when you're held to ransom by the venal, the cranky or the issue-obsessive.'[49]

What made matters worse was that the pro-European members of Major's government – Ken Clarke, Douglas Hurd and Michael Heseltine – underestimated the depth and breadth of feeling in the parliamentary party about Maastricht. Indeed the 'bastards' in Cabinet were just as vexed about Europe as the backbench rebels. Hurd contends that it was not so much complacency among the senior ranks as a 'mixture of exhaustion and fatalism' within the government. 'It was more a case of a rabbit stuck in the headlights; so much energy was taken up by the Maastricht votes.'[50] Major removed the whip from eight of the rebels in November 1994: it was a move that did him more harm than good. As the government's majority almost completely disappeared, a sense of paralysis in office pervaded. Its room for manoeuvre was now extremely limited. Senior ministers were exasperated. 'The rebels thought all you had to do was take an anti-European position, be beastly to foreigners and the world would flock to your side,' said one. 'It was never true. It was a fantasy.'

'Put Up or Shut Up'

'I am not prepared to see the party I care for laid out on the rack like this any longer . . . It is time to put up or shut up.' With those words, Major stunned his party on 22 June 1995. His last throw of the dice was to resign as party leader, prompting a leadership election to resolve differences, restore discipline and reassert his authority after three years of infighting. It was an extraordinary move for a sitting Prime Minister. When the Whip had been restored to the eight rebels in April on the promise of loyalty, they had circulated the television studios boasting of their success. Major felt he could never trust their word again, and realised that a leadership challenge in the autumn was highly likely. He feared that the party conference would descend into farce, undermining everything the government was trying to accomplish. 'The only way to exorcise that was to resign and determine where parliamentary opinion really rested,' he recalls.[51]

Once it was clear that Michael Portillo was not going to stand for the leadership, only one Eurosceptic member of the Cabinet challenged Major: John Redwood. The Welsh Secretary believed that if there was 'no change' in leadership there was 'no chance' at the next general election. Redwood launched his campaign surrounded by the leading rebels, many of whom were held in contempt by Major and loyal members of the Cabinet. The effect was unfortunate: 'You can practically hear the flapping of white coats,' one of Major's campaign team remarked. But Redwood attracted the support of eighty-nine MPs, mainly from the right of the party, while twenty more abstained. Two hundred and eighteen voted for Major. He prevailed, but it was not an overwhelming vote of confidence. If it is assumed that almost all of the hundred or so ministers backed the Prime Minister, then up to half of backbench MPs had failed to vote for him. 'The message that I would give to every Conservative . . . is that the time for division is over,' Major declared on the steps of Number 10 after the result had been announced. 'It made him seem weaker to the public,' one leading rebel recalled. 'It may have bought him some parliamentary time, but the worst thing was that it left us with more stories about a Prime Minister whose party was not behind him.' Major's allies were unrepentant. 'You cannot deal with unreason, and on Europe there was no middle ground, no meeting point with them – they were utterly intransigent and intractable,' recalls one. 'Whatever they may have said, most of them wanted us out of the EU, but they didn't say that because that was beyond the pale.'

It was soon apparent that Major's victory had not put an end to the government's problems. A string of further by-election defeats, and the defection of three Tory MPs to Labour or the Liberal Democrats, undermined the Prime Minister's attempts to show that he was back in command. Fatal for a government struggling to hold itself together was the accumulation of crises outside its control. An uneasy truce in Northern Ireland which Major strove to achieve in 1994 came to an end in February 1996 when the IRA exploded a massive bomb in London's docklands. Suggestions the following month of a link between BSE, or 'mad cow disease', and a form of human brain disease led to a catastrophic decline in the sales of British beef at home and a worldwide ban on its export by the European Commission. The government's policy of 'non-cooperation' with the EU in retaliation became the subject of ridicule.

As the party gathered in Bournemouth in October 1996 for its last annual conference before the election, Major and his Cabinet tried to put on a brave face. Speaking up against Europe and defending the Thatcherite inheritance would almost certainly be a crowd-pleaser. 'We should be proud of the Tory tax record but [not forget] that people needed reminding of its achievements . . . It's time to return to our tax-cutting agenda,' the new prospective parliamentary candidate for Stafford, David Cameron, declared in his first speech from a conference platform. Playing to the gallery, he set his sights on the Labour leader, Tony Blair. 'The socialist Prime Ministers of Europe have endorsed Tony Blair because they want a federalist pussycat and not a British lion. It is up to us in this party, in this country, to make sure that lion roars, because when it does no one can beat us.'[52] The audience lapped it up, although Ken Clarke, who was sitting behind Cameron, did not look amused.

After finding himself out of a job when Norman Lamont resigned in May 1993, Cameron had been snapped up by the new Home Secretary, Michael Howard, who appointed him one of his special advisers. If Cameron's experience at the Treasury had toughened him up, the Home Office under Howard was no place for shrinking violets either. It was one of the few areas of government where a minister was actively driving an agenda, often against the grain of civil servants and commentators – Howard was unapologetic about tightening penal policy, famously saying that 'Prison works.' Cameron enjoyed working for Howard, although he considered himself much more of a liberal than his boss. Even so, his fifteen-month spell under Howard's wing at the Home Office had given him a flavour of politics at the sharp end of Whitehall. Cameron's eye for detail and flair for words

31

were put to use by his new boss, but more importantly Howard valued his capacity for hard work. Working for Howard also provided an insight into the rapid rise of the Shadow Home Secretary, Tony Blair. In the late summer of 1994 Cameron left the service of a beleaguered government for the private sector, joining Carlton Communications, a media company which owned London's weekday ITV station, Carlton Television. Under the watchful eye of the charismatic chairman Michael Green, Cameron was soon promoted to be the company's director of corporate affairs. However, his heart was really set on becoming a Tory MP. In January 1996, when two shortlisted contenders for what seemed to be a reasonably safe Tory seat dropped out, Cameron was called to interview at the last moment. 'I must admit that my first thought was that, at twenty-nine, he was too young. But then he spoke and it was obvious that he was the best candidate,' recalled one of the stalwarts of the Stafford Conservative Association.[53]

While Cameron's star rose, it seemed that anything that could go wrong did go wrong for the party in power. Major had seriously considered calling an election in autumn 1996, but decided to hold off until March or May 1997, the last date at which it could take place. While the competence of the government had long been called into question, the misdemeanours of a handful of Conservative MPs further damaged the party's reputation in office. In a speech prima-rily about education, Major declared that it was time to go 'back to basics' by restoring values of decency and respect in communities across the country. Unauthorised briefings from junior staff in Central Office claimed that he was actually talking about personal morality rather than education. Major was incensed. When several ministers were exposed in the press for having extramarital affairs, 'back to basics' suddenly blew up in the government's face. Allegations of 'sleaze' also came to haunt the party. Investigations by the *Guardian* revealed that two Conservative MPs, Tim Smith and Neil Hamilton, had taken cash in brown paper envelopes from the owner of Harrods, Mohamed Fayed, for asking parliamentary questions, while Jonathan Aitken, like Hamilton a minister in the government, became embroiled in damaging allegations about receiving hospitality at the expense of associates of the Saudi royal family. To the public, these matters tarred the whole party with the same brush. There was a firm impression that the Conservative Party was synonymous with a culture of greed and arrogance that had taken root during the Thatcherite heyday of the 1980s.

Outmanoeuvred and Outclassed

While the Major government headed for the rocks, the Labour Party was undergoing a revolution of its own. Neil Kinnock's resignation following the 1992 election defeat prompted a period of soul-searching for the party. Kinnock's successor, John Smith, was a capable parliamentary performer, but his strategy was largely to ride the wave of growing discontent with the government. He believed that 'one more heave' would be enough to deliver victory at the next election. A small group of Labour politicians were not so convinced. They realised that the party had to change even more drastically than it had under Kinnock. Among them were Gordon Brown, the Shadow Chancellor, Tony Blair, the Shadow Home Secretary, and Peter Mandelson, the party's former Director of Communications, who had become an MP in 1992. Their ambition to modernise the Labour Party would come a step closer on 12 May 1994.

Cameron was enjoying a pint of beer outside the Two Chairmen pub in Westminster when he heard about John Smith's death earlier that day. In shock, he turned to a colleague: 'This means Tony Blair will be leader of the Labour Party,' he declared. 'He'll move it onto the centre ground and we'll be stuffed.' It was a sound prediction. The path was clear for the Shadow Home Secretary to emerge as the front-runner to replace Smith, after his friend and colleague Gordon Brown stepped aside (a decision that would haunt Brown for the rest of his career). Blair possessed immense skills as a communicator, and he also had youth and charisma on his side. He, Brown, Mandelson and Alastair Campbell, the former tabloid journalist who became Blair's press secretary, formed a powerful clique at the top of the party.

'New Labour' would extend its appeal across the political spectrum, unlike the old party of the left. It sought to blend the modern economic agenda that had been entrenched by the Thatcher–Major governments with a passion for social justice, redressing the inequalities that had arisen during the 1980s and 1990s. New Labour would position itself as the 'One Nation' party of British politics. Rewriting Clause IV of the party's constitution, stripping it of the commitment to public ownership of industry, was a clear signal to the electorate that the party had changed. Presentation was crucial. While Kinnock had done the heavy lifting in abandoning unpopular policies, it was now for a new generation to take a symbol like Clause IV and rebrand Labour for the wider electorate. By accepting aspects of the Thatcher revolution, including the sweeping reforms of the trade unions, restructuring of the economy and a tough stance on law and order, the party manoeuvred itself onto fertile electoral territory. Learning the lessons of the disastrous 'shadow budget' in 1992, Labour pledged not to increase income tax and committed itself to Tory spending targets for two years if elected. The leadership took absolutely nothing for granted: there would be no room for ideological purity or reckless dissent in the New Labour project. Hungry for power after eighteen years in opposition, the party loyally followed its new leadership.

For an embattled government, the advent of New Labour presented considerable practical and philosophical challenges. 'I attended many meetings with John Major in Number 10, and while we were sitting there four or five major governmental decisions had to be made while we were having a discussion about the next manifesto,' recalls Daniel Finkelstein, who joined Central Office in 1995. 'There comes a point when you're holding a coalition together with a tiny majority that the wider political picture becomes secondary.'[54] Central Office was reorganised, but it could not match New Labour's state-of-the-art war room at the heart of its Westminster headquarters in Millbank Tower. The Conservative election machine, which had been so formidable in previous campaigns, was completely outclassed.

New Labour presented a far more fundamental problem to the

Conservatives. 'We knew Tony Blair would be a formidable opponent,' recalls William Hague, who was promoted to the Cabinet in 1995. 'He had the right appearance and attitude at the right time. It made our political strategy that much harder. The Cabinet found it very hard to decide how to attack New Labour.' It was a dilemma that caused many of the Tories' brightest brains to falter: they could not find a convincing response to being outmanoeuvred. 'It was clear Blair was giving us a political nervous breakdown because we weren't sure what we stood for, and trying to define ourselves in contrast to him was extremely difficult,' recalls George Bridges, the youthful Assistant Political Secretary in Number 10 between 1994 and 1997. 'He was picking up Tory principles that he felt were appealing to middle England and playing them for all they were worth.'[55]

Central Office strategists and election planners went through contortions trying to decide how to attack New Labour. Guided by research showing that the public believed that Labour had indeed changed, they argued that it was a change that heralded new dangers. 'New Labour, New Danger' became the catchy slogan inspired by the party's advertising agency, M&C Saatchi, accompanied by a poster showing Tony Blair's 'demon eyes' lurking behind red curtains. It was partly inspired by Steve Hilton, who had left Central Office after the 1992 general election to become an apprentice of the advertising guru Maurice Saatchi. But the attack on the opposition had a flaw, as Finkelstein admits: 'It showed that we didn't actually know what we thought was wrong with New Labour, and that the only way we could fight them was by pretending in our own heads that they were dangerous.'[56] There was confusion about the approach throughout the party. Central Office staff became frustrated that Major would veer from one line of attack to another. 'He followed what we used to call the Coca-Cola strategy, which argued that Labour was copying us, as Cola Light, and that we were the real thing. We repeatedly tried and failed to get him to understand that you couldn't say they were dangerous and copying you at the same time.'[57] Yet Major was convinced that the public would see through the 'froth' of Blair, which contrasted with the late John Smith, who he believed was a politician of substance.

The fact was that the party was in total disarray about how to attack the resurgent opposition. Some senior figures believed that Blair was a left-winger in disguise, while others tried to portray him either as a puppet of the old left or as believing in nothing at all. 'Of all the iterations we went through, the one thing that never occurred to anybody was that Tony Blair might actually mean it,' Andrew Cooper admits. 'We completely underestimated him and the New Labour project.'[58] Very few on the Tory side understood what they were up against. 'Tony Blair was an extremely accomplished, protean, shape-shifting politician who managed brilliantly to appeal to old Labour voters and simultaneously to huge number of middle-ground Tory voters in 1997,' Boris Johnson reflects.[59]

When an exhausted John Major finally called the general election on 17 March, his party had long lost the will to govern. It lay tired, divided and discredited. 'I love my party in the country, but I do not love my parliamentary party,' Major later admitted.[60] 'For much of the time I didn't feel able to say exactly what I thought because I needed to keep the party together. It was my continuing nightmare that the party would split. It always felt like two horses pulling in opposite directions, and you were pulling back on both sets of reins at the same time, which was very uncomfortable.'[61] Indeed, by placating the demands of the 'oddballs who came out of the wood-work' after 1992, as one former whip put it, Major found himself in an intolerably weak position.

As Prime Minister for six and a half years, John Major had survived longer than most of his predecessors in Number 10 Downing Street. In many ways he was given a 'hospital pass' in November 1990. The economy was deteriorating and the government was struggling to find its poise after the political disaster of the poll tax. Major cannot escape culpability as a senior member of Mrs Thatcher's adminis-tration, sharing in the collective responsibility for the failures of its later years, but he was determined to draw a line under a period of huge upheaval. By promising to create 'a country at ease with itself' and attempting to reconcile the increasingly polarised positions within his party, he steered the Conservative Party to calmer waters for a time. His decency and straightforwardness endeared him to the wider party, and indeed to many in the country. His mandate in 1992, which was built on the highest ever popular vote (admittedly on a high turnout), was testament to his skilled management of a party in office that was seriously fraying at the edges.

Winning the 1992 general election was in fact a Pyrrhic victory for John Major and the Conservatives. Faced with such a small majority and an increasingly hostile press climate, the Prime Minister would inevitably find it harder to ride the 'two horses' of European opinion within the party. While his purpose was to govern the country, others recklessly indulged themselves in a civil war the wounds of which would take years to heal. After 1992, longevity would be his government's greatest enemy, as the public tired of some in the parliamentary party, whose arrogance and obsession with Europe became abhorrent to them. Lesser men would have buckled under the strain of leading a party seemingly intent on destroying itself.

But even allowing for his scant room for manoeuvre, Major could have taken a firmer and more decisive line with those who sought to cause so much trouble, and have been less thin-skinned about what others, particularly virulent critics in the press, thought of him. By restating the more harmonious vision of Britain he espoused on becoming Prime Minister, he might have been able to create some light amid the darkening clouds after 1992. Despite his achievements in forging the Northern Ireland peace process, conquering inflation and passing on a secure economy in May 1997, he could have been more forceful in articulating a positive vision for the party.

Whatever John Major could and might have said or done, the public wanted change, and voted for it. New Labour was ready to assume the reins of power, while for the Conservative Party a journey into the unknown was about to begin.

TWO

Lost in the Wilderness
May 1997–June 2001

The suddenness of losing power is very brutal. After eighteen years in office, opposition was a strange and lonely place for the Conservative Party. Bereft of ministerial cars, red boxes and armies of civil servants, the surviving 165 Tory MPs would somehow have to regroup. In the dying days of government, the party often looked as though it would break apart over divisions on Europe. Yet to John Major's credit he held it together. The price, however, was a catastrophic electoral defeat.

Leaderless and Powerless

'When the curtain falls it is time to get off the stage, and that is what I propose to do.' With those words, John Major tendered his resignation as leader of the Conservative Party on Friday, 2 May, before going to Buckingham Palace to offer his resignation as Prime Minister to the Queen.

As he then headed to The Oval to watch Surrey play cricket, he left behind him a party in a state of shock. There were many Tory MPs who wanted to see him resign the party leadership immediately, but he was held in affection by the grassroots in the country. Stripped of the responsibility of running the country, some of his allies argued strongly that he could steady the party's nerves in opposition. Lord Cranborne, his chief of staff during the election campaign and Leader of the Lords, and Alistair Goodlad, the Chief Whip, pleaded with him that the party had a better chance of staying together if he remained as leader until the autumn. It would give time for the party to elect his successor and to come to terms with defeat. 'It would be terrible,' Major retorted, 'because I would be presiding with no authority over a number of candidates fighting for the crown. It would merely prolong the agony.'[1]

The agonising had already begun in Central Office. As a triumphant Tony Blair made his way up Downing Street in bright sunshine on his first day in office, the young guns in the Conservative Research Department stared gloomily at the television screens. 'We just didn't know where to go or what to do,' recalls one. Others, like George Osborne, a twenty-five-year-old former member of the CRD and special adviser to Douglas Hogg, the outgoing Minister for Agriculture, understood the magnitude of events. 'Curiously, George was quite excited,' recalls a friend. 'He was on the losing side, but he sensed this was a big moment in British politics.' Little did Osborne know how long it would take for his party to come to terms with the events of that day and the night before.

The new House of Commons offered little solace for Conservative MPs. As they filed onto the opposition benches for the first time since 1979, they must have felt like an endangered species. The chamber overflowed with the amassed ranks of the 419-strong Parliamentary Labour Party. As caretaker Leader of the Opposition, John Major hastily assembled a Shadow Cabinet. Having lost seven Cabinet colleagues, he could barely muster a full complement of shadow ministers to oppose Blair's Cabinet. Several had to combine portfolios, including Major himself as leader and Shadow Foreign Secretary, after Malcolm Rifkind's defeat. There were no MPs from Scotland or Wales to serve as Shadow Secretaries of State.

A triumphant Blair rubbed the Conservatives' noses in their defeat. As he delivered his first speech at the dispatch box as Prime Minister, two Tory Eurosceptic MPs, Bill Cash and Sir Michael Spicer, rose to their feet at the first mention of Europe. The government benches heckled and laughed at their interventions, and Blair duly congratulated them and their fellow Eurosceptics on 'the magnificent part that they played in our victory'.[2]

There was a mixture of emotions within the surviving members of the parliamentary party. Some were relieved just to be there at all. 'Even people like Gillian Shephard with huge Tory majorities hung on by the skin of their teeth,' the former Home Office minister Ann Widdecombe recalls. 'Nothing will ever equal that defeat – it was shattering.'[3] Another survivor, Liam Fox, vividly recalls a senior colleague telling him in the Commons tearoom that it was 'wrong to assume that this was the worst it could get'.[4] A complete electoral meltdown had only narrowly been avoided. A third of the parliamentary party had majorities under five thousand – any further swing from the Conservatives to Labour or the Liberal Democrats would place their seats in peril. The other two thirds were more secure, but that presented another problem: complacency. 'The 1997 defeat was so bad that the party was reduced to a group of MPs who thought they could survive come what may,' says the former minister David Willetts, who was seen as one of the few leading intellectual lights left in the parliamentary party.[5] Reaching out to the majority of voters who had turned their backs on the Tories, particularly in marginal seats, would prove difficult, as so few MPs could claim to represent them.

The party had also suffered from the impact of the Referendum Party during the election. Formed by the Anglo-French billionaire financier Sir James Goldsmith, it pledged a referendum on Britain's continuing membership of the EU. Goldsmith had been unhappy that the Major government had not undertaken to hold such a referendum, although it had promised one on Britain's possible entry into the single currency. He invested millions of pounds of his own fortune to promote the new party. Although it polled only 800,000 votes (just 2.6 per cent of the vote), Goldsmith led a high-profile campaign and fielded 547 candidates, predominantly in seats where none of the other candidates favoured a referendum. Most of the seats it did not contest were held by Eurosceptic Conservative MPs (of whom many were swept away regardless). According to expert analysis, only a handful of Tory seats fell as a direct result of the intervention of the Referendum Party, although some contend that it may have cost the Conservatives between twenty and twenty-five seats.[6]

Nevertheless, the existence of Goldsmith's single-issue party was certainly something the Tories could have done without as they headed towards defeat in 1997.

What has never been revealed before is that Goldsmith was provoked into action by the maverick diarist and former Tory minister Alan Clark. Clark had retired from the Commons in 1992, disillusioned by the downfall of Mrs Thatcher. He was not a particular admirer of Major's, and was firmly on the Eurosceptic wing of the party. He soon regretted his decision to leave politics, and as the Major government's problems worsened, he was desperate to find ways of reviving the Tory cause. An old friend of Goldsmith's, Clark was aware that the financier was becoming increasingly disenchanted with the party's policy towards Europe. During a visit to Goldsmith's ranch in Mexico in February 1994, Clark took it upon himself to suggest that the Conservatives might offer a referendum on Britain's membership of the EU at the next general election. Goldsmith was apparently led to believe that Major himself sanctioned this. But when he subsequently asked Major whether he was going ahead with his 'promise', the Prime Minister was aghast, telling him he had no such intention. Goldsmith accused the government of bad faith, and prepared to launch his own campaign and party. 'The Referendum Party was an entirely Alan Clark ramp,' a senior Tory figure insists. 'Clark had no sanction to make any such deal.'

Desperate to return to the Commons, Clark was elected as Tory MP for Kensington and Chelsea in the 1997 election, without opposition from the Referendum Party. Goldsmith died a few months after the election, while Clark's revived parliamentary career was cut short by his death in September 1999. Alan Clark was an idiosyncratic Tory on the right of the party, who was best known for his philandering and his vivid diary account of the Thatcher years. But his cameo role in the dying days of the Major government, which further fanned the flames of the European debate, deserves a footnote.

Shortly after the election, some commentators, including the former Irish Prime Minister Garret FitzGerald, asserted that the

Conservatives lost primarily because over four million of their 'natural supporters' either stayed at home or voted for the Referendum Party. A powerful myth was born which had the effect of reinforcing complacency among senior figures in the party, such as the Eurosceptic former Party Chairman Norman Tebbit, who argued that the road to recovery lay in mobilising this hidden mass of Tory support. These claims were hotly disputed by the party's private pollster, Nick Sparrow of ICM, whose research showed that 3.5 million former Tory voters had switched directly to Labour and the Liberal Democrats. But a significant number of Tory MPs were more inclined to believe the Tebbit version of events. 'Some of the new MPs thought that getting rid of John Major and firmly opposing Euro entry would herald a return to popularity,' recalls Ken Clarke. 'But they had no experience of opposition, and they acted as if nothing had happened.'[7] Clarke was one of only thirty-six Conservative MPs who had been in the Commons before Margaret Thatcher led the party to power in 1979.[8] Alongside the lack of experience of opposition, the prevailing mindset was that the party would be returned to office once the electorate realised the error of their ways. As one MP, Liam Fox put it, 'Too many people thought after 1997 that we were having a glorified time-out.'[9]

The 'Anyone But Ken' Leadership Contest

John Major's sudden resignation propelled the party into an immediate leadership contest. The most likely front-runners were already out of the race: Michael Heseltine suffered further heart problems immediately after the election, while Michael Portillo was not even in Parliament. The surviving 'big beasts of the jungle' from Major's Cabinet entered the ring. Ken Clarke's support came mainly from the pro-European wing and the centre of the party, while Michael Howard, Peter Lilley and John Redwood pitched their appeals to the Eurosceptic right. William Hague, the young Yorkshireman who had served in the Cabinet for just two years in the relatively junior role of Welsh Secretary, considered his options. He initially accepted an offer from Howard to be his deputy and Party Chairman, but was persuaded by friends that Howard would not win. He quickly cut himself loose from the deal, and decided to stand for the leadership himself. Howard had been tainted by an outspoken attack from one of his former colleagues at the Home Office, Ann Widdecombe, who said that he had 'something of the night about him'. Howard's tough stance on law and order as Home Secretary had won him plaudits from the right, but he had become a polarising figure both inside and outside the party.

Hague saw an opportunity to present himself as the candidate who could make 'a fresh start', as the youngest candidate and the one least associated with the old regime. But footage of his speech as a sixteen-year-old Young Conservative to the 1977 party conference would haunt him. 'Half of you may not be here in thirty or forty years' time, but I will be and I want to be free,' he had declared, with Mrs Thatcher applauding in the background. Like Major in 1990, Hague had the advantage of having the fewest enemies within the parliamentary party, and like Major he had risen from humble beginnings. As a comprehensive schoolboy in Rotherham he had been a member of a rare species: a Young Conservative in a traditional Labour-supporting area where iron and steel were the staple industries. He was inspired by the speeches of Winston Churchill, collected volumes of Hansard and spent hours learning great political speeches by heart, a talent that would serve him well in years to come. A prodigious student at Oxford and a successful management consultant at McKinsey's, Hague was destined for a successful political career. In 1989, aged only twenty-seven, he had been elected to Parliament as MP for Richmond, in his native county. At the time of the 1997 leadership contest this was still the last time the party had won a by-election.

Hague was affable and, crucially, he was a Eurosceptic. Having pledged not to join the single currency 'for the foreseeable future' in his leadership campaign, he appealed to the growing ranks of sceptics on the Tory benches. He was also largely untainted by the struggles over Maastricht. Projecting himself as the youthful candidate who could modernise the party and reform its creaking organisation, he attracted support from the younger generation of Tory party workers and former ministerial aides. Among them was George Osborne, who became an enthusiastic member of Hague's campaign team. 'George felt William was the only candidate to take his argument to the country and get a professional campaign going,' one insider recalls. 'We tried to involve the party more and make the argument that it had become out of touch.'

Another young Tory to take an interest in Hague's campaign was the defeated candidate for Stafford, David Cameron. Cameron and the younger Osborne vaguely knew each other from the Major era, but the five-year age difference meant that they had moved in slightly different circles. 'David was the hot-shot special adviser while George was a lowly person in CCO to begin with,' observes a mutual friend, and as Osborne made the step up to being a ministerial aide, Cameron had left his equivalent role at the Home Office for fresh and well-paid pastures at Carlton. But when Cameron went to support one of Hague's campaign events he felt like a spare part, and decided to concentrate on life outside politics. While Cameron's involvement with the party in Westminster receded, Osborne's was about to intensify as Hague's campaign gathered momentum.

Standing in the way was Ken Clarke. Clarke was one of the few senior Conservatives of whom the public had a favourable impression after the landslide. He was credited with having managed the economy reasonably well after taking over as Chancellor from Norman Lamont in 1993, steering it towards low inflation and modest growth after the difficult years of recession. Laid-back and straight-talking, his fondness for Hush Puppies, jazz, birdwatching and the odd cigar endeared him to the public, if not to some of his more strait-laced colleagues, and opinion polls and surveys of constituency chairmen showed him to be the popular choice for leader in the country. To Tory MPs, Clarke's main asset was his ability to perform both in the Commons and on the airwaves. 'He was the big beast who could knock down Labour,' says Widdecombe, one of Clarke's supporters. 'He did extremely well, appealing beyond the pro-European wing of the party. After all, he had been a reformer in the Thatcher–Major governments in health and education. So we took it for granted that he could win.'[10] In the first ballot, on 10 June, Clarke duly emerged as the front-runner with forty-nine votes to Hague's forty-one. Howard and Lilley were knocked out of the contest.

But ultimately Clarke's pro-European views would be his Achilles' heel. Knowing that his attraction to the idea of a single currency was anathema to a large number of Tory MPs, he made the fatal mistake of entering into a Faustian pact with the arch-Eurosceptic John Redwood, who remained in the race. On paper, it was a sensible move: Redwood had obtained thirty-eight votes in the first ballot, and if these were transferred to Clarke in the second, he would secure victory. But the partnership stretched credulity for many Tory MPs and commentators, and when Howard and Lilley promptly declared their support for Hague, he emerged as the unity candidate from the centre-right who could beat Clarke. By far the most important endorsement, however, came from Lady Thatcher, who was horrified that Clarke might win. Her very public declaration of support outside the House of Commons – 'It's William Hague. Have you got the name? Vote for William Hague to follow the same kind of government I did' – would prove decisive.

In the third and final ballot on 19 June, Hague emerged with ninety-two votes to Clarke's seventy. He had picked up almost all of Redwood's supporters, many of whom had been persuaded by Lady Thatcher's intervention. Nearly seven years after leaving office, her influence on Tory politics remained strong. The leadership election confirmed that being anything other than a Eurosceptic was an insurmountable bar to leading the party. This was the 'anyone but Ken' contest. The result defied the reality that Clarke was the most popular choice outside the confines of Westminster. 'We needed more time to think things through,' regrets Michael Simmonds, a Central Office official. 'All of the old ideological arguments about Europe were fought out in the leadership election. We needed to look at the country and realise why people didn't like us and start afresh, but we just didn't do that.'[11]

Starting from Scratch

At just thirty-six years old, William Hague was the youngest Tory leader since Pitt the Younger in 1783. Conservative MPs had skipped a generation in choosing him in preference to his older rivals, who carried too much baggage from the Major years. 'The depth of the defeat in 1997 was so great that the new leader would be deprived of any capital and credibility,' recalls Daniel Finkelstein, who became Director of Policy under Hague. 'William had to create that authority himself.'[12] Hague himself acknowledged the scale of his task. 'I thought it would be a long haul and it would take two parliaments to recover, but I also thought that there would be a chance of making reasonable progress by the next general election.'[13]

A few months after becoming leader, Hague received friendly advice from John Howard, the Australian Prime Minister, who had led his centre-right party to power in 1996 after thirteen years out of office. He was the first overseas leader Hague met after becoming party leader. After seeing Tony Blair in Downing Street, Howard visited Hague in the Commons, where he said, 'You know, William, there's only one thing harder than the first year in opposition.' 'What's that?' asked the Tory leader. 'It's the second. You've just got to understand how hard this is.'[14]

Hague tried to establish his authority by building a team capable of reflecting the balance of opinion within the party. So depleted were the ranks of Tory MPs that he did not have a huge pool of talent to choose from. 'If we did have a supply of wise people – who were they and where were they?' asks Finkelstein. 'Many were simply not present in the aftermath, having lost their seats, and others drifted off, not to be seen in the wake of the storm.'[15] Clarke refused to serve: 'William offered me deputy leader but we would have fallen out straight away.'[16] Their conflicting views on the single currency would have held up any meaningful progress on other issues, such was the strength of feeling about the issue. Clarke's return to the backbenches was a blow given his popularity in the country and among the party grassroots, as was the departure of Michael Heseltine, who decided to leave the frontbench following his heart problems. Hague did appoint nine former members of Major's Cabinet, including Peter Lilley as Shadow Chancellor, Michael Howard as Shadow Foreign Secretary, Brian Mawhinney as Shadow Home Secretary, Gillian Shephard as Shadow Leader of the Commons and John Redwood as Shadow Trade and Industry Secretary. Lord Parkinson, architect of Mrs Thatcher's 1983 landslide victory, made a surprise return as Chairman of the party. Norman Fowler, another veteran from the Thatcher–Major era, returned from the backbenches to shadow John Prescott's super department of Transport, Environment and the Regions. Hague promoted several figures from across the spectrum, such as the arch Maastricht rebel Iain Duncan Smith, who became Shadow Social Security Secretary, and pro-European David Curry at Agriculture. Others moving up to the top table included former ministers David Willetts and Francis Maude. Only Fowler could claim any real experience in opposition, having been in Mrs Thatcher's Shadow Cabinet before 1979.

Establishing an office for the new Leader of the Opposition was a lonely business. Hague relied on the help of former MPs like Seb Coe and Charles Hendry, who had worked on his leadership campaign. 'We just started from scratch. You tend to forget that once you have been in government that long, there is no structure waiting for you to go into opposition,' recalls Coe, a close friend of Hague's. 'We arrived in the opposition block in the Commons to find that the phones were disconnected. Blair had operated out of a high-tech unit in Millbank, and we only had Central Office, which looked like the scene of a car crash.' Hague asked the former Olympian to become his chief of staff, and Coe began to assemble a team to run Hague's private office, but it would take time for even the most basic duties to be fulfilled. 'It was not unusual for letters to be unanswered after six months,' he recalls.[17] Hague appointed George Osborne as his Political Secretary and Secretary to the Shadow Cabinet. It was all a far cry from the well-oiled Whitehall machine to which the party had had access for eighteen years. 'George didn't even have a proper list of phone numbers so he could let them know when the next meeting was,' a fellow aide recalls.

Life in opposition soon exposed the weaknesses of a party organisation that had fallen into disrepair. Archie Norman, a new MP, was given the task of revamping Central Office as Party Vice-Chairman. A former colleague of Hague's at McKinsey, Norman had successfully turned around the supermarket chain Asda. As a businessman-turned-politician, he was shocked at what he found. 'We had an old-style telephone exchange with two women connecting wires for us,' he recalls. 'Eventually, we installed a new telecom system. Even then we only had two computers connected to the internet in the entire building.'[18] It was no match for Labour's modern head-quarters in Millbank Tower, fitted out with the state-of-the-art campaigning tools including the 'Excalibur' computer, which enabled party officials to rebut attacks at the touch of a button.

Such was the shortage of funds that Norman enlisted friends to help redecorate the building at weekends. The Conservatives were effectively bankrupt: the general election had left the party £8 million in the red, and the auditors warned Lord Parkinson that they were not sure whether they could sign off the accounts. Norman and the new Party Treasurer Michael Ashcroft had to find £3 million of savings from the budget, mainly by making large staff cuts at Central Office, and Ashcroft personally bankrolled the party to the tune of £1 million a year between 1997 and 2001.[19] If it was not for his generosity and that of a few other wealthy donors, it is doubtful whether the party's central organisation could have remained a going concern.

Shaking up the Party

Hague's advisers were daunted by the task ahead of them. 'It was really difficult to know where to start,' Coe recalls. 'We weren't on anybody's radar screen, and nobody was thinking of building long-term relationships with us. It was going to be hard pounding.'[20] Archie Norman took the initiative by writing a memo to Hague outlining what he should do in his first hundred days. He urged the new leader to create a fighting party machine with a mass membership. 'I doubt that he thought it was the most pressing issue, but he was seized with the idea that he should be a reformist leader, and asked me to make it happen,' Norman recalls.[21] Hague saw the logic of party reform: 'We got on with these reforms at the beginning partly because I thought there was no point adopting a lot of policies when we had just been booted out of office after eighteen years. There was also a valid feeling that the MPs had let the party down by squabbling among themselves. We felt the grassroots needed to exert themselves.'[22]

The structure of the party was largely unchanged since the days of Benjamin Disraeli in the nineteenth century. The voluntary party in the country continued to be subservient to the leadership in Parliament. Archie Norman, who was soon promoted to Chief Executive of the party, began to sweep away the cobwebs and start afresh. He drew inspiration from New Labour's experience in opposition after 1994. An open-plan 'war room' would bring together campaign staff, press officers and the CRD. Just as Peter Mandelson made enemies with his make-over of the Labour machine in the early 1990s, Norman's businesslike manner was not universally popular. 'I was going to deliver it and I didn't mind how much resistance there was,' he recalls.[23] Parkinson played good cop to Norman's bad cop, helping to smooth relations. 'He had no flair for persuading people – he thought he was there to save politics, but he could not understand that he was a novice,' says Parkinson.[24] In reality, the party desperately required the dynamism of a new broom like Archie Norman to help revive it after years of decay.

On 23 July 1997, Hague used his first major speech as party leader to promise a 'democratic revolution'. His proposals would give members a vote in leadership elections, just as Labour had introduced 'one member one vote' in the early 1990s. He set the ambitious target of increasing party membership from 400,000 to a million within four years. For the first time the party would have a constitution, with the creation of a single board to take overall control over both the professional (Central Office and constituency agents) and voluntary (grassroots) wings of the party, although it would still be weighted heavily against the rank and file, with only five of the seventeen members representing the grassroots. Despite Hague's proclaimed desire for decentralisation, the board and its sub-bodies would actually centralise power within the party, extending the control of national officials over local associations. What most pleased the grassroots, however, were the plans to give them a vote in leadership elections.

Hague sought the party's endorsement for his election as leader and his six principles of organisational change ('unity, decentralisa-tion, democracy, involvement, integrity and openness'). As there were no alternatives on offer, this 'back me or sack me' ballot, held just before Hague's first conference as leader in October, was supposed to be low-risk. Nevertheless, almost a fifth of the membership rejected their new leader, on a paltry turnout of just 44 per cent.

The greatest obstacle to Hague's 'democratic revolution' was his parliamentary party. MPs fiercely defended their right to elect the leader. Some proposed an electoral college to include party members, with MPs retaining the lion's share of the vote. Hague was happy to allow the grassroots to vent their fury at the parliamentary party. Many were unhappy at being let down by the sleazy behaviour and divisions among MPs that had preceded the landslide defeat. The first party conference after the election would see fireworks. 'I deliberately let them rebel and gave them half a day at conference to do that, and boy, did they rebel,' recalls Hague. 'They demanded a bigger share of votes in the leadership election and they told off the MPs in no uncertain terms.'[25] When Sir Archie Hamilton, the Chairman of the 1922 Committee, the body that represents backbench Conservative Members of Parliament, rose to speak in defence of MPs he was booed and heckled. The mood suddenly changed. MPs finally relented on the issue, agreeing to a two-stage process whereby they would vote in a series of ballots to select the final two candidates, who would go forward to a ballot of all party members.

Democracy had come to the Conservative Party, but it came at a time when members were leaving the party in droves. Membership had fallen from one million in 1987 to 400,000 in 1997, while the average age of party members, which had been sixty-three in the early 1990s, continued to rise.[26] A shrinking party in the country could now exert real influence, but this presented new problems.

'Entrenching your changes in a democratic party is the right thing to do, but democratising an unreconstructed party and then trying to change it is incredibly difficult,' argues David Willetts. 'The leadership tried too hard to attempt to please the Tory press, which had an agenda that was resistant to change.'[27] It was a criticism that rang true: Hague's reforms looked good on paper, but they overlooked the fact that the real work that needed to be done was in changing the party's policies and broadening its appeal.

In his first year as leader, Hague succeeded in performing one of the largest overhauls of the party organisation in over a century. In February 1998 a ballot of the membership almost unanimously approved his 'Fresh Future' reforms. But few in the outside world would even notice, let alone give him credit. 'I had some confidence that we would soon get going again. Our first party conference was very successful. The first few months did seem to go to plan, but then it became apparent that none of that was making any difference in the country. Whatever we did, it just wasn't cutting through to the voters at all,' Hague recalls. In fact Hague had wanted to go much further in changing the public face of the party, which was predominately male, white and middle-class. There were only thirteen female Conservative MPs after the 1997 election. 'We wanted a woman on every candidate shortlist, and there was a lot of resistance amongst MPs and activists, and so we dropped that to win acceptance of the constitution,' Hague says regretfully. 'We should have had a bigger row and forced it through, but at that time things like that were regarded as very un-Conservative.'[28] Had he been bolder, the public might have taken more notice. It was a mistake that he would make a habit of repeating.

The first tests of public opinion after the election did not bode well. Basking in its honeymoon, Labour recorded average opinion poll ratings of 55–60 per cent for the rest of 1997, while the Conservatives languished at 23–26 per cent.[29] Blair's satisfaction ratings as Prime Minister broke all records. 'I don't know if there was anything we could have done about this,' recalls one of Hague's senior aides. 'We were bit-players in the drama in which Tony Blair was the main character.'

Although the Conservatives retained the safe seat of Uxbridge in a by-election in July 1997, the next time voters went to the polls the party would get the shock of its life. Having lost Winchester, a traditionally safe Tory seat, to the Liberal Democrats in the general election by only two votes, the defeated Conservative MP, Gerald Malone, forced a by-election in November 1997 after contesting the result in the courts. The party's director of campaigning in Central Office, Tony Garrett, told senior staff on the morning of the by-election that the result would be 'too close to call', and agents on the ground in the cathedral city believed that there would be only two thousand votes in it either way. When the votes were counted, the Liberal Democrat MP, Mark Oaten, was returned with a majority of over twenty thousand. 'It was a huge eye-opener. There was a tendency for us to think that the electorate would wake up after the general election and feel that they had overshot the mark,' recalls Francis Maude, who was then Shadow Culture Secretary. 'Here we were giving them the chance to say, "Sorry guys, we didn't mean to do it," and put right what was meant to be a Tory seat. A lot of colleagues just didn't get it. There was something deeply wrong; we were totally in denial.'[30] Maude, who had been out of Parliament between 1992 and 1997, was one of a small number of MPs around the Shadow Cabinet who began to recognise how unpalatable the Conservative Party had become, and how powerful the mood for change in the country really was.

Getting Round the Kitchen Table

For all the changes to its organisation, the Conservative Party had not come to terms with defeat. Inside Central Office there were a few figures who understood the depth of the problem, and realised that the party's relationship with the electorate had completely broken down. In an organisation sapped of intellectual energy and drive, they cut lonely figures. Among them was Andrew Cooper, who had overseen the party's private polling since early 1996. Having previously worked for the former Labour Foreign Secretary David Owen, who helped to form the breakaway SDP in 1981, he became a supporter of John Major at the 1992 general election before joining the centrist think tank the Social Market Foundation (SMF) as head of research. Daniel Finkelstein was another former member of the SDP and director of the SMF, who joined Central Office in 1995 to develop policy. Finkelstein and Cooper were two of the brightest officials in Central Office: they had as sophisticated an under-standing of public opinion as anybody in the party. Hague appointed Finkelstein to direct policy, while Cooper was given the unenviable task of devising a strategy for recovery.

Cooper had been influenced by Michael Portillo's speech at a fringe event at the 1997 party conference. Portillo's lecture, 'The Ghost of Conservatism Past, the Spirit of Conservatism Future', was a blunt assessment of how the party had come to be regarded in the 1990s. His shock at how he himself seemed to embody the party's unpopularity had caused him to consider what had gone wrong. Cooper shared Portillo's analysis: 'Although there were clearly parts of the Conservative government's record that led to its defeat, the reaction on the doorstep during the 1997 campaign was more about the party's character, not about its beliefs. They disliked our motives and us as people,' Cooper says.[31] The party had become completely estranged from ordinary people's lives and concerns. His research showed that the majority of people had accepted that a dose of Thatcherite medicine had been necessary to cure the economy of its industrial relations ills and the scourge of inflation. In fact, the party was credited with the economic recovery in the mid-1990s, despite the calamity of Black Wednesday, and some polls during the 1997 general election showed that Major and Clarke were more trusted to manage the economy than Blair and Brown. But the state of the public services, principally health and education, had emerged as a key public concern during the 1990s. Instead of responding to this, the party became obsessed with Europe, holding a conversation with itself rather than with the voters.

An aficionado of American politics, Cooper seized on a phrase used by the senior Democrat Congressman, Dick Gephardt, to explain why the Republican Party had done so badly in recent mid-term elections. The Republicans had become obsessed with impeaching President Clinton for various misdemeanours in office, rather than tackling the 'kitchen table issues' that mattered to people. 'We needed to think about what ordinary hard-working people talked about around the kitchen table, and show that we shared their values,' says Cooper. His strategy paper 'Kitchen Table Conservatives' starkly laid out the deep-seated perceptions of the party. It suggested 'ten-thousand-volt shocks', bold, dramatic gestures 'to make people sit up and go, "Wow, that's surprising, we wouldn't have expected them to do that." '[32] Cooper unashamedly borrowed from New Labour's polling guru and chief strategist Philip Gould, whose recent book *The Unfinished Revolution* charted his party's long spell in opposition and its recovery. Cooper recommended that Hague do the following: 'a high profile expulsion by the [party's] ethics and integrity committee ([which says] we will not tolerate sleaze); an impatient confrontation with the Carlton Club (we are inclusive); a speech saying that we deserved to lose the general election (we are not arrogant and we are listening); a clear position on reform of the House of Lords (we have changed)'.

When Cooper presented the paper to Hague, Chief Whip James Arbuthnot and a number of other close aides in November 1998, the leader lapped it up: 'I agree with almost every word of it.' 'I wish I had asked him which words he disagreed with,' Cooper now says. He was surprised at how little discussion there was. 'Unless anyone objects, this will be our strategy,' Hague instructed. A few days later, Cooper made another presentation to Hague and the full Shadow Cabinet. 'From now on I want you all to be clear that I shall promote and reward exclusively on how closely you stick to this strategy,' Hague declared. After this, no one was willing to express outright opposition to the paper, and in the discussion that followed everyone tried to find something in the paper that they could be positive about. But it was clear to Cooper that they were unconvinced. Sure enough, many of Hague's colleagues ignored the new strategy in speeches, parliamentary questions and media appearances. Hague instructed Cooper to have one-to-one meetings with the

Shadow Cabinet to find out what their reservations were. Only one, Gary Streeter, the Shadow International Development Secretary, appeared to understand what was expected: 'So what you're saying is that we need to do everything differently?' 'Yes, exactly,' Cooper replied.[33]

Hague encouraged groups of backbench MPs to go to Cooper's presentations at Central Office. They left unimpressed. Many blamed the election defeat on John Major for being 'weak and useless' or 'not right-wing enough', or felt that Tony Blair had 'pulled the wool over people's eyes, nicked our policies and millions had stayed at home rather than vote for us'. Disappointed with the complacency of Conservative MPs, in January 1998 Cooper wrote a follow-up paper entitled 'Conceding and Moving On', a phrase taken straight out of *The Unfinished Revolution*. New Labour had understood that the Conservatives had won the argument on some issues, particularly the Thatcherite settlement of the economy and the demise of trade union power, and so had to 'concede and move on'. Only by 'letting go' could Labour really change. This argument touched a very raw nerve. While many backbenchers dismissed Major's leadership, frontbenchers who had served in his government were not prepared to have its record traduced. 'We should have taken a strong line: we had left with a golden economic legacy and said that nobody can manage the economy better than we can. That should have been our robust approach,' argues Ann Widdecombe, one of the most colourful former ministers from the Major years. 'We disowned the past, and it was the single biggest mistake we made – we began making it with William Hague and have been making it ever since. We went crawling around saying, "Oh no, we're terribly sorry, we really are going to change," and the question was, to what and from what, and nobody really had an answer.'[34]

It was a view that resonated with the rank and file, who detested the thought of 'doing a Blair' to their party. In 1997 Hague had begun to make amends with the electorate by apologising on behalf of the Conservatives for taking the country into the ERM, leading to the débâcle of Black Wednesday. However, the party's own research showed that most voters did not think the Tories had apologised at all. The irony was that the most vociferous defenders of the Major government happened to be those who had been most critical of the Prime Minister at the time. 'No matter how often you replay the video of the last election, we always get wiped out,' was Finkelstein's riposte to an argument that showed that many senior Tories simply refused to have an honest debate about how their party had lost, and what its purpose was in the modern world. This was no longer a world torn by the divisions of the Cold War: the bogeymen of the left were now few and far between, but many on the right had failed to notice.

By the spring of 1999, the 'Kitchen Table' strategy had been reduced to Shadow Cabinet discussions about appearance. 'We had great debates about whether we should wear suits and ties or open collar shirts on TV,' recalls one shadow minister. 'There was not really any profound discussion about the real issue which was the character and perception of the party,' says Oliver Letwin, who had been elected as a new MP in 1997. 'I remember feeling utterly alone. It wasn't a discussion that anybody was having. Colleagues weren't talking about it, nor were the think tanks. We talked about other things, like Europe and tax, but not that.'[35] Emotionally, many MPs had been so stunned by the 1997 defeat that they were unable to 'let go' and understand what the country really thought of them.

Responsibility for the demise of the 'Kitchen Table' strategy lay with Hague himself. As leader, he failed to convince his senior team of its merits, despite his enthusiastic endorsement. Neither did he lead by example. 'It still puzzles me that he never followed it,' says Cooper. 'I frequently found myself challenging him on things he did and said, pointing out that they did not accord to the strategy. He had been elected leader on a reforming ticket, but he is not by nature and temperamentally a modernising person; he's traditional in most of his instincts and attitudes – he loves the rough and tumble of politics. It was almost like he wanted someone to give him an off-the-shelf way of doing it.'[36] Hague himself confessed to not being fully convinced by Cooper's strategy: 'It was thoughtful and correct, but it was an incomplete analysis. It was more a public relations strategy, as it didn't really tell us what to do – it was more of a diagnosis than a prognosis. I didn't find anything in the "Kitchen Table" stuff that was going to give us success then – maybe it would ten years later, but there was no guarantee we would be around in ten years' time.'[37]

In fact, Cooper's strategy was more operational than Hague suggests, and included a set of guidelines for Hague and his shadow team to follow. He advised them to start 'talking about the future, not the past', 'using the language of people, not politicians' and 'being *for* things and people, not just *against* them'. These suggestions may not necessarily have been a panacea, but at least they offered an avenue that Hague could have pursued.

Ultimately, Hague was not confident enough to lead a thorough rethink of the party's position. Almost two years into the job, his leadership was not secure. In December 1998 he had suffered the humiliation of the Tory leader in the House of Lords, Lord Cranborne, brokering a deal with Tony Blair to save ninety-two hereditary peers whose seats in the House of Lords were threatened by proposed constitutional reforms. Hague was opposed to the government's plans to remove the right of all of the 750 hereditary peers to sit in the Lords until the party formed its policy towards reforming the Upper House. Cranborne's secret deal with the government left Hague no choice but to sack him, but the episode gave the impression that he was not in control of his party.

Hague was also painfully aware that the party's average poll ratings showed no sign of improvement, stubbornly hovering below 30 per cent. The traditional Conservative-supporting newspapers cried out for vigorous opposition to the Labour government, but Blair was enjoying a prolonged honeymoon as the economy continued to grow. Feeling the pressure, Hague urged the Shadow Cabinet to be more combative. 'We were providing a running commentary, saying no to everything, so that people could remember how negative and rude we'd been about Labour at the end of each week, but had no better idea about how a Conservative government would make the world a better place,' laments Willetts.[38] 'William's big problem was that he was not strategic – he was flying by the seat of his pants all the time,' says another frontbencher. The central question about how the party tackled its past would soon erupt into a full-blown row that threatened Hague's increasingly precarious position.

Lilley's Taboo and Hague's Wobble

With Hague and his Shadow Cabinet unconvinced by the 'Kitchen Table' strategy, coming to terms with why the party had become so unpopular would be far from straightforward. The next opportunity arrived when Peter Lilley, Hague's deputy, tried in vain to draw a line in the sand under the party's Thatcherite inheritance. This exposed a real taboo within the party about acknowledging the limits of the Thatcher revolution while understanding how the political landscape had changed since her fall. The conservative commentator Andrew Sullivan adeptly summed up the tension when he wrote that the Tories were 'as culturally inept as they were economically successful. They created the substance of the new country but they couldn't articulate it.'[39]

Lilley had been associated with the Thatcherite wing of the party. His notorious rendition of 'I've got a little list' from Gilbert and Sullivan's *The Mikado* at the 1992 party conference included a jibe at 'young ladies who get pregnant just to jump the housing queue'. It was a performance that would be played over and over again on the airwaves, much to his embarrassment. However, he was also one of the party's clearest thinkers, alongside Willetts, and his attempts as Major's Social Security Secretary to reform the welfare system in the 1990s had earned him respect throughout Whitehall. Hague asked him to conduct a review of policy in June 1998, when he relieved him of his role as Shadow Chancellor while promoting him to the deputy leadership.

Lilley embarked on a consultation exercise called 'Listening to Britain', in which shadow ministers would meet nurses, teachers and other members of the public and ask what mattered to them. He was not encouraged by his colleagues: 'They all wanted to stand up and give a speech. I said, why start off giving a speech if you are there to listen?'[40] What Lilley could distil from his review helped to inform the R.A. Butler Memorial Lecture which he delivered at the Carlton Club, the social hub for Tory grandees, on Tuesday, 20 April 1999. By coincidence, on the same evening over a thousand Conservatives would descend on the Hilton Hotel in Park Lane for a dinner to celebrate the twentieth anniversary of Mrs Thatcher's first election victory. Both the timing and the substance of Lilley's lecture set the stage for a damaging row inside the Shadow Cabinet. 'Once he gave it all hell let loose,' recalls Willetts. 'No one realised that it was lighting the blue touchpaper.'[41]

Lilley argued that the party had settled the economic and industrial questions of the 1980s on its terms, and now the debate had moved on to the state of the public services. This chimed with Cooper's analysis. In characteristically logical fashion, Lilley sought to underline the point. 'We were associated in the public mind, rightly or wrongly, with hostility to the public sector,' he recalls. 'As far as the NHS was concerned there was a feeling that we wanted to flog it off to our friends in the City and make people pay at the point of care. They were absurdly false caricatures, because we had never done any of those things whilst in power.'[42] Only if the party succeeded in 'slaying the myths' about privatising the NHS through the back door would the public begin to listen to what it had to say about reforming the public services. 'It was a way of getting onto gentler territory for the electorate, but those messages were a little too early in the life of a badly dented and uncertain party,' says Coe.[43]

Various drafts of Lilley's speech had been circulated to Hague and the Shadow Cabinet, but much as with the discussion over the 'Kitchen Table' document, there was surprisingly little debate before it was given. 'We let it go through without enough attention because we were thinking about other things,' claims Hague.[44] It is more likely, however, that no one bothered to read it properly. Lilley's speeches were not known for creating much press coverage, and in view of the clash with the Thatcher anniversary dinner, it was decided that key sections of the speech would be briefed to the papers as a major statement about the direction of party policy. The press had a field day over the timing. Headlines such as 'Tories: We Won't Privatise Hospitals' on Monday would be succeeded on Tuesday by 'Tories: We're Abandoning Thatcherism'.

Lilley believed that lobby journalists, particularly those from *The Times*, had their own agenda: to destabilise Hague's position before local elections in May. But some of those inside Central Office were incredibly angry. They believed that the speech gave the impression that the party would no longer contemplate private-sector involvement in the public services, which even Blair's government was considering. For the party's Membership Director, Michael Simmonds, it was a point of political principle. He decided to leak an earlier version of the speech to *The Times*, and was promptly dismissed after an internal inquest. 'It showed us at our worst, because we had a serious contribution to the philosophical debate, and we had an opportunity to have a good debate,' laments Ann Widdecombe. 'Instead we had the press in full cry saying it was a departure from Thatcherism, which is not what Peter had said, and a situation where the boys in Central Office were playing a game of personality politics. All it did was portray us as unfit for government.'[45]

But there was more to the row than game-playing. Lilley's speech touched on a raw nerve, which stemmed from the bitterness over Mrs Thatcher's downfall. 'It was a sizeable moment,' recalls Coe. 'I was with William the morning after the speech, on our way to Liverpool, and although he was always calm under fire, his serenity was at full stretch. The way the media dealt with it, added to the strident voices in the party, meant that this was serious. It was fairly bleak.'[46] When the Shadow Cabinet met later that week, several senior figures expressed their indignation. Francis Maude, Lilley's replacement as Shadow Chancellor, was angry that the ground had not been better prepared. 'I think you should calm down, Francis,' Hague told him. 'No, sometimes you shouldn't be calm,' Maude retorted. 'This is a time for panic!' Michael Howard, the Shadow Foreign Secretary, was even more scathing: 'This is the most dangerous and damaging speech I have ever read in my entire career.' Some of those present were struck by the ferocity of Howard's reaction. 'It chimed in perfectly with the criticism that Labour had always made of the Thatcher government, which we had always resisted. I didn't hold back,' Howard recalls.[47]

Regardless of the fact that it had not been Lilley's intention to repudiate Mrs Thatcher's achievement, the row revealed a real reluctance among influential senior figures to accept that the world had moved on since her day. Lilley believes he could have done things differently: 'I was responsible for it, and there was an unexpected response, so I don't blame anyone else. I would still have said it, but I would have done some different preparation to calm down the loonies.'[48] For others, the speech was a turning point. 'The Lilley episode was a terrible warning,' says Willetts. 'It raised the "no entry" sign over various party taboos, and it made it much harder to make changes to policy.'[49]

The row was the last thing the party needed before the local elections. 'It genuinely did rock Hague's leadership, because it brought to a head the fact that we were doing badly,' Finkelstein recalls.[50] It revealed ineptitude and division at the top of the party, while the Tory press, disillusioned with the state of the opposition, scented blood. More fundamentally, the leadership had reached a fork in the road: either Hague could develop the arguments that Cooper and Lilley had advanced, or he could side with the majority opinion inside his Shadow Cabinet, and not question the party's Thatcherite inheritance. One way would involve more soul-searching with no demonstrable short-term gain, while the other would mean playing familiar tunes to keep the press and the party faithful onside. Hague and his team chose the latter, and in doing so they lost any chance they had to address the causes of the party's unpopularity.

To Blair and his aides in Number 10, it was a defining moment. 'When Peter Lilley attempted to catapult the Tory party forward and was rebuffed, we all thought, "Great – we've got quite a long time left in office," ' recalls one senior Labour adviser. 'We knew exactly what was being played out from our own experience in opposition;

it was that Lilley was saying to his party, "It's about us, we've got to change," and the rejection of that view told us that the Tories were several years away from being a threat. They obviously just didn't get it.'

For Hague, survival became the primary motivation. He was comforted by the fact that his robust exchanges with Blair at Prime Minister's Questions cheered up his backbenches. Many Tory MPs left for their constituencies at the end of the week feeling that Hague had outwitted Blair, but they were painfully aware that his public profile outside the bearpit of Parliament paled in comparison to Blair's. Images of the youthful leader wearing a 'Hague' baseball cap at a theme park, or attending the Notting Hill Carnival, attracted ridicule, as would his claim in August 2000 to have drunk fourteen pints of beer a day in his youth. 'Once the story became us failing to pick ourselves up off the floor, these incidents came to be seen as the cause of our problems, which they weren't,' Hague laments.[51] He had done himself few favours following the death of Diana, Princess of Wales in August 1997, when his wooden statement appeared out of touch in comparison with Blair's emotional reaction. While Blair, once again, articulated the mood of the nation, Hague could only offer the suggestion that Heathrow be renamed 'Princess Diana International Airport'.

Most seriously for Hague, the party's focus groups found that voters thought he was a weak leader, and had to be replaced if the party's ratings were to improve. As criticism of Hague's leadership grew, he himself began to have serious doubts about his position. There had been modest gains in the local elections in May 1999, but still the party only polled 33 per cent of the vote, lagging well behind Labour. Members of the Shadow Cabinet were either confused or angry about the direction in which Hague was taking the party. 'I really wondered if we could keep it together at all. I wondered if there would be an open division in the party, or if I would have to stand down as leader,' Hague recalls.[52] Between late April and early May, he wobbled. Something would have to be done to lift his spirits and boost his position.

Turning Right

Just as Hague's confidence reached its lowest ebb, he received encouragement from two new additions to his team. Nick Wood, a hardened lobby correspondent with *The Times*, and Amanda Platell, a former editor of the *Sunday Express*, were appointed to bolster the party's media operation. Hague realised that the coverage of Peter Lilley's speech had been a disaster. He lacked a 'heavyweight' figure to handle the media since assuming the leadership, and his advisers kept pressing him to find 'our Alastair Campbell'. Campbell's press operation from Number 10 was vastly superior to anything the Tories could muster. Indeed, Campbell and Mandelson regularly ran rings around Tory announcements or press releases. In the plain-speaking Australian Platell, Hague finally found someone who knew and could speak to newspaper editors on their own terms, and could take on the party's most hostile critics in the press.

Both Platell and Wood were shocked at what they found when they arrived. 'It was clear to me from the beginning that William's agenda was quite fuzzy,' Wood recalls. 'It just didn't translate into an easy message for people to understand.' They realised that there was very little time to turn things around if Hague was to survive: the next electoral test would be the European Parliament elections in June. 'If we did badly in the European elections, then that would have been the end of William Hague.'[53]

By May 1999 Hague had at least managed to defuse some of the tension surrounding the European question, in particular whether Britain should drop Sterling in favour of the Euro. At his first party conference as leader he pledged to oppose doing so for the 'foreseeable future'. It was a line that was bound to come under pressure, given the strength of feeling on both sides of the divide. The crunch point had come two years earlier, when during a four-hour meeting of the Shadow Cabinet on 24 October 1997 it was agreed that the party would oppose membership of the single currency during the current Parliament and the next. David Curry and Ian Taylor, both prominent Europhiles, promptly resigned from the Shadow Cabinet. They were followed a few months later by the former Cabinet minister

Stephen Dorrell. The new policy was solidified by a ballot of party members in 1998. 'For a number of months Eurosceptics and Europhiles, from Teresa Gorman to Ken Clarke, were regularly coming in to see him to persuade him to move in their direction,' says Coe. 'But in the end they all knew that he would not move from the stake he placed in the ground.' The uncertainty of the Major years had disappeared. 'The range war just petered out. We had occasional sniper fire, but it ceased to cause anywhere near as much damage as before.'[54]

George Osborne, Hague's Political Secretary, also sensed that a 'potentially fatal civil war' on Europe had been averted. Yet he feared that it might erupt again in October 1999 when Michael Heseltine and Ken Clarke shared a platform with Tony Blair at the launch of 'Britain In Europe', the embryonic 'Yes' campaign for a referendum on joining the Euro. Indeed, Osborne wondered at the time whether this could have been the moment that the Conservative Party split in two, as Labour did when the SDP formed in 1981. But the departure of leading Europhiles from the Shadow Cabinet, and their dwindling numbers on the backbenches, had given Hague the space to allow the hardened Euro policy to settle.

Now the leadership could use the European elections to present the party's Eurosceptic credentials. Hague promised radical reform of the EU and a halt to further integration, encapsulated in his own slogan, 'In Europe, not run by Europe'. His aides, particularly Platell and Wood, believed this would resonate with public opinion and the grassroots. 'We constructed as hard-hitting and noisy a campaign as we could,' says Wood. 'William was totally comfortable with the message.'[55] The election results on 13 June were widely perceived to be a success for the party, which came first in a nationwide election for the first time since 1992, with 36 per cent of the vote and thirty-six MEPs. Although turnout was a dismally low 24 per cent, the result gave a huge fillip to Hague's confidence. Enthused by the campaign, supporters had come out to vote. It proved to be a crucial turning point for Hague: 'I thought that if we lost the European elections I would have outlived my usefulness and maybe it would have been time for me to go. As it turned out we did very well so that thought went away pretty quickly.'[56]

Hague and his aides were convinced that pressing the Eurosceptic button would lead to future success. The campaign had cemented the influence of his new media advisers. 'Amanda became by far the most influential adviser to William for the rest of the Parliament,' one aide recalls. Platell and Wood now saw their job as being to protect and promote the leader at all costs. There would be a harder line to policy and presentation, while any argument that challenged the leadership's position was rapidly dismissed. Platell soon made enemies; in fact she came to be loathed by some in Central Office. Andrew Cooper, who failed to see eye to eye with her after she joined in March, left four months later. Peter Lilley left the Shadow Cabinet in June. 'William summoned me and said, "The last few months have been extremely destabilising and nearly led to the end of my leadership, and so if one us has to go it has to be you," which was fair enough,' Lilley recalls.[57] Michael Howard, Gillian Shephard and Norman Fowler also departed from the Shadow Cabinet, further sapping Hague's frontbench team of experience. Cecil Parkinson had already left in December 1998.

Loyalty to Hague was now paramount. It came at the expense of any attempt to mount a plan for recovery in the long term. Platell in particular 'waged war against anyone who she suspected was not totally loyal to him', another aide remarked. She skilfully courted the editors of the tabloids, despite the *Sun* having already given up on Hague and the party – on the eve of the party conference in 1998 he was portrayed on the paper's front page as the famous Monty Python dead parrot with the headline: 'This party is no more . . . it has ceased to be . . . this is an ex-party. Cause of death: suicide.'[58] Hague's new media advisers sought to project him as a 'tough guy' who understood the concerns of ordinary people. Together with Nick Wood, Platell formed an alliance with Seb Coe, Hague's chief of staff, and from the summer of 1999 Hague trusted their advice much more than that of the Shadow Cabinet. Some were concerned that he had become too reliant on a close-knit team of young advisers. 'I remember going to an away day,' says Parkinson. 'There were only six of us there. I asked halfway through, "Where does the Shadow Cabinet fit into your thinking?" They were convinced that just this little group could do it on their own.'[59]

Platell and Wood encouraged Hague to take a line on issues that would play well with the tabloid press. Support for Tony Martin, a Norfolk farmer who shot dead an intruder breaking into his house, brought favourable coverage in the red-tops and the *Daily Mail*, but attracted criticism in other quarters. 'Amanda rehabilitated William Hague, but not the Conservative Party,' one former party aide observed. It was a press strategy designed to secure 'core' supporters, but it did not impress swing voters. 'It was a shift towards a more robust kind of conservatism that spoke for the silent majority,' Wood insists.[60] Policy documents such as the *Common Sense Revolution* included measures to crack down on ill-discipline in schools and bogus asylum seekers. It was hoped that a tough stance on law and order and a commitment to lower taxes, through a 'tax guarantee', would be music to the ears of supporters. Hague memorably said that 'If the Common Sense Revolution was a person it would be Ann Widdecombe,' the tough-talking new Shadow Home Secretary. 'It mattered more to party members that the leader was coming out with things that they agreed with than the fact that the party was not doing so well,' admits Rick Nye, who joined Central Office as Director of Research in 1999. 'It was the height of our introspection.'[61]

Only once did the Conservatives overtake Labour in the opinion polls – during the fuel crisis in September 2000. This owed more to the government's unpopularity over high petrol duty than to any faith in the Tory alternative. Three years into government, New Labour had survived its first domestic crisis, when protesters blocked access to oil refineries, leading to a shortage of fuel. Voters were prepared to give Blair the benefit of the doubt after the crisis ended, and the polls soon reversed. Although the Conservative Party made some progress in local and European elections, its performances in parliamentary by-elections continued to be abysmal. A dire warning came at the Romsey by-election in May 2000, when a rock-solid Tory majority fell to the Liberal Democrats. If there was a moment at which to pause and question whether the approach pursued since the European elections was working, it was after the result in Romsey. The leadership pressed on regardless.

Portillo Returns and Disharmony Reigns

Victory at the Kensington and Chelsea by-election in November 1999 provided one glimmer of hope, even though it was the party's safest seat in the country. The death of the veteran diarist and Tory MP Alan Clark paved the way for Michael Portillo to return to the Commons. Hague hoped that Portillo would strengthen the front-bench team; it was a sign of his continuing vulnerability that he extended the invitation so soon to a man who was widely seen as a rival for the Tory crown. 'William had suffered a huge amount of undermining, which was compounded by the fact that we had a king across the water in the shape of Michael Portillo,' says Widdecombe. 'Everywhere I went, including Tory associations around the country, people asked me, "Have we got the right leader?" and there were a lot of people waiting for Michael to take over.'[62]

The former Defence Secretary had embarked on a great deal of soul-searching after his dismissal by the voters of Enfield Southgate in 1997. A series of television documentaries, including a journey by train across Spain tracing his family roots, had helped to rehabilitate his public image. He had also embarked on a political journey since his defeat, in an attempt to come to terms with why his party had been so comprehensively rejected. Hague's team were not entirely convinced that his journey was complete. Soon after Portillo returned to Parliament, Nick Wood had lunch with him. 'I asked him what he thought we should be doing, and he replied that he didn't know. I then reeled off what we were planning to do, and he said absolutely nothing,' recalls Wood. 'So I went back to William and said that he seemed happy with everything. In reality, he wasn't happy at all.'[63]

Within two months, Hague invited Portillo to replace Francis Maude as Shadow Chancellor. Maude had failed to land any blows on Gordon Brown, and had given a huge hostage to fortune when he predicted that Britain was heading for a 'downturn made in Downing Street' at a time when, apart from the bursting of the dot.com bubble, the economy showed little sign of slowing. Hague felt that Maude had not given him the support he expected from a Shadow Chancellor, and considered removing him from the Shadow Cabinet in the reshuffle. At Portillo's insistence, Maude was kept on board, taking over as Shadow Foreign Secretary.[64] Portillo quickly made an impact as Shadow Chancellor, reversing the party's opposition to the minimum wage and the independence of the Bank of England, two of Labour's most popular economic measures since 1997. However, he found a hardened opponent in Brown. 'This was a Chancellor of the Exchequer who at that stage was at the top of his game, publicly and professionally,' says Coe. 'Neither Francis nor Michael could lay a glove on him.'[65]

As the leadership prepared for the final party conference before the general election, which was expected in spring 2001, one last effort was made to broaden the party's appeal. Hague formed a new strategy group of senior shadow ministers and aides. Two new MPs, Tim Collins and Andrew Lansley, also joined the group. They had been at the heart of the successful 1992 general election campaign, and would become prominent figures in planning for the 2001 election. The strategy group discussed how the party should respond to the public's continuing concerns over the state of the public services. While the government had been surprisingly cautious since 1997, sticking to Conservative spending plans and avoiding major reform, there was a strong view that the Tories should not even talk about health or education, because the public was far more inclined to trust Labour in those fields, as opinion polls had indicated, and they could not win the argument. Portillo and Maude, who had formed an alliance, disagreed, as did Archie Norman, who had recently been promoted to the Shadow Cabinet as Shadow Environment Secretary. 'It became clear that we were completely empty on these issues, especially health,' Norman recalls. 'On education we did have one or two flagship policies on grammar schools and liberating universities by raising endowments, but that was about it.'[66]

Personality clashes and divisions over social issues soon came to the fore. The tensions focused around Portillo. 'Once he returned the party was immediately divided,' recalls one colleague from the Shadow Cabinet. 'I did not recognise the Michael Portillo I knew from before.' The stage was set for tensions to boil over at the conference in Bournemouth in October 2000. The mood had been upbeat until the Shadow Home Secretary, Ann Widdecombe, delivered her keynote speech. A combative performance in which she outlined a 'zero tolerance' approach to drugs established her as the conference darling. During her speech she announced fixed-penalty fines for people caught with cannabis, a policy that had not been discussed in full Shadow Cabinet. Widdecombe insists that it had gone through the 'proper processes', and that Hague had signed the policy off. However, as soon as the press were briefed on the day of Widdecombe's speech, an argument developed about whether those caught would receive a criminal record. The police questioned how the policy could be enforced, and Widdecombe believes her colleagues used the controversy as an opportunity to attack her.[67] The row descended into farce when the *Mail on Sunday*, prompted by a former Central Office official, asked members of the Shadow Cabinet whether they had taken cannabis in their youth. When several replied that they had, the policy collapsed. The Shadow Cabinet could not agree about a supposedly flagship policy at its last conference before the general election. It gave the impression of a party in total disarray and utterly unfit for office.

The newspapers, particularly the traditional Tory-supporting papers, were now filled with stories about splits between 'mods and rockers' in the Shadow Cabinet. Social conservatives like Widdecombe and Duncan Smith were pitted against Maude and Portillo, who took a more liberal stance on issues like gay rights. Widdecombe insists that the press, particularly *The Times*, which she claimed had become 'a Portillista rag', exaggerated the tensions. 'We used to be a relaxed broad Church as a party on these issues, and in my view they didn't need to be resolved, but we were being portrayed as divided and we went along with it,' she says.[68] Yet the tensions were palpable. The decision to oppose Labour's repeal of Section 28 of the Local Government Act, which prohibited the promotion of homosexuality in schools, had already driven a wedge through the parliamentary party, and had provoked the defection of Shaun Woodward to Labour in December 1999. More liberal members of the Shadow Cabinet, like David Willetts, believed that the party had become deeply disengaged from social trends in the country since the 1980s and 1990s: 'We got to a point after 1997 that we knew what to say about privatisation, but when for example we were asked about divorce rates, there was a completely incoherent muddle.' The backlash over 'Back to Basics' in the early 1990s had inhibited Conservative politicians from addressing such issues, Willetts argues. 'Nobody had thought it through properly. Some people said that married couples should stick together and that there should be tax breaks for marriage, while others said divorce was part of modern life and politicians shouldn't talk about it.'[69]

The tensions that consumed the Shadow Cabinet had taken on a poisonous aspect. Hague's authority was once again under question, and his aides, principally Platell, believed that Portillo, Maude and Norman had a subversive agenda. 'Amanda's battle with Michael was very destabilising. She took the view that he was plotting against William, and so set out to spite anybody who might be on his side,' Daniel Finkelstein recalls.[70] By now the relationship between Hague and his Shadow Chancellor and Shadow Foreign Secretary had completely broken down. 'I did have a difficult time with Michael and Francis in that period,' says Hague. 'I didn't particularly feel that they were team players at the time, and I don't think they felt I was loyal to them, even though I was.'[71] Portillo and Maude felt that they were being regularly briefed against in the press by Platell and Wood, and that Hague refused to do anything about it. When Hague challenged them to prove it, which was impossible, he said that he could not act without proof, which they took to mean that he was, at best, complicit.

Such was the level of mistrust between Hague and his two senior colleagues that resignation threats were issued over the appointment of backroom staff. Hague's advisers took great exception to some of Portillo's confidants and advisers. 'I managed to hold them together, and if they threatened to resign I largely ignored them. I wasn't going to deal with such stupidities, and refused to speak to them,' says Hague.[72] According to one senior member of staff at Central Office, this led to the appearance of an 'upstairs downstairs' mentality, with Maude and Portillo considered highly disingenuous.

Hague also became increasingly frustrated that his Shadow Chancellor failed to suggest ideas to help the party recover. 'Some of Michael's thinking tended to change by the week,' recalls one of Hague's aides. 'This was more about Michael's journey than the rehabilitation of the party.' Portillo's friends noticed that he had lost his enthusiasm for the cut and thrust of party politics. 'Michael almost immediately regretted coming back into Parliament,' says one. 'He told me that he had enjoyed each year of his adult life more than the previous one, until that year. He thought there was lots of intellectual nonsense going on. He also didn't particularly rate William.'

Staring at Defeat

The Conservative Party was heading for another electoral drubbing. Despite the tensions at the top of the party, Central Office was at least ready for the campaign. During the months leading up to the election there were some successful publicity efforts, including posters with the slogan 'You've paid the taxes, so where are the nurses/teachers/police?' This was one of the few attempts to campaign on the public services, and chimed with the party's private polling, which revealed the public's concerns over the lack of progress made by Labour. Andrew Lansley had planned it as the theme for the pre-election period, and some in the party felt it was a message that should be pushed right up to polling day, advice that was turned down.

After a delay caused by an outbreak of Foot and Mouth Disease, Tony Blair announced on 8 May 2001 that the election would be held on 7 June. For all Hague's faults as leader, he had presided over an overhaul of the machine to ensure that the party would survive.

The first week and a half of the campaign went relatively well. The party faithful had developed a strong affection for Hague, and there was a degree of *bonhomie* within his close team as they criss-crossed the country by helicopter. Yet any feelings of optimism were illusory – voters often walked away at the sight of blue rosettes coming towards them. Senior figures were already contemplating what might happen after the defeat. 'Holding them together in the campaign was hard – for several of them their first instinct when the going got tough was to reach for the lifebelts,' says Coe.[73]

Experienced figures in the parliamentary party were not hopeful. 'The 2001 campaign was the most ridiculous we have ever fought,' Ken Clarke recalls. 'People were not interested in saving the pound, and we avoided the major issues. It was like Labour's doomed campaign in 1983.'[74] The 'Keep the Pound' roadshow, inspired by the perceived success of the European elections campaign, was designed to arouse interest in the campaign: Hague's advisers hoped that his appearance on the back of a lorry holding up a pound coin would galvanise party supporters. Yet for many voters, the fact that Labour had already committed to holding a referendum on the single currency made Hague's rallying cry seem utterly irrelevant. 'Keeping the pound' was not the issue on which votes would turn.

On the eve of the campaign, Hague had told the party's spring forum in Harrogate that Labour's re-election threatened to turn Britain into a 'foreign land'. The author of the speech, Daniel Finkelstein, was alarmed that it was briefed to the press that 'foreign land' implied concerns over immigration and asylum, as well as the impact of a federal Europe. Labour immediately jumped on the speech as peddling a sinister agenda. 'It wasn't William's fault, and it was not an attempt to say immigrants would turn Britain into a foreign land,' insists Finkelstein. 'We were always careful with language. I am the son of two refugee immigrants, and we would never have written something like that. I don't think I have ever been as depressed about anything in politics as that.'[75] But the damage had been done. To the outside world it appeared that the Conservatives were hopelessly trapped in a tawdry sideshow of their own, unconnected with the Britain of 2001.

When Mrs Thatcher addressed a rally of the party faithful in the closing days of the campaign, Hague hoped she would lift morale. She urged them to turn out for the party, warning that another Labour term in office would lead to the 'progressive extinction of Britain as a nation state'.[76] Labour responded with posters of Mrs Thatcher's trademark perm superimposed on Hague's bald head. It was the most memorable poster of the entire campaign, making the Tory leader look weak and un-prime ministerial. The Conservative campaign, masterminded by Lansley and Collins, sought to revive the appeal the party had enjoyed in Mrs Thatcher's heyday. It was nothing more than an ersatz Thatcherism, a bizarre caricature of the campaigns she had fought in the 1980s. The 'Keep the Pound' campaign may have resonated with some of the party's supporters, but talk of 'bogus' asylum seekers left a bitter taste in the mouth. 'We were seen as anti-foreign and anti-everything. It became increasingly difficult to see what we were pro, except perhaps Britain,' says Archie Norman.[77]

On the issues that most concerned voters, such as the state of the public services, the Tory campaign completely unravelled. After the Shadow Chief Secretary to the Treasury, Oliver Letwin, had suggested to the *Financial Times* that £20 billion of spending cuts could be found, rather than the official party figure of £8 billion,[78] Gordon Brown raised the spectre of huge Conservative cuts to the public services. Labour's relentless focus on its investment versus 'Tory cuts' struck a chord. Brown's 'dividing line' on spending in 2001 had become the reverse of the Conservative attack on 'Labour's tax bombshell' in 1992. Voters were prepared to give Blair a second term: the economy was prospering and the government had done little to alienate the moderate Conservative voters it had so successfully courted before 1997. In contrast, the opposition looked hopelessly lost, drifting towards another crushing defeat at the hands of New Labour.

Could William Hague have done more to avoid defeat? He admits that the party 'sacrificed some long-term effort for some short-term victories. But we had to make sure that we survived in 2001: many people thought that the party would not make it through at all.'[79] The furore surrounding Peter Lilley's speech and the European elections in spring 1999 were vital turning points for Hague's leadership and the Conservatives' journey in opposition. After pursuing a course in which he sought to modernise the party's decaying organisation and commissioning the 'Kitchen Table' research, Hague panicked, and found comfort in a more populist groove advocated by his new media aides. When Lilley confronted his colleagues with some home truths, they took fright and wrapped themselves in a cloak of complacency. Hague's weakness was that he listened to those whose interests lay purely in propping him up, rather than considering the long-term future of the party. The leadership had steered the party to a relatively more settled position on the single currency, one of the burning issues immediately after the 1997 general election, and one which had plagued the Conservatives ever since the downfall of Mrs Thatcher. Like John Major, Hague had managed to find a way through, but his formula chimed much more with the weight of opinion within the party. Even so, the spectre of a split, which Major so feared, had continued to loom for a time. Although the party had just about survived in one piece, this did little to impress an electorate that had tuned out from what the Conservatives had to offer.

As voters went to the polls on Thursday, 7 June 2001, in fewer numbers than at any general election since 1918, there was a deep sense of foreboding in Central Office. Had they done enough to bring out even their most loyal supporters? Out on the stump, the mood was not promising. 'Everyone knew it was going to be a bloodbath,' recalls one of the party's footsoldiers. 'It was really a case of holding on to what we had and trying desperately hard to make some inroads.'[80] Canvass returns on the eve of polling day suggested that the party might be left with just 120 MPs, adding to the losses of the landslide in 1997. Hague was braced for a devastating defeat: the only question was whether it would sound his party's death knell.

THREE

Staring Into the Abyss
June 2001–October 2003

As the first results came in, it became clear that the Conservative Party was heading for another calamity. William Hague had hoped to make a few dozen gains and a modest increase in the party's share of the vote, the measure of progress that would persuade him to continue as leader.[1] In fact the party had gained just one seat, leaving it with 166 MPs, and increased its share of the vote by one point to 31.7 per cent. After 1997, it was the Conservatives' second-worst result since 1832. Yet the nightmare of losing twenty or thirty more seats had not materialised. As Hague flew down to London from his count in Yorkshire, he began to write his resignation speech, despite pleas for him to stay in the name of stability. As after the landslide defeat in May 1997, the party struggled to compose itself following a crushing defeat. If ever there was a time for an inspired leader to lift the Tories out of the gloom, it was now.

Hague Falls

Standing outside Central Office in bright sunshine on Friday, 8 June, William Hague admitted defeat. 'I believe strongly, passionately, in everything I've fought for. But it's also vital for leaders to listen and parties to change. I believe it is vital the party be given the chance to choose a leader who can build on my work, but also take new initiatives and hopefully command a larger personal following in the country.' He was painfully aware that he had become just the second Tory leader in over a century not to serve as Prime Minister. Many had believed after the Labour landslide in 1997 that victory four or

75

five years later would be a near-impossibility, but past performance showed that the Conservatives were capable of staging impressive recoveries. In the general elections that followed the great landslide defeats of 1906 and 1945 the party made up enough ground to challenge for power next time round. In January 1910 the Conservatives gained 116 seats, while in 1950 they recovered eighty-eight. The gain of a solitary seat was a dismal performance by comparison.

Tony Blair had achieved what no other Labour leader had done: a large enough majority to ensure a second full term in office. Despite a sharp fall in turnout to only 59 per cent, a post-war low, he had received another huge overall majority of 167 seats. With increased majorities in almost all of the constituencies gained from the Conservatives in 1997, New Labour crushed the Tories in large swathes of the country – particularly in their heartland of the south-east. Although they won one seat back in Scotland, the Conservatives failed to recover in Wales, and had slipped into third place in Manchester, Liverpool and many other northern cities. The Liberal Democrats not only won seven more seats from the Conservatives, but came a close second in many of the Tory strongholds in the south and west of England.[2] The Conservative Party's woes were compounded by an electoral system that worked to Labour's advantage. But the harsh reality was that almost one and a half million fewer people voted for the party than in 1997. Beneath the headline figures, the Conservatives were falling back even further.

The one consolation from the 2001 general election was the emergence of a handful of Tory MPs from a new generation. Elected in safe rural seats, they would be the future of the party, set apart from a parliamentary rump comprised of former ministers and backbenchers in the autumn of their political careers. Among them were David Cameron and George Osborne. After three years trying unsuccessfully to secure a winnable seat, Cameron finally persuaded the Witney Conservative Association to adopt him as their candidate in April 2000. Shaun Woodward, who had worked alongside Cameron at Central Office in the 1992 general election campaign, had represented the Cotswolds constituency since 1997. Woodward defected to Labour in December 1999 in protest at Hague's stance on Section 28 and other social issues. 'It's not me who left my party. My party left me,' he regretted at the time.[3] While Woodward was parachuted into a safe Labour seat, Cameron found a new political home in true blue Oxfordshire. Victory in Witney was cold comfort for David Cameron: his party lay in tatters. The new MP had some sympathy with his outgoing leader. If Hague had continued with the 'fresh start' theme of 1997, the result in 2001 might have been even worse, Cameron contends, but at least he would have set out on the right path.

Hague had told only three people that he would resign if he failed to reach his desired target of seats for the election: his wife Ffion, Seb Coe, his chief of staff, and the Chief Whip, James Arbuthnot. When news of his intention to resign began to circulate among senior figures in the early hours of the morning of 8 June, colleagues were in a state of shock. Despite the infighting that had blighted his Shadow Cabinet, many hoped that Hague would remain in post for a while to ensure stability after the expected defeat. 'Michael Portillo was very cross with me when I told him; that was the final straw for him,' says Hague.[4] Portillo was already on the way to the airport to fly to Morocco to consider his own future. After eighteen months of mistrust between them, their relationship had completely broken down; they would not even speak to each other for another seven years.

As Portillo headed for Morocco, several other colleagues in the Shadow Cabinet appealed to Hague to reconsider. 'I wanted him to have another shot at it,' recalls Iain Duncan Smith. 'I tried to persuade him before he went out to the cameras. I stopped trying once I realised he was tired and adamant that he was going.'[5] Nick Wood and Amanda Platell, Hague's loyal media advisers, also urged him to stay, arguing that he was held in great affection by the grassroots. Yet taking on the leadership of his vanquished party was a burden that was perhaps too great for the William Hague of 1997. As one former Cabinet minister commented, 'The sadness for the Conservative Party is that William Hague was put in [too soon]. It was rather like opening a very good wine several years before it should be drunk, and you don't get the best out of it.'[6]

Shocked, Frightened and Hollowed Out

William Hague's sudden departure left a vacuum at the top of the party, just as John Major's had done four years earlier. Instead of the complacent attitude that arose after 1997, senior figures inside the party had little to console themselves with. '2001 was by far the worst result,' says Lord Strathclyde, who became Tory leader in the Lords in 1998. 'I was one of those in 1997 who thought that the pendulum would swing back. After 2001, it seemed to be completely stuck.'[7] 'There was a state of panic; the party didn't know where to go,' recalls Liam Fox, then Shadow Health Secretary.[8] Hague's Shadow Social Security Secretary, David Willetts, laments the fact that there was 'no grown-up discussion of why we lost so badly for a second time. We were getting straight into another leadership election, and because of the fear of appearing divided there was no collective understanding of what had gone wrong. I think we were too frightened of it all.'[9]

The mood in Central Office was despondent. Among those to leave was Daniel Finkelstein, who had been head of policy before standing in Harrow West, a leafy seat in north London that the Conservatives lost in 1997. He would have become an MP had the party made even the smallest of inroads into Labour's majority, but out on the stump, Finkelstein soon realised that the party's campaign was doomed. Like Norman Tebbit, Mrs Thatcher's Party Chairman in the 1987 general election campaign, he compared the party's predicament after 1997 to that of Marks & Spencer. Tebbit's point had been that by dropping traditional lines in favour of more trendy, fashion-conscious items, M&S had alienated its core customers but failed to attract new ones. In 2001, Finkelstein drew a different conclusion: 'M&S was frequented by suburban women whose fashion sense and lifestyle had completely changed. Its sales began to fall because it did not change with its customers, and was committed to the same way of doing things.' It was precisely the same for the Conservative

Party, he argued. 'The party decided after 1997 that it needed to sack the voters and get a new set who were more willing to go along with what it wanted to say to them.' Indeed, M&S only restored its fortunes by broadening its range to accommodate old and new styles.

Instead of pursuing what many commentators labelled a 'core vote' strategy, the party failed to understand what its 'core' supporters – suburban, professional and middle-class (the so-called 'ABC1s') – wanted. 'When a Conservative Party starts attacking the "liberal elite" then you know you're in trouble, because they had actually been a traditional source of support. Ironically, the party had contributed a lot to the fact that these people had changed,' says Finkelstein.[10] New Labour appeared to be listening to voters' concerns about the state of the public services, while the Conservatives had left them unanswered. As a result, the middle classes deserted the party. In 1983 the Conservatives led Labour among ABC1s by 40 per cent. By 1992 that lead had fallen to a still healthy 30 per cent, but by 1997 it had collapsed to 5 per cent, and it was a mere 3 per cent four years later.[11] Only among working-class voters, the DEs, was there a small increase in Tory support, which produced the minuscule rise in the party's overall share of the vote. Such was the solidity of Labour's support and the lowness of the Conservatives' base among these voters that it hardly made a difference.

The party had become trapped in a warped version of its past. 'We had become a neo-Thatcherite party, not a Conservative party,' argues Archie Norman, the outgoing Shadow Environment Secretary. 'We were following an ideology that her disciples developed after she fell, but it wasn't what she believed in the 1980s.'[12] By pushing an agenda which stressed concerns about asylum and immigration, keeping the pound and raising the spectre of Labour's 'foreign land', the party's 2001 election campaign was fought on a narrow platform, and seemed to be aimed purely at 'striving' working-class voters. Mrs Thatcher had succeeded in picking up many of their votes in the 1980s, but she knew that their support was not enough by itself to win an election, and her initial success lay in appealing to both the middle and the working classes. William Hague's election campaign in 2001 was a parody of hers in 1979 or 1983. It was not only out of step with an earlier generation of Thatcherites, but was lost on an electorate that had moved on.

Despite Hague's ambition to revive Conservatism as a grassroots movement, the campaign exposed how thin and aged the party had become on the ground. 'There was a crisis of DNA in the party – it was left with the old, who were too infirm to be the footsoldiers of campaigns, but who actually kept the party ticking over in various places,' one party official observed. Elderly activists were loyal and hard-working, but they were too few in number to sustain a healthy presence in many constituencies. Many local associations, particularly in constituencies which for years had not returned a Conservative MP, had ceased to function as organisations capable of fighting an election campaign. Elderly members were accompanied by a younger generation of activists enthused by Mrs Thatcher's view of the world. 'The young ones socialised only with each other, and were obsessive about politics as well as being socially and culturally tone deaf,' another insider remarked. 'Association meetings were dominated by the old, who weren't necessarily prejudiced or bigoted, but out of step with public opinion on social issues, and a younger set who were atypical of their generation.'

The messages of the 2001 campaign resonated with a hard core of Tory activists, but those who helped to keep the party in touch with the world of work, through the professions, private industry and the public sector, simply drifted away. Disillusioned with or uninterested in a party so far removed from power, fewer and fewer were drawn into Conservative circles. 'There was a lost generation of bright young types who came into political maturity at a time when the party was in decline,' says a party official. 'If you combine this with the disengagement of the broader public from politics you have a perfect storm for the Tory Party struggling to survive in the country.' Along with injections of cash from a small group of donors, the hollowed-out grassroots had helped to keep the party alive after 1997. Now it would be left to the emaciated and estranged ranks of the Tory Party in the country to make the decision about William

Hague's successor. For the 166 Tory MPs returning to Westminster the contest had already begun.

The Peasants' Revolt

The ensuing leadership election, the fifth in twelve years, would not provide the constructive debate that the party so desperately required. As in 1997, five candidates stood: Michael Ancram (Party Chairman after Parkinson retired); Iain Duncan Smith (Shadow Defence Secretary); David Davis (a former minister who had been on the backbenches since 1997); Ken Clarke, who threw his hat into the ring for a second time; and Michael Portillo. With the exception of Clarke and Portillo, all of them appealed to the right of the parliamentary party. Both Duncan Smith and Davis were devotedly Thatcherite and Eurosceptic, while Ancram had a small following among social conservatives. Clarke drew his support from the centre of the party, as well as the dwindling number of pro-Europeans.

Portillo's return to the frontline had been a jarring experience, not least because of his bruising encounters with some of Hague's aides. Even before then he had had doubts about re-entering the political fray. Shortly before returning to Parliament in November 1999, he revealed that he had experienced gay relationships as a young man, an admission he came to regret.[13] Confiding with friends in February 2001, four months before the general election, he gave ten reasons for not wanting to be party leader, including his declining appetite for politics, the pursuit of other interests and a feeling that the party would not be willing to be led in the direction he would wish to take it. Shrugging, he concluded, 'Well, there isn't anybody else.'[14] When he set off for Morocco just after the election defeat, he told friends that he would not stand, but while he was there Francis Maude rang several times to tell him there was a strong tide of support building in his favour. When Stephen Dorrell, a former Cabinet minister from the centre of the party who had backed Ken Clarke in 1997, called to say that he would support him, his mind began to change. On his return to Westminster he resolved to go for it.

Portillo met with Maude and Archie Norman on the Monday after the election, and told them, 'We are going to win this, and win it on our terms. We are going to be uncompromising.' The party had to come to terms with modern Britain, he insisted. Its position on social issues, such as Section 28 and support for marriage through the tax system, had to be reconsidered. Portillo soon gained the support of a number of frontbenchers, including David Willetts and Oliver Letwin, and his campaign manager, Maude, collected further declarations of support from most of the Shadow Cabinet. Portillo also had the support of some of the brightest of the 2001 intake, including David Cameron. Despite being caught up in the Hague–Portillo rivalry, Hague's former Political Secretary George Osborne saw the need for change, and supported Portillo as the right candidate for the time.

Within days Portillo had become the front-runner. But in a series of meetings with undecided backbench MPs he did not make it easy for himself. When a potential supporter, Graham Brady, asked him about all-woman shortlists for selecting parliamentary candidates he refused to rule them out, even though those close to him knew he did not favour them. 'I wasn't happy with his response that "The end justified the means," ' Brady recalls. 'He just wanted a completely free rein to do whatever he saw fit. I then joined the David Davis campaign.'[15] Portillo's tactics would soon backfire. 'He wasn't going to campaign in the conventional fashion or dilute his views in any way,' recalls Michael Gove, a columnist at *The Times* who had written a biography of Portillo in 1995. 'He was essentially saying that the party needed to change profoundly, and unless they could accept his message and understand fully what they were getting into, he would not stoop to conquer.'[16]

Nevertheless, most of Portillo's campaign team were brimming with confidence, insisting that he had nearly a hundred MPs on board. But some were not so complacent. 'I raised my eyebrows when I heard some of the names being mentioned by senior MPs running the campaign,' says Mark MacGregor, a former parliamentary candidate who joined the campaign to organise events. 'For example, I saw William Hague on a list of possible supporters, but Hague had seriously fallen out with Portillo during his time as leader. There was a presumption that MPs would vote for Michael simply because he was the candidate backed by virtually the entire Shadow Cabinet, and that Clarke could not win support because of his views on Europe. Ironically, Duncan Smith was barely even given a moment's consideration.[17] Doubts were also emerging elsewhere in the camp. 'He didn't produce a forward-looking agenda that people could galvanise around,' recalls Archie Norman. 'When we met in my house before the first round, we said we had to have a policy narrative to make it clear what he stood for. Michael was pretty reluctant, but by then he realised it was too late anyway.'[18]

When the results of the first ballot were announced, Portillo emerged in the lead with forty-nine votes. To everyone's surprise, Duncan Smith came second with thirty-nine, and Clarke third with thirty-six. Davis and Ancram, who were tied on twenty-one, both withdrew from the contest. Portillo's lead was nowhere near as large as his campaign team had expected. 'They assumed there would be a wave of support, and when it didn't happen they didn't have a plan B,' Mark MacGregor recalls.[19] For Portillo, it was a defining moment. 'He didn't want to win, because it proved his point about the party not wanting to go where he wanted to lead it,' says his friend the former Tory aide Andrew Cooper.[20] He consulted his team about whether to pull out, but was persuaded to remain in the contest.

While Ken Clarke's campaign had had a faltering start, Iain Duncan Smith had made a surprisingly strong showing. The tactical flaws of Portillo's campaign had provided an opportunity for Duncan Smith to court the right. The Thatcherite and Eurosceptic wing of the party, who would have once flocked to Portillo, were now unconvinced about his candidacy. 'The out-and-out-moderniser package was too much for those who in earlier years had been ardent supporters,' Maude admits. 'He lost his old constituency without gaining enough new people.'[21] Paul Goodman, a newly elected MP, observed that 'There was a massive campaign to sign up the great and the good – the aristocracy of the parliamentary party, one might say – but it overlooked the peasants. Perhaps inevitably, a revolt followed, led by Iain Duncan Smith and managed by Owen Paterson, John Hayes and Bernard Jenkin.'[22] They believed that Duncan Smith would speak up for them and the backbenchers.

Iain Duncan Smith had made his name as one of the Maastricht rebels in the Major years. Before he succeeded Norman Tebbit as MP for Chingford in 1992, he had a career in the army and in business. He became a thorn in the side of the Whips' Office as a serial rebel during the passage of the Maastricht Bill.[23] Pinstriped and balding, Duncan Smith was not one of the most colourful characters on the Tory benches. Yet he was a competent and at times impassioned speaker, leading to a number of approaches to join the government, all of which he turned down. After the landslide defeat in 1997 he won promotion as Shadow Social Security and then Shadow Defence Secretary, and remained loyal to Hague. Many MPs were astonished when he put himself forward as a candidate to lead the party. Despite his loyalty in opposition, his reputation as a rebel remained, and very few considered him leadership material. 'I left Central Office with Iain after William Hague announced his resignation,' recalls Andrew MacKay, who was Shadow Northern Ireland Secretary at the time. 'As we were walking through Westminster, he said: "This is an awful dilemma, Andrew, because I've got to stand for leader to stop Portillo." I was exhausted, but thought, "This cannot be serious." Of all the people I sat around the Shadow Cabinet table with, this decent man was least equipped to do it.'[24] MacKay tried to dissuade him, but Duncan Smith had made up his mind.

Duncan Smith's campaign organisation soon eclipsed that of his rivals. 'We made a tremendous effort working on the new intake. We got a lot onside because the Portillo camp threatened them, and that wasn't a successful tactic,' says Owen Paterson.[25] The 'IDS' camp thought Portillo's campaign was overbearing in its approaches to new MPs, while its pitch was superficial and fixated with politically correct issues of little importance to traditional Tory supporters. Duncan Smith believed that the party had to stop arguing about Europe and broaden its approach: it had to engage with the state of the public services and concentrate on social problems. He also genuinely believed that only someone with impeccable Eurosceptic credentials could lead the party in this way.

When Tory MPs voted in the second round, Clarke came first with fifty-nine votes, ahead of Duncan Smith on fifty-four and Portillo on fifty-three. Portillo was knocked out of the contest by one vote, leaving Clarke and Duncan Smith to go to the final round, which would be decided by party members. It was an astonishing result: Duncan Smith had successfully led a peasants' revolt against the establishment. Many Tory MPs could not bring themselves to vote for Portillo, and a sizeable number of them had voted for Clarke, who picked up twenty more votes than in the first round, as a way of preventing Portillo entering the nationwide run-off. Any lingering interest Portillo might have had in leading the Tories evaporated. Within minutes of losing the vote in the Commons, he sent a text message to Andrew Cooper: it read, 'The slave is free' in Latin. 'I seemed to unite people against me in antagonism,' was his verdict as he announced his intention to leave frontline politics for good.[26]

Michael Portillo's personal and political journey had proved far too much for many backbench Tory MPs. His prescription for a modernised party, forcing it to accept social change, was simply too bitter a pill for them to swallow. 'He had a clear sense of what was wrong with the party, but not the country,' says Willetts. 'He campaigned against the obscurantism and atavism of the Conservative Party, but it became a preoccupation to liberate the party from a caricature of itself. Issues like attitudes to gay people were more important to the party than the country, which had largely accepted that things had moved on. The leadership campaign became a battle for the soul of the party disconnected from where the country stood in 2001.'[27] Many in the Shadow Cabinet understood that these issues had to be confronted, but the rest of the party did not. It was a battle that would continue to rumble in the party, while the rest of the country looked on bemused.

Another issue that continued to preoccupy the party but not the country was Europe. Hague had settled the dispute over the parliamentary party's position on the Euro, but for the Eurosceptic press and the grassroots, European integration still stirred the loins. Portillo's exit ensured a choice between the avuncular Clarke, whose pro-European views they largely disliked, and the relatively unknown Duncan Smith, whose Eurosceptic credentials were comfortably reassuring. Many of Portillo's supporters at Westminster had little option but to back Clarke, but MPs had little influence in a contest that would be decided by ordinary party members. 'We all retreated back into our comfort zones,' recalls Oliver Letwin. 'One lot of people went for Ken and were arguing that we just needed to revert to the golden days, and the others went to IDS to avoid falling into the Europe trap.'[28] Once again, a large number of MPs believed that Clarke would lead them into a distinctly uncomfortable pro-European position.

Drawn out over the long summer recess, the contest became drained of energy. As Clarke and Duncan Smith attended membership hustings across the country, there was little to excite the media, apart from the visible awkwardness between the two candidates. Their personal styles could not have been more different: Duncan Smith was serious but wooden, whereas Clarke was jovial but complacent. 'We didn't do many televised debates because there was so little public interest. We did one on *Newsnight*, and nobody ever asked us to do it again, because it was a pretty turgid affair,' recalls Duncan Smith.[29]

Duncan Smith's campaign won the support of party donors and, crucially, of the *Daily Telegraph*, which under the editorship of Charles Moore represented the most vocal of Tory activists. Duncan Smith's commitment to ruling out membership of the single currency for good played well with a paper that flew the standard for Euroscepticism. 'We were probably rather boring on the subject, and made ourselves the noticeboard,' Moore concedes. 'We could have said that Ken Clarke was the best candidate even though we didn't agree with him, but it would have been a regression if he had won. I do regret the factional negativity that crept in over Europe – it isn't good for papers to bash all the time.'[30] Although he had topped the poll of MPs in July, Clarke did not fancy his chances. 'The problem was that the change of leadership rules made it difficult for me. In 1997 the membership was more supportive, but did not have a vote, and in 2001 the MPs were more supportive, but they did not have the final say.'[31]

As the contest drew to a close in late August, Duncan Smith was in confident mood. Polling of Tory members showed that he had a commanding lead over Clarke. In July the Duncan Smith campaign commissioned focus-group research which showed that activists believed that Clarke 'had not uttered a single word to help during the [2001 election] campaign'. Other comments were very revealing of the mood of the party membership after the 2001 defeat: 'I'm very disappointed with the electorate'; 'People were brainwashed to vote Labour by the papers and the BBC'; and in order to win, the party had to 'just sit it out for the next four years, educate the voters and they'll see we're right in the end'.[32] For a constituency with views like those, it would not take much for a candidate from the right of the party, like Duncan Smith, to attract support. In fairness to his campaign, he tried to talk about the state of the public services and the need for reform, but these were not issues that excited the average Tory member as much as Europe.

Like William Hague in 1997, Iain Duncan Smith received the crucial endorsement of Lady Thatcher. In a letter to the *Daily Telegraph* on 21 August she wrote that he would restore the party's 'faith and fortunes', and warned that Clarke's pro-European views would lead to confusion and contradiction within the ranks: 'I simply do not understand how Ken would lead today's Conservative Party to anything other than disaster.'[33] John Major and Michael Heseltine came out in favour of Clarke, but Thatcher's influence with the party faithful remained strong. Eleven years after leaving office, her interventions, although fewer and farther between because of her declining health, continued to resonate with a large swathe of the party.

Once again, Europe would swing opinion within the party, although it mattered little to how most people voted at general elections. Clarke did not help his own cause. 'Ken's campaign managers got frustrated with him because every time they tried to steer him away from Europe he would just go back to it and make some comment about it,' says Duncan Smith.[34] 'Europe was his undoing,' admits Ann Widdecombe, a rare Clarke supporter from the right. 'People mistrusted his views on the subject, because he was seen as a troublemaker and had shared a platform with Blair in support of the Euro. But people couldn't get their heads round the fact that you could have a view contrary to most in the party and still serve because that view was not going to prevail.'[35] Like Portillo, Clarke was not prepared to change or even tone down his message. 'I wasn't going to compromise my views by saying things that I didn't believe in,' he insists.[36]

Long memories about Clarke's role in Mrs Thatcher's downfall also harmed his prospects. He had been one of the Cabinet ministers who told her in November 1990 that she had little chance of remaining as leader after the first ballot, and ardent Thatcherites would never forgive such 'treachery'. 'I believe this did him far more harm than the European issue,' says Don Porter, a respected figure as Chairman and President of the National Convention, the body which represents the voluntary wing of the party. 'Unlike some others who were less sincere, Ken was at least honourable and told her exactly what he felt, but that did him long-term damage.'[37]

In September 2001, the grassroots finally delivered their verdict. When the postal ballots were counted, 155,933 had voted for Iain Duncan Smith and 100,864 for Ken Clarke. Duncan Smith had won by a margin of three to two. It was an emphatic victory that appeared to give him the authority to lead the party through to the next general election.

A Leader in the Shadows

A day before the new leader of the Conservative Party was due to be announced, the world changed. As Iain Duncan Smith sat in his Commons office on 11 September 2001, news broke of a plane flying into the North Tower of the World Trade Center in New York. When a second plane hit the South Tower seventeen minutes later, he rang

William Hague to ask if the announcement of the result could be postponed. Normal politics was put on hold. Tony Blair had been addressing the Trades Union Congress in Brighton. 'This mass terrorism is the new evil in our world today,' he declared in a short statement before retuning to Number 10.

While the events of 11 September would cast a long shadow over the election of the new Tory leader, Tony Blair would find his stride as an international statesman. 'Nobody was interested in us: it was the biggest crisis to hit the Western world, and nobody cared about an opposition party that had a new leader,' Duncan Smith recalls.[38] When the leadership ballot result was announced in a low-key event in Central Office on 13 September, the media's gaze was fixed on events thousands of miles away.

Nick Wood, who continued in his role as press secretary to the party leader, becoming a close confidant of Duncan Smith, thought that the crisis would play to the strengths of a leader who had been Shadow Defence Secretary and had close contacts in Washington. Duncan Smith had planned that his first speeches would be about domestic policy, signalling a change of emphasis, but now he would have little opportunity to make them. 'The whole landscape changed,' remembers Wood. 'It looked good for him to go to Number 10 for meetings with the Prime Minister, but it was frustrating for us as we couldn't get into domestic affairs. Politically it was not good for us at all.'[39] An impotent leader of the opposition could only watch as the Prime Minister received plaudits for his shuttle diplomacy after 9/11. 'Oppositions die on foreign affairs. It was very difficult to make headway because the public weren't interested,' recalls Duncan Smith. 'I found it incredibly difficult to make a mark, when the news was wall-to-wall Tony Blair every night. I didn't get a look-in.'[40]

Failing to make an impression in the first weeks and months of his leadership was only one of the problems to beset Duncan Smith. Despite his convincing victory in the ballot of party members, he had won the support of only a third of the parliamentary party in the final round of MPs. It was hardly a solid foundation on which to build authority. 'We had Iain Duncan Smith because he wasn't anybody else – he wasn't me, or Portillo or Clarke,' says Widdecombe.[41] Long-serving Tory MPs also resented his rebellious behaviour during the Major years, while his lack of ministerial experience (he was the first party leader not to have served in the Cabinet) was a concern for many. Former whips and ministers questioned why they should demonstrate loyalty to a man whose disloyal behaviour had caused them so much consternation in the past.

Duncan Smith's first Shadow Cabinet leaned heavily towards the right of the party. A number of heavyweights returned to the fold, including Michael Howard as Shadow Chancellor and David Davis as Party Chairman. Michael Ancram and Oliver Letwin were promoted to Shadow Foreign and Home Secretaries respectively. There were very few counterbalancing voices from the centre or pro-European wing of the party. Portillo, Maude and Clarke all refused to serve, and Hague returned to the backbenches, although unlike Portillo he did not rule out a future in frontline politics. Bernard Jenkin, the only former member of Hague's Shadow Cabinet to support Duncan Smith in the early stages of the leadership election, took the defence brief, while the arch-Maastricht rebel Bill Cash became Shadow Attorney General. 'The appointment of Bill Cash is the final proof that the lunatics have taken over the asylum . . . grief will follow,' was the verdict of one disillusioned MP.[42] Like Hague, Duncan Smith lacked a close ally in the Shadow Cabinet to act as a troubleshooter and command respect across the party. While Thatcher had Whitelaw and Major had Heseltine, both Hague and Duncan Smith lacked a serious heavyweight figure to protect them.

What undermined Duncan Smith even further was the weakness of his private office. He relied heavily on supportive MPs such as Owen Paterson, his Parliamentary Private Secretary, and John Hayes, both of whom had very little experience in advising party leaders. He also lacked a chief of staff or a permanent Political Secretary. Jenny Ungless, his first appointment, departed after a few months as chief of staff, despairing at his way of working. 'It was bit of a ragtag army that came in with him, and a lot of them left very quickly,' Rick Nye recalls. 'His working methods were chaotic and he couldn't keep time: meetings would often overrun.'[43] As Director of the CRD, Nye was one of the few figures in Central Office Duncan Smith trusted, along with Greg Clark, who headed a new policy unit. In an attempt to stretch a hand out to his rivals for the leadership, he appointed Mark MacGregor, from the Portillo campaign, as Chief Executive.

Vulnerabilities on Display

There were some parts of the party machine that showed signs of life under Iain Duncan Smith. A more considered approach to domestic policy took root. Clark's policy unit was modelled on Mrs Thatcher's Number 10 Policy Unit. He developed a three-stage process to policy-making: identifying problem areas; dispatching shadow ministers and aides to European countries to learn from their experience; producing consultation documents in advance of preparing the next manifesto. Health was an area which received much more attention than before: *The Wrong Prescription*, *Alternative Prescriptions* and *Setting the NHS Free* were the most significant pieces of work in the field that the party had produced in years. Clark and Nye were conscious of the party's weakness in this area. 'It was a very collaborative process. We agreed that we shouldn't rush into making detailed policies, otherwise people would think that we hadn't learned from our mistakes,' Clark recalls.[44]

To the surprise of many in the party and the press, Duncan Smith did not concentrate on European issues. 'We wanted to broaden things out – our strategy was to talk about the public services,' he says.[45] At Prime Minister's Questions he invariably probed Tony Blair about health, education and transport, as well as foreign policy, which often dominated proceedings. But backbenchers were unimpressed by his performances: Duncan Smith struggled to rival Blair, who was in confident form at the dispatch box following his second election victory.

One of the more striking new arrivals at Central Office was Dominic Cummings, who had led the embryonic campaign against joining the single currency, as Director of Strategy. Young and enthusiastic, he had firm views about what had to change. 'I knew from my research at the "No" campaign that people thought the Conservatives were immoral, incompetent and weird, and didn't care about the things that mattered to them,' he says. 'My first memo to IDS said that we need to explain the failure of public services. To his credit, he said he agreed with it.' [46] In March 2002 Cummings produced another memo for Duncan Smith and senior members of the Shadow Cabinet in which he urged 'a single campaign for the period until at least July – "why public services are failing the most vulnerable in society" '.[47] 'Helping the Vulnerable' became the theme for the party's spring forum at Harrogate in March 2002.

This struck a chord with Duncan Smith, touching on his beliefs as a devout Catholic. 'Initially it was a personal thing for him, but by complete chance he was also about to make these visits to Glasgow in the spring,' recalls Cummings.[48] Rick Nye had recently suggested the idea of a visit to the Easterhouse and Gallowgate areas of Glasgow, which had some of the most deprived estates in the country. Deep in Labour's Scottish heartlands, this was not natural territory for a Tory leader. Organised in conjunction with 'Renewing One Nation', a party group with close links to faith-based organisations, Duncan Smith's visit to the city took place on 1 February. He was struck by what he saw – the run-down housing, visible signs of drug abuse and general lack of hope. 'It was a real eye-opener for IDS,' recalls Greg Clark.[49]

Nye and Cummings found an ally in Tim Montgomerie, a Conservative activist who was running the Conservative Christian Fellowship, another group which had access to faith-based charities. 'One day I went for a walk around Central Office, and I wandered downstairs into the basement where I could hear voices,' Cummings recalls. 'I found Tim Montgomerie and two other people sitting among the pipes and central heating boilers. Their office was literally in a bunker underneath Central Office. I sat down and started talking with them, and Tim said, "I really agreed with the helping the vulnerable stuff and I really hope you persuade Iain to do it." '[50] Cummings suggested that Montgomerie help write some of Duncan Smith's speeches, and from that point onwards he became an increasingly important source of advice and encouragement for the leader.

Many in the party, including some of Duncan Smith's inner circle, were sceptical about 'Helping the Vulnerable'. There had been a tradition of Tory evangelicals ever since William Wilberforce and the Earl of Shaftesbury, who were primarily concerned with the condition of the poor. But it was a tradition that had become lost during the Thatcher years. 'I didn't really get it all. It was very vague and woolly and largely consisted of IDS walking around housing estates,' recalls one close aide. 'The press were baffled, because we hadn't found a way of giving it any coherence.' Many members of the Shadow Cabinet were also perplexed, although Oliver Letwin's speeches about the 'conveyor belt to crime' and the decline of the 'neighbourly society' were consistent with the approach. Liam Fox, the Shadow Health Secretary, thought the strategy was not given a context, such as stressing the role of the family, in lifting people out of poverty.[51] The Party Chairman, David Davis, insisted that the 'helping the vulnerable' phrase was actually his invention. 'There were some people who didn't want to get it, and there were others like Howard who said that the vulnerable people in his constituency in Folkestone were more worried about illegal immigrants coming in from the Channel Tunnel,' says another senior party official.

It was clear that the new message failed to excite the majority of Tory MPs. 'It really threw my party; they really didn't get it,' Duncan Smith regrets. 'We hadn't quite figured out all of the detail because we were trying to feel our way forward, but the concept was very alien to the Conservative Party. They wanted me to talk about tax and Europe, but I just felt that we needed to spend time on these subjects to let the public know that we were broader than this narrow party that they perceived. Now I realise it was a radical step to far.'[52] With the eye of the media firmly focused on the 'war on terror', Duncan Smith struggled to get his message across to the public. He was aware that the weekly theatre of Prime Minister's Questions was not the right forum in which to convey the strategy, particularly as Tory MPs had become used to Hague's virtuoso performances from the dispatch box. However, the communicator was as much to blame as his target audience. Duncan Smith failed to get his message across because he failed to present it imaginatively and convincingly. Many in the party may not have 'got it', but forging such a different agenda would require deft communication skills, which he lacked.

Like Andrew Cooper after his attempts at persuading the Shadow Cabinet to adopt his 'Kitchen Table' strategy in 1998, Dominic Cummings began to lose faith in his masters. 'The left of the party never had a strategy for anything, and complained that the Eurosceptics were idiots and didn't understand what we were on about in helping the vulnerable,' he says. 'The right said that if we bang on louder about tax, Europe and immigration we'll punch through, and they thought the Tory Party could never be about the public services. And then there were the Portillistas.'[53] The latter believed that Duncan Smith's prescription was along the right lines, but that he lacked the political skills to drive it through. Shifting opinion within the party towards an agenda that talked about the vulnerable would be far from easy for such a divided party. There was simply no appetite for it. Despite Duncan Smith's commitment, his lack of authority was a considerable handicap to advancing his cause.

Uninspired by the 'helping the vulnerable' mantra, the Shadow Cabinet sought clarity on other issues. They decided to oppose the government's plan to introduce top-up fees in higher education, and to pledge to restore the link between the state pension and earnings. 'There was a sense that we were becoming far too populist in adopting these positions,' one frontbencher recalls. Taxation became a particular source of tension between Duncan Smith and Michael Howard, the Shadow Chancellor. Howard wanted to reassure voters that the party would prioritise spending on public services above tax cuts. Opinion polls showed that the public were concerned about public services, and were sceptical about any party that promised to cut taxes. But Duncan Smith, under pressure from Thatcherites in the parliamentary party and from the Tory-supporting papers, the *Daily Telegraph* and *Daily Mail*, pressed for tax cuts. The right questioned whether Howard's position provided enough 'clear blue water' between the Conservatives and the government, which had recently announced massive increases in public spending, particularly in health and education. 'The pressure from outside to mount a tradition-ally Tory approach was quite forceful, and there were pressures on Howard to make concessions, but he was adamant,' a close aide recalls. The issue was never really resolved by Duncan Smith, leaving an unhealed wound at the heart of the party. Relations with his Shadow Chancellor had deteriorated, with Duncan Smith privately consid-ering Howard to be a 'panicker'. The 'peasants' who had catapulted Duncan Smith into the leadership were seriously worried that their man was unable to establish a clear position. The dispute also confirmed that for many Tory MPs, upfront tax cuts, like Euro-scepticism, had become an article of faith.

By July 2002, when Duncan Smith undertook his first reshuffle, the Shadow Cabinet was not a happy team. The principal casualty was David Davis, the Party Chairman. According to one of Duncan Smith's close aides, who encouraged him to appoint Davis to the chairmanship, 'They just didn't hit it off.' 'Iain wasn't that bad at managing the overall Shadow Cabinet, but when it came to managing the big beasts, like Davis, who has an ego the size of a planet, it didn't work,' the aide regrets. 'They needed to be blood brothers, and they weren't, and we were in a weak position. Iain felt that Davis's heart wasn't in it and he wasn't pulling his weight.' Davis insists that he played a full role in managing the party organisation after the heavy defeat of 2001. 'There was no tension to speak of between Iain and me for much of the year, but it wasn't an easy time politically,' he recalls. 'It was permanent struggle in terms of the media and the public perception of Iain. There were tensions in Central Office caused by some of the people he brought in who wanted to modernise and change the party. So quite a lot of my job in those days was trying to manage all of this as best we could.'[54] Davis had taken some bold decisions, such as severing formal ties with the right-wing Monday Club, and made efforts to attract more women and ethnic minority parliamentary candidates.

However, by the summer of 2002 some in Duncan Smith's team and the Whips' Office suggested that Davis be moved from Central Office. They used the fact that he had gone on an early-summer holiday to Florida in July as a reason to suggest that he wasn't fully committed to the job, even though Davis had agreed to hold the fort at Central Office during August and September (an arrangement he had also made during his previous role as Chairman of the Commons Public Accounts Committee). Davis was furious when he learned in Florida that he was being demoted to shadow Deputy Prime Minister John Prescott's Department of Local Government and the Regions. When he returned from holiday, he discovered that a briefing campaign against him was well under way. 'It was being pushed by a mixture of the ultra-modernisers and some of Iain's people,' he recalls.[55] After agreeing to take up the new post, he issued a strong statement outside his constituency home in which he lambasted a 'cowardly campaign of character assassination' against him, based on a 'tissue of lies'. 'Vendettas, character assassination have crippled three previous Tory leaders. We cannot allow this to happen again,' he declared.[56]

Some in Central Office suggest that Davis's work-rate was not the issue. 'Iain decided he couldn't work with David Davis any longer, but the idea that he did not work hard was really just an excuse,' Mark MacGregor says, adding, 'But I suspect David thought he would have made a better leader.'[57] 'It went downhill for IDS from that point,' says Paul Goodman, a backbencher. 'In the wake of David being moved, I remember reading quotes in the press to the effect of "Friends of David Davis say that if you're going to kill a big beast you must do so with one shot." The turn of phrase sounded remarkably like David Davis himself.'[58]

The moment Davis left Central Office, Duncan Smith's personal ratings, which had remained steady since September 2001, began to fall. Davis believes that the rot set in then. 'The same people who got rid of me would then destroy him,' he says.[59] It was clear from Duncan Smith's botched reshuffle that all was not well within the Shadow Cabinet or Central Office, as became increasingly evident over the next few months. Duncan Smith's standing had been weakened, egos had been bruised, and to the outside world the party looked hell-bent on destroying itself from within. The turmoil would only intensify from here on.

The 'Nasty Party'

The party conference in Bournemouth in October 2002 would provide an opportunity for Duncan Smith to recover his standing. The party's private polling showed that although he was not quite as unpopular as Hague, he had made very little impression on the public. Duncan Smith sought to address the state of the public services for those in disadvantaged communities by inviting representatives from charities and organisations from outside the party to speak at the conference, and Greg Clark's policy unit produced a broad-ranging document, *Leadership with a Purpose*, containing twenty-five specific proposals. But all eyes were on Duncan Smith.

'Never underestimate the determination of a quiet man,' he told the delegates in his main speech. 'Some people say it was a mistake, but it expressed the truth about him,' Nick Wood says.[60] The audience applauded enthusiastically, but the commentators and sketchwriters were underwhelmed. 'If you were to read [his] speech, it would actually seem a great deal more interesting than it was when he delivered it . . . IDS's address is actually a straightforward repudiation of the social consequences of Thatcherism,' wrote David Aaronovitch, who was among the kinder critics, in the *Independent*.[61] 'He just couldn't compete with Blair,' says one frontbencher. 'The man just couldn't communicate.' While Blair received plaudits from across the world for his oratory after 9/11, Duncan Smith was not cut out for the conference stage, let alone the world stage.

If Duncan Smith had failed to set the conference alight, the performance of his new Party Chairman, Theresa May, would do just that. One of the few women to join the depleted ranks of the parliamentary party in 1997, May was among the party's most able performers. Within two years Hague had promoted her to the Shadow Cabinet to take on the education brief, where she began to foster more harmonious relationships with teaching bodies. She was one of the few Portillo supporters Duncan Smith thought highly of, and after Davis's demotion she became the first woman to chair the party. Wearing what became her trademark leopardskin high-heeled shoes, May gave her debut speech as Chairman. It stunned the conference:

'Yes, we've made progress, but let's not kid ourselves. There's a way to go before we can return to government. There's a lot we need to do in this party of ours. Our base is too narrow and so, occasionally, are our sympathies. You know what some people call us: "the nasty party".' The party faithful were dumbstruck. Without naming names, she took aim at those who had brought the party into disrepute. 'In recent years a number of politicians have behaved disgracefully and then compounded their offences by trying to evade responsibility. We all know who they are. Let's face it, some of them have stood on this platform.' The audience in the conference hall – both party members and the assembled media – would have known whom she meant. The fall from grace of Jonathan Aitken and Jeffrey Archer, and even the damage to John Major's reputation after former minister Edwina Currie exposed their affair that autumn, were but a few incidents they might have identified.

If this was not enough, she then accused some in the party of trying to 'make political capital out of demonising minorities', and charged others with indulging themselves in 'petty feuding or sniping instead of getting behind a leader who is doing an enormous amount to change a party which has suffered two landslide defeats'. She excoriated Conservative association selection committees who seemed to prefer candidates they would be 'happy to have a drink with on a Sunday morning' to those who could have broad appeal.

May won the respect of some inside and outside the Shadow Cabinet for giving a painful, if honest, assessment of the party's predicament. But other senior figures, such as the former Party Chairman Lord Tebbit and the Shadow Chancellor Michael Howard, were left reeling. 'It was ludicrous – it is only since that speech that the shorthand for the Tories has been the nasty party,' insisted Howard.[62] He was wrong: there was a growing body of evidence from focus group research undertaken after the 2001 general election which showed that many people did regard the party as just that.[63]

Duncan Smith seemed unsure of how to respond. 'He knew about it beforehand, but as he was so focused on his own speech I don't think he had time to think about what the repercussions would be of the Chairman criticising the party like that,' recalls Mark MacGregor, the party's Chief Executive, who helped to draft May's speech.[64] But Nick Wood insists that Duncan Smith was shown a draft of the speech without the 'nasty party' line.[65] The episode unsettled the party and its imperilled leader even further. It also strained relations between the Chairman and the leader, an axis that was essential to the party's well-being. More revealingly, it was an illustration of how sensitive the party was about dealing with its past, let alone the present. This was not a party at ease with itself.

For the 'quiet man' at the helm, the noise of discontent would only grow louder. The conference had not given the Conservatives the lift they so desperately needed. 'Helping the Vulnerable' had not enthused the party, May's speech had lowered morale and the polls showed the party flatlining between 29 and 32 per cent. Labour enjoyed average ratings around the mid-forties, while the Liberal Democrats, with their popular leader Charles Kennedy, were only five or six points behind the Conservatives.[66]

In October, Dominic Cummings left Central Office after only six months as Director of Strategy. Despite having the ear of the leader, Cummings had lost faith in those around him and their willingness to accept his agenda, particularly Duncan Smith's influential press secretary Nick Wood. In a confused chain of command, Cummings wanted to take a much more proactive approach to communications, making greater use of television. 'We just got to a stage of paralysis,' he recalls. 'Senior people didn't know what they were doing – they hadn't run complex organisations or done strategic communication involving serious market research, broadcasting and advertising. Everything was about tomorrow's newspapers. I wanted a revolution; Nick Wood didn't. Iain had said he wanted that too, but it was soon clear he didn't, so I left.'[67] Despite the severe strains among his team, Duncan Smith failed to heed, or even to see, the warning signs. One senior aide recalls a conversation from around this time, in which he tried to alert Duncan Smith to his weakening grip on the party. 'I'm afraid to say, Iain, I think things are going to go badly wrong for you, and the Conservative Party will get rid of you.' Duncan Smith laughed. 'You think that because you don't understand the Conservative Party – they will never get rid of me.'

Modernisers Emerge

When Iain Duncan Smith won the leadership, many of Michael Portillo's supporters had held their heads in despair. For all Duncan Smith's overtures about public service reform and helping the vulnerable, they did not believe he could carry the party with him. While Duncan Smith enlisted a few leading lights from the Portillo campaign, including Oliver Letwin, who became Shadow Home Secretary, and Mark MacGregor, who became Chief Executive of Central Office, others in the Portillo camp were utterly disenchanted. Jonathan Marland, a businessman who stood as a candidate in 2001, had given financial support to the Portillo campaign, and was friendly with a number of senior figures in the party, including Francis Maude, who left the frontbench when Duncan Smith was elected. 'Francis and I were in deep gloom after IDS won. There was very little new blood in the parliamentary party and there was a risk of coming third at the next election. We couldn't rescue it under Duncan Smith and I was tempted to support someone who would start a new party. The wheels were just coming off.'[68]

Maude refused to accept that the failure of the Portillo campaign meant the end of a 'modernising' agenda for the party. While the leadership contest was being played out between Iain Duncan Smith and Ken Clarke in August 2001, Maude and Archie Norman decided to set up a campaigning organisation that would argue for change in the party. At the same time David Willetts, another Portillo supporter, was independently considering setting up a think tank. Maude and Norman floated their idea with Rick Nye from Central Office. Nye suggested marrying the two ideas along the lines of the Democratic Leadership Council and the Progressive Policy Institute, which had helped propel Bill Clinton to the 1992 Democratic presidential nomination in the United States, espousing centrist 'New Democrat' positions and supporting sympathetic candidates in Democratic primaries. A strong influence on New Labour in its infancy, the 'New Democrats' model was now inspiring Tory modernisers a decade later. With financial backing from Jonathan Marland and others, Maude, Norman and Willetts asked Nye to get the project off the ground. Nye was tempted, but decided to stay within the party machine under the new leadership.

The sister-organisation idea took off in November 2001, with the launch of X-Change, an independent think tank which would develop policy ideas, and C-Change, an organisation campaigning to make the case for change inside the party. 'We needed to persuade people of the need to change. We wanted to create an intellectual ferment on the centre-right as there had been in the 1970s, but the old think tanks had too much baggage,' Maude says.[69] There had been little intellectual vibrancy among Conservatives outside the parliamentary party since the early 1990s, either among think tanks such as the Centre for Policy Studies or the Institute of Economic Affairs, or in the columns of right-wing commentators. They suffered in comparison to the buoyancy of the centre-left, where the Institute for Public Policy Research had made its name as a nursery of ideas for New Labour in the 1990s.

Any positive thinking had been confined to a small circle of young Conservative activists in their twenties and early thirties. Unlike many party members of their generation, they were not yearning for a return to the Thatcher years, but felt that the party had completely lost touch with modern Britain. Nicholas Boles, an openly gay Westminster city councillor and businessman, Ed Vaizey, a lawyer and former member of the CRD and journalist Michael Gove all aspired to become Tory MPs. They tried unsuccessfully to launch a magazine called *Blue* before the 2001 general election, and shortly after the defeat they edited a book, *A Blue Tomorrow*,[70] which included essays by former officials and CRD alumni such as Andrew Cooper, Michael Simmonds and Steve Hilton (who after the 1997 general election left politics altogether to set up his own company, Good Business, which advised multinationals on ethical practice).

After leaving Central Office in summer 1999, Cooper had gone on to found the market research and polling company Populus (which later conducted polls for *The Times*). Using evidence from various measures of public opinion, he continued to advance the argument he had made in his 'Kitchen Table' paper: that the party had not adapted to the modern world. In his chapter in *A Blue Tomorrow*, entitled 'A Party in a Foreign Land', Cooper argued powerfully that the Conservative Party 'unchanged, cannot survive'.[71] Together with the contributions from the other young Tories who featured in the book, Cooper's essay became an important manifesto for those who sought to modernise the party. Out of the ashes of Portillo's failed leadership bid, they had emerged with a mission to change the Conservatives. They had a manual; now some of them were about to have a home.

Francis Maude appointed Nicholas Boles as founding director of X-Change (which was renamed Policy Exchange) and C-Change, and Boles set up shop with two others in a small room in the bowels of Westminster Central Hall. 'We were tiny and living hand to mouth,' he says. 'But we created a home for lonely voices in the wilderness. It was a physical and emotional space as much as anything.'[72] Relations with the party high command were distinctly cool. 'Policy Exchange was like the Polish government in exile – they didn't engage with us,' Nye recalls.[73] The new think tank devoted much of its early effort towards 'localism', arguing for greater decentralisation of power to a local level, but failed to attract much support within the parliamentary party. Even those who were sympathetic to a modernising message, like the backbencher Nick Gibb, thought the think tank was 'in danger of acquiring a simple panacea through localism. There was a case for localism, but I worried that they weren't engaged in the bread and butter of politics, like improving standards in health and education.'[74]

The sister organisation, C-Change, attracted a number of centre-right activists in their twenties whose social liberalism made them reluctant to join often traditionalist local Conservative associations. C-Change's campaign to persuade the party to take a long, hard look at itself was spearheaded by Douglas Smith, later to become one of David Cameron's speechwriters, whose background as an arch-Thatcherite lent weight to his advocacy of modernisation. 'My epiphany came at the 2001 general election,' Smith explains. 'Until then I had been resistant to the arguments of Andrew Cooper, who was the original prophet of modernisation, but the election result made his case unanswerable.'[75] In an article for the *Daily Telegraph* in June 2001 entitled 'Selfish, Soulless and Smug', Smith offered an analysis of why the Tories had fallen into such disrepute.[76] This attracted the interest of Maude and Norman, who asked him to head up C-Change. Together with Andrew Cooper and Michael Gove he compiled presentations for Conservative MPs, but C-Change's most important audience was the party's grassroots, which it targeted at conference fringe events and constituency roadshows. 'Because I was from the right, I could persuade people that they weren't selling their souls by backing modernisation,' Smith says. 'It was not like rewriting Labour's Clause IV, where change was imposed from the top; this was about reaching a new understanding from the bottom up.'[77]

Supported by a mass of statistics from election results and opinion polling since 1992, C-Change's presentation 'The Case for Change' was launched at the party's spring forum in 2003 to an audience of voluntary party top brass: association chairmen and council leaders. Smith recalls, 'We told them that the relationship between the British people and the Conservative Party had become like a bad marriage: the party was shouting at the public, while the voters were preparing the divorce papers. I stood at the back of the hall observing the body language of the audience. People were open-minded and listened carefully. Some of them protested, but we made real progress.' Meetings with MPs in the Commons did not go so well. 'Quite a few of our MPs were very resistant – they tended to be of the old school that saw everything in left–right terms and couldn't grasp the modernising versus traditionalist argument. They were in denial: some of them were broadly comfortable with the status quo and had an emotional reluctance to accept that the party had to change.'[78] Francis Maude and Archie Norman had created a vehicle for a younger generation of modernisers, outside the parliamentary party, to set a new direction. But despite signs that the grassroots were prepared to listen, they were still just noises off for the leadership and many

103

others inside the party. Events centre stage would soon be far more arresting.

Desperate Man, Desperate Measures

As MPs returned for the new parliamentary session in October 2002, there was a sense that Duncan Smith's time was running out. His weekly exchanges at Prime Minister's Questions lacked any spontaneity or political charge. Suffering from a perpetual frog in his throat, he struggled to land any blows on Blair. Up to now he had been relying on his close parliamentary aides Owen Paterson and John Hayes, as well as Greg Clark and Rick Nye in Central Office, to help him prepare. Frustrated by his unwillingness to listen to their advice, Clark and Nye suggested that Duncan Smith call in four talented MPs from the 2001 intake: Boris Johnson, Paul Goodman, David Cameron and George Osborne. 'It was a very difficult time,' Goodman recalls. 'We met increasingly early on Wednesday mornings to prepare IDS, but he was very lacking in confidence.'[79]

Osborne and Cameron had experience in preparing leaders for the theatre of Prime Minister's Questions. In his role as Hague's Political Secretary, Osborne had played the role of Tony Blair when rehearsing for the exchanges. He had also helped to brief John Major shortly before the 1997 general election, as had Cameron before the 1992 election. Johnson, who was editing the *Spectator* at the time, often arrived at the meetings late and left early. Some in Duncan Smith's office thought the ambitious backbenchers were a little too big for their boots: 'They were pros and better at it than Iain, but thought they knew it all, and would talk over him in the meetings or put their feet up on coffee tables.' Duncan Smith's performances gradually improved, but he was still no match for Blair. 'You couldn't get more of an A-team than that, but it just didn't help,' says one of his aides. Boris Johnson and George Osborne looked on in awe as Blair despatched one Tory MP after the next in Prime Minister's Questions. At one point Osborne turned to Johnson and said: 'The simple reality is that the Conservative Party is not going to recover until Tony Blair ceases to be Prime Minister.'

Within weeks of returning to Westminster, the Tory leadership was engulfed in a crisis that revealed how little authority Iain Duncan Smith commanded in the parliamentary party. Conservative MPs were instructed to vote against the government's legislation to allow unmarried couples – both gay and straight – to adopt children. Traditionally such issues would be decided as a matter of individual conscience, without a party whip, but some of the more socially conservative voices close to Duncan Smith urged him to use the Adoption and Children Bill to take a stand. It set him on a collision course with MPs who held more liberal views about adoption and gay rights, particularly Michael Portillo and Francis Maude. The decision to impose a three-line whip ignited a row that blew open the divisions that had emerged since 1997, under Hague's leadership. The issues that split the 'mods' and 'rockers', or social liberals and conservatives, such as Section 28, had not lost their potency on the Conservative benches. Now there was unease that Duncan Smith had increasingly surrounded himself with advisers whose politics were shaped in large part by their Christian beliefs. 'They had a particular agenda that they wanted to push, which IDS had an ear to. It was always about getting voluntary groups involved, but they weren't interested in any groups who were not Christian,' recalls a party official.

The most prominent casualty was the Shadow Work and Pensions Minister, John Bercow, who resigned from the Shadow Cabinet in protest. Duncan Smith believed his resignation was more to do with a damaged ego, as he had been moved in an earlier reshuffle, than the principle at stake. Eight Tory MPs defied the three-line whip by voting with the government in the key Commons vote on 4 November, including Portillo, Maude and Clarke. But there was discontent among the new MPs, with Cameron, Osborne and Johnson abstaining. Osborne regrets that the vote came to be seen by Duncan Smith as a showdown with the 'Portillistas', and felt that the Conservative Party had become detached from modern Britain. To his disbelief, he was hauled up before the Chief Whip, David Maclean, to explain why he did not vote. 'George felt that he was somehow being made out to be an opponent of Iain's when this was not what it was about,' a friend recalls. It said something about Duncan Smith's lack of judgement that he was isolating those who were trying to help him.

The next day, 5 November, an act of defiance turned into a full-blown crisis, complete with its own fireworks. Duncan Smith had been due to make an announcement on social housing, but decided instead that he had to address the growing political crisis that threatened to engulf his leadership. Shortly before a hastily convened press conference at Central Office that morning, he consulted Theresa May, Oliver Letwin and senior Central Office aides Nick Wood, Rick Nye and Mark MacGregor. Letwin coined a phrase to sum up the situation: 'unite or die'. Nye and MacGregor were strongly opposed to the idea of issuing such a dire warning to the party, but Duncan Smith had made up his mind. 'The Conservative Party wants to be led,' he told journalists in the small press room at Central Office. 'It elected me to lead it in the direction I am now going. It will not look kindly on people who put personal ambitions before the interests of the party. My message is simple and stark: unite or die.' He promptly left the stage without taking questions. Reporters were dumbstruck. Standing at the back of the room, Nick Wood, Duncan Smith's press secretary, turned to Nye and whispered: 'It's over.'

Some of the reporters had been expecting Duncan Smith to resign there and then, but the only story they were left to write was about a leader making a desperate appeal to his own party in the full glare of the cameras. 'My concern was that the party was vulnerable and we had to stop this perpetual rowing over everything that the leader did,' Duncan Smith later insisted. 'They just weren't ready to be led.'[80] In truth, they were not willing to be led by him. He had dug a hole for himself by enforcing a three-line whip on an issue that was bound to inflame passions across the party. He then carried on digging by turning the episode into a question of leadership and party unity, which only highlighted his inability to lead the party with any confidence.

Perversely, Duncan Smith had put his finger on the malaise that had afflicted the party since the last days of Mrs Thatcher's premiership. Lack of confidence in the leadership and disunity had fostered the disloyal behaviour that had cursed Major and Hague. Now it was Duncan Smith's turn to try to pull rank. 'As a former Maastricht rebel, Iain was the last person to call on the rest of us to be loyal,' a member of the Shadow Cabinet recalls. It had been over a decade since the Maastricht Bill had passed through the Commons, but senior figures in the party had long memories. During the sixty-two divisions in the Maastricht debate Duncan Smith had voted with his own party on just four occasions, and with the Labour opposition on eleven. 'The establishment, which included the older generation of Europhiles, were horrified,' Owen Paterson, Duncan Smith's Parliamentary Private Secretary, recalls. 'They just thought, "Why on earth should we unite under you?" It all went back to the problem that he only got the support of a third of the parliamentary party.'[81] The bitterness over Maastricht had not gone away. Although the internecine warfare between Eurosceptics and Europhiles had diminished – mainly because the latter had dwindled in number and influence – the enmity between them lived on.

Interestingly, someone who might have had most reason to bear a grudge towards the beleaguered leader was surprisingly sympathetic. 'I was surprised when Iain became leader, because of the perception of him as a fundamentalist anti-European who was bound to focus public opinion solely on the European issue again, which had done so much damage in the 1990s and was still doing damage,' recalls Sir John Major. 'But it was nothing personal against Iain, and indeed he would ask to see me and we would talk about things, which was to his credit.'[82]

After Duncan Smith's desperate appeal for unity, the Shadow Cabinet lost all hope. 'Most people sitting around the table thought that they could do better than him,' Rick Nye recalls. 'The more pressure he was under, the more nervous he got and the more desperate he was to show he was in control. But he was being pulled in different directions, and he didn't have the intellectual confidence to hold to one side.'[83] 'He always wanted people to leave a meeting with a warm glow that he had agreed with them and that they would get what they wanted,' says Owen Paterson. 'He should have been tougher and more brutal from the beginning, but he's got this psychological need to make people compromise, and he always felt he could persuade them.'[84] Another remarked that 'There was always an attempt to muddle through, and that's really when it all started to break down.' It was clear that the Tory leader did not command the confidence of most of his Shadow Cabinet, let alone the parliamentary and voluntary party.

Ever since he became leader, Iain Duncan Smith was not happy with the party organisation he inherited. Central Office was tainted with memories of infighting and conspiratorial intrigue during the Hague years. 'There was a very uneasy feeling between the leader's office and the Chairman's office,' recalls Don Porter, then President of the National Convention, which represented the grassroots.[85] Duncan Smith's advisers believed David Davis had been primarily interested in empire-building during his time as Chairman, laying the ground for a future leadership bid (which Davis denies). Some of Duncan Smith's rivals were surprised that he appointed the Portillo-supporting Mark MacGregor as the party's Chief Executive in 2001, and for a while it was believed that Duncan Smith would preside over a modernisation of the party's organisation. But raising funds from party donors proved increasingly difficult. MacGregor and Stanley Kalms, the Party Treasurer, were forced to find massive savings in Central Office's budget, resulting in a further depletion of staff. Although the Policy Unit and CRD embarked on a long-term review of policy, many officials, particularly within the press office, were openly scornful of the need for modernisation. 'They were more interested in securing a positive headline in the *Daily Mail* than in helping to change the party's "nasty" image. This was compounded by the fact they didn't understand a proactive approach, they were too reactive,' says MacGregor.[86] MacGregor had made enemies early on. 'He wanted to achieve a revolution in the party and he didn't understand the subtleties of the voluntary party in the country – there were many fights behind the scenes,' recalled a senior activist.

Paranoia set in. Duncan Smith turned on his senior lieutenants in Central Office. Without warning, he fired the Chief Executive,

Campaign Director and Research Director on 14 February 2003. Mark MacGregor, Stephen Gilbert and Rick Nye departed in the 'St Valentine's Day Massacre'. 'Somebody close to him told him that the senior team in Central Office was plotting against him,' says one official. 'It was not true. He just believed it.' To everyone's astonishment Duncan Smith appointed Barry Legg, a fellow Maastricht rebel who lost his seat in 1997, to replace MacGregor as Chief Executive and to take on the role of chief of staff. Before entering Parliament Legg had been a Westminster City councillor during the time that Dame Shirley Porter, leader of the council, became embroiled in the 'homes-for-votes' scandal, when homeless families were moved into two London tower blocks that were known to be riddled with asbestos. Although Legg was cleared of misconduct when the district auditor investigated the affair, he was implicated for being aware of the 'party electoral reasons' behind the gerrymandering.[87] He had become a pariah for many in the party, and his appointment drew scorn from all quarters, including Michael Portillo. 'To surround yourself with lesser people and with people who agree with you is not a sign of strength,' he told the BBC. 'You don't look tall if you surround yourself by short grasses.'[88]

Aggrieved at the lack of prior consultation, the party board (the key decision-making body representing each section of the party) furiously objected to Legg's appointment. 'I made it abundantly clear that this was an issue on which I thought he had treated the board with contempt, and he could not just appoint somebody like that,' recalls Don Porter.[89] Even before the Legg appointment, representatives from the voluntary party had confronted the hapless leader with the reality. 'Iain, I've got to tell you, there's one thing that isn't working. There just isn't a perception out there of you leading the party,' one told him. At a hastily arranged meeting inside the Commons, the board set out their concerns to the Party Chairman, Theresa May: Legg had to go. May was in an uncomfortable position, torn between her loyalty to the leadership and the outrage of the board. She herself had only learned about the 14 February purge the night before.

Scenting trouble, journalists from the *Guardian* and BBC Radio 4's *Today* programme embarked on an investigation into Legg's past. They were aided by senior Conservative MPs who actively briefed against both Legg and Duncan Smith. On 6 May the *Today* programme broadcast revelations about Legg's key role in the 'homes-for-votes' scandal together with claims that he was involved in a decision by a major food company, Hillsdown Holdings (of which he was company secretary), to remove an £18 million surplus from a pension fund, an action which a High Court judgement described as unjust and unauthorised.[90] Legg disputed the allegations, adding that 'as both the ombudsman and the judge made clear, the trustees were right to be seeking to secure a greater proportion of the surplus for scheme members than the company was willing to offer'. Nevertheless, the headlines were highly damaging, not least because senior Tory MPs, including the former whip Derek Conway, were so outspoken against Legg. 'I think it's a wrong appointment. I think [Duncan Smith] allowed friendship to cloud his judgement, frankly,' Conway remarked.[91] The following day Legg resigned. The Campaign Director Stephen Gilbert, who was widely respected in the party, was also reinstated following protests from the board.

The two-month saga was highly damaging for the leadership. Duncan Smith had been forced to back down, demonstrating even further how weak his position had become. The party's finances were deteriorating, while the number of donations being made to the Liberal Democrats was rising dramatically.[92] Leading donors began to question why they should continue to fund a party that seemed in such disarray. One of them, Jonathan Marland, told Michael Howard, who was staying with him in Wiltshire, that the only alternative to disaster at the next general election would be for him to replace Duncan Smith. Howard angrily dismissed the suggestion.[93] He did not want to become involved in, or be seen to be involved in, any plotting.

Yet his demonstration of loyalty seemed out of touch with the views of many of his colleagues. Tory MPs were in a febrile mood. Crispin Blunt had become the first MP to openly call for Duncan

Smith to go, resigning his post as a frontbench spokesman shortly before polls closed on the 1 May local elections. 'We carry the handicap of a leader whom Conservatives in Parliament and outside feel unable to present to the electorate as a credible alternative prime minister,' Blunt said.[94] Although many of his colleagues agreed with him, no one else dared to rock the boat. The local election results were not quite as bad as had been predicted, but having lost confidence in the leadership, Tory MPs wondered just how long Iain Duncan Smith could last. In the meantime, their minds had become preoccupied with events far away.

From Baghdad to Brent East

The crisis that beset the Blair government and the rest of the world in the spring of 2003 did not leave the Conservative Party unscathed. The mission to remove Saddam Hussein from power in Iraq had far-reaching consequences for politics at home. From the outset Duncan Smith offered steadfast support to the Prime Minister in joining a US-led military campaign, and he agreed with Blair that bringing about 'regime change' in Baghdad was the 'right thing to do'.

Duncan Smith had strong connections with leading neo-conservatives in the Bush administration. 'Neo-cons in Washington had too much influence over too many of our people,' recalls Ken Clarke, an opponent of the war.[95] 'It was absolutely brainless neo-conservatism and it came at a high price,' says another frontbencher. 'Sucking up to George Bush was just ghastly, it was repellent. We should have opposed the war from the start.' Duncan Smith rejects any suggestion of being leaned upon in any way to deliver support for the key vote in the Commons on 18 March, which endorsed Blair's decision to commit British troops to military action against Iraq. 'I had contacts with the Americans, but nobody lobbied me,' he recalls. 'They were more likely to have been talking to Labour MPs, because the Conservative position was pretty clear by then.'[96] This position, on one of the most important foreign policy questions in years, had been reached after little debate within the party. Although Labour's divisions were laid bare for all to see, Conservative MPs were not exactly united in their support for military action. Sixteen voted against the war, and all the former Conservative Foreign Secretaries who spoke in public before the campaign – Geoffrey Howe, Douglas Hurd and Malcolm Rifkind – declared their opposition.

The government prevailed only with the support of the opposition, and the day after the vote Duncan Smith received a call from the US Vice President, Dick Cheney. 'I just wanted to thank you for resisting the temptation just to play political games, for doing what you all agreed was the right thing to do and to support the war,' Cheney told him. 'It was a huge temptation: we could have brought the government down,' says Duncan Smith. 'I still believe it was right not to have done that.' If the party had suddenly withdrawn its support for the government a political crisis would have ensued, engulfing both Labour and the Tories. If Blair had not secured the support of over half the Parliamentary Labour Party, and the government had then faced a motion of no confidence in the Commons, Duncan Smith would have withdrawn support: 'If that had happened, we wouldn't have been in the business of saving Blair.'[97] Ultimately, the Prime Minister carried a majority of Labour MPs, but he only won the vote with Tory support. Siding with the government over war with Iraq was the most controversial decision Duncan Smith took as party leader. Had he opted for a different course, it is unlikely that British forces would have joined the American-led invasion. Tony Blair's premiership might also have come to an abrupt end, and the history of the next few years would have been very different.

Although he believed it to be right, Duncan Smith's decision to hug the government close was a huge misjudgement in domestic political terms. As Iraq descended into chaos amid a power vacuum after the swift fall of Saddam Hussein's regime in April 2003, questions began to be asked about the lack of proper planning for the aftermath. The absence of weapons of mass destruction (WMD), on which the government had principally based its case for action, and the suicide of Dr David Kelly, a government scientist and expert on WMD who had been revealed as the source of a controversial report on the *Today* programme on 29 May which claimed that the government 'probably knew' it was wrong to claim Iraq's WMD could be deployed in forty-five minutes, raised further questions about the use of intelligence. The charge that Britain had gone to war on a false prospectus suddenly had a new potency. Opinion polls, which had initially showed that over half the public supported military action, despite the largest ever peacetime demonstration in London on the eve of the Commons vote, were now overwhelmingly hostile. As Dr Kelly's death plunged the Prime Minister into crisis in July, Duncan Smith launched a fierce attack of the government's handling of the affair. 'The government treated Kelly abominably badly, but it got caught up with its vulnerability over Iraq,' he says. He found it difficult, however, to land any real blows. 'In a sense we became damaged by the Kelly saga because we had supported the war.'[98]

By offering unqualified support to the government in the lead-up to the war, Duncan Smith had left his party politically exposed. The anti-war Liberal Democrats took full advantage of the government's unpopularity. Winning the safe Labour seat of Brent East in a by-election on 12 September, Charles Kennedy's party pushed the Conservatives into third place with only 16 per cent of the vote. In the 2001 general election the Conservatives had come second, comfortably ahead of the Liberal Democrats. Brent East focused minds back onto the domestic scene, and with it the Conservative leadership.

Blackpool Stormclouds

As delegates gathered in Blackpool for the annual party conference on Sunday, 5 October, the skies looked threatening. An autumn storm was approaching from across the Irish Sea. The Lancastrian resort had produced moments of high drama in the past: the shock announcement of Harold Macmillan's resignation as Prime Minister in October 1963 led to a week of frenzied speculation about who would succeed him. Forty years on, another leadership crisis was about to envelop the party. The conference was supposed to be the party's shop window to the electorate. In October 2003, it had the makings of a horror show by the seaside.

Details had emerged in the press that Duncan Smith had allegedly paid his wife, Betsy, a salary from his parliamentary staffing allowance for diary and secretarial work. Armed with apparently damning evidence, a former official from Central Office was determined to show that Betsy Duncan Smith had performed little or no work between September 2001 and December 2002 to justify her salary: 'I knew how damaging it would be. I decided that Iain was hopeless and could not do what he wanted to do, which was to transform the image of the party. Things were so bad that almost anybody would be better – at least they might be more competent.'

In June 2003, Michael Crick, an investigative journalist at BBC's *Newsnight* programme, was approached with details of the story. After four months of research, he put the claims to Duncan Smith's office in the week before the conference. The office issued a denial and threatened to sue the BBC if the story was broadcast. Although the programme pulled the story, the *Sunday Telegraph* reported details of the allegations on 5 October. 'Once it ran, we couldn't do anything about it. The story broke on the worst possible day – on the eve of the conference,' recalls Duncan Smith's press secretary, Nick Wood. 'It completely took over everything else.'[99]

A subsequent investigation by Sir Philip Mawer, the Parliamentary Commissioner for Standards, cleared Duncan Smith and his wife of all the charges. But the damage had already been done. 'It was a complete stitch-up,' Duncan Smith insists. 'The whole idea was to create a firestorm around me that would make it impossible for me to continue against the backdrop of the Brent East by-election.'[100] The 'Betsygate' story acted as a catalyst for a further series of events that would lead to his downfall. Party officials and representatives of the grassroots were bracing themselves for an imminent coup. 'As soon as I arrived a senior party official came up to me and said, "You must prepare yourself this week for the leader going," ' Don Porter recalls.[101]

As the President of the National Convention, Porter was charged with organising the conference. He did his best to lift morale by hosting a huge party for over twelve hundred activists on the Tuesday evening. Ironically, it was called 'Celebrating Success'. It had the desired effect of cheering the activists, but the bars and corridors of Blackpool's Winter Gardens soon filled with talk of plots. A number of MPs and party officials from Central Office were determined to act. Some seasoned MPs were despairing. 'Everyone knew that we could not win the election with IDS as leader,' one recalls. 'It was a horrible conference, absolutely vile. It was a party with a smell of death about it. I couldn't wait to get away.'

Duncan Smith's aides felt helpless. 'The atmosphere was very fraught,' Owen Paterson remembers. 'Everything had broken down and the whips were going crazy.'[102] All discipline had gone, apart from the veneer of gentility displayed inside the conference hall. The Whips' Office was supposed to ensure that the conference went smoothly. George Osborne was now a junior whip, despite the smack on the wrist he had received after the gay adoption vote. As the eager new recruit updated David Maclean, the Chief Whip, with almost hourly reports about the febrile mood among MPs, he was stopped in his tracks. 'I don't want to hear any more,' Maclean told him. 'I know it's bad!'

As the rain lashed against the windows of the Imperial Hotel, the main conference hotel on the seafront, Duncan Smith's team began to rewrite the speech they had been preparing for several months. Danny Kruger and Tim Montgomerie worked through the night trying to find the words that would do enough to ensure their leader's survival. 'It was very tense but very exciting,' recalls Kruger, who had been research director at the centre-right think tank the Centre for Policy Studies before joining Duncan Smith's office as a speechwriter. 'We eventually rewrote it, but it didn't help when the printer broke down – it was chaos.'[103] Montgomerie had become Duncan Smith's chief of staff following Legg's departure in May, providing the support that the leader had lacked from the beginning. 'The tragedy for Iain was that he had finally got a good team together,' Paterson regrets.[104] It was too little too late.

Duncan Smith was in combative mood as he walked onto the conference stage. He immediately went on the attack, lambasting the failures of what he called 'Blair World'. 'My mission is to take the Conservative Party back to government. I won't allow anything or anyone to get in my way. We must destroy this double-dealing, deceitful, incompetent, shallow, inefficient, ineffective, corrupt, mendacious, fraudulent, shameful, lying government – once and for all.' In an attempt to see off his critics, he continued: 'I say to everyone here today: You either want my mission. Or you want Tony Blair. There is no third way. The quiet man is here to stay, and he's turning up the volume.' Yet he said very little about his alternative vision for the country, unlike the previous year. The faithful, however, rallied by his attack on Labour and the Liberal Democrats, were generous in their applause. But the speech had descended into farce as members of the audience closest to the podium leapt to their feet seventeen times during its course. These obviously choreographed ovations smacked of desperation – for weeks afterwards, the official responsible was greeted with standing ovations from staff whenever he entered party headquarters.

Shocked by the amount of plotting going on, David Cameron had been glad to leave the conference after just one day. He had rushed back to London from Blackpool to care for his eighteen-month-old son Ivan, who suffered from a rare condition, Ohtahara Syndrome. Born in April 2002, Ivan was David and Samantha Cameron's first child. His epileptic fits and spasms often required hospital treatment. Cameron watched the speech from his son's bedside in St Mary's Hospital, Paddington. The only television available was a tiny black-and-white set with virtually no sound, limitations that appeared to improve Duncan Smith's performance. Cameron initially believed that the speech had gone fairly well, until a friend called to put him straight. 'It was a car crash,' he told Cameron bluntly.

'I will fight, fight and fight again to save the country that I love,' Duncan Smith had declared as he tried to rally his party. Loyal MPs and whips tried desperately to spin the speech in the best possible light, but even Duncan Smith knew that his fighting talk would not end the speculation about his position. 'Iain thought it was good but not quite good enough,' Kruger recalls.[105] In fact, it was unquestionably a poor performance, and many in the party considered it the final straw. 'As I was waiting for my train out of Blackpool two senior MPs phoned me to ask about getting some research done into which of the obvious alternatives to IDS would be the best to rally round,' recalls Andrew Cooper.[106] It was only a matter of time before MPs would take matters into their own hands.

The Whips Take Control

When MPs returned to Westminster a few weeks later, mutiny was in the air. Duncan Smith's last throw of the dice at the conference had done nothing to allay concerns among the parliamentary party. Many felt that he just could not speak to the electorate, and lacked charisma. The contrast with Tony Blair's skills as a communicator, and the realities of the twenty-four hour media age, did not help his cause. His opponents were determined to rid the party of its leader, fearing his survival in office would only harm the party's already dismal electoral prospects.

Many MPs, including those who had voted for Duncan Smith in 2001, vented their frustrations to the whips. Their traditional role was to relay backbench opinion to the leadership, while remaining steadfastly loyal. Balancing these loyalties was now no longer possible. Despite public proclamations of support for Duncan Smith, the Whips' Office could not stand idly by. David Maclean, the Chief Whip, who had played a key role in securing the leadership for Duncan Smith (having originally backed David Davis), took the unprecedented step of going on television to tell conspirators to fall into line. 'I will be asking if they want to be hard-working MPs, who get behind the leader, or not. Because if they don't, they should go and work in industry,' he warned. But privately Maclean had long lost confidence in Duncan Smith and his ability to improve the party's fortunes. He contemplated resigning, but was persuaded by friends to stay to resolve the party's troubles. 'He had decided enough was enough,' said one. He was now driven by 'guilt that he supported and ran [Duncan Smith's] campaign in the first place'.[107]

The Chief Whip's broadcast appeal for discipline provoked dissident MPs into action. He would prove to be the kingmaker. On Wednesday, 22 October, Maclean told Duncan Smith that support was ebbing away and that he should consider stepping down.[108] When the leader rejected the Chief Whip's advice, the whips took matters into their own hands, encouraging MPs to do 'what they thought was best for the party'. Under the leadership rules introduced after 1997, if 15 per cent of the parliamentary party, which in 2003 amounted to twenty-five MPs, wrote to the Chairman of the 1922 Committee it would be sufficient to force a vote of confidence in the leadership. Over the following weekend several leading donors, including the spread-betting millionaire Stuart Wheeler, said they would refuse to fund the party while Duncan Smith remained in charge.

Duncan Smith's fate was decided on Tuesday, 28 October. Francis Maude announced on the *Today* programme that he had written to Sir Michael Spicer, the Chairman of the 1922 Committee, asking for a confidence motion. One by one MPs delivered their letters by hand to Sir Michael Spicer's office in the House of Commons. 'It was like watching the inevitable unfold,' says one MP. 'By now frontbenchers, backbenchers and whips all became conspirators.' Maude's intervention may not have been necessary: by 10.15 a.m. Spicer had already received more than twenty-five letters – some reports suggest that he actually received nearly forty.[109]

Duncan Smith summoned his aides and senior frontbenchers to his Commons office, where he saw them individually. It was reminiscent of Mrs Thatcher's fateful meetings with members of the Cabinet in November 1990. Some urged him to resign rather than stay on and fight a confidence vote. 'Many people went in to tell him the game was up, but I thought there was a chance he could still win the vote,' recalls Nick Wood. 'A lot of people were dismayed that he took it to a vote.'[110] He decided to persevere. At 2.15 p.m., the embattled Tory leader appeared outside Central Office with senior Shadow

Cabinet colleagues to announce that MPs would vote the next day, Wednesday, 29 October.

When the vote took place, the parliamentary party brought about Duncan Smith's downfall by ninety votes to seventy-five. The comparatively narrow margin was surprising. 'I can remember one colleague saying he would vote for him on the day because he didn't want him to be humiliated, but he knew he would be kicked out anyway,' says a senior MP. 'Then I was worried in case everybody did this.' Divided, dispirited and in despair, Conservative MPs had deposed a leader who had been in office barely two years. It was only the second time since 1900 that a party leader in opposition had been removed before he had the chance to fight a general election. Duncan Smith took his place in the pantheon of Tory history with only Austen Chamberlain for company. In 1922, the party had rebelled against Chamberlain in protest at continued Conservative partici-pation in David Lloyd George's coalition government, originally formed in the midst of the First World War. After the famous meeting of Tory MPs at the Carlton Club on 19 October 1922, when a majority voted against remaining in the coalition, Chamberlain resigned as party leader and Lloyd George's government collapsed. The Conser-vatives returned to power one month later under a new leader, Andrew Bonar Law. Lloyd George was to be the last Liberal Prime Minister. Within two years the Liberals, a once rock-solid party of government, crumbled at the polls before drifting into obscurity as the third party of British politics. The fate that befell them was looming over the Tories on the dark autumn evening of Wednesday, 29 October 2003. The circumstances may have been different, and there was no immediate prospect of a general election, but this was a party staring into the abyss.

FOUR

False Dawn
November 2003–May 2005

Shortly after seven o'clock on the evening of Wednesday, 29 October 2003, flanked by senior members of the Shadow Cabinet including Michael Howard, Theresa May and Oliver Letwin, Iain Duncan Smith made a short resignation statement outside Central Office. 'The parliamentary party has spoken, the announcement has been made, and I will stand down as leader when a successor has finally been chosen. I will give that leader my absolute loyalty and support.' The faces around him could not have been more sombre. 'I fought to keep IDS because, whatever the difficulties, it seemed to me that the trauma of removing a leader would lead us into a period that would destroy us with yet another battle for the leadership,' Letwin recalls. 'Standing there, I really did think that we were seeing the annihilation of a party that was capable of functioning in the future.'[1]

No Hope

After toppling yet another leader, the party was in a fractious and directionless state. 'If Duncan Smith had won the confidence vote we would have limped on to the general election, and could well have ended up with a lower share of the vote than the Liberal Democrats, and that would have been it,' a senior figure reflects. 'It was like the decline of someone with a terminal illness: every now and then there would be a sharp deterioration and the patient would have fallen to the next level.' The alternative, which MPs had chosen that day, was a bloody battle for the leadership: a nightmare scenario that seemed just as unpalatable as holding on to the incumbent.

Unlike the situation during the traumatic removal of Mrs Thatcher thirteen years earlier, the party no longer had the cushion of office and all the levers of power at its disposal. Like Mrs Thatcher, Iain Duncan Smith felt betrayed by a parliamentary party which he thought had lost its senses. Yet self-preservation had overcome any residual loyalty Tory MPs might have felt to a leader they never really accepted. The party had suffered two crushing defeats in 1997 and 2001. By October 2003, nothing other than a catastrophe at the next election seemed possible.

Iain Duncan Smith had been elected as leader of the Conservative Party because of who he was not, rather than because of who he was. He was neither Michael Portillo nor Ken Clarke. He was a decent man who held strong views about Europe and the state of society, but he was not a leader-in-waiting. He gained acceptance because too many Tory MPs despised the thought of being led by either a man they felt had lost his political nerve and deviated into unfamiliar territory, or by a man who was regarded as having too much nerve in holding on to his pro-European views. Iain Duncan Smith was an accidental leader. He understood that the party had to broaden its focus after the 2001 defeat, and by steering away from the subject of Europe and concentrating on reforming the public services to 'help the vulnerable' he tried to carve out a new direction. But too many in the party, and in the country, were unwilling to listen to his message.

Tony Blair's assumption of the role of international statesman after 9/11 only magnified Iain Duncan Smith's unsuitability for the leadership of his party. In the wake of the demoralising defeat in 2001, the Conservatives desperately needed a politician who could unite a divided party, provide a clear sense of purpose and command national appeal. Portillo and Clarke may have fulfilled some of these criteria, but they were also flawed. Duncan Smith, it soon transpired, could not fulfil any of them. Finding himself incapable of reconciling intractable views and belligerent personalities in his Shadow Cabinet, his fledgling agenda began to sink. Like the country, his colleagues were uninspired by his public performances. The 'Betsygate' allegations were highly damaging, but Duncan Smith's speech in Blackpool was the final nail in his coffin. Tory MPs had come to the inescapable conclusion that their leader was unelectable.

Just how bad was the condition of the Tory body politic in the autumn of 2003? Electorally, modest progress had been made in local elections in the spring: there were 560 more Conservative councillors than before, and the party polled 35 per cent of the projected national share of the vote. However, this was well short of the 40 per cent that an opposition party needed to attract to be a contender in a general election. Performances in by-elections continued to be dire, with Brent East proving that the resurgent Liberal Democrats had established themselves as the main vehicle of protest against the government. Organisationally and financially, the Conservatives were in decline. Donations had dried up, and Central Office had become the scene of bitter infighting. The grassroots felt that they had become dislocated from the party in Westminster, as the Barry Legg episode had so visibly proved.

The clearest demonstration of the party's failure in opposition was its inability to benefit from a government that had begun to lose the benefit of the doubt. Duncan Smith's decision to give his party's unequivocal support for the war in Iraq meant that the Conservatives had no credibility in holding to account a government policy which was rapidly unravelling in the late summer and early autumn of 2003. As far as the public was concerned, the opposition were at best silent, and at worst complicit in one of the biggest foreign policy failures since the Second World War. While Labour's poll ratings began to fall to 36–37 per cent, the Conservatives remained stuck on 31–33 per cent during September and October. Only the Liberal Democrats, who had opposed the war from the outset, benefited, as their ratings rose to 25 per cent.[2] As Tony Blair's standing as Prime Minister and his party's popularity began to falter for the first time since 1997, the Tories under Iain Duncan Smith were imploding. It was an untenable position for an opposition party to be in.

What made the atmosphere so utterly desolate as the storm clouds gathered around Iain Duncan Smith's leadership was the lack of hope. There was a sense that nothing and no one could lift the Conservatives out of the depths of despair. For a party that once commanded the heights of British politics, it had become a question of survival.

The Coronation Coup

The darkest hour is always before dawn, and so it was for the Conservative Party in late October 2003. As Duncan Smith's leadership came crashing to an end, a concerted effort was already under way to fill the approaching vacuum. At the forefront of the minds of the MPs who had brought him down was the desire for a quick succession. A drawn-out leadership contest was too appalling to contemplate. MPs soon came to the view that the Shadow Chancellor, Michael Howard, was the only figure capable of commanding authority within the parliamentary party. He had held Cabinet posts under Margaret Thatcher and John Major, including Home Secretary, and had served under Hague and Duncan Smith. Friends and colleagues had been urging him for some time to challenge Duncan Smith, but he had refused even to consider it. 'I didn't plan to stand,' he insists. 'I was trying to persuade people to vote for Iain Duncan Smith right up until the end. But when it was clear that wasn't going to happen, people asked me to consider it, and I decided to go for it.'[3]

Two senior figures in the Shadow Cabinet, Liam Fox and Oliver Letwin, were instrumental in persuading him to go for it. Fox had been Howard's Parliamentary Private Secretary when he was Home Secretary in the early 1990s, while Letwin believed Howard had the necessary seniority to lead the party. 'To avoid disaster, it became clear to me and some others that we needed to club together and have someone of unimpeachable authority,' Letwin recalls.[4] Fox was equally clear: 'We needed a return to stability. I told Michael Howard that this could happen only if the leadership could be won quickly.'[5] What eventually trumped Howard's loyalty to the leadership was the argument that Letwin, Fox and others were making. One of his confidants recalls that he was finally persuaded to stand by the following appeal: 'We don't give a shit if you don't want to do this, it's your duty – get on with it.'

Michael Howard did not suffer from a lack of ambition. As one of the few survivors from the Thatcher and Major era, it appeared that his frontbench days were over in 1999 when he stepped down from Hague's Shadow Cabinet. Returning as Shadow Chancellor under Duncan Smith two years later, he revived a long career at the summit of Tory politics. Howard had come a long way since his humble beginnings in South Wales. His parents were Jewish émigrés from Eastern Europe who had settled in Llanelli, an industrial town near Swansea, where they became successful shopkeepers. Like several other senior politicians born during the war years, he went to a grammar school and then on to university. At Cambridge he developed a passion for debating, and soon joined the University's active Conservative Association, becoming President of the Cambridge Union Society and meeting future political colleagues including Ken Clarke, John Gummer, Norman Lamont and Leon Brittan. They became known as the 'Cambridge mafia'. In 1975 he married the model Sandra Paul, who had appeared on the front cover of *Vogue* and included Frank Sinatra among her glamorous friends and acquaintances.

After a successful career as a barrister, becoming a Queen's Counsel in 1982, Howard joined his Cambridge friends (and rivals) in the Commons a year later. Catching the eye of Mrs Thatcher, he quickly won ministerial promotion, although some of his decisions were not without controversy. As Minister for Local Government he accepted an amendment to a bill in 1988 that became known as Section 28, which prohibited the promotion of homosexuality by local authorities, particularly in schools. When the Blair government sought to repeal Section 28 after 1997, the Conservatives opposed them (it was eventually repealed in March 2003). He had also managed to steer another controversial piece of legislation through the Commons: the Community Charge. Mrs Thatcher had rewarded him with a seat at the Cabinet table, as Employment Secretary.

As John Major's Environment and then Home Secretary, Howard

was one of the most proactive members of the government. In the latter role he took a tough line on crime, famously declaring that 'Prison works.' He was known for his ability to get things done, his diligence and his forensic eye for detail, but some found him abrupt and, occasionally, abrasive. As Home Secretary he repeatedly clashed with judges and prison reformers, and his reputation came under serious question over the sacking of Derek Lewis, the Director-General of the Prison Service, after a prison breakout in 1995. When a critical inquiry into several prison escapes was published on 13 May 1997, Howard faced a relentless interrogation from Jeremy Paxman on BBC2's *Newsnight* programme.[6] The infamous exchange, in which Howard refused to answer the same question fourteen times, marred his subsequent bid for the leadership.

Worse, the former Prisons Minister Ann Widdecombe, who worked under Howard at the Home Office, accused him of deliberately misleading the Commons over the dismissal of Lewis, which Howard strongly denied. She was quoted in the *Sunday Times* as saying that Howard was 'dangerous stuff' and that there was 'something of the night about him'.[7] It was a phrase that quickly caught the public imagination, contributing to a sinister, Count Dracula-like image (which the impressionist Rory Bremner parodied to considerable effect) that Howard would find hard to shake off. Ending up in last place with a derisory twenty-three votes in the 1997 leadership contest, Howard was deeply bruised. While he was respected as a politician of weight, his public persona was not one that voters warmed to. He reminded them of a discredited Tory government that they had only just voted out of office in a landslide.

Six years on, the Conservative Party was in a very different place. Although the 'something of the night' attack still lingered, Michael Howard was one of the few senior Tory politicians left who was willing and able to lead a party with an even more tarnished reputation. His stock within the parliamentary party had been strengthened by some robust exchanges with Gordon Brown at the dispatch box. He had landed some blows on the Chancellor, which was more than could be said for his predecessors since 1997. Now he was presented with an opportunity to restore his leadership ambitions and resurrect a party in a grave state of disrepair.

Although he maintained his loyalty to Iain Duncan Smith privately and publicly in the days leading up to the vote of confidence, Howard had begun to assemble a small group of allies and confidants to plan for a potential leadership bid. The first thing he did was ring up Rachel Whetstone, his talented special adviser at the Home Office in the 1990s, who was working for the public relations firm Portland. 'I'm not going to do this job without you,' he told her.

Whetstone was just about to go on holiday to Ecuador, but her old boss persuaded her to be his Political Secretary after she came back. Brought up in the genteel surroundings of the Sussex countryside, she came from a wealthy family with impeccable Thatcherite credentials. The granddaughter of a former RAF officer who made millions from intensive chicken farming and who helped to found the leading free-market think tank the Institute of Economic Affairs, Whetstone had politics running through her veins. The works of Milton Friedman and Friedrich Hayek, both important intellectual influences behind the Thatcher revolution, filled the bookshelves at home. At Benenden School and Bristol University she honed her fierce intellect and insatiable appetite for political argument before embarking on a career at the Conservative Research Department in 1990. Rising quickly through the ranks, becoming head of the Political Section in 1992 (when Cameron left for the Treasury), Whetstone established a reputation as a sharp operator who took few hostages. Howard was not bluffing when he said he could not do the job without her. Few others were able to give him such candid and blunt advice. With the help of Whetstone, Oliver Letwin and a few others, Howard quietly began to plan for a leadership bid. Despite invitations to join them, Cameron and Osborne were reluctant to become involved, thinking it would be counter-productive to be associated with any plans in the shadows.

There was one major obstacle to Howard's chances of success: David Davis. Like Howard, Davis had supporters in the parliamentary party who urged him to stand, and having failed in 2001, he was determined to have another attempt at the leadership. During the weekend before the confidence vote on 29 October that would bring down Duncan Smith, Davis sounded out opinion among a few friends in the parliamentary party. Among them was Graham Brady, who had supported his 2001 leadership bid but had become Howard's parliamentary aide in January 2003. 'He phoned me and I intimated that I thought Howard was the best option,' recalls Brady.[8] Brady's view was an important litmus test for Davis, as he felt that some of his supporters could live with Howard. Meanwhile, others like Eric Forth, the Shadow Leader of the Commons, continued to gauge opinion within the party.

Davis and his allies were deeply resentful of the way he had been sacked as Party Chairman. Yet he had remained in the Shadow Cabinet, and he voted for Duncan Smith in the confidence ballot. 'One or two people tried to drag me into the plot against Iain but I refused to get into that,' he says.[9] In any event, his supporters began to prepare for a leadership bid in anticipation of Duncan Smith's departure. Others senior figures also began to manoeuvre themselves into position, including Michael Ancram, the Shadow Foreign Secretary, and Tim Yeo, the Shadow Environment Secretary.

As MPs began casting their ballots in the confidence vote on the morning of Wednesday, 29 October, Howard had a brief discussion with Davis in the Commons. The Shadow Chancellor had already discussed what to say with his close supporters. Some MPs, including Oliver Letwin, had urged him to compromise and offer Davis the deputy leadership. Whetstone sharply disagreed. 'Do not offer him anything. If you want to do it, it's got to be on your own terms,' she urged him. Howard was courteous but firm when he met Davis, confirming that he would stand, but saying that he would not be interested in any deals. The meeting broke up with Howard not knowing what Davis was going to do. Half an hour before the result of the confidence vote was declared, Davis rang Howard to say that he would not be standing.[10] He had decided to make a statement outside the St Stephen's entrance of the Commons within minutes of the ballot result being announced at Central Office. 'I wanted to stop the whole process dead – if that had not happened, then others in the game would have probably manoeuvred themselves into position,' says Davis. 'It needed shock and surprise, so I couldn't tell anybody – not even Michael or my own friends – until very late on in the day.'[11]

Davis's allies, including Eric Forth and Derek Conway, a former whip from the Major years, were incensed. Why turn down the opportunity to go for a job he coveted, they asked. Davis claims that he had actually made his mind up the previous day, but wanted to find out where Howard's intentions lay. 'There had just been a European Football Championship qualifier match between England and Turkey, where there had a been a fight on the pitch, and it continued in the tunnel afterwards,' he recalls. 'I told my friends that a leadership election, which would have a sharp edge like the others, would be like the fight that goes on into the tunnel. It would run into the next general election, which was only a year or so away, and Labour might go early to catch us when we were barely out of it.'[12]

His allies told him they were sure he would win, but he was adamant that a damaging contest would only drag the party further down. In fact they were wildly overstating their case: Davis had after all secured just twenty-one votes in the 2001 leadership election, and there were a number of members of the parliamentary party who were determined to stop his candidacy at any cost. Several senior colleagues, including Francis Maude, had also warned him that he risked being another isolated leader if he failed to carry the majority of the parliamentary party in a leadership ballot.[13] Like Duncan Smith, he might have won the confidence of the wider membership, but he could not be sure of having the support of a majority of MPs sitting on the green benches behind him. Such an unenviable prospect may well have been enough to place his leadership ambitions on hold.

Shortly after Davis declared his intention to stand aside for Howard, Tim Yeo rang Howard to say that he too would not be standing. For a brief period there was speculation that Eric Forth might enter the race, but when Fox, Letwin and Stephen Dorrell, a former Cabinet minister, issued a joint statement in support of

Howard it was clear that the path was clearing for the Shadow Chancellor. Within an hour of Duncan Smith losing the vote, Howard had emerged as the 'unity' candidate.

The following morning, on Thursday, 30 October, David Maclean resigned as Chief Whip. In a letter to all Tory MPs he wrote: 'Now that we have a leadership election it is vital that the whole Whips' office is, and is seen to be, neutral and impartial. I cannot let my past commitment to [Duncan Smith] give rise to any suggestion that the office will not operate with the highest standards of neutrality and my departure will make that abundantly clear.'[14] Others were not so convinced of his neutrality. 'It was a bizarre thing to do – no Chief Whip should leave a sinking ship,' recalls a former whip. 'But he saw that Howard was the only person who could stabilise the party. After all, Maclean had been Howard's right-hand man at the Home Office – they go back a long way. It was all orchestrated.' Amid the turmoil of Duncan Smith's demise, the Whips' Office had discreetly steered the way for Michael Howard's coronation. For his part, Maclean wished to observe the 'old Conservative rule that Chief Whips should do their duty and never talk about it again'.[15] But there is no doubt that he presided over a very old-fashioned Tory coup in order to prevent a potentially fatal power vacuum engulfing the party. The person who could have stopped that coup in its tracks was David Davis. He might not have won had he triggered a contest, but to his credit he put party unity first. Not for the last time he passed up an opportunity to seize the reins of the party he so aspired to lead.

The Saatchi Gallery Spirit

The Howard team soon rallied a large number of MPs (David Cameron and George Osborne among them) as well as figures from the worlds of business and marketing to their cause. Campaign funds of £75,000 were raised overnight.[16] Seizing the moment, Howard's team decided to launch his leadership bid later that day, 30 October. At 6 a.m. they began looking for a venue, and decided on the new Saatchi Gallery in County Hall, the former home of Greater London

Council, across the river from the Commons. Evoking the name of the Saatchi brothers, whose advertising agency had played such a role in earlier Conservative election victories, against the backdrop of a modern art gallery seemed to fit the bill. Huge expectations were riding on Howard's speech at the launch that afternoon. The night before, Rachel Whetstone asked Steve Hilton to come up with a draft. Although the speech he prepared had the right modernising message, she realised it would not work for Howard. She rang Francis Maude, one the few 'modernising' voices within the senior ranks of the parliamentary party, who knew Howard well, and asked him to redraft it. Together with Nick Boles from Policy Exchange, Maude worked through the night to knock it into shape.

To their surprise, Michael Howard delivered the speech almost word for word the following day. He promised to lead the party 'from its centre', and expected the support of every colleague. 'There will be no place for ancient feuds or rankling discords,' he declared. In a passage that could have been delivered by Michael Portillo two years earlier, he said: 'At its best we are a party broad and generous, broad in appeal and generous in outlook; a party capable of representing all Britain and all Britons . . . There can be no no-go areas for a modern Conservative Party.' 'We won't hesitate to give credit to the government when it gets things right,' he promised. 'We won't oppose for opposition's sake. People want better than that.' This was not the combative Michael Howard of old. 'I've learnt that if we want to persuade people, we need to preach a bit less and listen a bit more. I've learnt that just winning an argument doesn't on its own win hearts and minds. I've learnt that politicians won't be respected by the public unless they respect each other, and that people won't trust us unless we trust them.'[17]

The Saatchi Gallery speech was what Maude and other like-minded modernisers had yearned to hear from a party leader ever since Portillo's failure in 2001. But for Howard it meant something more immediate: 'I was trying to give the hope to the party that a moment had come when new leadership could turn things round.'[18] Maude came to regret that there was not more discussion about the speech in advance. 'I wish when he read it that I'd stood over him and said, "You've got to mean it." This was not just a speech; this was a strategy that had to be followed. I think he heard the music, but he didn't internalise it.'[19]

Rachel Whetstone could not believe how well Howard had delivered the speech. However, she was painfully aware that when answering questions from reporters afterwards he gave an important hostage to fortune. She had warned him that he would be asked whether he would stand by the policy positions set in train by Duncan Smith. 'I told him, "You've got to ditch the old policy agenda and say we're going to have a policy review," ' she recalls. 'The old policies included things like finding an island for asylum seekers, which was crazy, and opposing university tuition fees, which was illogical. Michael said that he couldn't drop them, as he had been Shadow Chancellor. Therein lay his inability to get away from the old Tory Party.'[20]

To the audience of Central Office staff and an assortment of MPs and other supporters, Howard's answer to the policy question was lost amid the uplifting spirit of the occasion. His words immediately stamped his authority on the parliamentary party, deterring any undeclared rivals, including Ken Clarke, from throwing their hats into the ring. The assembled media were taken aback. 'He symbolised Thatcherism to the party in a way, and yet the people around at his launch were those who we now regard as modernisers,' a seasoned editor recalled. 'I remember seeing the people there and thinking, "This is a serious moment." The key thing was that young people with careers and earning potential were coming back to work for the Tories, and that was such a contrast with IDS.'

By the end of the day almost a hundred Tory MPs had publicly pledged their support for Howard's candidacy. When nominations closed the following week, on Thursday, 6 November, Michael Howard was declared leader unopposed. He was the third leader in opposition since 1997. With a debilitating leadership election having been averted by a coup to crown him as leader, the tiniest glimmers of hope began to appear.

The Grown-Ups are Back in Charge

Michael Howard's coronation presented opportunities that neither of his predecessors since 1997 had enjoyed. He understood that restoring order to a demoralised and fractious organisation was an immediate priority. 'It was encouraging that the party was behind me, and it helped impose a sense of discipline on the party, which was badly needed, as the previous years had been very damaging.'[21] He appointed Stephen Sherbourne as his chief of staff. An experienced operator, Sherbourne had served as Margaret Thatcher's Political Secretary in Number 10. 'There was no underestimating the scale of the task – we needed to show the outside world that the party was back in business, credible and could be taken seriously again,' he recalls.[22] Together with Whetstone, who became Howard's Political Secretary, Sherbourne recruited a brand-new team to occupy a suite of offices adjacent to the Palace of Westminster. Only one member of Duncan Smith's private office, Jonathan Hellewell, who oversaw correspondence, was retained. 'Stephen Sherbourne played a vital role in keeping everybody calm,' recalled a senior party official. 'He professionalised the private office and gave the whole thing an air of seriousness. This was so important, because there was an attitude everywhere that we had become a laughing stock.'

Rachel Whetstone became a pivotal figure in the new regime, throwing herself wholeheartedly into the job. Howard entrusted her with the responsibility of enforcing his will across the parliamentary party, and she had little patience for MPs who strayed from the party line or uttered anything that might be interpreted as defeatist. 'Michael and Rachel wanted to win, but some in the parliamentary party didn't – they just didn't have the hunger for it,' recalls Daniel Ritterband, a former Saatchi & Saatchi ad man whom Sherbourne and Whetstone recruited as their special assistant.[23] 'There was no complacency. Rachel didn't care if she ruffled feathers; the party needed a kick up the backside.' While some recalcitrant MPs resented the smack of firm leadership, many were comforted by the fact that at last someone was in charge. 'There was an attitude that with Michael

Howard they had got the grown-ups back,' Sherbourne recalled. 'There was a real sigh of relief within the party.'[24]

Howard also introduced a new team to run Central Office. Breaking with tradition, he appointed co-chairmen, rewarding loyal supporters Liam Fox and Maurice Saatchi. Fox took charge of campaigning, constituencies and handling the media, while Saatchi presided over strategy. Having conceived some of the most successful Tory advertising campaigns since the late 1970s, the advertising guru, famed for his large tortoiseshell glasses, was revered by many in the party (although some who had worked closely with him in 1997 were not so confident about his organisational abilities). Central Office was reorganised into three departments: research under Greg Clark and David Willetts; marketing under Will Harris; and communications under Guy Black (with the assistance of George Eustice). Black was another member of the 'Smith Square set' from the late 1980s and early 1990s to return to the fold. As a former Director of the Press Complaints Commission he brought with him an impressive range of media contacts. Two other CRD alumni were also enlisted: Steve Hilton, who as a former of protégé of Maurice Saatchi had gone on to launch a successful consultancy called Good Business, came back on a part-time basis to assist Saatchi on strategy; and George Bridges, Major's former Assistant Political Secretary in Downing Street, was appointed Director of the Research Department. On 11 November the party took the symbolic step of announcing that it would sell the lease on 32 Smith Square after forty-five years. The move would release much-needed funds for a cash-strapped party, which would seek modern, state-of-the-art new headquarters elsewhere in Westminster, leaving behind a building that had become associated with discord and intrigue.

Howard had created a tight-knit team to run his office and manage Central Office. His regime had the hallmark of Tony Blair's operation in opposition before 1997: decision-making was confined to a small group of powerful advisers, whose influence rivalled and often exceeded that of the Shadow Cabinet. In another departure, Howard appointed a much smaller team to sit at the top table than had his predecessors. A Shadow Cabinet of twelve (instead of twenty-six under Duncan Smith) met several mornings a week. 'In the early days it worked very well to collectively make sure that we had a daily view of what was happening, what we should be initiating and responding to. It gave us a great deal of flexibility,' Sherbourne recalls.[25]

Howard rewarded those who had either stood aside or helped his smooth succession. David Davis was made Shadow Home Secretary, Oliver Letwin promoted to Shadow Chancellor and Michael Ancram remained as Shadow Foreign Secretary. Tim Yeo was given overall charge of the public services, combining health and education – a brief that was considered to be too wide for one spokesman, given its electoral importance. David Maclean was reinstated as Chief Whip in recognition of his enduring loyalty. In his Saatchi Gallery speech Howard had appealed to all the 'talents' in the party to step forward and serve. However, he obliged Duncan Smith's parting wish that Francis Maude should remain outside the Shadow Cabinet, given his alleged involvement in his demise. This deprived the new leader of a key personality, as did the absence of Ken Clarke, who wished to remain on the backbenches. Michael Portillo also declined an invitation to return to frontline politics, although he had supported Howard's bid for the leadership. With his passion for party politics long since gone, Portillo announced on the day after Howard became leader that he would stand down as an MP at the next election to pursue other interests. Howard was determined to minimise dissent and to welcome figures from across the party into the fold. Clarke, Hague, Duncan Smith and John Major would meet as a 'council of wise men' to offer their advice to the new leader, and two thirds of the parliamentary party were given frontbench roles or posts within the party hierarchy.

Within a few weeks, Michael Howard had begun to rebuild confidence. 'At the end of October we could have gone under in many ways – ideologically, structurally and financially – but Michael turned the tide,' recalls Guy Black.[26] In Number 10 the mood was apprehensive, as the government realised that it was facing a very different beast at the top of the Tory Party. The two party leaders went back a long way. Blair had shadowed Howard at several points during the Thatcher and Major years before he became Labour leader in 1994. 'Our view was that Howard was a serious figure who you needed to respect,' says Matthew Taylor, who was Blair's head of policy. However, Blair sensed that his old adversary's character flaws and history would become apparent for all to see. 'I once had a very funny exchange with Tony about Michael Howard,' recalls Taylor. 'What he said was, "The thing about Michael Howard is that initially people don't like him, when they get to know him a bit more they like him, but when they *really* get to know him they're not sure again." I said to Tony, "Well that's the reverse of you, then!" That was the perception of Michael Howard: that he wasn't as crudely unattractive to the voters as some people thought, that he was more credible, but that deep, deep down people still didn't really want him to be Prime Minister.'[27] It was a conundrum that some of Howard's closest aides understood only too well. Their task was to project him as a leader with both credibility and a mission, in the hope that voters would look at him afresh.

What's the 'Big Idea'?

Having restored some semblance of order, Howard now had to devise a strategy for the next general election, which many expected to be held in spring 2005. With barely eighteen months to play with, this would be his only chance to press the reset button. His team decided to use a series of speeches and advertisements to present the 'new' Michael Howard to the country. He would personify a party that had turned a new leaf, continuing the theme of the Saatchi Gallery launch. The first example of this approach was a two-page newspaper advertisement in January 2004 entitled 'I Believe', which set out sixteen core beliefs in a personal manifesto. In an attempt to portray Howard as a forward-looking leader who understood voters' concerns, it contained statements such as, 'I believe that every child wants security for their parents in their old age' and 'I believe in equality of opportunity. Injustice makes me angry.' It also chimed with the Thatcherite instincts that 'The people should be big. The state should be small' and that 'Britain should defend her freedom at any time, against all comers, however mighty.'[28] 'It was a symbolic attempt to show that we were back out there,' says Guy Black, who promoted the advertisements. 'We wanted to show he was a leader who had core beliefs that you wouldn't necessarily immediately associate with him, as they were much more liberal than you might expect from the Michael Howard of old who suppressed prison riots and introduced Clause 28. It made an impact.'[29]

The relaunch continued in February, when Howard delivered his 'British Dream' speech in London. In a highly personal and heart-felt address, he talked about how his family prospered in Britain having settled as immigrants, initially in the East End of London and then in South Wales. He described discrimination as 'one of the worst ways in which people are denied control over their own lives'. It was a theme he reiterated a few months later in Burnley, where the far-right British National Party had established a foothold on the local council. Denouncing the BNP's aims, he declared that 'We are a stronger and better country, rich in our cultural diversity, because of the immigrant communities that have settled here.' He softened the party's approach on various social issues, committing it to supporting the government's Civil Partnership Bill, which gave same-sex partners many of the rights enjoyed by married couples and pledging to introduce measures to improve childcare. The party even held a 'gay summit' at Westminster with lesbian and homo-sexual groups, something that would have been unthinkable only a few years before, given the controversy surrounding unmarried adoption and Clause 28.

The New Year polls showed encouraging signs of progress – one even put the party at 40 per cent, ahead of Labour. 'There was a window of hope for a few weeks when we genuinely believed we would win the next election,' recalls Ed Vaizey, one of Howard's speechwriters.[30] Others, like Richard Stephenson, who represented the grassroots on the party board, were more cautious. 'The bounce came from a feeling of stability and confidence, rather than any genuine restoration of fortunes. All of a sudden there was a firm hand on the rudder.'[31] Indeed, the average poll ratings showed a modest improvement, from 32 per cent in November 2003 when Howard took over, to 35 per cent in March 2004.[32]

Projecting an impassioned Michael Howard was perhaps the easiest of the tasks of the new team. Determining the direction of party policy and convincing the public that the Conservatives were a credible alternative government would prove much harder. Sherbourne admits that the early initiatives did not add up to a coherent policy. 'They were like stones in a pond creating ripples of interest. The problem was that they didn't hang together, and it was hard to know where they were going.' He blames the lack of time: 'It was like getting on a moving train which was just about to arrive – it was hard to plan anything.'[33]

A more fundamental obstacle was Howard himself. In April his senior advisers, including Whetstone, Sherbourne, Bridges, Saatchi and Hilton, met at his constituency home in Kent to discuss strategy. There was a feeling that some of the early momentum had been lost, and the polls were beginning to slide. Howard expressed his frustration. 'What do we do?' he asked. 'I've been giving these speeches for the past few months, but we're stuck.' They argued that he had to define a vision for the party, and that there was a 'lack of a big idea'. Maurice Saatchi asked Howard what his 'moral purpose' would be as a potential Prime Minister.[34] 'I know what my political beliefs are,' he responded, 'but it smacks of vanity to go on about them. I want to be the country's problem-solver – that will be my strategy.' One of those present recalled: 'The die was cast then. We were not going to have a strategy.' Another said: 'We were fucked. We never had a strategy.'[35] 'The problem was that Michael as a person did not have a political philosophy other than a classical Tory view of freedom and individual responsibility,' recalled a close aide. 'So we did not have a philosophy that could be applied to things like the environment or international development.'

The lack of a compelling message led to a confusing approach to policy. Much of the detailed work begun under Duncan Smith was continued, but what was left of his efforts to reposition the party as a champion of 'social justice' quietly disappeared. Howard had never been keen on the idea. In January 2004, Duncan Smith expressed his frustration that moving the party onto different territory was 'like shining a pencil torch into a dark void. There is just a little bit of light coming through on this one, but we need to do a lot more work on it. There is still more understanding required.'[36] But the policy contradictions and weaknesses that existed under Duncan Smith continued under Howard. On the one hand the party continued to oppose university top-up fees, while on the other it developed policies, unveiled in summer 2004, that would give people the 'Right to Choose' to use public money to spend on private education or healthcare, which they could supplement themselves if necessary.

The 'Right to Choose' policies failed to make an impact. George Bridges admits, 'They were very radical, but we didn't have the time to take on board what the research told us about the public's attitude to choice – that they wanted choice, but it was a struggle to show how it would improve standards and outcomes.'[37] The policies also suffered from being too complicated to sell to the public. 'We had an advertising campaign in June and July to explain them, but no one really understood them,' says Black.[38] Research undertaken by ICM, which conducted the party's private polling, showed that people felt the Tories were still on the side of the better-off, rather than ordinary people, particularly when it came to the NHS. Very few people could even identify the party's ideas on health and educa-tion, let alone understand them. In order to make the point, ICM displayed a large lemon on the front cover of its report to the party.

Adding to this lack of clarity was the leadership's response to the electorate's cynicism about politics. Spurred on by Howard's eager-ness to be the nation's 'problem-solver', Steve Hilton and George Bridges, alongside Johnny Heald from the market research firm ORB, planned an intensive summer of focus group research to establish people's real concerns. It revealed that voters were very suspicious of politicians who made easy promises. They felt unable to distinguish between New Labour and the Conservatives, but felt 'let down' by Labour's 'broken promises'. While they were content with the general state of the economy, they were dissatisfied with Labour's record on asylum, crime, the public services and tax. This reinforced Howard's view that people wanted 'action, not words', but it also showed that voters were far from convinced that the Conservatives could do any better than Labour.[39] For Howard, this provided an opportunity to go on the offensive and exploit Labour's weaknesses. 'He felt he needed bullets to kill the enemy with – that was his approach to policy,' one adviser lamented. Hilton and Bridges began to work on an idea that they hoped would address the problem of voter cynicism, while taming some of Howard's desire to go on the attack. As they devised a game plan, events intervened to bring out the Michael Howard of old.

The Long Shadow of Iraq

Howard was an experienced performer in the Commons who enjoyed the parliamentary knockabout. He had risen to prominence in the 1980s and early 1990s as an adversarial frontbencher capable of landing blows on Labour opponents, including a young Shadow Home Secretary called Tony Blair, and as Shadow Chancellor he had found the measure of Gordon Brown far more than any of his predecessors. To the delight of Tory MPs he skewered Blair in one of his first outings at Prime Minister's Questions as leader.

Blair was in his weakest position since coming to office: Iraq continued to divide the Labour Party, and he faced a massive back-bench rebellion on university top-up fees, which had not been included in its manifesto in 2001. Blair tried to make the case that variable fees would widen access to universities. 'This grammar-school boy will take no lessons from that public-school boy on the importance of children from less privileged backgrounds gaining access to university,' Howard retorted, to loud cheers from his own side.[40] His bravura performances lifted morale on the backbenches, but his first major test would leave them disappointed.

The former High Court judge Lord Hutton had been asked by the government to inquire into the events leading up to the death of Dr David Kelly. Hutton's report had the potential to damage the Prime Minister, particularly as his inquiries had uncovered information that undermined the original case for war and raised questions about the government's conduct. This would be an opportunity for Howard to combine his forensic skills as a lawyer with his mastery of the Commons to expose the weakness of Blair's position and possibly precipitate his resignation.

Shortly after he became leader Howard assembled a 'special unit', which included former Cabinet ministers David Hunt and Peter Lilley, to prepare for the report. 'We had material prepared for the various approaches that the report might take,' Sherbourne recalls. 'Everyone was firing themselves up for Hutton to attack the government.'[41] 'We were on horseback with our bayonets at the ready. We thought the report would bring Blair down,' Black added.[42] Various scenarios were planned for, from a total indictment of Blair through to criticisms of the intelligence handling. Crucially, no contingency had been made for a complete whitewash.

Howard enlisted the services of a former protégé from his time at the Home Office, David Cameron. He discreetly asked him to prepare a dossier ahead of the report's publication, believing that Cameron's eye for detail would be put to good use. Howard had promoted Cameron to Deputy Chairman of the party on becoming leader in November 2003. Having spent five months in a junior frontbench role under Duncan Smith (as deputy to Eric Forth, who was then Shadow Leader of the Commons), the thirty-six-year-old MP was now brought right into the heart of the new leader's inner circle, joining many of his closest friends and former colleagues from the CRD, including Rachel Whetstone and George Bridges. Cameron spent almost two months familiarising himself with thousands of pages of evidence to the Hutton inquiry. It would all be in vain. On the eve of the report's release, its main findings were leaked to the *Sun*. Blair and his colleagues would be exonerated, and the BBC strongly criticised.

At 6 o'clock the following morning, 28 January 2004, Howard and

Cameron were invited into the Cabinet Office to preview the report. When they returned to the Commons, their faces were ashen. 'I was not expecting it to be a whitewash. We had to make a very quick decision about what to do,' Howard recalls.[43] Various drafts of Howard's response to Blair's statement in the Commons later in the day had been prepared. 'Do you think I should change it?' Howard asked Sherbourne. 'No,' he replied. 'If you change the speech now, we don't know how it will all work out.'[44]

The speech had been prepared on the assumption that Hutton would be very critical of the government. This assumption now lay in tatters, yet Howard chose to deliver his script largely unaltered. Having listened to Blair's statement, Tory MPs sat glumly as Labour MPs hissed the Leader of the Opposition. 'People were thinking, "Has he lost the plot?" ' one of Howard's aides admitted. Howard and his team had misjudged the mood. 'Everybody felt awful when we left at the end of the day,' another recalls. The press were scathing: 'The Prime Minister wiped the floor with Mr Howard,' wrote Alice Miles in *The Times*. 'Mr Blair was putting him on the spot about Hutton, not the other way round.' Charles Moore was equally scornful in the *Daily Telegraph*: 'It was pitiful watching poor Mr Howard trying to squeeze poison from some parenthesis in paragraph 947b (or wherever).'[45]

The Hutton Report had denied Howard a precious opportunity to take advantage of the government's troubles. Blair had escaped condemnation, while the episode rebounded on the Tories. It confirmed that Iraq would be a poisoned chalice for Howard, just as it had been for his predecessor, and underlined to MPs and the party in the country the difficulty their new leader would have in reviving their fortunes. 'Hutton was the moment the door closed,' Ed Vaizey reflects. 'We just felt so demoralised that Blair had the measure of the moment and got through such an amazing scandal that should have brought down the government.'[46] Undeterred, Howard was determined to press on. 'It was the first major setback, but he just kept going,' recalls Black. 'Nothing affected his confidence.'[47] Indeed, he was far more assured when the report was debated more extensively in the Commons a week later. The whole affair had more of an effect on David Cameron's confidence. He had invested months of hard labour trying to find incriminating evidence, but to no avail. His leader had been wrongfooted. 'David was very deeply involved in it, across the strategy and the tactics, and has since become almost paranoid about anything to do with Iraq and intelligence,' recalls a colleague from the time. 'I think he was so badly burnt by the whole experience that he doesn't want to go anywhere near these sorts of things again. It had a profound impact on him.'

Overconfidence may have been to blame for Michael Howard's next intervention over Iraq, a week later, on 5 February. When it was revealed that British soldiers had died because of inadequate equipment, Howard called on Blair to resign. He was genuinely outraged, but his team felt that he had overplayed his hand. 'It's not a good idea to call on somebody to resign unless you know they definitely will,' recalls Black.[48] They also felt the matter had not been properly discussed – Howard fired his shot during a radio interview while on a trip to Portsmouth. 'It was a mistake,' Sherbourne adds. 'He was genuinely angry but it came across as too glib.'[49] Relations between Tory high command and the Bush administration deteriorated sharply: overtures had been made to arrange a visit to the White House later that year, but nothing had been fixed. When reports in the papers suggested that Howard would not be welcome, his office decided not to pursue the visit further. Given President Bush's unpopularity in Britain, Howard's aides did not believe they were losing out much on the kudos of a trip to Washington. Nevertheless, being shunned so publicly was an irritation they could have done without.

The question of how to handle the continuing fallout from the war caused serious ructions within the inner circle. Howard felt the new inquiry into the intelligence on WMDs by the former Cabinet Secretary, Lord Butler, would provide a further opportunity to attack Blair. The Tory leader had withdrawn the party's formal involvement in the inquiry in March because he thought its terms of reference were too restrictive. Guy Black was alone in urging

Howard to go on the offensive, while others in the team, primarily Rachel Whetstone, advised him to steer well clear of the issue. She had supported the original invasion in 2003, but by the time she began working for Howard she realised it had been a mistake. 'If you're not prepared to admit that supporting the war was wrong, you have to stay quiet, Michael,' she told him.[50] 'There was a lot of disagreement about how we played it,' Black recalls. 'I was of the view that the next general election would be an election about Iraq, and I always said that to him. I felt that the liberal media that generated the debate would want to make it a referendum on Iraq. In such a referendum we had nothing to say, because we supported it. I thought Butler was an opportunity to reverse our policy and say that we were misled as much as anybody else.'[51] The opinion polls now showed that a majority of the British people felt they had been deceived, and that the war had been a terrible error.

When the Butler Inquiry was published in July it was indeed far more critical of the government than Hutton, stating that the evidence for WMD was 'limited, sporadic and patchy'. Black advised Howard that this would be his last chance before the election to take a bold step. An interview with the *Sunday Times* would provide such an opportunity, but he only went halfway: 'If you look at the terms of the motion put to the House of Commons on 18 March [2003], it placed a very heavy emphasis on the presence of weapons of mass destruction in Iraq. So I think it is difficult for someone, knowing everything we know now, to have voted for that resolution. I think I would have voted for a differently worded resolution that would have authorised war . . . I am still in favour of the war.'[52] Howard's carefully worded position was hedged around with caveats. Black was disappointed: 'He rang me and said he was sorry, as he wanted to go further but couldn't.'[53] Whetstone was even more despairing that her boss had tried to have it both ways: 'It was a lawyer's answer – dancing on the head of a pin, and then we got hammered in the Commons,' she recalls.[54]

Once again, Blair turned the tables on his opponent. 'The public will respect people who were honestly for the war, and they will respect people who were honestly against the war: they will not respect a politician who says that he is for and against the war in the same newspaper article,' he told the Commons.[55] Tory MPs felt they had been given conflicting signals from the leadership. 'Support for us went down, as it looked like we were a tricky bunch of politicians trying to absolve ourselves of blame,' one senior MP recalled. Howard's chief of staff realised how damaging the leader's intervention had been. 'It was a critical moment because all of our problems – shortage of time, the frustration at not making headway in the polls and being tactical rather than strategic – were all of a sudden encapsulated in this interview,' Sherbourne admits. 'For a long time Labour didn't know how to play Michael, but they then thought the opportunistic line would resonate with the public.'[56]

Struggling to Break Through

The polls were showing that the party was nowhere near the level it needed to be at less than a year before a possible general election. Although Labour's popularity had tumbled as discontent over the government's policies on Iraq and university tuition fees began to bite, the Conservatives returned to their flatline position of 30–31 per cent by June.[57] There was some comfort in the local elections results that month, when the party made gains in London (despite failing to win the mayoralty of London from Ken Livingstone) and in parts of the Midlands and the North-West. For the first time since the 1980s, the Conservatives made modest advances at Labour's expense in metropolitan boroughs. But these were overshadowed by failure in the European Parliament and parliamentary by-elections.

The leadership hoped to capitalise on a growing hostility among voters towards the European Union. The government had ruled out a referendum on the controversial European Constitution, which set out a framework of rules to govern the EU. The Tories attacked the proposed Constitution as a federalist invention, and demanded the referendum that Labour had resisted. Under pressure from the Eurosceptic press, in April 2004 Blair pledged just such a referendum after EU negotiations were concluded, thus depriving Howard of powerful ammunition ahead of the European elections in June. The party was vulnerable to a resurgent United Kingdom Independence Party (UKIP), which had recently recruited to its ranks Robert Kilroy-Silk, a smooth-talking television host and former Labour MP. UKIP advocated complete withdrawal from the EU, a position with which many Tory voters and activists (and a number of Tory MPs) sympathised.

Despite performing better than Labour on polling day, the Conservatives' share of the vote and total number of seats fell, as voters chose UKIP as a vehicle for protest. Not only had Howard failed to match Hague's success in 1999, the result also showed that the party's thunder on Europe had been stolen – by both Blair and UKIP. 'We did well in the local elections, but we lost the propaganda battle over the European elections. It should have been seen as a disaster for Labour, but they managed to turn around people's perceptions so that it was seen as a loss of momentum for us,' Howard says.[58] But the bad news for the Tories went beyond mere perceptions. Although Labour had fared badly, the Conservatives had failed to make a breakthrough. 'This means you can win a three-figure majority at the next general election,' Labour's chief pollster and strategist, Philip Gould, told Blair. It was enough to restore Blair's confidence. Between mid-April and 10 June, he had wondered whether to stay on as Prime Minister, given his mounting problems. Gordon Brown's allies were pressuring Blair to name a departure date, his personal ratings had fallen to their lowest point since 1997 as the situation in Iraq remained bleak, and concerns for his family's welfare weighed heavily on his mind. The June elections were a critical fillip.[59]

While Blair resolved to carry on, Howard's problems were about to get worse. In July's by-elections in the Labour seats of Leicester South and Birmingham Hodge Hill, the Conservatives performed miserably, dropping to third place in both. Despite armies of Tory MPs and activists marching on both constituencies, the party went backwards. Howard had talked up the Conservatives' chances of success, especially in Leicester, where they had held a seat in the 1980s. Insult was added to injury in September when the party came fourth, behind UKIP, in the Hartlepool by-election. The *Daily Telegraph* condemned the result as 'the worst by-election perform-ance by an official opposition in modern history'.[60] 'It was clear to the outside world that we were in no shape to win a general election,' Black recalls.[61] In desperation, Howard reshuffled his Shadow Cabinet, which had already reverted to its traditional size. In a move interpreted as an attempt to fend off the threat from UKIP on the right, Howard brought back the Eurosceptic John Redwood as Shadow Trade and Industry Secretary. 'It was symptomatic of "What can we do now?" so we had a reshuffle,' one senior aide recalls. 'Redwood probably was a mistake, but Michael really wanted him back – after all, John actually had some ideas and did some work. We had 166 MPs, and so many were "has beens" and "never will bes". There were so few of any calibre.'

Timetable Tensions

By the autumn, a general election was looming. Time was running out for Howard to reverse the party's fortunes. Despite moving to new offices in Victoria Street in Westminster in the summer, party headquarters continued to suffer from organisational problems. The co-chairmanship of the party had not been a success. 'I didn't think it would work from the start,' one of the incumbents, Liam Fox, recollects. 'Our roles were not efficiently delineated from the start.'[62] 'In reality they were both terrible administrators and found it difficult to divide up responsibility – no one was in charge day-to-day,' remarked one of Howard's aides.

Fox's co-Chairman, Maurice Saatchi, was to play a central role in preparing for the annual conference at Bournemouth. Howard hoped that Saatchi's creative flair would give the party a much-needed boost on the eve of the run-up to the election campaign. Following on from their focus group work, Steve Hilton and George Bridges produced a plan for the conference period. Over the summer they gave a presentation to Saatchi and Howard, proposing the idea of a 'timetable of action'. It was similar to Ronald Reagan's initiative during his 1980 US presidential campaign, when he pledged to issue a series of specific executive orders within hours of arriving in the White House. Such a plan would show voters exactly what to expect from a Tory government, which could then be held to account in the most transparent way. Hilton knew that Howard was a fan of Reagan's, and of American politics in general, and Saatchi was very much taken by the idea. 'This was the old Tory virtue of pragmatism. It was as good as we could get to overcome the fact that we didn't have an ideological point to make – because there wasn't any ideo- logical difference between the parties,' Saatchi recalls.[63] It also tapped straight into Howard's preference for 'getting things done' rather than lofty political rhetoric. The idea was favourably received by focus groups, and Saatchi and Howard encouraged Hilton to develop it into the main theme for the conference.

Hilton decided to join forces with his old friend David Cameron, who had been promoted to the Shadow Cabinet in June as head of policy coordination in place of David Willetts, who was also Shadow Work and Pensions Secretary. Cameron would now play a central role in preparing the party's next manifesto, reporting directly to the Tory leader. At thirty-seven, he had reached the top table of Tory politics, and had an opportunity to frame the party's platform for the election. During a few days away in Devon in August, Hilton and Cameron produced the 'Timetable for Action' based on the party's focus group findings. It was designed to meet public concerns about hospital cleanliness, more police on the beat, tougher discipline in schools and tighter controls on immigration, among other things.

These were not the sort of issues on which a new Prime Minister could deliver results by centralised *diktat* in a matter of hours, so in order to ensure credibility, Hilton and Cameron set out their 'Timetable for Action' over a period of weeks and months. When they presented this to Saatchi, he hated it, feeling that the extended timetable meant the idea had lost its drama and power, and become boring. Hilton could not believe that his idol had taken the Reagan initiative quite so literally. Saatchi asked Guy Black to devise a rival 'Timetable for Action' with a far shorter time horizon. He had the backing of Howard, who believed that clarity was essential to his emphasis on accountability.

Matters came to a head a few weeks later, in September, when Howard's team met in Portcullis House, adjoining the Commons. Saatchi blasted the Hilton–Cameron timetable. Rachel Whetstone argued that it was the only practical way to implement the idea, while Black sided with the Party Chairman. Tempers frayed on all sides, and some at the meeting were struck by how dismissive Saatchi was towards Cameron. 'He had known us all since the 1992 general election when we were all kids and he was this amazing guru, but he couldn't adjust to the reality that we were players now, and that the power was moving to a new generation,' one of those who was present at the meeting in question remembers. After the meeting, several of the team laid into Saatchi, and the next day Saatchi and Hilton had a blazing row in Saatchi's office in party headquarters in Victoria Street. Hilton stormed out, after which Saatchi sent him an email saying, 'You are no longer my special adviser.'

While Hilton carried on with his work for the party, which had grown far beyond the part-time role envisaged in late 2003, Saatchi became less involved with the preparations for the conference. 'From that point Maurice started not to show up to meetings, whereas Liam was always there as a trouper,' recalls one of Howard's closest aides.

One of Saatchi's most visible contributions was to oversee a revision of the party's old 'torch of freedom' logo from the 1980s. Soviet-like in design, the updated torch was intended to demonstrate a desire for action by being gripped firmly by a muscular fist. The 'Timetable for Action' was adjusted to reflect Saatchi's preferences, although senior aides were not enamoured with the final version, which some felt was 'an uneasy compromise'.

In the final days of preparation for Howard's conference speech, George Bridges suggested boiling down the timetable into a straightforward message that could be conveyed by party workers on the doorstep during the election campaign. Building on the party's research, Howard's aides came up with ten words: 'Lower taxes, cleaner hospitals, more police, controlled immigration, school discipline'. Howard then added an eleventh, 'accountability', which was intended to tackle voters' cynicism. 'In boiling it all down, we sacrificed some of the broader agenda,' regrets one of his aides.

Howard's conference speech exuded confidence and was reasonably well received by the media and the grassroots, but behind the scenes all was not well. The polls spoke for themselves: the party was stuck stubbornly on 31 per cent in October, nowhere near the level needed to contend for power, whereas Labour had recovered to 38 per cent.[64] Howard knew that something drastic had to be done.

Crosby Takes Control

With six months left before the general election, the party machine was demoralised and dysfunctional. Central Office was rudderless and unfit to fight the campaign. The former Party Treasurer and donor, Michael Ashcroft, was so incensed by Saatchi's claim during the conference that the party was ahead in the majority of top target seats that he commissioned his own research, which revealed the party to be in a much worse position. He presented his findings to Howard in a note entitled 'Don't believe the bullshit.' It showed that the party was spreading itself too thinly, rather than focusing on the seats it might actually win. Ashcroft had already begun to recruit several former Central Office figures, including Stephen Gilbert, to run his own operation to support candidates in target seats. It was a sign of the party's disarray that one of its leading donors decided to invest so heavily in a separate campaign outside the party machine.

In desperation, Howard reached out to an Australian campaign guru named Lynton Crosby, who had masterminded several election victories for the Australian Prime Minister John Howard. Michael Howard had known Crosby since the late 1990s, and had asked him to review the party's operations shortly after he became leader. 'Essentially I said there was lack of clarity over their strategy,' Crosby recalls. 'The research also showed that the AB professional classes saw Labour as more economically competent, which is something we never overcame.'[65] Hoping that Crosby's track record in campaigning would give the party a much-needed fillip Howard asked him to become Campaign Director early in 2004, but he could not take up the position until October, shortly after the party conference season. When he came on board, Howard asked him to focus on crime and immigration, because he felt that as a former Home Secretary he had credibility in those areas, and the focus group research conducted by Steve Hilton and George Bridges had identified immigration as an important issue for voters. It was also an area in which Crosby had some campaign experience, particularly during the 2001 Australian federal election, when border protection was a hot issue.

Crosby immediately set about transforming the broken machine, establishing clear lines of authority and restoring a sense of purpose. 'The organisation just wasn't running as well as it could, and there were so many leaks, but we sorted that out,' he recalls. 'There hadn't been one central figure to make decisions.'[66] Renaming Central Office Conservative Campaign Headquarters (CCHQ), he channelled resources into promoting simple, clear campaign messages that would resonate well in marginal seats. 'He made a huge difference, and it was a shame he didn't arrive earlier,' Howard says.[67] The 'Timetable for Action' and the 'ten words' were refined into five simple campaign themes. 'It was obvious that Maurice would be marginalised pretty quickly,' says Black.[68] Saatchi was stoical about the changes: 'Liam and I handed over the campaign to Lynton.'[69] Within months, Crosby's dynamism had raised spirits in CCHQ: 'He brought the staff along with him and got the place humming for the first time in years.'

While Crosby fixed the machine, the debate about the party's election strategy intensified. The question of whether to offer tax cuts continued to divide Howard's senior advisers. Internal polling showed that while swing voters were not in favour of tax cuts, Conservative-leaning voters were hungry for them. Tory backbenchers also pressed hard for significant cuts. As Shadow Chancellor, Howard had asked City troubleshooter David James to examine ways of cutting 'wasteful' public spending. The new Shadow Chancellor, Oliver Letwin, had also pledged to match Labour's planned spending increases on health and education. Some urged Howard to make bold gestures on tax, such as abolishing inheritance tax altogether, while others feared that a tax-cutting agenda would lead the party down the same path as Hague's doomed 2001 campaign. When James recommended £35 billion of efficiency savings, Howard and Letwin pledged that £23 billion would be reinvested in frontline public services, while £8 billion would reduce government borrowing and £4 billion would finance 'targeted tax cuts'.

Straddling the internal debate over taxation and spending, this was a formula that sought to please everyone but succeeded in satisfying no one. Howard and Letwin believed that by pledging to match Labour's spending plans the party would stave off Gordon Brown's claim, used to such effect at the last election, that the Tories would cut investment in the public services. This led to another problem. The election strategy featured immigration as a prominent campaign theme. Strict controls on immigration were among the measures considered, including an Australian-style points-based system and an annual cap on the number of people entering the country. The government had been criticised for hugely underestimating the number of Eastern Europeans who would come to the UK after their countries joined the EU following a major accession treaty in 2004. 'Our polling showed that immigration was one of the most important issues facing the country, and that people thought we would be better at dealing with it,' one senior figure insists.

Howard's Young Turks on the Rise

Satisfied that he had a capable Campaign Director in place, Howard felt that the time for internal debate was over, and that he needed to present a harder edge to the party's policy positions ahead of the election. It was reminiscent of William Hague's final six months as leader: parking the party on territory that had a narrow but concentrated appeal, thus surrendering the centre ground to New Labour. Howard hoped that promoting the likes of David Cameron and George Osborne would inject fresh zeal into preparations for the election.

Although they knew each other reasonably well from the Major years, it was only after the 2001 general election, as new MPs, that Cameron and Osborne became good friends. Rather like Tony Blair and Gordon Brown after their election as two young MPs in 1983, Cameron and Osborne were eager to get themselves known, attending debates in the chamber and in parliamentary committees to scrutinise government bills. They independently decided to take a close interest in counter-terrorist legislation, which the then Home Secretary David Blunkett was steering through the Commons after the atrocities of 9/11. They sat together during hours of late-night sittings, and Osborne would offer Cameron a lift home most evenings. When Osborne decided to start cycling to Westminster from his home in Notting Hill, Cameron followed suit.

Their conversations often strayed onto the state of the party, as they traded insights from their days preparing Iain Duncan Smith for Prime Minister's Questions. Cameron and Osborne had loyally served the party, on and off, for over a decade, and they were now at the heart of Howard's preparations for the election the following year. Alongside Whetstone, Hilton and Bridges, they were increasingly important advisers to Howard behind the scenes. Unlike Cameron, who joined the Shadow Cabinet in June as policy coordinator, Osborne had not yet made it to the top table. However, he would not have to wait for long. Increasingly impressed by his performance as a junior Shadow Treasury spokesman, Howard promoted him to Shadow Chief Secretary three months later.

Cameron and Osborne's influence on Howard was regarded by many in the parliamentary party with a mixture of bewilderment and envy. Several long-serving MPs took great exception to the young turks. Reports in the press in July 2004 that a group of fourteen MPs – known as 'bed-blockers', including the former whip and ally of David Davis, Derek Conway, were being urged to step down to make way for fresh faces were angrily rejected. 'This is what we call the Notting Hill set,' Conway retorted, referring to Cameron, Osborne, Hilton, Whetstone and Ed Vaizey, among others. 'They sit around in these curious little bistros in parts of London, drink themselves silly and wish they were doing what the rest of us are getting on with.'[70]

Ironically, none of the so-called 'Notting Hill set' actually lived in the fashionable W11 postcode of London (although most were not far away). They were in fact highly ambitious and hard-working members of the 'Smith Square set' who had found favour in the Howard regime. They were friends outside politics, spending weekends together in London or the country, and going on holiday together, often on horse-riding treks (Whetstone in particular was a keen equestrian).[71] 'We used to discuss politics, but not always. It's not like we were political obsessives, like weird train-spotting anoraks,' says one. David and Samantha Cameron were not always present (especially after their first son, Ivan, was born), but occasionally joined the others on foreign excursions, including a weekend in Budapest to meet Hilton's Hungarian grandmother. Hilton and Whetstone were particularly close to the Camerons: Whetstone was godmother to Ivan.

On 17 August 2004 fifteen years of friendship were soured by the revelation in a gossip column that Whetstone had been having an affair with (Viscount) William Astor, a former government whip and opposition spokesman in the Lords who was married to Samantha Cameron's mother.[72] David Cameron was shocked when Whetstone confessed to the relationship with his stepfather-in-law, but Samantha made it clear that she never wanted to see Whetstone again. The affair made a tiny splash in a tabloid newspaper, and there was some reconciliation, but the episode caused a painful rift. Several months later Hilton and Whetstone became partners, but relations between Rachel and David, though amicable, were never quite the same again. Yet Whetstone would play a key role in Cameron's ascent nine months later.

As the election drew closer, politics, and more specifically the future of the party, began to dominate the group's conversations. It was clear to them that while Michael Howard may have rescued the party from the depths of despair, he was not going to transform its electoral fortunes. Howard's brief honeymoon provided an opportunity for the Policy Exchange and C-Change modernisers to influence a new direction for the party, but they would soon be disappointed. While they enjoyed closer links with the Howard regime (Whetstone was on the board of Policy Exchange), they were still on the fringes in terms of influencing party policy. On the socially conservative wing of the party, the 'Easterhouse modernisers', so-called after Duncan Smith's visit to Glasgow in 2002, formed the Centre for Social Justice (CSJ) in June 2004. Duncan Smith approached Christian and charity organisations to examine aspects of Britain's 'broken society' such as drug abuse, family breakdown and poverty. It was an agenda that found little favour under Howard. There was some attempt to find common ground between the different modernising strands during 2004, when Tim Montgomerie, Duncan Smith's former chief of staff, arranged a few meetings under the banner of 'The Change Alliance' at which the future of the centre-right was debated. Members of Policy Exchange, CSJ and Reform (a new think tank set up to explore public service reform) exchanged views, but little came of the initiative other than lip service being paid to placing the disadvantaged at the top of the party's agenda.

A more fertile debate about the party's future was taking place among the 'Smith Square set' (especially Cameron, Osborne and Hilton), who had become utterly convinced of the case for modernisation. They had met a few times to discuss the future even before Howard became leader in November 2003. 'We were trying to work out was going wrong with the party,' Nick Boles, who was director of Policy Exchange, recalls. 'We often met for dinner at David's house in North Kensington, and sometimes I had people round for take-away pizza at Policy Exchange in Westminster.'[73] Daniel Finkelstein, who was now a leader writer at *The Times*, remembers the conversation returning time and again to one topic: how to recover after the next election. 'The critical thing we all had in common was that we were all schooled in defeat in 1997, then in 2001, and we were almost certainly heading for another one next time round. We were huddling together for warmth, trying to find a way out of the cold.'[74]

Joining them on several occasions was the original prophet of modernisation from the early Hague years, Andrew Cooper, who kept his finger on the pulse as director of the polling company Populus, the pollster for *The Times*. Cooper's experience with Michael Gove in presenting their *Case for Change* argument, through C-Change, to activists and MPs had made some impression, but that was all. Cooper and Gove reiterated their concern that the Conservatives had not learned the lessons of the 1997 defeat. Osborne and Cameron, in particular, asked them to specify ways in which the party could change. 'There was a sense of frustration because they kept on asking me for a policy area to show that we were modernising,' Cooper recalls. 'But it was more about our priorities, tone of voice and behaviour. At the end of these dinners there was no consensus about how this would happen.'[75] Michael Gove, a columnist at *The Times* who was on the lookout for a safe Tory seat, was equally frustrated. 'I was impatient. My view was that the case had to be made for change, and that the people who understood it had to discuss it,' he recalls. 'It had to be about our demeanour – for example, Prime Minister's Questions did not have to be a shouting match but a constructive dialogue. It was a real turn-off to people.'[76]

When the group met over dinner in Mayfair in July 2004, the conversation became more intense, exposing stark differences of opinion. 'People sat around knowing that Howard was doomed. David and George had just joined Howard's top team, so they were less inclined to rock the boat,' recalls one present. 'I thought they were far too conventionally-minded about it all.' That summer Steve Hilton had become convinced that the party had to change, not least because his intensive focus group research had revealed the party's unpopularity on many fronts – not least the credibility of its policies on the public services. The public were far more interested in greater public service investment than in promises of upfront tax cuts that could not be kept. 'You do realise that if we don't win the election, we're going to take over the whole thing?' Hilton confided in Bridges on the way back from one particularly dispiriting session.

But who exactly would take over, and how? Among the circle of friends, just two were MPs: David Cameron and George Osborne. 'There were powerful advocates of change in those discussions – Danny [Finkelstein] and Michael [Gove] for example, but there wasn't a great corpus of [modernising] MPs, and that was one of the problems,' recalls one. 'There were a few others on the back-benches who were interested in modernising the party, but what was interesting is that a group of MPs disliked us, even though they professed to be modernisers themselves.' Not only had they attracted the wrath of the parliamentary old guard, through the likes of Derek Conway, but they were not particularly popular even among those who agreed that the party had to change. Some thought they were arrogant and dismissive of long-serving backbenchers, while others envied their access to the leadership.

There was also a certain amount of scepticism within the original 'set' of friends, including Cameron himself. He understood that things needed to change, but wondered just how fast the party could go down the road of modernisation. 'David later confessed to me that he often found it puzzling, some of the things we were talking about,' recalls Finkelstein.[77] Nick Boles says of Cameron's caution: 'It took him quite a while to realise what bad shape the party was in, because it had always given him the best job opportunities. He was the golden boy, so it was hard for him to see that the party was dysfunctional and out of touch with people. Having said that, it's also true that he is slow to change his mind about things, and has settled views. He is a small "c" conservative in many ways – it took lots of things to make him realise what was wrong.'[78] Gove believes that Cameron also felt obliged to defend the leader who had just promoted him to the Shadow Cabinet. 'His attitude was that you had to be loyal to your captain until he falls.'[79]

As the general election approached, the gatherings became less frequent. Gove and Boles were off on the campaign trail, having been selected as candidates, while Cameron and Osborne were drawn into the campaign at the party's headquarters in Victoria Street. Andrew Cooper believed that little had been achieved by their discussions. However, on a rare occasion when they met at Cameron's house in

February 2005, the prospect of an imminent defeat had focused minds. Over pizza, they wrestled again with the party's problems. Hilton drove the conversation, urging his friends to think more imaginatively about the world after the election. He believed that although there was a shared analysis, there was no shared solution. 'We have no clear answers,' he told them in frustration. Finding them might take years. 'The universal assumption was that the next leader would probably not be a modernising one. There was no talk of anyone in our circle becoming leader,' Finkelstein recalls.[80] Another said: 'We didn't think we would be running the party in two or three years' time. Ten years' time seemed more realistic.' Little did they know how soon events would overtake them.

The Victor Meldrew Campaign

As the 'Smith Square set' debated the future of the party by night, by day they prepared for the election campaign. At the beginning of 2005 the renewed discipline and vigour instilled by Lynton Crosby was producing results, and the mood in CCHQ was upbeat. During February and early March the party gained substantial media coverage for policy statements on immigration and asylum, crime, pensions and hospital cleanliness, after outbreaks of hospital-acquired infections such as MRSA. Howard used individual cases in Prime Minister's Questions, including that of the pensioner Margaret Dixon, whose shoulder operation had been repeatedly postponed, to raise the state of the NHS. With Blair on the defensive, the Conservatives felt a new sense of optimism. 'We were trying to personify the big public services issues, which was effective. There was some momentum and buoyancy, and the polls weren't in a desperate position,' Guy Black recalls.[81]

Nevertheless, the party was in a weak position after the dire 2001 general election result. It needed a huge swing of 10.5 per cent from Labour to win an overall majority of one. Crosby ruthlessly concentrated on 900,000 swing voters in the 150 marginal seats that could turn the election, although some former party officials believed that he had failed to reverse the Saatchi policy of targeting too many constituencies to be able to allocate resources effectively. New regional call centres and a computerised 'Voter Vault' system, bought from the Republicans in the United States, would identify the voters the Tories needed to attract. The Ashcroft operation also stood to benefit the party, ploughing resources into forty-six seats he believed Conservative candidates had a chance of winning. Activists on the ground were far more motivated than they had been four years earlier, while the Shadow Cabinet fell in behind the leadership. The party was in better shape, organisationally, to fight this general election than any since its victory in 1992.

Howard's team felt that the government was in its weakest position since 1997. The troubled relations between Tony Blair and Gordon Brown continued to affect morale within the Labour Party, and Blair's announcement in September 2004, after a heart scare, that he would serve a 'full third term' but would stand down ahead of a fourth general election had not lanced the boil. With Iraq also continuing to harm the government, opinion polls on the eve of the campaign showed that Labour's lead over the Conservatives had narrowed to one or two points.[82] 'As the campaign drew near, there was a sense of excitement,' recalls Daniel Ritterband. 'We could feel some movement in the country, but we didn't know how far it would go.'[83] In fact it was illusionary. The fundamental obstacle, as Crosby had acknowledged all along, remained the buoyant state of the economy, which left little room for the Conservatives to persuade voters that they would be more competent at managing the nation's finances than Labour. The Tories had to try to make headway on other issues, which they decided meant crime and immigration. Any tactical advantage the party may have gained in the first few months of 2005 would soon be undone, entirely as a result of self-inflicted wounds.

The first of these showed that one of Howard's perceived strengths, imposing discipline on the party, could backfire under pressure. The leader had shown his capacity to be ruthless in November 2004 when he dismissed Boris Johnson as Shadow Higher Education Spokesman after revelations in the press about an extramarital affair. In late

March 2005 *The Times* reported Howard Flight, a party Vice-Chairman, saying at a private dinner that the party had plans to go beyond the proposed saving of £35 billion in public spending over the course of the next Parliament. Howard's chief of staff, Stephen Sherbourne, had warned Flight to stay 'on-message' before the dinner, conscious of the problems caused by Oliver Letwin's comments about spending cuts in the 2001 campaign. Howard not only dismissed Flight from his position, but insisted on his deselection as a candidate at the election. Some members of Flight's local association in Sussex were outraged. 'I think it was the right thing to do,' says Howard. 'It was going to cause considerable embarrassment to us during the campaign, and I heard that Alastair Campbell even did a jig in the room when he heard about Howard Flight's comments.'[84] Flight eventually made way for a new candidate, but the episode divided the parliamentary party.

Flight's gaffe presented Labour with a gift on the eve of the campaign, adding ammunition to their strategy of portraying the opposition as having a secret agenda of spending cuts. Crosby had advised Howard to be tough on anything that could harm the party's campaign, but the decision to make an example of Flight turned an embarrassment into a media frenzy. Whetstone in particular felt that Howard should act decisively. 'If you dig deep into the psyche of those people at that time, they were always looking for a "Clause IV moment",' Black reflects, referring to New Labour's reforms of the party's constitution in 1995. 'Even that late on there was a view that if they made an example of someone, then that would be the moment.'[85] Howard was similarly ruthless with other candidates who appeared to step out of line. One, Danny Kruger, who had worked in Iain Duncan Smith's office, was forced to stand down as a candidate in Blair's own seat after having been reported as calling for 'creative destruction' in the public services, a technical economic term that had obvious potential for further embarrassment. As it happened, Kruger had been standing in for David Cameron at the annual lecture of the Centre for Policy Studies when he made the comments. Cameron pleaded with Howard not to push Kruger out, but to no effect. It was not the last occasion on which he and others would privately express doubts about the direction of the campaign.

Once the campaign was under way in early April, the Conservatives made the running by launching their manifesto ahead of Labour. Despite the furore over the deselection, there was an expectation that Crosby would make this a competitive campaign. But it very quickly emerged that his relentless focus on certain messages was not supported by detailed policies. The manifesto, entitled *Are You Thinking What We're Thinking? It's Time for Action*, which was also the slogan for the first half of the campaign, was one of the thinnest the party had ever produced at only twenty-eight pages. The five themes of controlled immigration, lower taxes, more police, cleaner hospitals and school discipline, emblazoned on the front, had been publicised to the media and the electorate over the previous four or five months, and there was precious little that was new in the manifesto, apart from an introduction which Cameron and Gove drafted to present in the best possible 'modernising' light.

'We thought we didn't need lots of complicated policy documents because we had these key themes,' reflects Black. 'If you just repeat the same old things the press have nothing new to write and they will go out and write about someone else.'[86] 'Our campaign tried to hook onto people's concerns, but they were all non-economic. We were in a bind over Iraq and the economy, and so we didn't have a narrative,' Sherbourne admits.[87] Questions were also raised about a strategy that seemed to feed on people's fears. 'Are you thinking what we're thinking?' could be interpreted as a 'grubby conspiracy: whispered words, and noses tapped' about concerns over uncontrolled immigration.[88] Michael Portillo dismissed the party's platform as nothing more than a 'Victor Meldrew manifesto'.[89] Indeed, this was a campaign that began to resemble the grumblings of a grumpy old man, shaking his head in disbelief at the nature of twenty-first-century Britain.

Controlling immigration through tighter border controls, yearly quotas and caps was the subject of one of Howard's early speeches in the campaign. It attracted huge media attention during the first two weeks, despite attempts to move onto other territory. 'I don't think they worked out how to put the genie back in the bottle, having raised immigration, and they didn't know where to go with it,' recalls one seasoned reporter. 'Howard kept saying, "I haven't talked about it for four days," but what he didn't understand was that whatever was on his "grid" wasn't necessarily driving the news agenda. People raised it on the doorstep because they heard it on the news two weeks ago, and so there was a lag. It harmed their prospects because it reinforced the loss of support to the Liberal Democrats, who were trying to project a moderate appeal.' Polling organisations began to notice that there was a direct correlation between the party's focus on immigration and a drop in its support, especially among professional and middle-class women voters. Ever since Enoch Powell's infamous 'Rivers of Blood' speech in 1968, most politicians had either avoided the issue or treated it with caution. But Howard felt strongly that it was an issue that needed airing. What made it so toxic in 2005 (and indeed in 2001) was that the message was coming from a party that was discredited in the eyes of many voters or was seen as having other, more sinister motives.

Whether Howard liked it or not, the issue dominated the first half of the campaign. Senior figures within the party were increasingly uncomfortable. 'Immigration was becoming a major theme, and it was difficult,' says Ken Clarke. 'It was an important subject, but it had to be handled with care.'[90] Howard and his advisers were worried that the other messages of the campaign were being completely drowned out. 'The mistake we made was that we had little to say in week two, because we were saving announcements for later in the campaign,' recalls George Eustice. 'The press then filled the gap with their own stories about immigration.'[91]

The press had some reason to do this. An unnamed member of the Shadow Cabinet told the *Guardian* of his concern that 'we should not turn into a single-issue party'.[92] Some in Howard's team thought Cameron was the source of this comment, although others did not believe he would have briefed against the leadership. Whatever the truth, Cameron was certainly unhappy. 'I think David was quite uncertain – he was a good friend of Rachel's and Steve's, and he expressed reservations about some issues like immigration, but he didn't express them to me,' says Crosby.[93] 'There was unease from both him and George. There was a point when it went over the top,' recalls Michael Gove.[94] Indeed, Cameron rang a colleague in Howard's inner circle to say that the emphasis on immigration had gone too far. 'I really think you're overdoing this,' he said. Osborne shared his concern that the narrow focus on immigration was depressing, but held his counsel.

The last week of the campaign was dominated by the events leading up to the Iraq war, as immigration began to fade as a hot issue. The revelation of the Attorney General's advice to the Cabinet in March 2003 on the legality of going to war without a second UN resolution had the potential to damage the government even further, following claims that he had been leant on to recommend military action. But Tony Blair managed to ride the storm, claiming that the 'smoking gun has turned into a damp squib'.

The Conservatives responded with a poster: 'If he's prepared to lie to take us to war, he's prepared to lie to win an election.' It looked as if the party had misjudged the moment once again, and Howard was left exposed. 'It was a terminal point in the campaign,' recalls a senior Howard aide. 'A lot of liberal voters just said "No." We knew from our research that you could say that Blair didn't tell the truth, but voters didn't like him being called a liar, because they thought that was rude. They were different things. However, when we signed it off (without Michael being there), we weren't concentrating, we decided it on the fly, and it was a total cock-up.' The 'liar poster' only reinforced the ambiguity and apparent shiftiness of the Tory leadership's stance on the war. The chief beneficiaries were the Liberal Democrats, whose leader Charles Kennedy derided Howard's attack as 'claptrap', the Conservatives having been 'the principal cheerleaders for George Bush and Tony Blair in this war in the first place'.

Howard returned to his Folkestone and Hythe constituency in Kent the night before polling day. He had become a lone figure in the Tory campaign, as a result of a decision by Crosby and others in his team to present the election as a 'presidential contest' with Blair. Oliver Letwin, the Shadow Chancellor, had become much less visible as the campaign wore on, as he was having to fight his tightly contested seat in Dorset. His deputy, George Osborne, had made far more appearances, banging the campaign drum in the media from party headquarters in London, as had Cameron. They both felt obliged to take to the airwaves, particularly as their concerns about the campaign's narrow focus only increased as the weeks passed. In contrast, Labour's campaign was rejuvenated when Gordon Brown joined the Prime Minister on the campaign trail, sharing ice creams and jokes as if the rivalry between them had never existed. Brown had also backed Blair over Iraq during a crucial press conference. In the closing stages of the campaign Howard declared that voters would wake up to a 'better, brighter Britain' on 6 May if the Conservatives were elected the day before. It was the Tories' only positive message of the campaign.

When the exit polls at 10 p.m. showed that Labour was on course to win a third term with a majority of sixty-seven, there was little doubt of the nation's verdict. Whetstone and Sherbourne joined Howard and his wife Sandra in Kent to watch the results. There were a few bright moments early on, such as a gain in Putney in south-west London, which if repeated across the country would have led to a hung Parliament. For the first time since 1983, the party was making some advances and Labour was losing seats. 'The mood was resigned without being depressed; it wasn't funereal but it wasn't elated,' Sherbourne recalls.[95] But the inescapable reality was that Labour was heading for a third term in office, for the first time.

Back at CCHQ, the mood soon turned sour as results across the country edged Labour closer to the winning post. 'I'm leaving,' Maurice Saatchi told his staff in the early hours of the morning. As the marginalised Party Chairman walked out into the deserted streets of Westminster, party workers looked on. 'He was a lost soul. It was a sad sight, a beaten man,' one recalled. The sun was rising on another fine spring day, just as it had when the Conservatives suffered their crushing defeat in May 1997. Once again the party seemed condemned to the wilderness. It could not afford another false dawn.

FIVE

Signs of Life
May–December 2005

On Friday, 6 May 2005, Britain woke up to a familiar scene. New Labour remained in command while the Conservative Party lay vanquished. But 2005 differed from 1997 and 2001 in at least one important respect. Labour might have won, but Tony Blair's third victory engendered little enthusiasm in the country. 'Blair Limps Back', ran the front-page headline on *The Times*, while the *Guardian* warned, 'Time is Running Out'.[1] The rest of the press agreed that Labour had had a narrow escape – their majority was halved, and they had captured only 36 per cent of the vote, the lowest ever share for a victorious party. Unimpressed by the choice they faced, only 61 per cent of voters had turned out at the polls. 'Very few people liked us, but it came down to whether more people disliked the opposition more than they disliked us,' recalls a senior aide to Tony Blair. 'This was not an election for the Conservatives to win, it was one for us to lose.' The Conservatives remained marooned on 33 per cent, just 0.5 per cent better than the dire result four years previously. The party made a net gain of thirty-three seats, but with only 198 MPs it was nowhere near the 329 needed to form a majority. The Tories had not gone into meltdown, as some had feared during the nadir of October 2003, but they were now in uncharted territory. Another four or five years on the opposition benches would spell the longest continuous period out of office (twelve or thirteen years) since 1832. The question now was whether Michael Howard would succumb to the ignominy of defeat and resign at once, like the fallen leaders before him.

'You Can't Go Now'

Those around Howard had been braced for defeat. 'Michael never dropped his guard, but in our hearts we all knew it would be very tough,' Stephen Sherbourne, his chief of staff, recalls. 'Our only hope was for something unexpected to happen.'[2]

Howard himself had already made his mind up about what he would do in the event of a decisive defeat. As they watched the first results on television on the evening of Thursday, 5 May, he told his wife Sandra and his two closest aides, Stephen Sherbourne and Rachel Whetstone, that he would resign the next day. 'I thought that by the end of the next Parliament I would be nearly sixty-nine, and that would be a clear disadvantage, and I had also banged on about accountability during the campaign, and I had to be accountable,' he recalls.[3] Then came the bombshell. He wanted to step down as soon as a leadership election could take place, preferably within a month, and at least before the summer recess began. 'We were all so tired, and I didn't really think that much of it, and I felt by that point that Michael had done enough personally,' Whetstone recalls.[4] Her mood soon changed.

After Howard and his aides returned to London following the count in Folkestone in the early hours of Friday morning, a state of panic descended on party headquarters. At 7.30 a.m. Whetstone had started to write the leader's resignation speech. When Lynton Crosby, the Campaign Director, discovered what she was doing, he burst into a fury. 'This is lunacy – we've got to stop him,' he implored. If Howard left now, Crosby argued, the 'whole thing would be left in chaos'. It would also take the shine off the thirty or so candidates who had won seats from Labour. Whetstone was now certain that Howard had to delay his departure. She recalled that when he became leader he had promised supporters that he would change the leadership election rules, which William Hague had introduced, so that the final say would be given to MPs rather than to the wider party membership. Howard believed that his successor needed to have the majority support of Tory MPs, unlike Iain Duncan Smith, whose election had exposed the flaws in the system. This could happen only after the general election was over, and would take time.[5]

Far more importantly, Whetstone was convinced that David Davis was ready and waiting to succeed Howard. This was something she and others around the Tory leader were determined to avoid. Whetstone and Davis were two big personalities who did not see eye to eye: she leapt on anything she disliked about him as a sign of treachery to her boss, while he did not see why he should take orders from young, unelected advisers. For Whetstone, the final straw came towards the end of the election campaign. There had been a miscalculation over the party's plans to increase police numbers. Oliver Letwin rang Davis to say that the funding arrangements had to be changed, but Davis insisted that he did not want to change the position ahead of an interview for *The Jeremy Vine Show* on BBC Radio 2 the following day.

Late in the evening, Davis rang Howard's team, who were staying at the Mandarin Hotel in Knightsbridge. 'I am not happy with Mr Letwin's figures,' he told them. 'When your Shadow Home Secretary is calling your Shadow Chancellor "Mr Letwin", you know that you've got a bloody big problem,' one of his aides recalls. Howard was in his white dressing gown preparing for bed when he heard about the contretemps, and decided to ring Davis himself. After a sharp exchange in which he defended Letwin, Howard hung up the phone. His closest aides were deeply unimpressed. 'I had lost all respect for [Davis] at that point,' one recalls. 'He was a little prima donna.'

Tempers were inevitably frayed at the height of the campaign, and Davis had other things on his mind, including a fight to hang onto his own precarious majority in Yorkshire. He points out that he was the only shadow minister to have conducted a number of televised debates on home affairs with his Labour counterpart, so he could hardly be accused of being disloyal. However, some of Howard's closest advisers interpreted the episode as evidence that Davis could not be trusted with the leadership of the party. Yet he did not stray from the party line when he appeared on the radio the following day. 'While David was a difficult colleague in private, he played by the rules in public,' Stephen Sherbourne observes.[6] But what had happened behind closed doors during the last days of the campaign would directly influence what occurred in the immediate aftermath of defeat.

On the morning of Friday, 6 May, Michael and Sandra Howard, Stephen Sherbourne and Rachel Whetstone sped through south-west London in Howard's official car. They were on the way to Roehampton to greet Justine Greening, the new MP for Putney, to celebrate one of the few successes of the night. Sandra and the others pleaded with Howard to reconsider. 'You can't go now: you'll just hand it on a plate to David Davis,' they told him. 'They tried very hard to persuade me not to say anything at all,' Howard recalls.[7] Whetstone frantically attempted to convince him that he shouldn't specify a timetable for his departure. 'Whatever you do, leave it open,' she insisted.[8] After a heated conversation, he agreed not to tie himself down to a date.

In front of an audience of activists in Putney, Howard announced that he would stand aside sooner rather than later, after the party had an opportunity to consider changes to the rules for electing a new leader. The faces of the crowd turned to stone. 'My announcement took the sting out of the bad result for Labour,' he admits. 'They had won with a working majority, but they had lost a lot of seats, so there was no rejoicing from them. But it was a shock to the audience, the media and a real shock to the party.'[9] When they returned to party headquarters, staff looked utterly depressed at the prospect of an acrimonious leadership election just as there had been after Major and Hague resigned. 'I can't believe we're going straight back to everything that happened before,' one exclaimed to Howard's aides. As chief of staff, Sherbourne, bore the brunt of the complaints. 'I spent the whole afternoon fielding phone calls from all the bigwigs in the party saying, "What the hell has he done?" '[10]

At a gathering at Jonathan Marland's house in Knightsbridge a few days later, dismayed friends and senior aides piled the pressure on Howard. 'We all forcefully tried to dissuade him,' Marland recalls. 'We asked him to reconsider and buy himself more time and then have an orderly handover.'[11] 'He was very bloody-minded,' says another who was present. 'He started to dig his heels in and said that he wanted to go before the party conference in the autumn.' Only Sherbourne agreed with Howard that he would have to go sooner rather than later, once the leadership election rules had been changed. Howard had made his mind up. He had given the past eighteen months to pulling the party out of the mire; now it was time for others to take charge.

What had he achieved in that year and a half? Howard took comfort in the fact that the Conservatives actually polled 57,000 more votes in England than the Labour Party – a statistic that cruelly exposed the imbalances of the electoral system. But a serious analysis showed that the party failed to make any meaningful electoral recovery at all. Even though they were psychologically important to the party, the thirty-three Tory gains provided an illusion of progress, disguising the fact that 2005 was the third worst election result for the party, in terms of the share of the popular vote, since 1832 (after 1997 and 2001). There were still fewer Tory MPs than Labour's 209 under Michael Foot at the party's nadir in 1983. While there had been a small swing of 3 per cent from Labour to Conservative since 2001, there was little appreciable uplift in Tory support where it mattered. As in 2001, the Tories had piled up votes in seats they already held.[12] Indeed, in many of the party's thirty-one gains from Labour there was a larger switch in votes from Labour to the Liberal Democrats than to the Conservatives.[13] In five of England's nine regions the Conservative vote actually fell, and it declined overall in constituencies being defended by Labour and the Liberal Democrats. Some progress was made in Wales, where the party recovered a foothold of three MPs, but not in Scotland, where just one seat was retained.

The resurgent Liberal Democrats had prospered from their opposition to the war and the popularity of their leader, Charles Kennedy. They had the largest number of seats (sixty-two) for a third party since 1929, had replaced the Conservatives as the principal opponents to Labour in many northern towns and cities, and had pushed them into third place among the twenty-five to thirty-four age group. The most striking measure of the party's complete failure in 2005 was the fall in its core vote. Many derided the Tory campaign for pursuing a 'core vote' strategy, but in fact for the second time running the Conservatives ran an election campaign that actually drove away their traditional middle-class supporters. The party's lead among the ABC1s (professional, managerial and skilled working classes) fell to just 1 per cent, a far cry from the 30-40 per cent leads achieved in this sector of the electorate between 1979 and 1992.[14] Nothing had been learned since the party's crushing defeat in 2001.

The most perceptive Tory MPs were chastened by the results. Moderates like David Willetts, Damian Green and Stephen Dorrell agreed with prominent modernisers such as Francis Maude that many people in the party still did not comprehend the weakness of the party's position. They asked Michael Gove (who had just become an MP) and Andrew Cooper, the arch-moderniser and chief pollster for *The Times*, to produce an updated version of C-Change's *Case for Change* presentation, which they would present to MPs in the Commons later in the summer. It would be entitled *Shock and Awe*, after the American bombing campaign on Baghdad during the Iraq war.[15]

Meanwhile, the post-mortem began. 'The 2005 performance was the least defensible, in the sense that we could have done better,' argues David Willetts.[16] There had not been much love lost between Howard and Ann Widdecombe following her 'something of the night' attack in 1997, but she was not alone in her withering assessment of his contribution. 'Michael got Central Office in hand, and he did it quite well, because it had become such a hotbed of machination, backbiting and factionalism. But that was all he did. What else did he do? The results in 2005 were hardly anything to shout home about.'[17] Iain Duncan Smith argues that his successor moved the party in a 'different direction to the one I had started. His campaign seemed to the public and the media very negative.'[18]

Towards the end of Michael Howard's resignation statement on the morning of Friday, 6 May, he said: 'At its best [the Conservative Party] is broad and generous, broad in its appeal, generous in its outlook . . . A party capable of representing all of Britain and all Britons.' These were exactly the same words he had used to launch his leadership at the Saatchi Gallery on 30 October 2003.[19] But what had happened to the positive, moderate tone he had espoused then? As Francis Maude remarked, the Saatchi Gallery speech was 'a strategy that had to be followed. I think he heard the music, but he didn't internalise it.'[20] Howard had repeated the same error that Hague made midway through the previous Parliament. Having initially flirted with a more inclusive approach, he reverted to territory that was more comfortable to him.

It so happened that that territory was remarkably similar to Hague's in 2001. Tirades against the government had some effect in shaping public opinion, but the lack of an inspiring vision for the country (whether it was summed up in a 'Timetable for Action' or in ten words, plus 'accountability') undermined the credibility of the Tory alternative to Labour. 'Michael could never restrain himself,' says one of his closest advisers. 'He is actually a liberal to his finger-tips on social and economic matters, although he has strong views on immigration, but he couldn't resist scoring tactical political points against Blair which actually got us nowhere.' The one subject that might have shown a different side to Michael Howard was his passion for protecting the environment, which emerged from his negotiating role at the Earth Summit in Rio de Janeiro in 1990. To their regret, his advisers persuaded him to give it a low priority.

Michael Howard worked harder than most to bring about a recovery in the Conservative Party's fortunes. But his reputation from the Thatcher and Major years continued to haunt him, as the Labour Party knew full well. 'Michael Howard was a pretty good person to have as a bogeyman – he worried people,' one former Number 10 aide recalls. Whatever his achievements in office, Howard's reputation as Home Secretary during the 1990s evoked memories of an unpopular administration. It was a handicap that he candidly admits to. 'I recognised that in order for the Conservative Party to win, it had to persuade people that it had changed, and I tried to do that to some extent with some of the things I said and did, but I don't think I was the best person to convince them, because I was so closely associated with the previous government.'[21] He was not alone in reaching that conclusion. During his failed bid for the leadership in 2001, Michael Portillo realised that anyone who had been part of the Major government would not be able to convincingly present a changed Conservative Party to the electorate.

Whatever Michael Howard's character flaws and his misjudgements as leader, the party owes its survival to him for bringing it back from the brink in the autumn of 2003 and averting a complete catastrophe in 2005. 'When he took over, no one could have put together a plan to change perceptions of the party, considering the disaster we were inheriting,' insists one senior figure. The confidence of MPs, activists and party donors could not have been lower in the bleak period leading up to the Blackpool conference in October 2003. Under Howard the Conservatives were on life support, badly in need of intensive care. Apart from a few ultra-loyalists to the former regime, most senior figures believe that the party could have suffered a significant loss of seats in a devastating defeat had there not been a change in leadership. A further loss of seats could have consigned the party to decades in opposition, and possibly to terminal decline as a force capable of competing for power. 'Michael Howard has a very good claim to have saved the party,' says one moderniser. 'He didn't embody modernisation, but he instilled discipline and stopped the rot. He was purposeful and persuasive internally.'

Like Neil Kinnock's during Labour's difficult years in the 1980s, Howard's leadership restored a sense of stability to his party. He was essentially an unelectable leader of an unelectable party, but for the first time in years that party began to look competent and more united. 'We all owe an eternal debt of gratitude to Michael Howard for getting the buses to run on time,' says Oliver Letwin. 'He enabled us to get through to the 2005 election in a workable way.'[22] The grassroots and party activists marched along to Howard's tune. The same could not be said for all of the parliamentary party, of whom a large number were distinctly apathetic. 'You had a lot of Tory MPs who thought that they had pretty safe seats, and thought that it was pretty unlikely that we would win, who greeted defeat with remarkable apathy,' recalls Boris Johnson, who had entered the Commons in 2001. 'I don't think [the third defeat] shook the foundations of the Tory Party in the way that people might have expected. The Tory Party is meant to be a party of power, and if you keep it out of power for such a long period you will eventually produce quite sensational cravings.'[23] If the party was to satisfy its hunger for power, it would now need a leadership election like no other in its recent past.

The Reluctant Predator

In the days that followed Michael Howard's decision, news filtered back to the leader's office that David Davis's allies in the parliamentary party were impatient to get on with a leadership election as soon as possible. They saw the rule change as a crude attempt to thwart the man who had stood aside for Howard in 2003. During his short tenure as Party Chairman under Duncan Smith, Davis had built up a following among the grassroots on the right of the party who he thought shared his views. 'The counsel I would have for people talking about a rule change is that the public will see it as irrelevant, and that it will not necessarily produce the result intended. We've got a lot to do, and that's a distraction,' his ally Derek Conway warned.[24]

Filled with ambition, David Davis was a natural predator, determined to win the Tory crown. Born in 1948 to a single mother, and raised on a council estate in Tooting, south London, he was adopted by a Polish Jewish print-worker who had strong trade union links. After passing the eleven-plus exam he went to a local grammar school, where he often got into scrapes, breaking his nose three times (in a rugby match, a swimming pool accident and a fight on Clapham Common).[25] He read molecular and computer sciences at Warwick University, and gained further qualifications from the London Business School and Harvard University, before a successful career in business (becoming a director of Tate & Lyle). A fitness fanatic, he enjoyed extreme sports, including mountain climbing, and was a member of a Territorial Army unit of the SAS. Attracted to a party which he believed rewarded success and self-reliance, he was elected to Parliament in 1987. He rose quickly through the ranks, first as a skilful government whip, and then as John Major's Minister for Europe, entrusted with steering through the beleaguered Maastricht Bill. Establishing a reputation as a Westminster bruiser, Davis made as many enemies as friends (the latter ranged from the diarist and former minister Alan Clark to Blair's chief spin doctor, Alastair Campbell). Having turned down an offer to serve in William Hague's Shadow Cabinet, Davis chaired the powerful Public Accounts Committee, holding the government to account far more than the official opposition. Hague was uncomfortable with Davis's presence on the backbenches. According to one of Hague's close aides, he declared, 'That man will never be leader of the Conservative Party.'

Following Davis's unsuccessful attempt to win the leadership in 2001, he became Iain Duncan Smith's first and short-lived Party Chairman before being demoted to shadow John Prescott's department. Although Davis was rewarded with the role of Shadow Home Secretary after standing aside for Howard in October 2003, there was little love lost between the two men by the following summer. Yet Davis proved to be an asset as a fearless politician who could claim ministerial scalps, including that of the Home Office minister Beverley Hughes.

This did not prevent a number of serious disagreements with the leadership, not least on the party's position on proposals for identity cards. When Howard decided to support the government's Bill to introduce them in November 2004, he could not be confident of Davis's support, or that of several others. Davis had consistently opposed the cards on civil libertarian grounds, whereas Howard had proposed a voluntary scheme as Home Secretary. 'I was caught by surprise at a meeting of the Shadow Cabinet when it was the only item on the agenda,' Davis says. 'I thought Michael had changed his mind and joined my side of the argument, but he had clearly reverted to his original opinion. They thought I might resign, but I wasn't going to. I said that I would do what I had to do, and devised a strategy that ensured we would oppose it at third reading.'[26] Davis then devised five tests as a condition for the opposition's support for the second reading of the Bill. When it came to the Commons vote on 20 December, ten Tory MPs defied the leadership by voting against, while a number of others abstained, including David Cameron, who had previously told Howard that he could not support the Bill. Interestingly, Davis reluctantly toed the party line, whereas Cameron, who shared his opposition to ID cards, was absent on the day of the vote. With the election on the horizon, there was little appetite for divisions to spill into the open.

Within days of the election defeat, Davis's allies mobilised in the shadows. He had not confirmed his intention to stand, but some, including supporters in the Whips' Office, were keen to establish him as the front-runner well before the contest even began. A plot to oust Howard was being hatched, just as it had been against Duncan Smith. All Davis's supporters needed to do was persuade thirty or forty Tory MPs to write to Sir Michael Spicer, Chairman of the backbench 1922 Committee, to trigger a vote of confidence in the leadership, as had happened in October 2003. Yet there was a major problem: Davis himself. He was surprisingly reluctant to go in for the kill. 'From the outset, David didn't want to get the forty names together, even though there were people who were prepared to do that,' says Iain Dale, the Westminster publisher who became Davis's chief of staff shortly after the election.[27] 'We already had one leader ousted in that way, and I just thought it wasn't proper,' Davis asserts.[28] Those MPs who were prepared to support him were intensely frustrated. 'Why didn't David declare his candidacy straight away?' asks one. 'We should have either persuaded Howard to stand down sooner in May, or have forced a confidence vote the following month. There was shocking complacency among his people – it was terrible politics.' The immediate aftermath of Howard's resignation represented the best opportunity for Davis and his allies to strike, yet it was slipping through their fingers.

Howard's Parting Shot

Howard's close aides, however, were taking nothing for granted. As far as they were concerned, the predator lurking in the Tory jungle had to be stopped. They feared that Davis would impose an unpleasant regime upon the party. Howard knew that he was not in a strong enough position to sack Davis from the Shadow Cabinet, but there was a vacancy for the Shadow Chancellorship, as Oliver Letwin had decided to take a back seat after a tortuous campaign. Demoralised after unhappy tours of the television studios as a frontline spokesman, which most agreed had not played to his strengths, he was far more comfortable working behind the scenes on policy detail.

The resulting reshuffle of the Shadow Cabinet presented Howard with an opportunity to fire a parting shot at Davis. By promoting the new generation, namely George Osborne and David Cameron, to senior roles he could at least increase the likelihood of a contest, rather than a coronation. 'There could be no excuse for second thoughts six or nine months down the track. I wanted to give the candidates the best possible opportunity to prove themselves,' Howard recalls.[29] Over the weekend he began to plan the reshuffle with his two principal aides, Rachel Whetstone and Stephen Sherbourne. 'He wanted a changing of the guard,' Whetstone recalls. 'He didn't want to have a big reshuffle, but he wanted the top team to look new and different.'[30]

What of the members of the new generation who were about to be thrust into the limelight? It appears that they did not have great expectations. Just before the general election, Cameron, Osborne and Hilton had discussed what would happen after the expected defeat. Osborne and, to a lesser extent, Cameron had played increasingly prominent roles as campaign spokesmen on the airwaves. They hoped for some kind of promotion after the election, but however bad the result, they agreed on one thing. 'The party had to change, but David and George needed to have a common position about what would happen next,' recalls a close confidant. 'They believed that Michael had to carry on as leader for years to give stability to the party: they needed lots of time to develop a new argument. This was the best way for the party to renew itself.' As the results came in on election night, both looked on from their constituencies in despair. The party may have been gaining seats, but that was little consolation. A defeat was a defeat. 'I clearly remember George said to me at the time, "My God, I did not come into Parliament to spend my entire time in opposition," ' a close friend recalls. 'He knew that the result was unforgivably bad, because after eight years in opposition, and with the Iraq war seriously denting Blair's popularity and standing, the party pretty much got the same result as before.'

When Osborne and Cameron heard that Howard had decided to resign, everything changed. The understanding they reached just before the election had become redundant. 'The feeling was, "Now what?" ' a mutual friend recalls. As soon as Howard delivered his statement, senior frontbenchers began to position themselves behind the scenes for the leadership election, whenever it came. David Willetts, the Shadow Work and Pensions Secretary, and Oliver Letwin, the outgoing Shadow Chancellor, were anxious that someone had to stand against Davis.

Letwin felt strongly that the party had to change in order to survive, and believed that Shadow Health Secretary Andrew Lansley stood the best chance as standard bearer for modernisation. Lansley had been Norman Tebbit's Principal Private Secretary during the mid-1980s. As director of the CRD during the 1992 general election, he led the 'Smith Square set' into battle against Labour. Like his apprentices from the CRD, he had become persuaded after the 2001 general election campaign (which he himself played a significant role in directing) that the party needed to change course. Among other things, he argued that it had to find a broader social spread of parliamentary candidates.

David Willetts was toying with standing, and did his utmost to persuade Osborne not to commit to supporting another candidate for the time being. When Letwin approached Osborne that weekend to ask him to back Lansley, he went away empty-handed. Willetts was not the only MP taking a cautious line. Friends of Cameron and Osborne from the 2001 intake, like the junior whip Greg Barker, also strongly encouraged them not to announce their support for any candidate at such an early stage. It was welcome advice, but there was no question that they were about to blot their copybooks by prematurely declaring their intentions.

During the same weekend, David Cameron was weighing up his future. Only forty-eight hours had passed since the election defeat, and he claims that he was not inclined to stand in the immediate aftermath. At thirty-eight, he had been an MP for only four years, and had joined the Shadow Cabinet less than twelve months before. Surely this was not enough experience for him even to contemplate the top job? As a young father of two young children (Ivan, his three-year-old son, who required twenty-four-hour care, and Nancy, who was eighteen months old) there were other demands on his life. But he was not going to rule anything out just yet. Steve Hilton joined the Cameron family at their constituency home in Dean in the Cotswolds over the weekend. As they mulled over Michael Howard's resignation and the immediate future, one question emerged – should Cameron go for it? Hilton very quickly sensed the direction of his friend's thoughts. Sentences prefaced with 'If I did stand . . .' made it clear what his inclinations were. Having initially dismissed the idea of a leadership bid, Cameron was now giving it serious thought.

By Sunday, Michael Howard was coming to a decision about the reshuffle. He decided to offer Osborne, rather than Cameron the Shadow Chancellorship. He had been impressed by Osborne's performance as Letwin's deputy (Shadow Chief Secretary to the Treasury), particularly during the election campaign, feeling that he had done well in teasing out Labour's economic policy weaknesses, something the Tories found particularly hard to achieve.

Cameron had not made quite the same impact during the campaign, and had not impressed the leadership with his criticism of the campaign's tone on immigration. Having formerly thought that Cameron was best placed to succeed him at some point, Howard began to have doubts about his former protégé's seeming lack of ambition in the autumn of 2004, when he turned down his offer to become Party Chairman. Howard had thought that Cameron would shine in the role, and that the appointment would be a solution to the failed experiment of co-chairmen in charge of

Campaign Headquarters, but Cameron had said he didn't feel able to take on the responsibility while caring for his disabled son. Some of those close to Howard speculated that the real reason might have been Cameron's desire not to be blamed for the impending election defeat, while others felt that he did not want to be seen as the 'Central Office boy who became the ultimate apparatchik'.

As far as Howard was concerned, Cameron needed more time to raise his profile and find his voice, while Osborne, who despite sharing Cameron's unease about aspects of the campaign did not express them openly, deserved a bigger promotion, having demonstrated prodigious talent and drive. 'Michael felt David didn't really have balls in the way that George did,' says one senior aide to Howard. 'The problem with David was that he was seen as a bit fluffy within the party, so if he was going to run, Michael felt that a good type of a job would be something like Work and Pensions, where he could really show that he had the kind of capacity to roll up his sleeves.' Taking on difficult areas like benefit reform would give Cameron the chance to do just that.

Howard had known Cameron for longer than Osborne, and had promoted him to the Shadow Cabinet first, so it was all the more remarkable that he was about to encourage the more junior of the two to stand against Davis. There may be more to this than meets the eye. Although Cameron claims that he initially rejected the idea of standing after the defeat, he may well have calculated long beforehand that he stood a better chance of succeeding Howard whenever he stood down by deliberately creating some distance from the leadership as the general election approached. Turning down the party chairmanship before what many regarded as a doomed election campaign, and watching others take on the poisoned chalice of the Shadow Chancellorship would ultimately give him a better chance of securing the top job. This suggests that, far from lacking in ambition, there was a ruthless streak to David Cameron that would surface time and again in the years to come.

Rachel Whetstone had encouraged her boss's instinct to promote Osborne, agreeing with him that Osborne had made a better fist of the election campaign. Realising that Osborne would need some time to think about the offer Howard was about to make, Whetstone decided to tip her friend off. When she rang him on Sunday afternoon, he was stunned into silence. 'And he wants you to run, George,' she told him. 'Michael thought that if you were going to stand for the leadership, you had to be able to show that you could beat Gordon Brown – and this was the job to do it,' an insider recalls. As soon as he got off the phone, Osborne rang two of his oldest political friends. He did not call David Cameron, but he already knew from an earlier phone conversation with him that he was seriously considering a campaign for the leadership himself, which he supported.

Osborne was aware that taking on Gordon Brown was fraught with risk, particularly as the economy was showing few signs of faltering. 'Six Shadow Chancellors have been crushed by Brown, and I'm only thirty-three,' he told them. 'My whole career could be over by the time I'm thirty-four or thirty-five!' But he soon decided that this was not a job he could turn down. 'In politics you've just got to go for it and see what happens,' he confided in one friend. And the suggestion that he take a shot at the leadership? 'He was completely taken aback,' another friend recalls. 'He never planned to run. He may have been tempted, but from what he told me he was sure that he didn't want to do it.'

After surprising Osborne with the news, Whetstone rang Cameron. 'Michael wants you to take on the work and pensions brief, David,' she told him. Cameron was stunned, and rejected the offer immediately: 'I want something I can be creative with – what about education?' Whetstone said she would inform Howard about his preference. 'I was told he wanted education – I just offered him what he wanted,' says Howard.[31] Although the education brief was not particularly prestigious in the eyes of many in the party, Cameron thought it would give him a platform to raise his profile ahead of the leadership contest. He had taken an interest in the education of children with special needs since becoming an MP, not least because of his son's condition.

The following day, Howard formally offered Osborne the role of

Shadow Chancellor, which he accepted. 'I want you to be my successor, George,' Howard told him. Osborne said that he was flattered and would think about the leadership, but would not commit to anything. Cameron is clear that Howard did not make the same proposition to him during his meeting that morning. It is not clear whether Cameron had encouraged Osborne to take on the Shadow Chancellorship in their discussions over the previous forty-eight hours, but when he heard that he had accepted it he was relieved, as if Osborne had declined the job, Howard might have offered it to him instead. While Cameron enthusiastically took on the more junior role, his ambition to stand for the leadership was growing by the day.

Howard unveiled the new Shadow Cabinet on Tuesday, 10 May. After four years on the backbenches he brought back Francis Maude, the arch-moderniser whom Duncan Smith had requested him not to promote after his downfall. Maude would become the new Party Chairman, responsible for changing the leadership rules. David Davis remained in his post as Shadow Home Secretary, and other familiar names were also retained: Letwin decided to remain in the Shadow Cabinet, taking the environment brief; Lansley stayed at health; Willetts moved to energy and industry; and Liam Fox was promoted to Shadow Foreign Secretary. A few older hands returned, like Malcolm Rifkind, who became Shadow Work and Pensions Secretary after returning to the Commons as MP for Kensington and Chelsea (replacing Michael Portillo). However, Osborne's and Cameron's promotions caught the headlines more than anything else. Other members of the Shadow Cabinet were far from pleased. 'The insiders came up the inside track,' remarked one. 'Howard set the backdrop for a Cameron–Osborne coup to take over the party by delaying the contest. He teed them up in key positions and gave them time to plan. It was an absolute Howard plot. There was massive resentment that others had been passed over.'

Cameron Steps Up

Cameron and Osborne now had a decision to make. Osborne knew that Cameron had all but made up his mind to stand for the leadership. 'After Howard forced George to think about running, he thought about it for a bit and then decided that he had to make the job of Shadow Chancellor succeed, because if he didn't he would be finished,' one mutual friend recalls. 'Also, David said that one of them should challenge David Davis, and not let this be a walkover. It was obvious that David was really in a place where he wanted to go for it, whereas George wasn't even remotely thinking like he was.' Oliver Letwin, who kept in close touch with both in the week after the reshuffle, agrees: 'George was definitely a potential leader, but my impression is that he thought all along that David had the edge,' he says. 'From an early stage when Cameron made clear he was going to stand, George was behind him.'[32]

Cameron says that there was no single person whose advice tipped him over the edge, but the views of his wife, Samantha, and his wider family were crucial. Samantha told him that if he had the right ideas and knew what needed to be done, then he should get on and do it. His brother gave him similar advice. The views of his closest friends in politics, including Osborne, were also important. The following week, Osborne decided to rule himself out once and for all. 'I am making it clear, I would not be a candidate,' he told the *Daily Telegraph* on Friday, 20 May.[33] When pressed on whether he had made a deal with Cameron, similar to that purported to have been made between Tony Blair and Gordon Brown in 1994, he denied it. The night before, he had rung Cameron, and during the course of the conversation Cameron had said, 'If you choose not to run, George, I want you to run my campaign.' A short while later, Osborne rang back to say that had just told the *Telegraph* he was ruling himself out, and that he would support Cameron in his bid. No agreement was even made about whether Osborne would stay on as Shadow Chancellor in the event of Cameron becoming leader.

With his friend out of the running, the path was clear for Cameron to finally make up his mind. Two of his closest friends and allies, Steve Hilton and Michael Gove, urged him to stand. Greg Barker and Oliver Letwin also encouraged him, as did Lord Harris, a prominent party donor, and Andrew Feldman, a university friend and businessman who would help with fundraising. It was an audacious decision, but one taken with a dose of realism. 'He didn't think in any way that he was going to win, but he was up for it,' Letwin recalls.[34] The tiny group of parliamentary supporters and other friends standing behind him began to prepare a putative leadership bid, even though Cameron would not make a public declaration until the middle of June.

To the party establishment, let alone the party in the country, which had hardly heard of either of them, there was considerable surprise that Cameron or Osborne were even considering throwing their hats into the ring. 'I thought initially that David wasn't ready,' recalls Jonathan Marland, who was Party Treasurer at the time. 'But early on in the campaign he demonstrated his qualities which would make him the obvious choice for leader. George, who proved his true colours during the election campaign, was probably too young at thirty-three, and couldn't have done it alone.'[35] Comparisons in the press with Tony Blair and Gordon Brown after they entered the Commons in Labour's defeat in 1983 provoked jealousy among many Tory MPs. '[They] are OK as individuals,' said one. 'But as a group they exude the kind of smugness that has lost the Tory Party so much support since the 1980s.'[36] Cameron would clearly have his work cut out if he was to persuade the majority of the parliamentary party to support him.

No Longer the 'Learning Moderniser'

Hadn't Cameron been Michael Howard's right-hand man and the author of the 'Victor Meldrew' manifesto? 'He learnt from experience that it was not a manifesto which worked in winning votes,' says friend and ally Ed Vaizey in his defence.[37] By the time Cameron was appointed to the role of head of policy coordination in June 2004, many of the campaign policies, such as the patient's passport, were either well in train or about to be signed off by the leadership. 'Those weren't his ideas,' Nicholas Boles insists.[38] Cameron's role was more as the midwife of Howard's enervated policy prospectus than its creator. He argues that the introduction to the manifesto which he wrote with his friend, the journalist and then prospective parliamentary candidate Michael

Gove, was relatively modernising, while admitting that at the time he was a 'learning moderniser'. Yet he cannot wholly escape culpability for playing a key part in producing one of the most threadbare and narrowly focused manifestos the party had ever produced. Cameron does not in any way claim to be responsible for the conduct of the 2005 campaign and its focus on immigration, but he cannot totally dissociate himself from it. He was loyal to his party leader, despite expressing unease about the conduct of the campaign at several points. Having previously turned down the party chairmanship, he was not going to rock the boat to such an extent that his future prospects would be put in doubt. As we have seen, Cameron was playing the long game.

Even friends like Nick Boles did not see how Cameron could claim to be the standard bearer for modernisation. Long before the election, Boles had expressed his doubts about whether an Old Etonian like Cameron could credibly lead the party, and he had been unimpressed by his early caution. Writing in the *Evening Standard* just after the election, Boles argued that someone from the right with a personal story of 'social mobility' would be better placed to sell modernisation to more traditional Conservatives.[39] In David Davis, he thought, with his journey from a south London council estate to frontline politics, there was a contender who could strike a chord with the party and the country. Rising from humble origins had been an asset to other Tory leaders, from Edward Heath and Margaret Thatcher to John Major and William Hague. After the party conference a few months later, realising that he had backed the wrong horse, Boles wrote to Cameron about his former doubts. Cameron replied: 'I think you're right that it took me quite a long time to get here, but let's hope that like slow cooking the result in the eating will be much better, stronger and more convincing.'[40]

The most important influence on Cameron's political outlook was the impact of the third successive electoral defeat. '[It] took him from being sceptical about the claims of us modernisers to being embracing of them,' says Boles. Finkelstein agrees: 'When he got it, he got it big.'[41] Others outside the 'Smith Square set' had already noticed signs of his unease about the narrowing agenda being pursued by the party's high command. 'David returned from campaigning during the Cheadle by-election shortly after the general election,' another modernising MP, Nick Gibb, recalls. 'He said to me that every time he put a leaflet through a door he just thought to himself, "That's another vote for Labour and the Lib Dems," because they were very core vote and very negative messages.'[42] Cameron no longer wanted to be on the losing side. Although late in the day, he came round to the view that the party had to modernise if it was to stand a chance of ever winning again. It was a view that came into even sharper focus in the months ahead.

From Bloodbath to Spring Awakening

While Cameron began to prepare for his leadership bid, Howard's authority ebbed away. Although the outgoing leader had created a breathing space, his aides were desperate to stave off a direct challenge from Davis's supporters before the end of July. If they could get through to the summer recess, it would be impossible for a contest to be triggered while the Commons was not sitting. The chances of Howard surviving until then, however, were diminishing by the day. When the new Chairman, Francis Maude, unveiled the proposals to reform the leadership election rules in a consultation paper entitled *A 21st Century Party* at the end of May, there was a bloodbath in the parliamentary party. The paper criticised the 'flawed' system introduced by William Hague in 1998 as 'expensive and protracted, causing maximum uncertainty and disruption', and said that it was 'wrong in principle and certainly damaging in practice for one group of people to have the power to elect the leader of the party and a different group of people to have the power to remove him or her'. 'Party members,' it continued, 'cannot know the candidates as well as the MPs. It is essential that the leader enjoys the confidence of Conservative MPs.'[43] There were also plans to merge moribund constituency associations, widen the membership base and introduce measures to improve MPs' 'work rate' and sense of discipline. Many MPs were deeply suspicious. Ann Widdecombe warned of the party becoming a 'Stalinist centrally controlled set-up . . . If it becomes too centralised then whoever controls the party will simply produce a Parliament of clones.'[44]

Backbenchers were even more resentful about the proposed changes to the leadership election rules, under which MPs could put themselves forward if they had the support of at least 10 per cent of the parliamentary party. If one candidate had over half the parliamentary party behind them, they would automatically be declared leader. If that did not happen, all the candidates would go forward to a vote of the National Convention, which would then produce a shortlist for MPs to choose from. Crucially, the one-member-one-vote system that had been extended to the wider party membership was absent from the proposals. A 'constitutional college' of MPs and party members would vote on the leadership's proposals at the end of September. It was clear that Howard would have to stay on as leader beyond the summer, which his aides had pleaded with him to do. The timing infuriated David Davis's supporters further.

The bitterness and recrimination of the Duncan Smith period had returned with a vengeance. The leadership's plans were roundly rejected at several meetings of the backbench 1922 Committee in May and early June: as Howard scanned the room for support on one occasion he could only find two MPs who were prepared to speak up in his support. From the right of the party, Edward Leigh criticised the way the leadership had dispatched Howard Flight after he had strayed from the party line just before the election, rousing backbenchers to bang their desks in approval. The 1922 Committee voted to return to the old system, whereby the parliamentary party had the final say in choosing the leader, but decided that party members would be formally consulted, although their preferences would not be binding. Although the vote did not bind the leadership, it gave the impression of a party squabbling about internal rules that mattered little to the outside world.

Howard cut a lonely figure as the backbenchers turned on him. 'It was horrible,' recalls one of his senior aides. 'Davis's henchmen on the committee were really cutting up rough.' At another private meeting between the 1922 Executive Committee and the Tory leader and his team, more blood was spilled. 'They were slightly overweight men in suits, incredibly pompous – complete jerks,' one of Howard's aides recalls. Rachel Whetstone stormed out of the meeting, telling one of the committee members: 'You lot never deserve to ever win an election again. I hate this party, and I hate all of you, and the way you have behaved is disgraceful.'

The efforts to reform the election rules were in total disarray. Senior figures including David Willetts, Theresa May, Andrew Lansley and Michael Ancram publicly attacked the leadership's intention to 'diminish democratic involvement', as did many of the fifty newly elected MPs, who represented a quarter of the parliamentary party. Iain Duncan Smith added his voice to the growing protest. Howard was now convinced that he had to stay on until after the conference in Blackpool if the party was to avoid another implosion. His aides felt that only if he could survive until then might the conference become not an outlet for recrimination, as it had been in 2003, but a stage for the leadership candidates to make their pitch in the full glare of the media and the wider party. A mature and calm debate seemed a long way off, however.

In the immediate aftermath of the election, a number of senior figures did not hold back from slamming the campaign. Even worse for the leadership was a stinging attack from the former Party Chairman, Maurice Saatchi. Writing in the *Sunday Telegraph* three days after polling day, he said that 'mere anger at the problems of the world we live in is not enough to convince the voters that the Conservative Party is fit to solve them . . . Last Thursday the electorate gave Michael Howard credit for the focus and discipline he has brought to the party. But the voters did not accept that the Tories have yet regained a sense of purpose.'[45] Saatchi's criticism was deeply resented by Howard and his team. 'It was disgusting,' said one. 'He was basically saying, "If only we listened to him." It left a lot of bad blood with Michael and all of us.' Saatchi had reason to be resentful himself, having been marginalised the previous year, but his argument hit a raw nerve: voters simply did not believe or trust in the

Tory alternative, because it was so bleak and lacking in vision. Michael Ashcroft's dissection of the election campaign and result, presented in a booklet entitled *Smell the Coffee: A Wake-Up Call for the Conservative Party*, was just as cutting.[46]

A sorely needed break in the clouds appeared in June. The leadership election could not begin until the rules were changed, but potential contenders and other senior figures began to lay their claim to the future of the party. In a series of pamphlets, media interviews and speeches to think tanks, they openly discussed the state of the party unfettered by the iron grip of the old regime. The starting gun had not been fired, but the potential runners and riders began to rehearse the arguments that would shape the coming leadership election. For his part, Howard was eager for a public debate to emerge, and despite the manoeuvrings of Davis's supporters the mood in the parliamentary party gradually began to settle. Howard asked Steve Hilton to present an analysis of the election results and a post-mortem of the campaign to MPs, including research revealing the full extent of the public's negative perceptions of the party. Gradually the animosity that had built up over the past few weeks began to relent. 'There was an openness in the party to debate where we were and what we should do to change that hadn't existed before – this was our Prague spring,' says David Willetts.[47] 'Everyone had time to express themselves, and we had a number of good potential leaders debate in a civilised way,' Liam Fox recalls. 'We had none of the rancour of 1997 or 2001, in which Europe had become the defining issue. It was a much more thoughtful period.'[48]

Margaret Thatcher called on the party to return to 'first principles', while Sir John Major insisted that it reclaim the 'centre ground'. Yet for the first time since her downfall, Lady Thatcher's influence had begun to recede. She had suffered several minor strokes, and her doctors advised her not to make too many public appearances. In one of the most thoughtful contributions to the debate, David Willetts argued that 'Modernising Conservatism' meant emphasising the need for a strong society as well as a strong economy, and that for far too long the party had not applied itself to questions of social justice and equality. The last eight years, he argued, had seen the party preoccupied with questions of leadership and organisation.[49] Influenced by the vitality of the American right, Liam Fox argued that freedom had to be placed at the heart of the party's agenda. In a speech to the think tank Politeia he declared, 'Freedom is our essence. Let freedom reign.'[50] Andrew Lansley suggested that part of the answer might be changing the party's name to 'Reform Conservatives', while Alan Duncan argued that the party had to shed its 'socially distasteful' and 'economically irrelevant' reputation.[51]

The emerging front-runner David Davis told an audience at the Centre for Policy Studies (CPS) that the party needed a 'new Tory idealism'. Davis's CPS lecture caught the media's attention because of his explicit appeal to the centre of the party. 'We should be a one-nation party,' appealing to women and ethnic minorities, he declared.[52] It was a similar pitch to that of Malcolm Rifkind, who also had his eye on the leadership. From the traditional right of the party, the backbencher Edward Leigh, who founded a new grouping called the Cornerstone Group, produced a pamphlet entitled 'The Strange Desertion of Tory England' in which he argued that the party had not been clear enough on Europe and low taxes. 'We must seize the centre and pull it kicking and screaming towards us,' he wrote. 'That is the only way to demolish the foundations of the liberal establishment and demonstrate to the electorate the fundamental flaws on which it is built – in contrast to the cornerstone of conservative philosophy. Then we must rebuild the Conservative alternative on that empire's ruins.'[53]

Pulling in the opposite direction was David Cameron's contribution to the debate. Steve Hilton, Michael Gove and Oliver Letwin helped him prepare several speeches on public services and 'the quality of life'. On 16 June, Cameron had hinted on Radio 4's *Today* programme that he was 'contemplating' standing, the first time he had signalled his intentions in public. He made his first major speech thirteen days later, on 29 June, to the think tank Policy Exchange, which by now had established itself as the spiritual home for the younger, more socially liberal modernisers. Born out of the discussions Cameron,

Hilton, Gove and Letwin had had earlier in the year, the speech, entitled 'We're All in it Together', concentrated on reviving social bonds and institutions, such as the family. Cameron argued that tax breaks for married couples would send a message to families that the state was on their side.[54] He spoke of 'a dynamic economy, a decent society and a strong self-confident nation' that was 'forward-looking, inclusive and generous'.

Cameron's performance failed to excite opinion inside the party, while many commentators were confused as to what type of Conservatism he was trying to espouse. Some erstwhile modernisers were not enthused. 'It was a very conventional analysis, and very centrist in the Conservative tradition,' Andrew Cooper, one of the prophets of modernisation, recalls. 'He wasn't the obvious modernising candidate.'[55] 'It was serious but dull,' concedes one of the speechwriters. 'The other speeches sank without trace, but they were important in working out our ideas and they were germs of things to come like "shared responsibility".' Some of Cameron's team were nervous. 'Do you think we can win?' Andrew Feldman asked Steve Hilton in the street outside Policy Exchange after Cameron's speech. 'I can't see how we can lose,' Hilton replied. Hilton knew his young friend was coming from nowhere, but he was overwhelmingly confident that the party would eventually see that Cameron was the right candidate with the right argument.

The Davis Juggernaut Rolls on

The young pretender for the Tory crown knew he had his work cut out. David Davis was the clear favourite, while events further afield had enhanced the chances of another seasoned performer, Ken Clarke. The 'No' votes in the French and Dutch referenda on the proposed EU Constitution on 29 May and 1 June made a referendum in Britain, which many had expected to take place in 2006, unlikely. The European issue, which had so harmed Clarke's chances in 2001, would no longer be such an obstacle to his hopes of making a third attempt at the leadership. On 19 June Clarke declared that he was 'keen to run', but would not make up his mind until later in the summer.

Meanwhile, preparations for Davis's bid were well under way. 'There was an impressive machine operating, and it looked as if it had garnered a large amount of support for Davis,' says Letwin. 'He looked very much in the lead.'[56] Preparation for the Davis campaign had even begun in January, well before the general election campaign, when a dozen or so MPs assembled at the Nottinghamshire home of former minister Andrew Mitchell, who would become Davis's campaign manager. Along with the former whip Derek Conway, Mitchell had a reputation for being a tough operator who knew his way around the parliamentary party and the Whips' Office. After the election, Davis called on the services of the publisher Iain Dale to be his chief of staff. Dale recruited several others to join the campaign, but this was to be an MP-led operation. 'There was a group of them who thought that if you didn't have the letters MP after your name then you were a second-class citizen,' says one.

MPs were given tasks ranging from promoting Davis in the media to rallying support within the parliamentary party. Nick Herbert, the former director of the think tank Reform and one of the brightest of the 2005 intake, was drafted to take care of Davis's speeches. He recruited James Frayne, who had successfully managed the 'No' campaign for a regional assembly in the North-East. Frayne immediately saw that there were problems. 'Success in campaigns is determined by a clear message and an effective decision-making structure that can adapt to change,' he recalls. 'We had neither. The lack of traction by the other campaigns meant we were never forced to address it.'[57] The closest Herbert and Frayne came to a theme was 'Changing Britain, improving lives', which sought to promote Davis as the politician who understood and cared about people's concerns. Davis was comfortable with the theme, but he was even more relaxed about rallying support within the party. 'David gave a few speeches about what he wanted to do, but he felt it would be improper to go further than that when the campaign hadn't even started,' says Iain Dale. 'Some people felt that this was a sign he wasn't prepared to be ruthless enough.'[58]

The inherent weaknesses of the Davis campaign would soon be

obscured by events in the real world. The terrorist attacks on London on 7 July propelled him onto the national stage, and his assured parliamentary and broadcast performances not only won plaudits within the party and from commentators and political opponents, but raised the profile of the Shadow Home Secretary in the public's mind – even more so than that of Howard as Leader of the Opposition. In the weeks that followed the '7/7' atrocity the public debate about the party's future was suspended, while the leadership campaigning in the shadows lost momentum. 'Davis was resurgent, and things became difficult for us,' Greg Barker, a Cameron supporter, admitted.[59] The fledgling Cameron campaign had not reached much beyond twelve to eighteen MPs by the start of the summer recess in late July. Cameron responded with a speech on foreign affairs and terrorism, as well as developing his brief on education. Even Michael Howard, who was publicly staying above the fray, began to have doubts about Cameron's chances. 'I was surprised that his campaign hadn't taken off. In the early stages he didn't succeed in making much of an impact.'[60]

One of the few sources of encouragement for Cameron was Oliver Letwin's public declaration of support on 2 July. The Shadow Environment Secretary and former Shadow Chancellor was the most senior Shadow Cabinet figure to have aligned himself with Cameron. 'Colleagues came up to me saying what a typically quixotic gesture it was to back David Cameron. So I wasn't alone in thinking we weren't going to win at that time.'[61] Letwin was a useful asset to the Cameron campaign. 'Oliver's early support was crucial,' said one insider. 'He was the Gandalf of our campaign, providing sound advice and intellectual weight. It gave confidence to David and the intimate team.' Letwin, however, was the only serious frontbencher to have come out in support of Cameron. Many senior figures, including Willetts, Lansley, Rifkind, Yeo and May, were either considering their own bids or lining up behind Davis publicly or privately. Most thought Cameron was simply laying a marker for a future bid, and was not in any way a serious contender. An important moment had passed, however. When Parliament rose for the summer recess at the end of July, there was huge relief in Howard's office and among the Cameron camp that Davis's allies had failed to trigger the vote of confidence that may well have ousted Howard. As long as Howard was still there, Cameron had a chance.

Feeling the Breeze of Blair's 'Indian Summer'

Undeterred by the lack of parliamentary support, Cameron and his closest team set to work on a campaign manifesto in late July and August. Their attempts to sketch out the themes for the campaign had met with mixed success. A lunch with the editorial board of *The Times* earlier in the summer had not gone well. 'They asked him lots of questions and, although he had his opinions, he hadn't really worked out how to craft them together into a clear message. An early speech was needed to set out a distinctive agenda,' recalls George Eustice, who left CCHQ, where he was Howard's press secretary, to join Cameron's campaign team.[62]

The speech to Policy Exchange tried to carve out a distinctive platform, but the Cameron team realised they needed to thrash out in much greater depth what a Cameron-led Conservative Party would be like. They gathered around the corner from CCHQ, at the London office of Robert Fleming (a financier and constituent of Cameron's who helped to raise funds for the campaign) and in Cameron's constituency home in the Oxfordshire village of Dean at the weekends. The campaign theme, 'Modern Compassionate Conservatism', emerged from these conversations, as did the slogan that was to feature on the campaign literature: 'Change to Win'. They agreed that opposing tuition fees and foundation hospitals and promoting the idea of a 'patient's passport' had to be dropped. As education spokesman, Cameron had already signalled his support for Blair's proposals to reform secondary education, which included plans to devolve more power to schools away from local authorities. Supporting the government when its reforms chimed with Conservative thinking would be more sensible, they thought, than opposing for opposition's sake.

Lessons learned from aspects of New Labour's success, and in particular Tony Blair's style of leadership, influenced their discussions. Gove and Osborne were particularly admiring of Blair's achievement in surviving the challenges of his second term and winning a third. They respected his stance on Iraq, but even more appealing was his mastery of communication and willingness to embrace market-based reforms. In February 2003, Gove had written in *The Times*, 'I'm afraid I've got to be honest. Tony Blair is proving an outstanding Prime Minister at the moment,'[63] and friends recall that during this time Osborne would refer to Blair as 'our real leader', a comment he insists was made in jest. Blair was enjoying his 'Indian summer' in July 2005. Once again he encapsulated the public mood after the London bombings, and he had used his charm to help the successful 2012 Olympic bid.

However, all was not well within the highest reaches of New Labour. Blair had survived an attempted coup by Gordon Brown's allies in the days immediately after the general election, but that would not be the end of the bitter rivalry beneath the surface. Blair knew he could not stave off the threat from Brown's ambition to succeed him for much longer. It was only a matter of time before something had to give. In October 2004 the Prime Minister had promised to leave Downing Street after serving a 'full' third term, but Brown and his allies were determined to force him out well before then.

For Cameron and his small team of supporters, the turmoil within Labour's ranks presented a possible opportunity. Blair had achieved electoral success by appealing to moderate former Tory voters, they thought, so why not build on that success? Oliver Letwin was key to the shaping of a new understanding. 'Tony Blair spotted that the Labour Party needed to change, and accept Mrs Thatcher's understanding that the free-market economy was the way to run the economy, but at the same time he realised that there were things that had been left behind by us – such as various social problems and the public services.' It was a revealing admission from a politician who had been inspired by the Thatcherite politics of the 1980s. 'These things had to be dealt with – [Blair] got that right – but the problem was that he didn't sort them out, certainly not to begin with, and later because Gordon Brown stopped him,' Letwin continues. 'Our task was to take it to the next stage and tackle them properly. This is what Modern Compassionate Conservatism would be about.'[64]

Cameron's team were now grappling with what others had tried and failed to do since 1997, from William Hague's early attempt to understand why the party had lost office (through the work of Andrew Cooper and Peter Lilley), to Michael Portillo's unsuccessful leadership bid and Iain Duncan Smith's mission to 'help the vulnerable'. 'We were having arguments about what had gone wrong with the party, the perception of it and what needed to be done to set it right,' says David Willetts. 'There had always been groups of us who have been trying to address this; the problem was making it happen.'[65] Cameron and his small team of supporters believed they had the answer.

During August, the campaign operation began to take shape. Two more members of the original Smith Square set came on board: Kate Fall and Edward Llewellyn, who were fellow alumni of the CRD. Another new recruit, Dan Ritterband, who had worked in Howard's office, joined Cameron's team as they gathered in Dean one hot weekend in August. 'It was a bit like the Kennedy compound in Cape Cod,' recalls Ritterband. 'There was a big Sunday lunch and children running all over the place. There were papers spread over the garden. This was not about men in grey suits behind closed doors, as the Tory Party used to be.'[66] Every last detail of the campaign launch was discussed. 'We wanted to bring a breath of fresh air to everything,' Ritterband recalls. Steve Hilton was in his element. Fuelled by Coca-Cola and cigarettes, he worked long into the night working on the formal campaign launch. He agreed with Cameron that the look and feel of the launch was crucial to marking him out from his rivals. 'Dave *is* the change' was one of his regular refrains at the time.

'We are Coming to the End-Game'
Despite the creativity in Dean, it had become the conventional wisdom in the press that David Davis was marching towards victory. Few columnists gave Cameron a chance, let alone considered backing

him, with the exceptions of India Knight in the *Sunday Times* and Suzanne Moore in the *Mail on Sunday*. On 31 August the field became even more crowded, when Ken Clarke finally declared that he would run for the third time. Backed by Tim Yeo, Ann Widdecombe and John Bercow, Clarke attracted support from across the party, and he could still count on his appeal in the country as a moderate who was capable of landing blows on Labour. The *Daily Mail* threw its weight behind him, giving him a handy boost. Clarke's intervention was a major blow for the Cameron campaign. 'It caused a problem for us, as there was a perception that if Clarke ran then David would have to concede and they would stand on a joint ticket, even though David never had any intention of being anyone's running mate,' says George Eustice.[67] Clarke had already asked Cameron to do just that, but the former Chancellor's advances were politely declined.

A second blow came when David Willetts, who had staked out a consistent position on modernising the party, announced on 15 September that he would not stand, but would back Davis. 'I was persuaded by Davis that he would be the leader with a better chance of changing the party – he was coming from the right and had the toughness to do it,' says Willetts.[68] Liam Fox had also entered the ring on 5 September with a pitch to the Eurosceptic right, promising to pull Tory MEPs out of the centre-right European People's Party (EPP) group in the European Parliament.

Many in the parliamentary party and the press now expected the contest to be between Davis and Clarke. The Davis camp claimed to have the support of almost half of the parliamentary party. 'We are coming to the end-game here with Clarke versus Davis. I think Cameron can now go away,' warned Alan Duncan, who abandoned his own putative leadership bid in July.[69]

Despite their efforts over the summer months, the pressure began to mount on the Cameron team. They had barely attracted any more supporters since July, and the campaign funds were practically non-existent. 'By September it did looked pretty bleak for us. There was a view that if Davis got ninety MPs then it would be all over and there would be a coronation,' recalls Eustice.[70] 'David very, very nearly pulled out, because he didn't want to be humiliated,' says a confidant. 'The irony was that his more sophisticated backers were the ones saying "You should pull out," whereas Greg Barker, who is a complete maverick, was the one who petulantly said "You must carry on." ' Even more surprising for Cameron was the nervousness of his campaign manager, George Osborne. 'Look, in a week's time you might have to admit it, you know,' Osborne told him. Others suggested that he sue for peace with Davis and aim for a senior position. 'I cannot allow that to happen,' he replied immediately. 'Someone's got to stop Davis,' one his team recalls him saying. 'I have to press on – if I win the leadership in 2010 or 2016, we'll be out for a generation.' It was a critical moment. Michael Gove was one of those who encouraged Cameron to stick to his guns, arguing strongly that he had to fight to win as the out-and-out modernising candidate.[71] Cameron was more determined to succeed than ever as the conference season drew closer.

Take-Off

As expected, Michael Howard's efforts to change the rules of the leadership election foundered on 27 September. The proposals failed to secure the necessary two thirds of the votes of the National Convention, despite Howard's warning in a letter to MPs two weeks earlier that if the rules were not changed the party would be thrown into a crisis. The party board would now agree a timetable for the contest, conducted under the existing rules, whereby MPs would vote to select a shortlist of two candidates in October before a ballot of members in early December. Expectations of a Davis victory increased, given his supposed support among the grassroots.

The Cameron campaign toyed with holding their launch during the Labour Party conference at Bournemouth, where the media would be assembled. 'We wanted to show that we were the people to take the fight to Labour,' Eustice recalls.[72] But deciding that this might be seen as too counter-intuitive, they decided instead to go for Friday, 29 September, just before the start of the Conservative conference at Blackpool. They were fully aware that this was the same day as Davis's planned launch. Andrew Mitchell, Davis's campaign manager, rang George Osborne to ask him to change the date, but Osborne held firm, calculating that going head to head would be more favourable to Cameron. It proved to be the right call.

Davis's performance in the staid setting of the Institute of Civil Engineers in Westminster was not a match for Cameron's at the Royal United Services Institute in Whitehall. Standing in front of his campaign slogan, 'Modern Conservatives', Davis delivered a heavily scripted speech to an audience of largely pinstriped MPs. The event reinforced the impression that Davis's support came from the establishment in the parliamentary party. 'In order to be able to change our country, the Conservative Party itself must change,' he said, but there was a sense that he was merely ticking boxes. 'Davis was reading out the safe speech of a front-runner – it wasn't really him,' recalls one seasoned hack. As journalists left for Cameron's launch, one of Davis's key supporters admitted to one of them, 'That was terrible.'

When the press arrived at the Cameron launch they were greeted with pop music, fruit smoothies and chocolate brownies. The contrast could not have been starker. The television cameras panned around a large, airy room filled with attractive young supporters. The Cameron campaign had borrowed £20,000 to spend on lighting, refreshments and a set. 'It couldn't have been more different to the classic committee job in a wood-panelled room at the event we had just been to,' one reporter recalls. Oliver Letwin opened proceedings with a short introduction. 'I stood there thinking to myself very clearly that we were not going to win, but this was the right place to be,' he later recalled.[73] With a spring in his step, David Cameron took the platform. He admitted that many Conservatives thought he was too young and inexperienced for the top job, before stating: 'I believe that if you have got the right ideas in your head and the right passion in your heart, and if you know what this party needs to do to change, then you should go for it. That is why I am doing this.' He spoke freely without notes, which gave his performance a spontaneous feel, but what impressed journalists more was that he took open questions afterwards until they had none left to ask. Even when someone asked about his views on the state of Iran's foreign policy, he gave an assured reply. He had meticulously prepared for this event, and it showed.

The press's expectations had been confounded, and they were unanimous in their verdicts on who had come out on top from the launches. 'I could see them physically sitting up and listening,' recalls one of Cameron's closest confidants. 'They had all come from Davis's event, and I could see the glee in their eye as they thought, "Here we go, here's fluffy Cameron with his smoothies." They thought Dave was finished before he took to the stage. At the end, they thought, "We had no idea he could do that." ' As far as the lobby were concerned, Cameron's leadership had just taken off.

Some of Davis's more perceptive supporters understood that this was a turning point. 'What the launch did was expose us as vulnerable,' recalls one of them. 'We thought that we would get through, because Cameron's campaign until then had been terrible. But ours was in trouble – Davis was never around, and everything was decided at the last minute.' 'We were the front-runners, so there was a natural tendency to play it safe,' recalls another, Paul Goodman. 'The problem, in retrospect, was that by 2005 modern Conservatism wasn't David Davis – as it was, I think, when he first bid for the leadership in 2001. It would be very hard to deny that David Cameron was closer to the zeitgeist.'[74]

The organisational weaknesses that had plagued the Davis campaign from the beginning would now begin to show. In contrast, a number of Tory MPs rang the Cameron camp to offer their support, and others began to donate money to the campaign. The contest was now officially under way after months of preparation. Although the Cameron team had established the perfect launchpad for Blackpool, they were under no illusions that David Davis was still the man to beat. As soon as Cameron left the launch, he returned to his house in North Kensington with Steve Hilton to work on the speech he would deliver at the conference the following week.

Blackpool Beauty Parade

There was a real sense of excitement as the Conservative Party gathered at Blackpool on Sunday, 3 October. It could not have been more different from the atmosphere two years previously, when talk of plots filled the air before Iain Duncan Smith's demise. Five months had passed since the election defeat, yet the mood among delegates and MPs was almost buoyant. The debate over the leadership election rules had been resolved, and the decks cleared for a conference that would be an open audition for the five contenders: David Davis, David Cameron, Ken Clarke, Liam Fox and Malcolm Rifkind. The activists were there to be wooed, just as much as the MPs. More importantly, they were prepared to listen to some uncomfortable truths.

The Party Chairman's opening address to the conference was a poignant occasion as Francis Maude delivered a withering assessment of the party's electoral advance since 1997. 'Now's the time to be brutally honest with ourselves,' he said. The Conservative Party had 'no God-given right to survive, let alone succeed'. 'Three times now we've asked people to elect us, and three times they said, "Thanks, but no thanks."'[75] Armed with a penetrating analysis of the 2005 election result, Maude spelled out in bald terms why the party had to change. Using charts that had been part of the *Case for Change* presentations in recent years, he pointed out that once a policy was identified with the party it immediately became less attractive to the electorate. 'Only one in three thinks the Conservative Party shares their own values,' he told a silent audience. The research showed that well over half of the British people still believed the party cared more for 'haves' than 'have nots', and that it was stuck in the past: 'Too often we sound like people who just don't like contemporary Britain.' Maude's speech was strikingly similar to Theresa May's 'nasty party' speech three years before, but this time the audience was much more willing to accept the analysis rather than sitting in disbelief. His overture set the tone for the remainder of the conference. It was now up to the rival candidates to attempt to win the hearts and minds of the party faithful. The Blackpool 'beauty parade' was about to begin.

The Davis campaign decided to make their candidate ubiquitous, attending every evening reception, drinks party and fringe event he could to press the flesh. Cameron attended fewer functions, but stayed for longer than Davis, who was whisked around by his team. The all-important party donors took note. Jonathan Marland, the Party Treasurer, remembers how on one occasion, 'Cameron talked to the donors and worked the room, whereas Davis spoke for half a minute and then left the room to go elsewhere.'[76] The Davis camp did little to endear themselves to those in and around the hotel bars. One party grandee remarked, 'His outriders were thugs and bullies who thought that they could do what they liked.'

Courting newspaper executives was also a priority for the candidates. Cameron's launch had given his campaign a real fillip, but he would be given a lesson in how difficult it was to win over some sections of the press, particularly on the right. At a dinner on Tuesday evening with senior journalists and editors from the Telegraph Group, he described himself as 'the heir to Blair'. Chiming with the thinking of Osborne and Letwin earlier in the summer, this was meant to portray the Conservative Party as the 'modernising wing of British politics', as one key player recalls. According to the then editor of the *Daily Telegraph*, Martin Newland, 'It was an absolute shocker, and the room went silent for a while. I said to him, "I understand exactly where you're coming from, but I wouldn't repeat it outside the room." Of course, the right-wingers reacted with deep silence; there was a shocked sensibility in there. But he was very unapologetic about it.'[77] It looked as if Cameron had misjudged his audience and rejected their Holy Grail, Margaret Thatcher's legacy. Osborne, who also attended the dinner, did not believe that Cameron had made a serious *faux pas* until the following day. He and Cameron should have realised that such a glowing reference to Blair would cause consternation in such company. But as it turned out, Cameron did not need the support of the Telegraph Group to win the leadership, unlike his predecessors.

Cameron had received a major boost the night before. BBC2's *Newsnight* had commissioned the respected American pollster Frank

Luntz to conduct a televised focus group examining the leadership candidates. The results were startling. To begin with most people could not even recognise Cameron, but the more they saw of his launch speech and other media appearances the more they warmed to him, in contrast to the other candidates. Crucially, his privileged background did not prove to be a problem. A *Guardian* ICM poll also indicated that he had raised his profile, but it was the *Newsnight* broadcast that made a significant impact at the start of the conference. Earlier opinion polls indicated that the public saw the leadership contest as a two-horse race between the well-known Davis and Clarke, with Cameron hardly registering. Indeed, Clarke was still regarded by the public as the most popular choice, a fact he had relentlessly pushed during speeches and interviews. Suddenly the mood changed.

The conference was turning into an American-style political convention as badges and campaign merchandise appeared all over Blackpool. When the Clarke campaign produced free bottles of mineral water blazoned with their candidate's name for delegates, Hilton spotted an opportunity: Cameron's bottles would have sparkling water. George Eustice recalls that Hilton spent every night of the conference 'designing and printing newsletters with a Cameron twist and then pushing them under people's hotel room doors at 6 a.m.'.[78] The Davis campaign's efforts at branding did not go down well. Girls wearing T-shirts with the slogan 'It's DD for me!' across their breasts caught the eye of tabloid photographers, but failed to wow everyone at the conference, especially the respectably dressed constituency chairmen and chairwomen.

The stage of Blackpool's Winter Gardens, the scene of so many important speeches over the years, was the platform on which the candidates would make their pitches to the party, the media and the country. Cameron's speech was to be on Wednesday, 4 October, the day before Davis's. Late on Tuesday evening, his team congregated in Hilton's room at the Imperial, the main conference hotel, to work on his speech. Like all the candidates, Cameron would have only fifteen minutes on the stage, and by 2 a.m. he realised that there was simply too much material, however well-prepared. 'It didn't flow, so David just decided to wing it off by heart as he did at the launch. He had a few notes and some bullet points,' says one of those present.

The Davis camp had their own problems. 'He was doing far too much at conference,' recalls a senior member of his campaign team. 'We didn't get what he wanted to say. He wanted to make it wholly about home affairs, which made it too modest. It should have been much more sweeping.' Davis's campaign manager Andrew Mitchell had long warned him that he could take nothing for granted: 'Before he went off in August I told him he needed to make a great speech about why he wanted to be Prime Minister and leader of the Conservative Party, but we were very slow in prodding him into action. Because we had great speechwriters we thought the speech would also be great, but you can't draft a speech by committee, and it came together very late in the day.'[79]

During the weekend before the conference, Paul Goodman sent an email to the rest of the Davis camp. 'I warned that the speech wasn't in a good state and that we could be looking at one of the great conference disasters.' The team recruited a speech coach and hired a lectern to help Davis rehearse in his hotel room, but there was nothing they could do about the competition. 'The Cameron strategy seems to have been to do nothing at conference – apart from make a smash-and-grab speech for the leadership,' recalls Goodman. 'The Davis plan was to do everything – lots of speeches and appearances. Due attention was paid to all of them, except the one that really mattered – the conference speech itself.'[80]

As Cameron walked with Greg Barker, one of the stalwarts of his campaign, along the seafront to the Winter Gardens on Wednesday morning, he barely said a word. He knew that this was his opportunity to capitalise on the success of the last few days. The atmosphere in the Empress Ballroom was alive with anticipation. Journalists, commentators, party workers and campaign staff were curious to see whether Cameron could repeat his performance at the launch, while the rank and file barely knew the man who walked out onto the conference platform.

'We meet in the shadow of a third consecutive defeat,' he told them, before mentioning their concerns about a 'bankrupted pension system' and 'powers passed to a European Union that nobody trusts'. He then confronted them with reality. 'We were defeated by a government that won fewer votes than any in history. But let's not blame the electoral system. Let's not take comfort in solid but slow progress. Let's have the courage to say: "They've failed – but so have we." ' It was a hard-hitting message, but one which was delivered with charm as Cameron walked freely across the stage. 'Because he wasn't looking down at his notes, people thought it was coming from the heart and so they believed him,' Andrew Cooper observed.[81] The lobby journalists and commentators to the right of the stage were captivated. 'After about two minutes of Cameron we suddenly stopped clucking away to each other and started to listen,' recalls a senior MP who was standing with the press. 'It was one of those rare moments. At that point, having quietly pledged to vote for Davis, I knew I wasn't going to do so.'

'We don't just need new policies or presentation or organisation, or even having a young, passionate, energetic leader – though come to think of it, that might not be such a bad idea,' Cameron continued as the audience laughed. 'We have to change and modernise our culture and attitudes and identity. When I say change, I'm not talking about some slick rebranding exercise: what I'm talking about is funda-mental change, so that . . . we have a message that is relevant to people's lives today, that shows we're comfortable with modern Britain and that we believe our best days lie ahead.' As he built up to the climax of his speech he appealed to the party to place its faith in a 'new generation': 'It will be an incredible journey. I want you to come with me.' The hall applauded wildly and the cameras flashed away as he kissed his wife Samantha and waved at the audience. 'We were all euphoric,' Barker recalled immediately afterwards.[82] Cameron and Osborne believed that the launch speech was actually the better of the two performances. Nevertheless, this would be a hard act for his rivals to follow.

Malcolm Rifkind had spoken the day before, delivering a spirited speech, as did Liam Fox and Ken Clarke, who followed Cameron on Wednesday afternoon. Clarke confidently declared: 'We search for leaders who will be seen by the public as prime ministers in waiting. Oh boy, have you kept me waiting.' Although the audience were cheered by his tub-thumping rhetoric, some thought it condescending to be told by a twice-defeated leadership candidate that they had kept him waiting too long.

The weight of expectation was now on David Davis, who took the stage the next day. After a passionate introduction about the threat posed by domestic terrorism in the wake of the 7/7 bombings, his speech lost momentum, although he stirred the audience when he described his personal story and his commitment to maintaining traditional British freedoms and family values. 'I know what it is like to live in a tough neighbourhood,' he declared. 'I grew up on a council estate. It is sixty-nine years this morning since my communist grandfather joined the Jarrow march against unemployment. So I wasn't born a Conservative. I chose to be a Conservative.' But the remainder of the speech felt overly scripted and stilted, in contrast to Cameron's more natural, off-the-cuff delivery. Party members were polite in their applause, but they had not been wowed. The press were not enthused either. Davis's team blames the spinning operation by Cameron's supporters in the media. 'They helped to ensure that a speech which was admittedly lacklustre was reported as downright bad,' says Goodman. 'I remember Danny Finkelstein and Bruce Anderson, both strong Cameron supporters, spinning vigorously after Davis sat down. To be fair to them, they didn't have to push very hard.'[83]

Immediately after his speech, Davis had lunch with his key lieutenants. 'I was with him, [his wife] Doreen and Derek Conway, and he was very quiet,' Goodman says. 'He clearly knew that there was a big problem, to put it mildly.'[84] It had been a disastrous forty-eight hours for the Davis campaign. 'We had dinner that night, and I knew we were profoundly wounded. In the coming weeks it became clear that we had lost,' recalls Andrew Mitchell.[85]

Party activists returned home stirred by a week that had not descended into chaos or infighting, unlike the Blackpool conference of two years previously. The beauty parade of candidates and the maturity of the debate had invigorated the wider party. It would now be up to MPs to make their choice.

Back to Westminster

In the space of a single week, the standings of the rival candidates had been transformed. Opinion polls registered a complete reversal of fortunes. 'We polled party members before and after the confer-ence, and David Cameron's rating doubled from 19 to 39 per cent,' recalls Peter Kellner of YouGov. 'I have never seen any figure in polling history move so fast.'[86] The field began to narrow as the deadline for nominations, 10 October, approached. Malcolm Rifkind soon with-drew in favour of Ken Clarke, while Liam Fox emerged as a serious contender, gaining support from the right. Cameron hoped that promising to match Fox's commitment to withdraw Tory MEPs from the EPP group in the European Parliament might curry favour with Eurosceptics, although it would also mean alienating the party's natural (and powerful) allies on the centre-right in Europe. It was one of the few specific commitments he made in the campaign, as he did not want to restrict his freedom of manoeuvre if elected. His closest confidants believe that Cameron made the EPP pledge because he had always disagreed with the party's membership of the 'federalist' grouping. Yet there was no doubt that it would help garner support from those who might not otherwise have considered supporting him, particularly those who were leaning towards Fox.

Cameron also refused to promise jobs to MPs in any future regime, unlike the Davis camp. However, there was one exception. On the first day of the new parliamentary session, the Cameron campaign announced that the Deputy Chief Whip, Patrick McLoughlin, a senior and well-respected figure in the parliamentary party, would become Chief Whip if Cameron won. 'It immediately gave people the impres-sion that it wouldn't just be boys with scooters,' Greg Barker recalls.[87] Cameron's whipping operation was already in full swing, ahead of the first ballot of MPs.

There was one issue that began to cause difficulty for Cameron – drugs. It had been sparked by a fringe event at the conference, when Andrew Rawnsley of the *Observer* asked him whether he had taken drugs at university. 'I had a normal university experience,' he replied. 'There were things that I did then that I don't think that I should talk about now that I'm a politician.' Drugs was an issue that had caused much controversy after the 2000 party conference, when a number of Shadow ministers admitted that they had smoked cannabis as students. It now came to plague the Cameron campaign as the press, led by the *Daily Mail*, called on him to come clean.

As a backbencher after 2001, Cameron had been more liberal than most of his party on the issue of drugs classification. Now under the scrutiny of a leadership campaign, the spotlight was on his private life. He decided to say that he was 'entitled to a private past'. It was neither a denial, nor a candid admission. 'Once he made a decision to stick to the formula, he stuck to it,' says Barker. 'We saw the drugs stuff as a test of his character under pressure. It impressed colleagues in the way he handled it. I think that it strengthened his confidence and his candidacy.'[88] Cameron also wanted to protect a close member of his family who had received treatment for drug addiction. When reports about this appeared in the press, he issued a statement saying how 'incredibly proud' he was of his relative. The swirling media interest gradually subsided. It was a difficult issue that could have derailed Cameron's leadership bid, but he calmly turned it to his advantage. He was helped by the fact that most of his rivals stayed above the fray. 'We did not want the campaign to descend into the gutter,' Andrew Mitchell, Davis's campaign manager, made clear.[89]

When MPs voted in the first ballot of the leadership election on 18 October, it was clear that Davis's support was crumbling. With sixty-two votes, only six ahead of Cameron, he was nowhere near reaching the support of half the parliamentary party. Fox won forty-two votes, while Clarke was knocked out of the contest with thirty-eight – a humiliating outcome for the man who had topped the MPs' ballots in 2001. Yet the result was even more of a blow for the candidate who came first. 'Derek [Conway] had his figures and

I had my own, but this was way beyond our worst-case scenario,' Iain Dale recalls.[90]

The Cameron campaign was on a roll. It tried to lure senior figures from the Davis camp, including David Willetts, who came very close to jumping ship. The main worry was Fox, who threatened to overtake Davis in the second ballot two days later by winning support from the right of the party. 'We were worried that Davis's votes would have transferred to Fox,' says Barker,[91] and Fox himself insists, 'We came very close to overtaking Davis.'[92] But in the event it was clear that many of Clarke's votes had gone to Cameron. In the second ballot he took ninety votes to Davis's fifty-seven and Fox's fifty-one. There was huge relief in the Cameron camp – they had fended off the Fox threat and, crucially, topped the poll, unlike Duncan Smith in 2001. They may not have won the support of half the parliamentary party, but it was a remarkable result given that so many had expected Davis to be the clear winner only weeks before.

With Fox eliminated, the campaign would now proceed to the television studios and the hustings, as the remaining two candidates sought the votes of party members across the country. The Davis campaign was in disarray. He discussed with Dale, Herbert, Mitchell and Conway whether he should withdraw altogether, and it was suggested that it might be better for the party to unite around Cameron. On the day of the second ballot, Dale had even prepared a statement for Davis to concede defeat. But Mitchell and Davis agreed to continue. 'At this stage we knew we would not win, but we were determined to come a decent second and ensure an orderly contest. There were advantages for the Conservative Party more widely as a result,' says Mitchell.[93] This came as a relief to Cameron, who wanted both to have the endorsement of the grassroots and to have time to work on his plans for the leadership.

Roadshow Harmony

Like the public debate about the Conservatives' future in the spring, the final round of the leadership election in the autumn energised the party. Cameron was now the undeniable front-runner and Davis the underdog, but the two candidates campaigned as if there was everything to play for. Davis had enlisted the help of Nick Wood, William Hague's and Iain Duncan Smith's former press secretary, to help him attract good headlines in the press. Several televised debates, unlike the stultifying affairs between Clarke and Duncan Smith in 2001, spurred public interest in the election. Both candidates prepared meticulously for their encounters in front of the television cameras. Cameron was put in the shade by Davis's confident performance on BBC1's *Question Time*, chaired by David Dimbleby. 'This is absolutely the worst time for the Conservative Party to imitate Tony Blair,' Davis proclaimed. In a more even exchange a few weeks later on ITV, chaired by Jonathan Dimbleby, Cameron accused Davis of offering the same 'core vote' strategy that had lost the party the last two general elections, and dismissed Davis's commitment to upfront tax cuts four or five years before the next general election, promising instead to 'share the proceeds of growth' between investment in public services and cuts in taxation.

Touring around the country for six weeks in late October and November, the two candidates developed a rapport. They had not known each other very well before the leadership contest, and there had been mutual suspicion between the two camps in its early stages, which had stemmed from the disputes of the Howard years. 'The whole campaign was neither particularly divisive nor fractious, because the two campaign managers got on well and because the Davids discovered, rather to their surprise, I think, that they found each other more likeable and amusing than they previously imagined,' Mitchell recalls.[94]

The Cameron camp were aware that Davis was performing well during the hustings, but that only served to lift the performances of their own candidate. 'They became a double act, like touring entertainers. Davis was more relaxed because he knew that he wasn't going to win,' one senior MP recalls.[95] In the final days of the campaign, it became clear which way the wind was blowing. 'Towards the end, when David Cameron got up to get off stage most people started taking photos in a way that didn't happen for Davis – there was an attitude that he was the future,' Barker recalls.[96]

The result of one of the most invigorating leadership elections the Conservative Party had experienced for decades came on Tuesday, 6 December. Cameron now had the declared support of well over half the parliamentary party, and crucially he had received the backing of Liam Fox and William Hague on 13 November. Hague's endorsement, in particular, reassured the party membership that Cameron would not 'betray' them. Grassroots opinion had changed since 2001. They had come to realise that the mistakes of the past four years could not be repeated, and many had been persuaded that changing the party's direction would not be a betrayal of Mrs Thatcher's legacy. They had reached this conclusion without the guidance of the Tory press: it was not until the day that the deadline for sending the postal ballots had passed that the *Daily Telegraph* became the first and last paper to endorse Cameron. 'We got there without the support of the press,' recalls a key member of his campaign. 'By the time they endorsed it was all was over.'

Davis had confirmed his reputation as a big player during the national tour, but it was Cameron's novelty that captured the imagination, as it had in Blackpool. 'The party showed that it realised the need to change, and David Davis, though capable, did not represent a change in the direction of the party and the spirit of its direction. It consciously chose a youthful leader who now offered a different direction,' reflected Tory grandee Douglas Hurd.[97]

The Royal Academy of Arts on Piccadilly in the heart of London provided the grand setting for the announcement of the members' ballot. Instead of a private declaration to the parliamentary party in a committee room in the House of Commons, the backbench 1922 Committee would break with tradition. Sir Michael Spicer, the Committee Chairman, would announce the result in front of a large audience and an array of cameras and microphones. 'We found out the result just before the announcement,' George Eustice from the Cameron campaign recalls. 'By that stage we were confident, but this was a convincing win, and David was pleased.'[98] At 3 p.m. the two candidates walked out onto the platform with Spicer to face a bank of flashing cameras. Spicer read out the result: 198,844 votes for Cameron, 134,446 for Davis. Cameron had won a resounding 68 per cent of the vote. 'I hereby declare David Cameron the new leader of the Conservative Party.' With those words, the heavy responsibility of reviving the party fell on Cameron's thirty-nine-year-old shoulders. It took the serendipitous combination of Howard's prolonged departure, the complacency of Davis's campaign and the audacious and artful persuasion of David Cameron to reach this pivotal moment. The last six months had shown that there was life in the old party yet.

SIX

Leaving the Comfort Zone
December 2005–December 2006

On 6 December 2005 the Conservative Party had chosen its fourth leader in just eight years. It was an extraordinary statistic, which underlined just how unsuccessful the party had been since the early 1990s. The Conservatives had now placed their faith in a man who had been an MP for less than five years. It was the most rapid ascent to the leadership of either major party in modern times: even Tony Blair had been in the Commons for eleven years before becoming Labour leader in July 1994. David Cameron had only joined Michael Howard's Shadow Cabinet in June 2004, and in scaling the heights of his party he had seen off far more experienced rivals.

After wooing the faithful in Blackpool, Cameron had become the acceptable face of change in the party. The members may not have warmed to everything he said, but they sensed his potential to restore their lagging electoral fortunes. With such a convincing mandate, he and his team now had the chance to reshape the Conservative Party after years of failure. The first few weeks and months would be crucial. Unlike the previous regimes, there could be no half-measures or missed opportunities. He had to prove that he could change the party in the eyes of the electorate, while taking it with him at the same time.

Mandate for Change
The declaration of the result at the Royal Academy had been meticulously planned. As at the September launch of Cameron's campaign, no detail was overlooked. Everything from the lighting and the

background music to the light-blue backdrop was geared for the television coverage, and both camps were determined to present a united front. The evening before, Cameron had told his team that 'There are no longer David Cameron Conservatives and David Davis Conservatives – we are all Conservatives.'

The margin of victory was in line with the Cameron campaign's expectations, but it was no less emphatic a mandate. Sixty-eight per cent may have been only 7 per cent more than Iain Duncan Smith received at the last leadership election in 2001, but the circumstances could not have been more different. Unlike in 2001, the final two candidates had developed a solid working relationship during the final stages of the campaign, and the occasion had not been over-shadowed by events elsewhere.

David Davis was magnanimous in defeat, and congratulated his rival handsomely. 'This has been a contest that is a preamble to us winning the next general election,' he declared audaciously. 'It has shown our party as democratic, intelligent, civilised, thoughtful, mature . . . in short, a party fit for government . . . I'm asking you to welcome the next Conservative Prime Minister, David Cameron.' Davis's words lifted the audience of party officials, donors, campaign staff, MPs and supporters. Deep down, he must have been bitterly disappointed not to win the prize he so dearly sought. And many in the party knew in their hearts that the party was far from ready for office. Yet for the first time since 1997, a ray of light had appeared at the end of a very long tunnel.

As at his launch event and in his speech at the party conference, Cameron delivered his first words as party leader without a script or an autocue. The spirit of the occasion was similar to William Hague's acceptance speech as leader in June 1997, and indeed to Michael Portillo's declaration that he was standing for the party leadership four years later, or Michael Howard's statement at the Saatchi Gallery in October 2003. Yet there was something different in the air. Unlike in the previous two leadership elections, Europe no longer dominated the argument. Both Cameron and Davis were avowed Eurosceptics, in line with the broad mass of opinion in the parliamentary party. Their campaigns had revealed strong differences on economic and social questions, but there was a sense that whoever won, the party had to rally behind him. 'It was time, just time,' says a senior frontbencher. 'It wasn't that Cameron had more authority than his predecessors when he won the leadership. People were thinking, "How many more of these bloody leadership elections do we have to go through?" We had to pull together.' This undervalues the mandate Cameron had just received. The case for modernisation had grown stronger with the passage of time: with each successive leader who did not address the party's tarnished reputation, the party faithful gradually had come to realise radical change could not be avoided. In David Cameron, they had voted by a large majority for a leader who had the potential to broaden the party's appeal far more than any of his predecessors. Although Davis was attractive to many of the grassroots, he lacked Cameron's forward-looking appeal.

'I said when I launched my campaign that we needed to change in order to win,' Cameron declared. 'Now that I've won, we will change.' The first goal he set would prove to be the most controversial. Confronting his party with an uncomfortable fact, the new leader said: 'Nine out of ten Conservative MPs are white men. We need to change the scandalous under-representation of women in the Conservative Party, and we will do that.' He followed with several hostages to fortune. 'I'm fed up with the Punch-and-Judy politics of Westminster, the name-calling, backbiting, point-scoring . . . when the government does the right thing, we will work with them.' There was no doubting Cameron's intent, particularly with regard to Blair's plans for school reform, but in fact it would not take long for him to succumb to the parliamentary knockabout he so derided. 'I don't want us to invent policies for newspaper headlines,' was another claim which would come back to haunt him.

He went on to repeat the core messages of his leadership campaign: there would be a 'full-bodied economic policy, not just a tax policy', public services would be well-funded, and the party would no longer peddle an 'opt-out culture of helping a few more people to escape' them. He reiterated his commitment to addressing climate change and the idea of a 'national school leaver programme', which he had trumpeted as Shadow Education Secretary. Then came the signal that he would try to confront the widely held perception that the party did not care about society. 'There is such a thing as society. It's just not the same thing as the state.' As everyone in his audience knew, this was a reference to one of the most quoted (and paraphrased) remarks made by Mrs Thatcher – 'There is no such thing as society.' Without directly repudiating her legacy, it was a clear indication that he intended to mark out different territory for the party. David Cameron may well have been a child of Thatcher, but this was an explicit recognition of the fact that the Conservative Party had to move on beyond the long shadow that had been cast over it since her downfall in 1990.

'If you want me, and all of us, to be a voice for hope, for optimism and for change, come and join us. In this modern, compassionate Conservative Party everyone is invited,' Cameron declared to rapturous applause. A real sense of euphoria swept the room: could this be the moment that the party put behind it the bitter recrimination and infighting of the past? Joined on the stage by his wife Samantha, who was seven months pregnant, the new leader savoured the moment. He knew that there were many tough battles ahead. Nevertheless, his campaign team hoped that his victory and his speech would send a clear and uplifting message to the party, and perhaps the country. 'He was not simply saying that we must be completely different from what went before,' says Ed Vaizey, a Cameron ally. 'It was more about stressing his optimism, his forward-looking nature and love of this country. The lesson we had learnt was that consistency would be of core importance.'[1] As the years ahead would show, this was a political virtue that could prove elusive.

'He Was the Future Once'

The next day David Cameron made his Commons debut as Leader of the Opposition. He had stood at the dispatch box only rarely since his promotion to the education brief, owing partly to the long summer recess, but he and Osborne were well-versed at preparing for Prime

Minister's Questions, and they had more than enough material with which to turn the much parodied 'heir to Blair' remark into an effective script. Cameron chose the subject of the government's plans for school reform, which as Shadow Education Secretary he had pledged to support. Blair's proposed 'trust schools', which would grant secondary schools more autonomy from local authorities, were similar to the 'grant-maintained' schools introduced during the last years of the Conservative government in the 1990s. He knew that Blair faced a large rebellion on the Labour benches, which threatened to obstruct the legislation in the Commons. Supporting the reforms would demonstrate that Cameron was serious about a more constructive approach to opposition on issues of cross-party agreement. It would also make life difficult for Blair by exposing him to attack from the rebels on the left of his party.

The Commons was even more boisterous than usual for Cameron's debut as opposition leader. As he rose to his feet, Tory MPs cheered and waved their order papers in support. 'With our support the Prime Minister knows there is no danger of losing his reforms in a parliamentary vote, so he can afford to be as bold as he wants to be – that's when he's at his best, or so I am told,' he declared, mocking Blair's claim a few years before that Labour was 'best when at its boldest'.[2] Faces on the government frontbench were noticeably glum. 'I want to talk about the future,' Cameron declared, before looking straight across at Blair. 'He was the future once.' Well-rehearsed and primed for delivery, the jibe hit its target. Blair's relationship with the Parliamentary Labour Party, and with his Chancellor, Gordon Brown, had been under strain since the general election. The Brownites were anxious that the Prime Minister step down much sooner than his declared intention to 'serve a full third term'.

Blair's body language was noticeably awkward during his first exchange with Cameron, perhaps because he felt his words had a ring of truth. He was reaching the end-game of his long rivalry with Gordon Brown, who was desperate to move into Number 10. However, Blair was determined to press ahead with his education reforms, even if he had to rely on Conservative votes in the Commons.

'Tony knew that this man was different – he got it, and the Tory Party was going to be a very different animal at the next election, and any attempt to attack them as the same old Tories would be doomed,' recalls one of Blair's Downing Street aides. 'On one level, he just admired the "You were the future once" line – he thought it was clever politics. But his view was that we had to go for Cameron on whether he was really up to it: was he a substantial enough person who could seriously change his party?' Blair may have identified both the tactical skill and the potential flaws of his new opponent, but for the remainder of his premiership he was unable to prevail in framing a counterattack. On the one hand, Blairites tried to exploit the new Tory leader's 'vagueness' on policy, while on the other the Brownites tried to label him an unreconstructed Thatcherite.

The more perceptive Cabinet ministers realised that they had a problem, as the uncertainty over when Blair was going to step down was likely to grow. 'We faced an opposition that was at last functioning, which meant that we had to refresh ourselves; but that was difficult, because we simply didn't know how long Tony was going to last,' said one.[3]

Cameron had got the better of Blair on his first outing at Prime Minister's Questions. However, he continued to watch and to learn from a Prime Minister who had no intention of leaving Number 10 just yet. 'David realised the wheels were coming off the Blair chariot in 2005 and that people were getting fed up with him,' a close confidant recalls. 'He relished his jousts with Blair, but often remarked that he had a lightness of touch and an ability as a politician that was something to behold.' Cameron may well have been exposing Blair's vulnerability after more than eight years in office, but he needed to look no further than the Blair of a decade earlier for inspiration on how to run a party in opposition.

Friends Reunited

David Cameron's preparations for the leadership were very different from those of his recent predecessors. Unlike them, he had the advantage of having ample time to plan what he would do in his first weeks and months. Spurred on by the expectation of an emphatic victory in the leadership contest, he and his closest colleagues began to plan for the first six weeks of his leadership in the final stretch of the contest. At the heart of his team were Steve Hilton, George Osborne, Michael Gove and Oliver Letwin. As the most senior figure of the quartet, Letwin would preside over a wide-ranging review of policy covering most of the key themes. Osborne remained as Shadow Chancellor, while Gove, having only just been elected as an MP, was given no formal role, although his candid advice and skills as a wordsmith remained important. Finally, Cameron asked Hilton to be his chief strategist. As one his oldest political friends, Hilton would have enormous influence over the direction of the 'Cameron project'.

Reuniting the Smith Square set of friends from the early 1990s, Cameron had already enlisted the help of Edward Llewellyn and Catherine Fall during the summer. Having assisted Chris Patten in Hong Kong and Paddy Ashdown in Bosnia Herzegovina, Llewellyn was a natural choice to be chief of staff of the new leader's office. Described as 'congenial but cautious', Llewellyn would bring order to the operation, assisted by Fall, who had worked in Howard's office and had been director of the think tank the Atlantic Partnership. The team set up shop in Norman Shaw South, the suite of offices Howard had occupied across the road from the Palace of Westminster. Cameron and Osborne had interconnecting offices, confirming the Shadow Chancellor's importance in the new regime. Cameron also lined up another friend from the Major and Howard years, George Bridges, to become Director of Research and a key conduit with party headquarters on 1 January 2006.

One notable absentee was Rachel Whetstone. She had played a crucial role in the promotion of Cameron and Osborne to the summit of the Tory Party, but the revelation in August 2004 of her affair with Lord Astor, Cameron's stepfather-in-law, made her *persona non grata*. Her probing mind and political realism would have been a real asset within Cameron's inner circle, but she now left politics to head Google's corporate communications in Europe. Apart from Whetstone, there was a degree of continuity from the Howard regime.

Steve Hilton, Kate Fall and George Eustice, who became Cameron's press secretary, had all played significant roles under Howard. However, no replacement was found for Guy Black, who had been Howard's Director of Communications, with overarching responsibility for relations with the media. Cameron also lacked someone to replace Lynton Crosby to take overall charge of Campaign Headquarters. These two vacancies would become painfully apparent in the months ahead.

The inner circle surrounding the new leader, which soon came to be known as 'Team Cameron', comprised the quartet of Osborne, Hilton, Gove and Letwin; Llewellyn and Fall who ran the private office; and Bridges and Eustice, who ran the party's political and media operation. What united most of them was their long history of friendship and, of course, their youth. None of them, with the exception of Letwin, had reached the age of forty. 'It was a very tight group from the very beginning,' says one aide who worked in the private office. 'George, Steve and sometimes Michael and Oliver would meet at David's house in Finstock Road [in North Kensington] on Sunday evenings to discuss where to go next.' The other characteristic they had in common was their class background. Many had attended the same schools and universities, principally Eton and Oxford. Llewellyn was an exact contemporary of Cameron's at Eton (and Oxford), while Bridges, who was slightly younger, and Letwin also attended the school. Much was made in the press about the return of the Old Etonians to run the Tory Party, evoking memories of the Macmillan and Douglas-Home era in the late 1950s and early 1960s, when a fifth of the parliamentary party had been to Eton.[4] Was the return of the 'Tory toffs' not a retrograde step for a party that had sought to shed its elitist image in the 1970s and '80s under Edward Heath and Margaret Thatcher, both of whom were seen as champions of aspiration and social mobility? Indeed, Douglas Hurd's Etonian education had been considered a factor that harmed his chances of succeeding Mrs Thatcher in 1990, in contrast to John Major's humble beginnings.

Fifteen years later, David Davis's roots could not have been more different from Cameron's, but the issue of class hardly made a difference in determining the outcome of the leadership election. Cameron's stock answer to suggestions that privilege should have barred him from the job was that it mattered more 'where you were going than where you came from'. There was no hiding the fact that he and many of his allies came from wealthy backgrounds, a perceived weakness that opponents inside and outside the party would be keen to exploit. The measure of Cameron and his allies' success would be in persuading the public and sceptical commentators alike that social privilege did not disqualify them from broadening the party's appeal beyond narrow and increasingly outdated class lines. Now that they had reached the top of the party, they had to rebut the claim that it was Labour that stood for 'the many and not the few'.

With a close unit of trusted aides around him, Cameron recognised that his Shadow Cabinet would have to reflect the balance of opinion and personalities in the party. Unlike his rivals, he had made a point of not promising any jobs during the early stages of the contest. On the day before the result was announced, he sounded out David Davis about remaining as Shadow Home Secretary. 'I told him that I was very happy to continue, or go back to the backbenches if he felt more comfortable with that, but I didn't want to go to defence, which was being talked about at the time,' recalls Davis.[5] While Davis continued in his post, Liam Fox was offered the defence brief. Davis's campaign manager, Andrew Mitchell, was given the international development brief. Ken Clarke was offered the role of Shadow Leader of the Commons, but chose to remain on the backbenches, where he could speak freely and pursue other interests. However, he would occasionally speak from the frontbench on constitutional matters, having agreed to lead a new 'Democracy Taskforce'. Sir Malcolm Rifkind had coveted the foreign affairs portfolio, having served as Major's last Foreign Secretary, but Cameron chose not to offer him the role. In not deferring to one of the party's elder statesman, the new leader showed that he was prepared to be ruthless. It was a telling indication of how he would manage his team in the years to come.

In his most high-profile appointment, Cameron announced that William Hague would be Shadow Foreign Secretary. 'We discussed it on and off a few weeks before the leadership election,' recalls Hague. 'When it looked likely that he was going to win, we talked again. I wasn't desperate to come back to frontline politics – it was a border-line decision for me, and I probably wouldn't have done unless David had been elected. The foreign affairs job was the only one I would come back for.'[6] Since resigning the leadership in 2001, Hague had carved out a career as an accomplished biographer and after-dinner speaker. His stock had risen within the parliamentary party and the rank and file, with his contributions to foreign policy debates in the Commons particularly noteworthy. Not only would he bring the wisdom of his experience, however difficult a period he had endured as leader, but he would be a reassuring presence at the top table for the party faithful. Cameron had not known Hague partic-ularly well up to this point, but he had enormous respect for the former party leader. Hague's importance to the new regime would grow by the day.

Nearly all who were asked to serve rallied to the cause. One man who could not be labelled a son of privilege was the new Chief Whip, Patrick McLoughlin. A former coal miner from Staffordshire, he was a rare breed on the Tory benches. McLoughlin was a long-serving figure in the party, having been a member of the Whips' Office since 1995 and an MP since 1986, and his promotion from Deputy to Chief Whip was reassuring to many backbenchers. Other figures from the generation above Cameron were also given leading roles, including the arch-moderniser Francis Maude, who continued as Party Chairman, and Andrew Lansley, David Willetts, Theresa May and Alan Duncan.

Cameron's 'Big Tent'

The eye-catching appointments came not so much in the new Shadow Cabinet, as in the wider net that Cameron cast for his review of party policy. Six main policy groups were set up to tackle the challenges he referred to in his acceptance speech: the 'quality of life', public service improvement, economic competitiveness, national and international security, globalisation and global poverty, and social justice. On his first full day as leader, Cameron would launch the social justice group on a visit to the East Side Youth Academy, a project for black teenagers in Newham, east London. He was accompanied by the man who had been deposed as leader barely two years before – Iain Duncan Smith. Like William Hague, Duncan Smith had grown in stature since leaving the leadership. His preoccupation with poverty and other social problems, such as family breakdown and drug abuse, through the work of the Centre for Social Justice (CSJ), had won him plaudits inside and outside the party. Shortly after the general election, the CSJ published a pamphlet, *Good for Me, Good for My Neighbour*, co-written by Duncan Smith and his former aide Danny Kruger (who subsequently joined Cameron's office as a speechwriter), in which they argued that the party could only recover if it 'cared about the way people lived their lives' and developed policies that would lift people out of poverty and deprivation.[7] Duncan Smith was now about to embark on an even bigger project with the CSJ: a 'state of the nation' audit.

As the leadership election drew to a close, Cameron had approached the former leader and said, 'Look, I think you are right about what you're doing and what you were trying to do as leader, and we were not generous enough as a party in supporting you on this. If I'm elected, will you pick this baton up for us?' Duncan Smith accepted in principle.[8] A few weeks before the leadership result was announced he told Oliver Letwin, who had been charged with directing the policy review, that he was willing to lead one of the six policy groups, on the condition that it would be outside the party's control and conducted in the public domain. He also asked to be joined by Debbie Scott, a respected figure in the charity world. Cameron and Letwin agreed to Duncan Smith's group having a greater degree of autonomy than the others. By making the announcement of the social justice group the first of his leadership, Cameron was demonstrating that the 'modern compassionate' Conservative Party he promised would draw heavily on the course that one of his predecessors tried and failed to set. In his new guise, Duncan Smith would become an increasingly influential voice in the new regime. It was an incredible transformation for a man many had written off only a few years before.

Over the next six weeks Cameron unveiled the other five groups, pacing the announcements across the Christmas period to maximise publicity. 'All our policies are under review,' he declared.[9] The policy review lay at the heart of the Cameron project to change the party. Not only would it seek to demonstrate to the outside world that the party was determined to rethink all of its policies, but it would provide a wide menu of options from which to choose in time for the next election. The new leadership called on the services of old and new hands, establishment and non-establishment, to head the policy groups. Peter Lilley, the former Cabinet minister and deputy leader who had tried to steer Hague's policy review after 1997, would take charge of the Globalisation and Global Poverty Group. He would receive advice from the rock star and activist Bob Geldof. This was a huge coup: Geldof's anti-poverty campaigns, beginning with Band Aid in 1984, had had a high profile worldwide; the most recent of them, Live 8, had influenced the government's approach before the G8 summit earlier in the year. Unveiled on 28 December, the announcement caught the media's attention during the relatively quiet period after Christmas.

Pairing former Cabinet ministers who were independent of the new leadership with experts who had little or no connection to the party would provide the template for the other four groups: the former Environment Secretary, John Gummer, was joined by Zac Goldsmith, son of the late Sir James Goldsmith (who founded the Referendum Party) and the youthful editor of the *Ecologist* and environmental campaigner, to run the Quality of Life Group; John Redwood (brought in from the cold after several years on the back-benches) would return to chair the Economic Competitiveness Group with Simon Wolfson, chief executive of Next clothing company; the former Health Secretary Stephen Dorrell would jointly chair the Public Services Group with Pauline Perry, a former Chief Inspector of Schools; and the National and International Security Group would be chaired by the former Defence Secretary Lord King and Dame Pauline Neville-Jones, a former chairman of the Joint Intelligence Committee. The unveiling of the groups and their chairmen attracted favourable coverage in the media, keeping the spotlight firmly on the new regime.

Oliver Letwin believed the policy review would inform the 'process of discovery' that Cameron had embarked upon as leader. 'We were trying not to make detailed statements about policy early on, because we wanted to state what kind of Conservative Party we wanted it to be,' he recalls.[10] The groups would try to provide answers to the challenges Cameron had identified at the Royal Academy on his first day as leader. Under his leadership the party would not confine itself to a narrow range of issues with which it had been associated for the best part of a decade.

Cameron acknowledges that opening up the policy review to outsiders presented risks: the groups could well come back with 'bad' ideas. 'He felt that we needed to engage with new ideas,' says a close aide. 'He said to us that it could get very messy and difficult.' The Cameron 'big tent' had been opened, and the hope was that people would begin to notice. 'We needed to correct the widespread perception that we weren't interested in poverty, climate change and the developing world, and that we were half-hearted about the NHS and not concerned with economic stability,' says Letwin. 'It's not that we hadn't addressed these subjects before; they just hadn't been given the prominence they deserved.'[11]

Shock Therapy

The policy groups were given eighteen months to report back, allowing the leadership a period in which to paint broad brush strokes. Travelling light on detailed policy in the first year of a four- or five-year electoral cycle was sensible politics for an opposition party. While Labour and the Liberal Democrats inevitably described the Conservatives as an empty vessel, an undeterred Cameron and his inner circle planned drastic changes to the party's image. They

223

had won a resounding mandate, and this might be their one and only chance. During a series of speeches in mid-December 2005 and early January 2006, Cameron and Osborne marked out the territory the party sought to occupy. In doing so, they sought to depart from some of the contentious and unpopular positions that had brought defeat at the last general election. Among the first commitments they made were promises to put economic stability above upfront tax cuts, to support a publicly funded NHS which provided 'free access to high-quality healthcare' rather than subsidising the wealthy to escape it, to allow greater autonomy for state schools without a return to selection through more grammar schools, and support for university tuition fees.

Cameron's speech on health at the King's Fund was instructive. When asked by reporters whether he would regret ruling out private insurance, he was unapologetic, showing a strategic certainty that his predecessors had lacked. Gone were the 'patient's and pupil's passports', or any hint that the party wanted a return to the old 11-plus exams and the desire to slash taxes without consideration for the state of the public finances. Even more striking was a commitment from Oliver Letwin that the party's aim should be to narrow the gap between rich and poor: 'We do redistribute money and we should redistribute money.'[12] In what was considered a snub to big business, Cameron also criticised WH Smith for promoting half-price Chocolate Oranges instead of real oranges at its checkouts. If individuals had to take 'social' responsibility for themselves and others, so should business, he argued. 'In the past Conservative governments were uncritical of big business. If we wanted to win, we had to show that a future Tory administration would be different,' insists one of Cameron's close aides. 'Every day, it seems, David Cameron finds some new Conservative household god to trash,' a leader column in the *Guardian* observed. 'All over the scene, the new Conservative hierarchy is repudiating the harshness of Thatcherite teaching.'[13]

The first ten weeks of Cameron's leadership were, in the words of Steve Hilton, intended to give the party 'shock therapy'. Others described it as decontaminating or detoxifying the brand, a phrase Hilton considered too negative. 'We devised a daily grid which listed everything we wanted to do up to the end of January,' recalls one senior aide to Cameron. 'It was all about showing, this is who we are, and not what people expected the Tory Party to be about.' In order to make this happen, the leadership and Campaign Headquarters would have to go into overdrive. Every Thursday or Friday the team would meet to finalise plans for the following week. Poring over the colour-coded grid of key themes, the operation felt 'like a general election campaign', George Bridges recalls. 'Everyone was working at breakneck speed; there was a real sense of excitement.'[14] At the heart of the operation was Hilton, whose frenetic energy infected the rest of the team. 'Steve was taken with this graph which showed how previous leaders had begun positively for the first three months and then perceptions about them would crash,' recalls George Eustice. 'It was a desire not to repeat previous mistakes and lose momentum that really drove him.'[15]

The early decisions Cameron took with Osborne were infused with Hilton's zeal. Following a political grounding at the Conservative Research Department in the early 1990s, Hilton was taken under Maurice Saatchi's tutelage before going into business. Brought back into the party fold by Michael Howard, Hilton was primed for Cameron's campaign. As chief strategist, he had an opportunity to put his ideas into practice, believing that they would be the antidote to the party's tired and discredited image. 'Steve understood how people reacted to us through his focus group work,' says Bridges, who had travelled around the country with him during 2004.[16] 'We were trying to establish a clear vision for what we wanted the party to be – it was all about attitudes and values,' says one of the inner circle. 'It was completely different to what Labour had to do, which was to abandon some of their core beliefs. Our basic Conservatism was still there, but we had to change our priorities and our personality as a party.' Those priorities were stressing the value of the public services, 'sharing' responsibility throughout society, and the importance of family life. Added to these was the idea of conserving the environment for future generations.

By projecting Cameron and the Conservatives as champions of the environment, Hilton was confident of arousing new interest in the party. Climate change had risen to the top of the international agenda in July 2005 when Blair hosted the G8 summit at Gleneagles. It made sense for the Conservatives to seize the issue from the Prime Minister as his star began to fade. To those who know Hilton and Cameron, this was not a cynical exercise. 'Although Steve is David's alter ego, the green agenda was entirely authentic to David. Both of them believed in it deeply,' says Andrew Cooper.[17]

From day one Cameron would embody the 'greening' of the Conservative Party, cycling to the House of Commons and erecting a wind turbine on top of his London home. In the most audacious publicity exercise of all, Cameron travelled with a camera crew to the Arctic Circle, where he sledged with huskies. The trip was mocked by critics, particularly as Cameron's own carbon footprint had grown by the fact that he had flown there. But it provided arresting images, and during the first few months of 2006 the public profile of the party began to change. There had been embarrassing setbacks, however: photographs of Cameron's shoes and briefcase being driven behind him in his official car as he cycled from Kensington to Westminster attracted considerable ridicule. Even the wind turbine installed on his house (at a reputed cost of £3,000) drew scorn – not everyone had the means to display their green credentials so overtly, and it was reported that such turbines produced only negligible amounts of electricity. But for younger voters, and middle-class voters who had fled the party for the Liberal Democrats (which had been the most environmentally friendly party) in recent years, it showed the Tories in a more positive light.

As a self-professed 'liberal Conservative', Cameron made an explicit appeal to Liberal Democrats to jump ship. While the government entered a turbulent period and Liberal Democrat MPs lost confidence in their leader, Charles Kennedy, the polls began to turn. In December 2005 the Conservatives jumped four points, to an average rating of 37 per cent. In some polls they reached the psychologically impor- tant 40 per cent barrier which an opposition had to pass to be in contention for winning office. Most significantly, the monthly average of opinion polls showed that the Tories had overtaken Labour (who fell to 35 per cent) for the first time since August 1992.[18]

The first real test of public opinion was fast approaching. In April 2006 Hilton and Bridges conceived the 'Vote Blue, Go Green' slogan ahead of the local elections in May. 'It was the most optimistic campaign we ever had,' recalled Bridges. 'I was a little more sceptical because I was conscious that we had to make it about making lives better by saving people money as well as saving the environment.' The campaign would encourage both modest measures such as recycling and more serious efforts to encourage energy conservation and less polluting forms of transport, such as hybrid or electric cars. The trademark phrase became 'It's not just the quantity of money that matters, but the quality of life'. Labour counterattacked with an election broadcast showing a chameleon called 'Dave' changing colours as he rode around on a bicycle. 'It was great for us, because it reinforced the fact that we were changing,' recalls Bridges.[19] It certainly did Cameron no harm.

Labour's mounting difficulties that spring also worked to the Conservatives' advantage. In April the government had been hit by Home Office fiascos, including confusion over the release of foreign prisoners and the Health Secretary, Patricia Hewitt, being jeered at a nurses' conference. The revelation of John Prescott's affair with his diary secretary was also damaging for the government. Claims that the Labour Party had accepted 'loans for peerages' before the 2005 general election continued to reverberate around Westminster, particularly as it became clear that these allegations reached all the way to Number 10. Blair's brief Indian summer after the 2005 election seemed ancient history. On the same day that the 'loans for peerages' story broke, the Prime Minister had to rely on Tory votes to get his much trumpeted education bill through the Commons. For a government with a healthy majority of sixty-seven, it was a harbinger of decline.

The government's difficulties could not have been more timely for the Conservatives. Achieving 40 per cent of the projected national share of the vote in town hall elections on 4 May, fourteen points ahead of Labour in third place, for the first time in any election since 1992 showed that the Cameron project was beginning to bear fruit. There was a palpable sense that the party was on the move, recovering ground that had been lost for well over a decade. 'The local elections were a very important moment,' recalls one of the inner circle. 'The results were not spectacular, but we were making progress.' There were signs that the Conservatives, rather than the Liberal Democrats, had become the beneficiary of Labour's unpopularity in office. Gaining 316 councillors and control of eleven councils, the party continued to recover in Greater London, south-east England and parts of the Midlands. The weak spots continued to be cities in the north of England, where despite the efforts of the new leadership (which included holding a Shadow Cabinet meeting in Liverpool and the party's spring conference in Manchester), not one council seat fell to its advance. Rebuilding a presence in urban Britain away from the South-East would not be easy. 'The local elections were a massive confidence boost, but we didn't take anything for granted,' recalls Bridges. 'We knew that we needed to do more in the North, and we were also aware that Labour's problems helped us. We had to keep going.'[20]

Searching for that Clause IV Moment

David Cameron was blessed with a six-month honeymoon as leader. His energy and determination to change and reposition the party had mostly impressed commentators in the media, and the favourable coverage he won contrasted with the appalling headlines the government was receiving. As Blair's authority was on the wane, his self-styled 'heir' was taking full advantage. If Cameron's comment at the *Telegraph* dinner in Blackpool the previous autumn had unsettled the right of the party, the fact that during his first few months as leader he seemed to emulate Blair – both in style and substance – caused further consternation among those in the party who were already nervous. The green campaign had given the party faithful something to sell on the doorsteps, but it was unfamiliar merchandise.

'The problem was that it was quite difficult to ask the blue-rinse brigade so soon after David became leader to campaign on green issues – they just didn't get it,' recalls Daniel Ritterband, who had worked on the Cameron leadership campaign and was now assisting Hilton at party headquarters.[21] Cameron candidly admits that many of the grassroots thought he had lost his senses when he launched the 'Vote Blue, Go Green' slogan. Yet he believes that they gradually took to it. In fact many activists tolerated the campaign because it seemed to be working. They may not have fallen in love with the idea of 'greening' their party, but they recognised its strength as a tactical exercise.

Despite the mood of optimism, Team Cameron realised that more had to be done to connect with the grassroots. 'There was a sense that the rest of the party didn't quite understand what we were doing, so we had to bring them onside,' recalls Bridges. 'We needed something to latch on to as a script.'[22] The party's internal polling also revealed that although David Cameron had made a favourable impression on the public, they still did not believe that the party as a whole had changed for the better. The green campaign had been a start, but decontaminating the Tory brand would need to be underpinned by much more than just Cameron's persona. Once again, the example of Blair's efforts to modernise the Labour Party became the subject of discussion. Rewriting Clause IV of the party's constitution, to show that it no longer supported the nationalisation of industry as a totemic goal, had been a means of demonstrating to the electorate that the party had changed. Taking the measure to a special conference of the Labour Party in 1995 increased Blair's standing with the public, proving that he had the courage to take on his party.

Cameron, however, did not believe that the Conservatives needed to have their own 'Clause IV moment'. 'He also felt that the first-generation modernisers, like Portillo, didn't succeed because they had a real contempt for the old party. David's view was that there was nothing wrong with our members, and that we shouldn't pick a fight with them,' recalls a former aide. In truth, he may well have been exasperated by their resistance to change. Osborne, in contrast, took far more inspiration from New Labour's experience in opposition. 'He frames everything we need to do in terms of "This is what Labour did." David felt that we had to rediscover things that we had always believed in, whereas George thought it was more about ditching unpopular ideas.' Osborne's desire to modernise the party was more marked than Cameron's. He was impatient, whereas Cameron, who had been jolted into action only after the 2005 defeat, did not have quite the same appetite for confrontations.

The deliberations ended in a messy compromise. On 28 February the leadership unveiled a consultation document entitled *Built to Last*, which restated many of the familiar lines from Cameron's campaign in the autumn and his first hundred days as leader. According to the document, the party aimed to create a 'dynamic economy, strong society and sustainable environment' by 'trusting people and sharing responsibility'.[23] It would be put to a ballot of party members for their agreement in time for the conference in October. Critics on the right were not enthused. 'Every one of those things could be listed in a Labour manifesto,' Lord Tebbit complained.[24] By and large Tebbit was correct. Much of the language did indeed echo the goals and priorities established by New Labour. But Tebbit's criticism rather misses the point. The document's greatest weakness was that it was a damp squib. *Built to Last* was no more than a rerun of Cameron's arguments during the leadership election. If the leadership had been bolder, it would have sought to make the case for change in much more explicit terms. Not only was the text vague, it lacked political punch. It could have advocated the 'ten-thousand-volt' shock treatment of the 'Kitchen Table' strategy that William Hague had failed to implement in 1998. Instead, it did not challenge the traditionally right-wing agenda that many of the modernisers believed was still the party's default position.

As for the rank and file, they were bewildered. Why were they being asked to endorse something that was being presented as a *fait accompli*? Only 29.6 per cent of the party membership bothered to vote in the ballot, hardly a ringing endorsement on the eve of

Cameron's first party conference as leader. *Built to Last* had become an embarrassment for the leadership. 'It didn't really work,' admits one of Cameron's former aides. Finding a balance between revitalising the party and offering constant reassurance was not going to be easy. Yet if Cameron was going to take advantage of his honeymoon and push the case for change to the wider party, this would have been the moment. It was a missed opportunity, and one for which the leadership took full blame.

Local Difficulties

If *Built to Last* had been a damp squib, challenging the traditional independence of local activists in choosing the party's MPs would really ruffle feathers among the grassroots. But it was a specific promise Cameron had made during the leadership election, when he had decried the lack of women and ethnic minorities in the parliamentary party (only seventeen women – just 9 per cent – and one black and one Asian MP were elected in 2005, out of a total of 198). All too often they were selected for seats that the party had no hope of winning: only three of the party's gains in 2005 produced women MPs. On becoming leader, Cameron imposed a freeze on the selection of candidates, to allow the party to draw up a 'Priority List' to compete for the 160 or so most winnable seats at the next general election. The target was for an equal balance of men and women, and a proportion of ethnic minorities (around 8 per cent) that reflected the general population. 'Until we're represented by men and women in the country, regardless of race or creed, we won't be half the party we could be,' he announced in a speech in Leeds. This 'positive action' plan was not about 'crazed political correctness', he said.[25] In April, Campaign Headquarters published new guidelines for local associations. They were also encouraged to solicit greater local involvement, possibly through American-style primaries. Crucially, the new rules would not be compulsory. Associations from the designated seats could still exercise the right to choose a local candidate from the larger list of approved candidates, rather than from the Priority List.

When the first names on the list were revealed in May, the press had a field day. The party chose not to publish what had become known as the 'A-List', but most of the names were posted on the ConservativeHome.com website. They included a sprinkling of celebrities, such as the actor Adam Rickitt from the television soap *Coronation Street*, and Zac Goldsmith, who was chairing the party's Quality of Life Policy Group. Many were labelled as 'Cameron's cronies'. They were primarily young and based in London, and often had very few connections with the seats in question. Local associations jealously guarded their historical independence in selecting candidates – after all, they would ultimately have to campaign for their candidate come the election. The Howard Flight affair just before the 2005 general election showed how divisive interference from the centre could be. Many associations were being asked to choose from a list of people they hardly recognised or felt were qualified to become MPs. 'This was heresy to some people in the party,' recalls a former member of Cameron's team. 'Any suggestion that we were loading the dice was abhorrent to them. It caused us a lot of problems, because we were treading on their toes and their self-interest.'

Meanwhile, a large number of candidates who did not make it onto the list became disenchanted. Many had pounded the streets come rain or shine for years. 'There were about 190 people who could have been MPs had we not done so disastrously in 1997, 2001 and 2005. They were very much the children of Thatcher and had seen their chances thwarted,' says one party official. 'Now here's David Cameron effectively telling them to get lost. The rage was very real.' Campaign Headquarters was inundated with calls from Tory MPs who had connections with disappointed aspiring candidates. 'They would say, "Can't you make an exception for so and so?" ' As the summer progressed, a number of local associations in the 'winnable seats' selected candidates who were not on the A-List. Would the party go further, and compel local parties to choose from the list? Francis Maude, the Party Chairman, was determined to press on, although he promised to review the arrangements after six months. 'None of us was ever satisfied with the progress, but there was a sense that we were getting there,' he recalls.[26] The seeds were being sown for a potentially damaging dispute between the grassroots and the leadership in the months to come.

Another internal matter that caused difficulty midway through 2006 was Cameron's pledge to leave the centre-right European People's Party (EPP) in the European Parliament. Many of the other Continental centre-right parties in the group, such as the German Christian Democrats, were supportive of further European integration, in contrast to the increasingly Eurosceptic position of the Tories. Those in Cameron's inner circle claim that he had been sceptical about the party's continuing membership of the EPP ever since the early 1990s, and he had made no secret of his Euroscepticism throughout his career. 'The big difference about our generation of moderates in the party was that you could be Eurosceptic and a liberal Conservative on other issues,' says Michael Gove. 'Until the late 1990s, that just wasn't the case.'[27] However, critics argued that withdrawal from the EPP would leave the party isolated in Europe. Indeed, it was naïve for the leadership to assume that there would be no long-term consequences to the move.

The new leader was obliged to make good on the promise he had made during the leadership election while courting support among MPs who might otherwise have backed David Davis or Liam Fox. 'It was undoubtedly made to guarantee the support of some colleagues,' recalls a former Shadow minister. 'They hadn't really thought about it. It was impossible to deliver it cleanly straight away. Our problem was that our MEPs had signed in blood only a few years beforehand that they would continue to sit in the EPP until 2009.' Added to this was the fact Tory MEPs were divided on how to proceed. Some were far more enthusiastic about European integration than their counterparts in Westminster, while others were even more Eurosceptic, and wanted to leave the EPP immediately. There was a real danger that the twenty-seven-strong group of Tory MEPs would split if Cameron went ahead with the decision to leave immediately. The prospect of forging an alliance with fringe parties on the right in Eastern Europe, whose controversial views on a range of subjects attracted growing attention from the Tories' opponents and from critics in the press at home, was also undermining the leadership's position.

The ill-thought-through commitment presented an unnecessary headache for Cameron and William Hague in the first few months of 2006. In July, the leadership struck a compromise. Cameron signed a declaration with the leader of the largest centre-right party in the Czech Republic to form a new non-federalist grouping in the European Parliament after the 2009 European elections. In the meantime, Tory MEPs would continue to sit in the EPP. Finding other credible partners on the right would prove to be problematic, but for the time being the deal diffused a source of tension.

Feeling the Strain

By July 2006, Cameron's honeymoon as leader was over. The first real warning sign came on 29 June. In May the unexpected death of Eric Forth, who had been a keen supporter of the Davis campaign, triggered a by-election in the safe seat of Bromley and Chislehurst, on the suburban border between London and Kent. It was the first by-election in a Tory-held seat since Cameron became leader. When the local association picked Bob Neill, a local member of the Greater London Assembly and a white, male lawyer, it was perceived as a snub to the leadership. Even though it was not in a Priority List seat, the by-election could have provided an opportunity to show off a new-model Tory candidate to demonstrate Cameron's desire to change the face of the party.

The campaign was fought on local issues, with Cameron's image barely featuring in the party literature. It is hard to say whether this, or local concerns about the candidate, made more of an impact. Whatever the cause, the party struggled to get out its vote, and a huge Tory majority of over 13,000 was reduced to just 633. The Liberal Democrats had come close to taking one of the Conservatives' safest seats in the country. 'It sent a real shock into the system,' recalls George Bridges.[28] Bromley and Chislehurst confirmed that for all the presentational effort over the past six months, the party's notorious track record in fighting by-elections had not changed. Campaign Headquarters had failed to monitor the situation closely enough on the ground. It would be another two years before the party machine cranked into action in by-elections.

Behind the scenes, the operation was showing signs of battle fatigue. The creative energy from Steve Hilton had been relentless. 'We just didn't have any time to have conversations about our long-term plans because of the speed we were going at,' admits Bridges. 'It was quite unsettling for some people in CCHQ.'[29] Nick Boles says, 'Steve was really the driving force behind the more radical ideas. There just weren't the resources to take things steadily, so it was a bit cobbled together in the first six months.'[30] Hilton's unconventional working methods often grated with party officials. Some complained that he would intervene at the last minute, disrupting planning processes that he had ignored until that point. He encouraged the party to spend large sums on advertising and website campaigns, seeking to create interest among young professional people who had never considered supporting the Conservative Party before. Highlighting personal debt (by means of a website offering advice through a calculator game) was just one initiative that absorbed much creative effort and money, but made little impact on the general public.

Not everyone was enthusiastic about Hilton. 'Steve has a brilliant creative mind, but his weakness is in his organisation. The sense of a dysfunctional organisation came from Steve,' recalls one. 'He didn't deal with CCHQ even though he was driving the agenda, so there was a real mismatch.' Another remarked: '*If* there was a clear map of where the party was going, it was *only* in Steve's head.' This was not so much to do with day-to-day decisions as with the big picture of where Cameron was leading the party. If the inner circle were unsure of where the Tories were heading, particularly in terms of how the Cameron project connected to basic Conservative principles, there was little hope for the rest of the party, let alone the media and the country. One MP jealously observed: 'Through David, Steve has moulded the Conservatives to his view of the world. The Tory party is a Hilton party, not a Cameron party.'

This overstates the case. Hilton's creative energy and passion were what the party had so desperately lacked for much of its time out of office. He may have been the driving force behind Cameron's efforts to change the party, but he was not the only influential voice in the Tory leader's ear. In his role as Cameron's Senior Political and Parliamentary Adviser, the former whip and long-serving MP Andrew MacKay could be relied upon to give candid advice as a key conduit with the parliamentary party. 'He wanted somebody around like me who had experience and who believed in the project,' he says. 'While he often took my advice, when he didn't it turned out he was right and I was wrong. He could make the right calls.'[31]

The real weakness in the operation rested with Campaign Head-quarters, which remained ill-equipped to maintain the pace that was being set by the leader and his team. Many mourned the loss of Lynton Crosby, whose three-pillared structure of research, campaigns and media had improved the efficiency of the organisation. In fact Cameron had held serious discussions earlier in the year with Crosby about a possible return, but they came to nothing. Crosby regarded taking on the job of Campaign Director or Chief Executive so far away from an election campaign as an obstacle, as was his growing consultancy in Australia and Britain. 'It was a shame – he knew all the research and understood the problems we had to confront,' recalls a senior Cameron aide.

Another problem was that Lord Ashcroft, whom Cameron had appointed as the party's Deputy Chairman in charge of polling research and target seats, was operating outside Campaign Head-quarters. Although there was a direct exchange of information via Stephen Gilbert, who was working alongside Ashcroft as the Director of Field Campaigning, with party high command, the fact that such an important aspect of the party's operation was outside the machine was a hindrance. 'Stephen was not totally integrated,' recalls an aide. 'It was like someone trying to fly an aeroplane with one of the first officers trying to fly the plane from the wing; we needed him on the flight deck.' George Bridges was a much-liked figure in the organi-sation, but he struggled to cope with an enlarged and sprawling brief as Director of Research and Campaigning. 'The structure became more complicated than it had been in the general election,' recalls one insider. 'The whole operation lost focus. It did not help that all of Cameron and Osborne's staff were in Parliament. No one was really in charge at Campaign Headquarters.'

The introduction of 'social action projects' was another way of attempting to demonstrate that the party cared about local communities and ordinary people. Hilton recruited Rishi Saha, a former member of C-Change, to run small-scale projects in target seats, with the local candidate and activists helping to refurbish a community centre or improve a public space for local residents. Even this met with resistance. 'There was a lot of protest to some of this from some of the rank and file,' recalls Bridges. 'They didn't want to be social activists.'[32] This would incense Hilton. 'Steve would get very angry, particularly when MPs did not agree with what we were doing,' recalls a party official. 'He rightly saw the disconnection between what David Cameron was saying and the rest of the party.' Nevertheless, the social action projects steadily began to take root at a local level.

Cameron's inner circle was beginning to feel the strain. No more was this apparent than in a speech Cameron delivered on antisocial behaviour and justice on 10 July. 'We have to have justice – we have to fight crime firmly and completely,' he told the audience at Iain Duncan Smith's Centre for Social Justice. He then argued that while 'the consequence of stepping over the line should be painful', society had a duty to encourage people to stay within the boundaries of good behaviour. 'I believe that . . . we have to show a lot more love,' he said. Young people wearing 'hoodies' were often blamed as the perpetrators of antisocial behaviour, but they had been neglected, he claimed. 'We – the people in suits – often see hoodies as aggressive, the uniform of a rebel army of young gangsters. But, for young people, hoodies are often more defensive than offensive.' Cameron's message had echoes of Tony Blair's declaration as Shadow Home Secretary in 1993 that Labour would be 'tough on crime and tough on the causes of crime'.

The speech was well received in some quarters, particularly by children's charities and commentators on the centre-left. Andrew Rawnsley, a columnist at the *Observer*, was impressed. '[Cameron] argued for a sophisticated approach which would concentrate as much on the causes of crime as on its effects. He invited his audience to empathise with why young people became troubled. In an arresting phrase, designed to get the headlines that it did, he said: "We have to show a lot more love." This was not the sort of phrase that anyone would dream of hearing from Michael Howard.'[33] But when Rawnsley's own newspaper coined the mocking phrase 'Hug a hoodie' the following weekend, Labour spin doctors seized upon it, and Cameron was dubbed a 'soft liberal' by traditionalists on the right. Sir Nicholas Winterton, the Tory MP for Macclesfield, was bewildered. 'I'm not sure what my leader is seeking to do. Perhaps he is trying to be more inclusive, but that does not mean pandering to people who are antisocial.'[34]

Cameron's speechwriters were unrepentant about the 'hoodie speech', although political damage had been done. 'David was not pleased, as he felt he had lost ground with the tabloids on the right,' recalls Danny Kruger, who helped to craft the speech. 'I'll never regret that, because I think what we said was right.'[35] It was the first notable setback for Cameron in his relationship with the press, particularly on the right. 'Some people lost confidence in us – it was a slap in the face,' recalls one former aide. 'A lot of Middle England Tories didn't like it. It was a misjudgement and gave the right a stick to beat David with, particularly the *Daily Mail*.'

Photographs of a hooded teenager pretending to fire a gun behind Cameron's back as he walked through an estate in Manchester the following February showed just how problematic the speech had been. The A-List and the EPP commitment had so far been contained as internal rows, but the hoodie speech attracted widespread, if undeserved, derision. The tabloid press saw it as an opportunity to take Cameron to task after months of largely favourable coverage. Trying to understand why 'hoodies' behaved in the way they did was a subject for which tabloid editors had little time. Had relations between the leadership and the wider party not been so unsettled after the local elections in May, the speech might have received a better press. Nevertheless, Cameron's stock was falling as Parliament broke up for the summer. His first conference as leader had to be a success.

Bournemouth Whimper

The most important development over the summer occurred within Labour's ranks. Shortly after Tony Blair returned to Downing Street after his summer break, a number of Gordon Brown's allies in the Parliamentary Labour Party called on him to announce the date of his departure. This attempted 'September coup' followed a difficult summer for Blair: his unwillingness to challenge Israel over the war in Lebanon and his plea to 'Let me get on with the job' had incensed his critics. After twenty-four hours of intense discussions with Brown on 6–7 September, Blair agreed that he would stand down as Prime Minister before the 2007 Labour Party conference.[36] It appeared that Brown could be in Number 10 within the year.

The news was greeted with joy at Tory headquarters. 'There was huge respect for Blair born out of fear,' says one party official. 'There was absolute euphoria when the plotting spilled out into the open in September 2006. We were desperate to get stuck into Brown.' Cameron and Osborne began to rehearse their lines of attack. At the Budget in March, Cameron had described Brown as an 'analogue Chancellor in the digital age', and throughout the year they had sought to present the Conservatives as the party of genuine reform. Osborne, in particular, tried to paint the Chancellor as a 'roadblock to reform' for attempting to scupper Blair's third-term drive for choice and private sector involvement in the public services.

The end of Blair's decade in power was at last on the horizon. This should have been enough to lift the opposition's spirits as they headed for Bournemouth. However, the makings of a fight between the leadership and the right of the party tempered the optimism. The principal source of debate at the conference concerned tax, a traditional Tory bugbear if ever there was one. Lord Forsyth's Tax Commission, which Osborne had set up when he became Shadow Chancellor under Michael Howard, was due to publish its final report on 19 October, after the conference. Its interim proposals suggested some scope for cutting income tax and corporation tax, as well as a raft of measures to simplify the tax system. Speculation was rife about how far Forsyth, a well-known former Cabinet minister and Thatcherite, would go after parts of his report were leaked on the eve of the conference. One of the earliest and most important commitments Osborne and Cameron had made was not to offer 'upfront' tax cuts at the expense of 'sound money' or economic stability. Voices on the right of the party used a series of fringe events to make the exact opposite case: that growth and stability came about because of low levels of taxation.

When Osborne took to the conference platform for his speech as Shadow Chancellor he pledged to 'share the proceeds of growth' between tax cuts and investment in services. 'Offering unfunded tax cuts in the previous two elections was not a silver bullet,' says one of Osborne's team. 'We wanted to signal our priorities – we were much broader than just being the party of tax cuts. We wanted to show that we would be responsible with the nation's finances and provide good public services. It wasn't just a tactical manoeuvre.' Osborne's speech was politely received by delegates in the conference hall.

Behind the scenes, the leadership had fought a significant battle on tax, which could have consumed the conference far more publicly than it did. 'We saw off the right on tax,' one of Cameron's closest aides asserts. 'George in particular felt that we had to get away from this obsession with tax cuts as the only doctrine in Tory politics worth fighting for. It was the right fight to have.' In many ways, resisting the temptation to promise unfunded tax cuts, particularly in the first year of a four- or five-year Parliament, should have been hailed as the party's Clause IV moment. Giving in to the pressure from the right would have given Labour live ammunition to fire at Cameron and Osborne. Indeed, the argument that they were not taking on the old guard in their party on a key touchstone of Tory politics would have immediately strengthened. The leadership prevailed, but did not push home its advantage. 'David doesn't have the instinct to confront the party, but likes to take people with him,' one former aide observes. To stamp his authority on the party, he would need to demonstrate that he had the stomach for a fight.

There were high expectations for the finale of the conference: Cameron's first speech as leader. His performance in Blackpool the year before had wowed the faithful. Now he had to argue that the party could not afford to rest on its laurels. There could be no let-up: much more needed to be done to persuade the public that the Conservatives were attuned to their concerns. A fundamental commitment to a well-resourced and comprehensive NHS would therefore be at the heart of Cameron's set-piece address. Yet the team struggled to find a coherent theme beyond this commitment. 'There was a real sense of not knowing what to say in advance,' recalls one of his speechwriters, Danny Kruger. 'Steve and I had a long meeting to knock out some ideas. It was his first speech as leader, but all the policies were out to review. The night before the speech everyone agreed it was no good. Steve just sat down through the night on his own working on it.'[37] Hilton had improved it, but it was still far too long.

Cameron was not prepared to risk another off-the-cuff perform-ance: this time he would use the traditional lectern. The passage of the speech that caught most attention referred to Cameron's own experience of the NHS, and the care it provided for his son Ivan. 'For me, it's not a question of saying the NHS is safe in my hands. My family is so often in the hands of the NHS. And I want them to be safe there,' he told the audience. 'Tony Blair once explained his priority in three words: education, education, education. I can do it in three letters: N. H. S.'

Cameron touched on other issues that resonated with the rank and file. He emphasised his commitment to the family and supporting it through the tax system. But some heads turned when he said, 'And by the way, it means something whether you're a man and a woman, a woman and a woman or a man and another man.' The audience applauded generously after he ended with a line that captured some-thing of the sparkle of his Blackpool debut a year before: 'Let sunshine win the day.' Although the team was reasonably satisfied, 'The press didn't go crazy. They thought it was flabby,' recalls Kruger.[38] It certainly lacked the bravura of Cameron's 2005 performance.

As David Cameron approached his first anniversary as leader, he had gone further than any of his predecessors since 1997 in ridding the party of its negative image. Venturing into new and 'greener' pastures, he had aroused interest in the Conservative Party. It was no longer being written off as an irrelevance or a defunct force in British politics. However, the party was still a long way from being considered a potential alternative government. Dragging it away from its comfort zone had been far from straightforward. Indeed, the sheen of Cameron's leadership had been tarnished after an unsettling few months halfway through 2006. If there was a lesson to learn from his first year in the job, it was that the goodwill of the party could not be taken for granted. 'It was secure, but obviously people had reservations that David and George were young and inexperienced,' recalls a former aide. 'They had given them the benefit of the doubt.' The year ahead would provide ample opportunity for any doubts about the direction of David Cameron's Conservative Party to rise to the surface.

SEVEN

The Great Escape
January–October 2007

In the ten years that Tony Blair had occupied Number 10 Downing Street, he had seen off three Leaders of the Opposition. None of them had come close to dislodging his grip on power. Only David Cameron would outlast him. Despite a brief period when Blair was in full command in the summer of 2005, his authority waned throughout most of the following year. Desperate to install their man at the helm, Gordon Brown's allies could not wait to get their teeth into the new Tory leader. They despised everything about Cameron, from his privileged background to the way he had captured the political initiative from the government; by contrast, the Blairites were flattered by his tributes to the outgoing Prime Minister. Cameron had made much of the running in 2006, while frustrated Labour MPs lost faith in the leader who had brought them three election victories. Their hope was that a change of leadership would revive Labour's fortunes and expose an opponent they saw as a shallow public relations man leading a party bereft of policies. Although they were relaxed about Blair's impending departure, there was anxiety in Tory high command about the succession. But however they tried to portray the Chancellor in public, nothing would prepare them for the way in which the summer would unfold.

Waiting for Gordon
Cameron, Osborne and the team met at the beginning of January 2007 to work on a strategy for the year ahead. The focal point would be the expected transition from Blair to Brown over the summer. The Chancellor's personal poll ratings were not particularly strong,

despite his being credited by many voters with having delivered a stable economy over the past decade. Virtually every opinion poll since November 2005 that had asked people how they would vote if Brown was Labour leader rather than Blair showed the Conservative lead going up.[1] The line the Tory leadership had spun in 2006 was that Brown would undo Blair's third term reforms, which it agreed with, and would be a 'roadblock' to further reform as an old-fashioned command-and-control politician. Osborne in particular felt that Brown's fêted skills as a strategist were overrated. This was not a view shared by many in Cameron's inner circle. Surveys of public opinion showed that voters did not understand the 'roadblock' analogy, nor did they believe that Brown was an unreconstructed left-winger. If anything, the most resonant criticism of the Chancellor was that he had been complicit at every stage in the unfulfilled promise of Tony Blair, and was a jaded figure.

Aside from Osborne, many in Cameron's inner circle were apprehensive. 'Nobody knew what Gordon was going to be like – it was a great political conundrum,' recalls one former aide. 'No one underestimates Brown; it is absurd to do so,' said another at the time. 'If he takes on a constructive reform agenda, then it would be hard to deny him the support that we have given Blair on education, for example.' Cameron felt that they should not reach any premature conclusions about how to prepare for a Brown premiership. 'You can't control what the others do. You can only control what you do,' he told them. 'We just don't know whether he'll go left or right. We have to go on ploughing our furrow and build our support.' After a long discussion about Brown, the Shadow Cabinet decided to adopt a cautious attitude. 'There was a consensus that he was smart, strategic and did not have all the negatives that had built up around Blair over a decade,' recalls David Willetts, then Shadow Education Secretary. 'There was a lot of trepidation.'[2]

A-List Deal

Attention soon turned to matters closer to home. In an interview with the *Daily Telegraph* to mark his first anniversary as leader in

December 2006, David Cameron made an insightful remark: 'I don't go out of my way to annoy anybody, but I want to change the Conservative Party and get us back to the centre ground.'[3] This explains why he had not claimed victory over the tax battle at the Bournemouth conference a few months before. Yet attempts to make the party more representative of the country had become a source of annoyance for some. The A-List of parliamentary candidates had met with stubborn resistance from local associations since its introduction the previous spring. Something would have to give. Some of Cameron's allies had been bullish about taking on vested interests in the party. 'David has made his position clear that we need more women and ethnic minority candidates, and will take whatever measures he thinks appropriate. If there has to be blood on the carpet, then he will see those changes through,' said one just before Cameron was elected in December 2005. Twelve months later, a quarrel with the grassroots had all the signs of turning nasty.

Some form of compromise would have to be reached if further acrimony was to be avoided. Local Conservative associations complained that the calibre of candidates on the A-List was variable, and refused to select those who appeared to have made it onto the list by dint of their association with the leadership or by mere celebrity. By January 2007, nearly half of the prospective candidates who had been selected under the new system were not actually from the A-List. However, some progress had been made: nearly a third of candidates selected were women, although this fell short of the desired 50 per cent target. Don Porter, who was elected as Chairman of the National Convention in March 2006 (and thereby Deputy Chairman of the party board), had set up a working party to investigate the efficacy of the A-List. As a senior figure representing activists, he was concerned that the leadership was not aware of the strength of feeling among the rank and file. Having consulted with association chairmen around the country, he presented his findings to Cameron at a meeting in the Commons in late January. Cameron listened carefully to Porter: theirs was a good working relationship. While acknowledging the progress that had been made in selecting more women candidates,

Porter calmly argued that local associations should be free to select from the entire candidates' list rather than just the A-List (albeit with the proviso of a minimum of half the interviewees being women at all stages of the selection process). He secured agreement to this after Cameron and his aides had considered the proposal. 'It completely took the sting out of the situation,' recalls Porter. 'The associations were very happy that they could choose from the whole list.'[4]

Although the deal effectively rendered the A-List redundant, it had made an impact. A number of senior figures, including Francis Maude, Theresa May, Bernard Jenkin and latterly John Maples, had strived to make the process work. In future the face of the parliamentary party would potentially look quite different. Seventeen women Tory MPs were elected in 2005. That number could rise to sixty or more if the party won power at the next election. 'It was "show, don't tell" modernisation – a subliminal message of change,' says a party official. 'It makes it harder for Labour to say that we did not look like the rest of Britain, as they had done over the past fifteen years.' Candidates like the black youth worker Shaun Bailey, and Priti Patel, a former Central Office staffer, might not have been adopted were it not for the efforts of the party machine to promote women and ethnic minority candidates. Francis Maude was satisfied with the measured progress. 'It was not as much as we would have liked, but I'd still settle for one third of women candidates and 7 per cent ethnic minority candidates without resorting to compulsion.'[5]

The Porter compromise was a face-saving deal for the leadership. Hilton advised Cameron not to let up over the A-List, but he refused to be drawn into a fight. Indeed, he admits that he thought the party might not have accepted the idea in the first place. However, this was a missed opportunity: sticking with the original concept, or a variation of it, would have given him the chance to demonstrate strong leadership and exploit the mandate for change he had received only thirteen months earlier. There had been progress, but it fell short of where modernisers wanted the party to be. Even so, the changed complexion of Conservative candidates was the most visible evidence that Cameron was modernising his party. It was something he would return to in the years ahead.

Struggling up North

The next big electoral hurdle was the elections on 4 May for English local councils, the Scottish Parliament and the Welsh Assembly. Like the local elections the previous year, they were of critical importance to the leadership. 'We set ourselves key goals for 2007 in getting more of the eighteen-to-twenty-five vote and gaining ground in the north,' recalls George Bridges, then the party's director of campaigns.[6] There was a huge mountain to climb in northern England. The Conservatives had been major players in the big cities of the north until the late 1970s. In 1975 they polled 50 per cent of the local election vote in Manchester; by 2006 it was down to 11 per cent. Similarly, in Newcastle the party scored 42 per cent in 1978, which had fallen to 7 per cent by 2006. On 18 January the party announced that it was setting up a Northern Board to help improve the party's perform-ance. Chaired by William Hague, himself a northerner, it was designed to give greater autonomy to the party's organisation in northern England to formulate campaigns and coordinate membership and fundraising.

Scotland and Wales had also become Tory deserts, where if it were not for the creation of the Scottish Parliament and the Welsh Assembly the party would have been denied any kind of representation. Despite several high-profile visits north of the border, Cameron struggled to court Scottish voters. His perceived 'poshness' may well have put them off, but there were more endemic problems. 'The organisation up there was completely ramshackle,' recalls Bridges. 'They didn't understand what we were trying to do at all, and I had absolutely no control up there as Director of Campaigns. It was a complete struggle, so they employed an extra person for us to liaise with, but it didn't make much of a difference.'[7] The situation in Wales was a little more encouraging, because the party had won three Welsh seats at the 2005 general election, strengthening pockets of support.

As the elections approached, all was not well at Conservative headquarters. Lord Ashcroft's polling research still remained outside party high command, while the lack of a permanent Chief Executive figure and Director of Communications weakened the whole operation. 'We needed to get Michael Ashcroft and Stephen Gilbert into headquarters,' recalls one senior official. 'We were going at break-neck speed in early 2007, but it was frustrating that there was a lack of coordination about who was doing what, and we were all so knack-ered.' Despite these weaknesses, the party gained 911 councillors and forty-nine councils, with a projected national share of the vote of 40 per cent in England (the same as in May 2006). Labour fared as badly as it had the previous year. The Conservatives could claim that they had the momentum, leading Labour by 13 per cent and taking numerous council seats from the Liberal Democrats. Some progress was made in parts of the north-west, particularly in Bury and Bolton, while there were signs of life in Sunderland in the north-east, but breakthroughs in the major northern cities remained elusive. In Scotland the party did no more than tread water, coming third behind the SNP and Labour with 17 per cent of the vote, whereas in Wales the party performed better, winning four Assembly seats from Labour.

It was a mixed set of results, confirming that a Cameron-led Conservative Party was on the road to electoral recovery in some parts of the country, but not in others. The nationalists in Scotland and Wales were the clear beneficiaries of Labour's poor performance, not the official opposition party in Westminster. Scotland continued to be a barren land for the Conservatives. Decades of decline north of the border would not be reversed overnight, but despite his campaigning efforts David Cameron had found a blind spot with the Scottish electorate. Even more concerning was that the party's average poll ratings were beginning to fall, from 39 per cent in March to 36 per cent in May, only three points ahead of Labour.[8] It was an unpropitious backdrop for Cameron's first major crisis.

A Storm Blows in
On 16 May David Willetts, the Shadow Education Secretary, would deliver a speech about the party's thinking on secondary schools. At

a meeting of the Shadow Cabinet when the speech was discussed, Willetts told colleagues that his primary intention was to state the party's commitment to city academies (which had been championed by Tony Blair as a way of reviving secondary education), while going one step further in freeing them from local authority control. It would be a further demonstration of how the Conservatives under Cameron would carry forward the Blairite agenda in education, in contrast to Brown's lukewarm support for academies. Cameron was happy with the speech. 'No one anticipated a problem,' recalls Willetts. 'The speech was seen by the key team in draft in advance. Nobody saw it as getting into a row about grammar schools. They read it as the latest Willetts speech on supply-side reform of education.'[9] One passage pointed to recent academic research suggesting that grammar schools were no longer a driver of social mobility. 'We must break free from the belief that academic selection is any longer the way to transform the life chances of bright poor kids. This is a widespread belief, but we just have to recognise that there is overwhelming evidence that such academic selection entrenches advantage, it does not spread it,' Willetts would say. Critics took this to be an attack on existing grammar schools.

David Cameron had stated his position on academic selection within a month of becoming leader. 'Under my leadership there will be no going back to the 11-plus, no going back to grammar schools,' he had said on 9 January 2006.[10] Improving standards in all three thousand or so secondary schools, and not just the 164 remaining grammar schools, would be the party's priority. This had caused a minor stir at the time, but in the full glow of Cameron's honeymoon it had failed to ignite much debate. 'We thought that it had been put to bed early on,' recalls MacKay. 'Even those who did not agree with it felt that there was at least a settled position.'[11] After all, not one new grammar school had been built during the Conservative Party's eighteen years in office after 1979. In 1997 the party's manifesto had pledged a grammar school in 'every major town where parents want that choice'. By the 2005 general election, however, the party only promised to 'make it as easy as possible for them to expand'.[12]

But Michael Howard's 'grammar school boy' versus Blair's 'public school boy' quip at Prime Minister's Questions had gone down well with the backbenches. Howard was not the only party leader to have benefited from a grammar school education – so too had Edward Heath, Margaret Thatcher and John Major. Regardless of the fact that the party had diluted its commitment to grammar schools over a number of years (albeit with greater emphasis when Cameron became leader), it was still an issue that touched a Tory nerve. It particularly rankled with grammar-school-educated journalists and commentators in Fleet Street, who sympathised with the rank and file in the country. Many believed that grammars provided a ladder of opportunity for bright children from poor backgrounds: an opinion poll in the *Daily Telegraph* showed that 49 per cent of people approved of a system based on grammar schools rather than the comprehensive system that had been introduced in the 1960s and '70s. That figure rose to 71 per cent among Tory voters.[13]

When Radio 4's *Today* programme led on the grammar schools aspect of Willetts's speech on the morning of Wednesday, 16 May, the omens were not good. Willetts had explicitly briefed the press the night before that his speech would be about city academies, not grammar schools. Some of his colleagues believe his 'intellectually rigorous' approach, rather like that of Peter Lilley's speech on the public services in 1999, did not make for good politics: 'The policy wasn't the problem, but David wanted to present the research and rub people's noses in it.' When he was asked about the research on *Today*, Willetts was not about to recant. The press operation at party headquarters was also slow off the mark to challenge the way his speech was being reported before it had even been delivered. One press officer blames the BBC for failing to realise that there was nothing new in the speech, but journalists could smell the making of a story. The likes of Simon Heffer at the *Daily Telegraph* were apoplectic, as were the eighty-five Tory MPs who had popular grammar schools in their constituencies.

When Willetts later appeared in front of a meeting of the backbench 1922 Committee that night, only two MPs spoke in his favour, while one backbencher after another rose to condemn his speech. It looked as though Willetts had been hung out to dry by his leader, who ironically was spending several days experiencing the life of a teaching assistant in Hull. The first frontbencher to publicly break rank was Graham Brady, the Shadow Europe Minister and a former grammar school boy himself. He insisted that grammar schools did increase social mobility, citing written answers to questions he had asked in Parliament. 'I felt that I ought to fly the flag,' he recalls. 'For those of us who had been defending these schools for decades, to have the shadow schools ministers attacking them was potentially devastating.'[14] Brady was duly reprimanded by the Chief Whip, but decided to remain in post because of his commitment to his Europe brief.

A row that showed no signs of abating was now turning into the first full-blown crisis for the new leadership. Cameron consulted his team over the weekend about how to respond. The consensus was that he could not back down: it was decided that he would use a press conference the following week to take a tough line on dissenters and ride out the storm. He described those who wanted to build more grammar schools as 'delusional'. It was the first time he had attacked his critics so publicly. 'This is a key test for our party. Does it want to be a serious force for government and change, or does it want to be a right-wing debating society muttering about what might have been?' he asked.[15] There was also some bullish briefing to the press that this would be the real 'Clause IV moment' as the leader faced down the 'backwoodsmen' in the party. 'In hindsight this was a mistake,' says one former aide. 'Our argument was actually quite nuanced – and so it fanned the flames and suddenly it became a "Tories in chaos" story.' Another admits that 'the language used to deal with the pro-grammar dissent was over the top and ill-judged'.

The row continued for another week before Cameron clarified that existing grammar schools would be safe under a Tory government, and proposed 'grammar streams' within schools (which meant setting pupils by ability for various subjects) as a way of mollifying his critics. It was too late to stop the resignation of Graham Brady on 29 May after the press office refused to comment on whether he would survive a forthcoming frontbench reshuffle. Brady decided that he would rather defend grammar schools (particularly in his constituency) than remain on the frontbench.[16] There was further confusion when another frontbencher, Dominic Grieve, suggested that more grammar schools could be built in his Buckinghamshire constituency if necessary: 'We must also ensure that if further grammar or secondary schools are needed they can be supplied within the county.'[17]

The whole episode gave the impression to the public that the party was in disarray over its education policy, with its leader incapable of preventing a bad situation from becoming even worse. Set against the backdrop of Tony Blair's announcement on 10 May that he would step down on 27 June, and an outward display of unity in the Labour ranks following his endorsement of Gordon Brown just before the May elections, the media spotlight shone firmly on a seemingly divided Tory Party.

The leadership had badly mishandled the situation. 'It was a storm that just blew up in our faces,' says one former adviser. 'Unlike the EPP problem or the battle over tax, which we had foreseen, this suddenly crept up on us.' But the way Cameron reacted had made matters worse. For his part, Willetts believes that Cameron held his line. 'David did not deliberately want to pick a fight with the party. Some people thought that's what my speech should have been about, but it wasn't going to be our Clause IV moment. Nevertheless, he knew that sometimes you can't choose your fights, and when they come along you can't ignore them.'[18] It just so happened that this was the wrong moment to pick a fight, as the polls began to slide in the wrong direction for the party. Added to the misgivings about the A-List, the crisis revealed just how much Cameron still had to do to bring the party with him. 'The grammar school row was a telling reminder that the Tory Party had not changed as much as it should have done,' says a frontbencher. 'It said more about the nervous state of the party – many were worried about betrayal of what the party stood for. The Willetts speech acted as a lightning conductor for that.'

The crisis also revealed that loyalty to the leadership within the party did not run deep. 'It was totemic because the party seemed to be drifting to lots of strange positions, and many of our supporters were simply bewildered,' says a disillusioned backbencher. Another MP, who was supportive of the leadership, thought that the episode spoke more about the complacency of the party than anything else. 'The indiscipline in the parliamentary party was still there, and the rank and file got stuck in. There was also a streak of Tory pomposity that we were going to be in power soon.'

The grammar school crisis brought into sharp relief a significant vulnerability: the perceived elitism of Cameron and his close circle. The right-wing press – and, for that matter, most of the liberal media – latched onto the issue of class that had reared its head during the 2005 leadership election. One of Ken Clarke's supporters, John Bercow, had unsuccessfully tried to make capital out of Cameron's privileged background in September 2005: 'In the modern world the combination of Eton, hunting, shooting and lunch at White's is not helpful when you are trying to appeal to millions of ordinary people.'[19] The comment almost certainly ended Bercow's chances of promotion under a Cameron regime, although it may have endeared him to Labour MPs, furthering his ambition to become Speaker. But the grammar school crisis, inevitably dubbed 'grammargate' by the press, did raise questions about Cameron's background and that of his inner circle, many of whom had been to Eton and other public schools. 'There was a sense that David Cameron and his closest advisers and colleagues in the parliamentary party came from a well-off elite,' says one frontbencher. 'The rich would always be OK, because they can exit the state system, and the poor get a lot of attention, but the people in the middle who were really struggling felt that their voices weren't being heard.' Columnists like Matthew d'Ancona in the *Sunday Telegraph* were scathing: 'There is something deeply distasteful about listening to the Cameroons preen themselves over their tough line on state grammar schools before, without missing a beat, they go on to discuss the selective examinations for top private schools facing their own children. The last thing

I would wish for is that the next election be fought along class lines, with Brownite Scots biffing English toffs.'[20]

Having struggled for so long to find grounds on which to attack the Tory leadership, Labour sensed its vulnerability to the charge that it was elitist. Given that his class and educational background had the potential to harm Cameron, the issue of grammar school education had to be handled with care. The irony was that Cameron and Willetts had committed the Conservatives to improving all state secondary schools, rather than an elite few.

The storm had abated by the beginning of June, but that did not calm the nerves of Cameron's team. 'We had slipped into a period of not being given the benefit of the doubt,' says one. 'Any problem or issue became magnified.' They noticed how seriously the issue threatened to divide the party, and how high passions ran. 'He was very aware of the accusation that he was an Old Etonian taking the ladder away from disadvantaged kids,' says Andrew MacKay. 'He was very uncomfortable with any talk of closing grammar schools down. He just thought it was unrealistic and impractical to build new ones. But like a fire, it rose quickly and died quickly.'[21]

The row also exposed continuing weaknesses in the Tory machine. The party still needed a Director of Communications to bolster the media operation, and a Chief Executive to get a grip on Campaign Headquarters. George Eustice had been a reliable press secretary since Cameron had become leader, but it was assumed that a senior press or broadcasting figure would take on a more overarching role. Although Alastair Campbell, Blair's former Director of Communications, was not seen as an exact role model, it was felt that a similarly persuasive character was needed to deal with an increasingly sceptical press.

Andy Coulson, the former editor of the Sunday red-top the *News of the World*, was hired as the party's Director of Communications and Planning on 31 May 2007. Ironically, Coulson's paper had published a photograph during the leadership election of a young George Osborne sitting next to a prostitute at a party with lines of cocaine on the table which had caused a stir just after the controversy about Cameron's alleged use of drugs. 'George brought Andy into the team despite having the most to object to because of the *News of the World* story, but he had developed a respect for him,' recalls one party official. Along with his contacts in the newspaper world, Coulson had other advantages. 'As an Essex man, we thought that he would always think, "How would this go down with white-van man?" '

Although he did not have a strong political background, Coulson's tabloid edge and populist insights would act as a counterbalance to the more considered approach of Hilton and Letwin. But Coulson carried baggage: he had resigned as editor of the *News of the World* in January 2007 after the paper's royal reporter, Clive Goodman, had been convicted of illegally tapping the phones of aides to the royal family. Coulson was cleared of any knowledge of the practice, but his appointment as the Tories' Communications Director only four months later raised eyebrows across the party and in the press, and indeed questions about his involvement in the controversy would resurface two years later. Nevertheless, it was hoped that Coulson would bolster the party's communications, which had been shown to be seriously deficient, not least during the grammar row. His arrival on 9 July did not come a moment too soon. 'He fitted in very well,' recalls an aide. 'It was obviously a difficult time, but he brought additional horsepower to the media operation, which we needed.'

Another important development was the integration of Lord Ashcroft's research operation into party headquarters. Cameron had been impressed with Ashcroft's 'smell the coffee' research after the 2005 general election, and as soon as he became leader he had appointed him Deputy Chairman to oversee the party's opinion research and target-seat campaign. However, the fact that Ashcroft and Stephen Gilbert, the Director of Field Campaigning, were working from a different location gave the impression that they were semi-detached from the rest of the party. After delicate negotiations, Ashcroft agreed to move his expanding operation in-house in June 2007, on the condition that all private research would be channelled through him. He would commission any polling, and it would be reported back through him personally, with little or no contact between pollsters and politicians. This was explicitly to prevent the politicians from 'cheating' on the research. 'Cameron benefits from far more opinion research than any leader has had before,' says Andrew Cooper, who as founder of Populus (a few years after he left Central Office) provides polling for the party, along with ORB and ICM.[22] 'Michael presents the evidence to them straight,' says a party official from within the Ashcroft operation. 'We use opinion research to find out what voters think, not to tell us what to think or to win internal arguments. David Cameron appreciates that.' The integration of these research tools would be put to the test immediately.

Party headquarters had recently moved from Victoria Street to more spacious offices at 30 Millbank, facing the River Thames (adjacent to the Millbank Tower where New Labour had its famous headquarters in the 1990s). The new location had a symbolic significance, replicating the journey from the party's dark days in Central Office to a location that had become synonymous with New Labour's electoral prowess. The organisation also reverted to the three-pronged structure of campaigns, policy and research, and media and communications that had worked well until the early 1990s, and under Lynton Crosby ahead of the 2005 election campaign. One departure from the inner circle was George Bridges, who after three and a half years working at the top of the party's organisation as Director of Research under Howard, and latterly in overall charge of media and campaigning, decided to reclaim his life outside politics in July. Bridges was one of the most talented political minds of his generation, and his absence was soon felt, although he kept in touch with Cameron and the others socially.

Enter the Clunking Fist

'The next election will be a flyweight versus a heavyweight. And however much he may dance around the ring, at some point he'll come within the reach of a big clunking fist,' Tony Blair had warned back in November 2006.[23] The Conservative benches burst into laughter, thinking it was a gaffe referring to Brown's awkward and

heavy-handed manner. But by the summer of 2007 frantic negotiations behind the scenes in Downing Street had smoothed the way
for Brown's succession, and peace had broken out between the Prime
Minister and the Chancellor, as well as their respective allies, for the
first time in years. A nasty surprise was also awaiting the Conservatives. On 26 June, on the eve of Blair's departure from Number 10,
it was announced that Quentin Davies, a Tory MP since 1987 and a
former member of the Shadow Cabinet (as Shadow Northern Ireland
Secretary between 2001 and 2005), was crossing the floor to the
government. In a letter to Cameron, Davies wrote: 'Although you
have many positive qualities you have three, superficiality, unrelia-
bility and an apparent lack of any clear convictions, which in my
view ought to exclude you from the position of national leadership
to which you aspire.'[24] It was the perfect fillip for Gordon Brown. A
pinstriped MP from the old pro-European wing of the Tory Party,
Davies had become steadily disillusioned with Cameron's leadership,
particularly on the EPP question. Although he was not a household
name by any stretch of the imagination, Davies's defection was timed
for maximum embarrassment to the Tory leader.

A week before Blair's departure, Cameron had tried to regain the
initiative. On 18 June he made a speech in Tooting, south London, in
which he pledged that the Tories were learning from 'New Labour's
mistakes' rather than copying them and abandoning Conservative principles. By applying those principles to 'new challenges', the Tories would
be the 'true force for progressive politics' in Britain.[25] It was another
audacious attempt to steal Blair's thunder. Cameron admired the Prime
Minister's determination to accelerate the city academies programme
and market-based reforms of the welfare system, and Blair himself
believed that his 'final two years have been my most productive'.[26] Nevertheless, the Prime Minister had accused Cameron of bearing 'the imprint
of the last person who sat on him', an attack that resonated with Labour
MPs, and more worryingly for Cameron, with many Conservative MPs
who were uneasy with the way he deliberately sought to praise the
outgoing premier. Was there nothing more to Cameron's world view
than a warmed-up version of New Labour, they asked.

Aware that the *Built to Last* exercise in defining a new vision for the party had been a damp squib, the leadership tried to respond to the growing criticisms that there was little to distinguish the Conservatives from Labour. They also tried to challenge the received wisdom in Westminster that Cameron was good at presentation, but light on ideas. In a series of speeches, Cameron talked about the notion of 'social responsibility', with individuals, community organisations, charities and businesses taking greater responsibility for the 'general well-being' of society, in contrast to Gordon Brown's desire to use the power of the state to shape it. This was to be the 'big idea' behind Cameron's Conservatism. 'The danger is that if you focus too much on individual freedom you allow society to become a free-for-all, and that has negative social and economic effects,' one of his closest advisers argues. 'There is no freedom without responsibility. This really meant a lot to us.'

Steve Hilton asserts that Cameron's speech to the party's spring forum in Nottingham in March came closest to defining the goal of his leadership. 'The big argument in British politics today is not about the free enterprise economy,' Cameron declared. 'It's about our society – because it's not economic breakdown that Britain now faces, but social breakdown.' 'General Well-Being' (GWB) was just as important as the Gross Domestic Product (GDP). 'The cost of not getting social policy right – in education, the welfare system and family life – would only rise in terms of higher taxes,' says one of Cameron's senior advisers. It was a coherent argument, and it chimed with the work that Iain Duncan Smith had been producing with his Social Justice Group. It also had a distinctly Conservative flavour, flowing from the One Nation tradition that had its roots in the Enlightenment thinking of Edmund Burke, the forefather of liberal Conservatism.

Cameron and Hilton were attempting to build an intellectual platform that was consistent with the early themes of the leadership campaign, but many commentators on the right were distinctly unimpressed. '[The party] is still in what might best be described as a naïve phase of political discourse and activity,' wrote Simon Heffer in the *Daily Telegraph*. Heffer was a well-known critic of the Cameron project, but now he was sharpening his pen. 'There is precious little evidence of seriousness. Where there should be policies, there are stunts. Where competence is required, there has been blithering obtuseness. And, all too often, such open wounds extend and join up with each other.'[27] The problem for Cameron was that Heffer was not alone in his trenchant criticism: many *Telegraph* readers and, in private, a large number of Tory MPs shared his view.

Cameron may never have been going to win over critics like Heffer and Tebbit, but he was vulnerable to the accusation of naïvety. His 'social responsibility' speeches were in many ways a work in progress. It was not an easy phrase to sell to political journalists, let alone ordinary voters. The real problem for the Tory leadership was that the window in which it could make an intellectual case for a 'New Conservatism' had already begun to close by the spring of 2007. In the wake of the grammar school row, speeches on the nature of Cameron's Conservatism were bound to fall on deaf ears. More importantly, the Westminster media's attention was fixed on the departure of one Prime Minister and the arrival of another.

On Wednesday, 27 June Tony Blair answered his last questions in the Commons as Prime Minister before going to Buckingham Palace to tender his resignation. The Davies defection provided a humiliating backdrop for Cameron as he prepared his last questions for Blair. Cleverly, he scarcely allowed the outgoing Prime Minister an opportunity to rub salt into the wounds. He paid generous tribute to Blair, who he said had 'considerable achievements to his credit'. After Blair's final words – 'That's it. The end' – Labour MPs rose to their feet in applause. Cameron and Osborne immediately joined the standing ovation, as, somewhat reluctantly, did the rest of the Conservative frontbench. Noticing that many of his backbenchers remained seated, Cameron gestured to them to stand. It was a poignant moment, illustrating the ambivalence towards the politician who had caused them so much difficulty for over a decade. A mixture of respect, fear and loathing had characterised the Tory reaction to Blair's leadership of the Labour Party and the country.

As Blair departed Number 10 for the last time as Prime Minister, a sense of trepidation descended on Tory high command. Gordon Brown stood on the steps of Number 10 declaring that he would do his 'utmost' to serve the country as Prime Minister. The former Chancellor's persona and style were very different from his predecessor's. Quoting George Orwell's *Nineteen Eighty-Four*, Cameron had warned that a Brown government would be 'like a boot stamping on a human face – for ever'.[28] But as soon as Brown entered Number 10, the mood could not have been more different. He somehow looked more composed and down-to-earth than either Blair or Cameron. 'When Blair went it was an anti-climax,' one former Cameron aide recalls. 'The Blairites were gracious, and Gordon got off to a good start. The media narrative turned in favour of the government, and we were utterly frustrated.'

Brown's first few weeks in Number 10 surpassed the Tories' worst fears. The Labour Party recovered its poise, encouraged by a Cabinet, hailed as a 'government of all the talents', that contained some of Blair's most loyal lieutenants as well as Brownites. Brown appointed figures from outside the Labour Party to ministerial positions, even inviting a couple of Tory MPs – the maverick former frontbencher (and future Speaker) John Bercow, to conduct a review of services for children with special educational needs; and Patrick Mercer, who would advise on security matters – into his own big tent.

Speculation about further defections to Labour began to mount. Brown's steadfast response within days of becoming Prime Minister to attempted terrorist attacks in London's West End and on Glasgow Airport reassured those who had been sceptical that he could rise to the moment. He further confounded expectations by announcing a diminution of his powers as Prime Minister, and pleased his backbenchers by ditching some of Blair's proposed measures, such as the introduction of super-casinos, and distancing himself from legislation enabling twenty-four-hour drinking. In contrast to the loucheness of Blair's Britain, Brown sought to project his 'moral compass' on the country. It was a strategy that warmed the hearts of the more socially conservative MPs on the Tory benches, as well as the right-wing press. 'Tories for Gordon' was a phrase that was suddenly bandied about Westminster. 'Not Flash, Just Gordon' was the imaginative Labour Party poster that seemed to capture Brown's seriousness.

More importantly for Cameron, the public mood changed. By June the Tories had already lost their lead in the polls for the first time since May 2006, with the two main parties level on 36 points.[29] 'We were very cautious, because there was a real desire for change in the country, and we feared that Brown could provide that newness,' recalls an aide. Indeed, Brown had uttered the word 'change' eight times during his short statement on the steps of Number 10 on 27 June. Senior figures in the Shadow Cabinet were concerned. 'We constantly told ourselves not to underestimate Brown, but we were surprised when he did even better than expected,' says Francis Maude. 'He seemed to have reinvented himself. It was a demoralising time for us.'[30]

In response, on 3 July Cameron undertook his first major reshuffle of the Shadow Cabinet since becoming leader. Osborne was given the additional task of general election coordinator, while the other senior figures – Hague, Davis and Fox – remained in place. Michael Gove was promoted to Shadow Schools and Children Secretary, while David Willetts was moved to take over a new brief covering universities and skills. Interpreted as a sideways move for Willetts after 'grammargate', the appointment was actually more about making space for Gove. Other entrants from the 2005 election also received promotion: Nick Herbert (formerly a member of Davis's campaign) to the Shadow justice brief, while Jeremy Hunt took over culture, media and sport. Dame Pauline Neville-Jones joined the frontbench as Shadow Security Minister, while Sayeeda Warsi was appointed community cohesion spokesperson, both being appointed to the Lords. The other significant move was the replacement of Francis Maude as Party Chairman by Caroline Spelman. Maude remained in the Shadow Cabinet as Shadow Minister for the Cabinet Office, but his move was seen as a demotion after the wrangling over candidate selection and other internal reforms. The reshuffle refreshed the top team, but scarcely made an impression on an increasingly sceptical electorate.

The first electoral test for Cameron in the new era came sooner than he would have liked with the death of the Labour MP for Ealing Southall in west London in June. A by-election was called for 19 July. It was not a seat the Conservatives hoped to win (having come third there in the general election), but it presented an opportunity to embarrass the new Prime Minister with a strong performance. Cameron was determined to make a decent fist of the by-election, making five visits to the constituency during the short campaign. A photogenic Sikh businessman, Tony Lit, was quickly selected for the seat following intense pressure from Campaign Headquarters. He had only joined the party recently – too recently for comfort, as it transpired: a photograph of him standing next to Tony Blair at a Labour fundraising dinner only a few weeks previously appeared in the weekend papers on the eve of the by-election. The final humiliation came when Lit, described as the candidate for 'David Cameron's Conservatives' on the ballot paper, came third with a mere 1 per cent increase in the Tory vote. Labour held the seat, as it did Sedgefield following Tony Blair's departure from the Commons, with the Conservatives slipping from second place at the general election to third. As at Bromley and Chislehurst a year before, the party continued its dire run of by-election performances. While Brown's honeymoon continued, Cameron's problems were mounting.

When it Rains, it Pours

'We mustn't lose our nerve,' Cameron told his team in the first few weeks of July. They tried to maintain a semblance of calm, but they knew the mood in the party was deeply unsettled. The new Prime Minister was attracting favourable headlines, while the Conservative leader was struggling to make any impact at all. In July, Labour moved into the lead in the polls, hitting 39 per cent, five points ahead of the Conservatives.[31] 'It was incredibly difficult,' recalls one of Cameron's senior aides. 'We really did struggle to get taken seriously. There was a switch in the air in Westminster. Brown managed to pull off a hell of a trick with the press, that he was a different man than they had known for the past ten years.'

It had been Brown's lifelong ambition to be Prime Minister, and he and his allies had been preparing the ground much more meticulously than Cameron's team had anticipated. Day after day Brown announced a new initiative or appointment to present a different type of government. By contrast, Cameron and his Shadow ministers were lucky to get a clip on the BBC's ten o'clock news. 'We knew that Brown hadn't really changed, and that he was the same old tribal politician who had fought his battle against Blair all the way,' recalls one of Cameron's aides. 'It was interesting – that kept us going in a funny sort of way. There were moments when we thought, "When is this going to end?", but there was never a feeling that this is all over.'

Cameron and his team had to plough on. A change of Prime Minister midway through a Parliament had put opposition leaders on the back foot in the past: Neil Kinnock's job had been made that much harder when Margaret Thatcher made way for John Major in November 1990. Unlike Kinnock, who had already undertaken a large review of policy by the time he faced a new Prime Minister, Cameron's policy review was still in progress. The policy groups were about to publish their final reports as planned, but the timing and nature of the policy review now took on a hazardous dimension. Although the review had given the leadership a breathing space in which to articulate the broad-brush themes it wanted to project in 2006, the party could not continue without any specific commitments. The purpose of the review was to provide the Shadow Cabinet with a range of policy options which would be sifted through by a newly created policy board comprising Cameron, Osborne, Letwin and Maude. The findings of the six main groups and the array of taskforces would provide a menu to choose from, while not binding the party in any way. This freedom of manoeuvre had already become an issue, most recently over the grammar schools débâcle, when David Willetts's speech appeared to be defining the contours of party policy before the relevant group had even reported.

'What was the point of establishing the [policy] commission, which has worked hard and intensively for over a year, with some of the best brains in the country who have given their time and expertise, if we are going to simply ignore their findings?' asked Nadine Dorries, an MP who sat on the Public Services Challenge policy group.[32] Matters were complicated further when the leadership launched another layer of consultation in mid-June – 'Stand Up Speak Out – the Nation's Despatch', which was intended to give the public a chance to inform party policy. 'We had so many conversations about it, and spent a small fortune,' recalls one party official. 'I told David and Steve that it wasn't worth it and it wouldn't work, but they wanted to go ahead with it anyway.' Like other initiatives intended to engage the public during this time, it sank without trace.

The publication of the first few policy group reports went according to plan. Iain Duncan Smith's Social Justice Group's report, 'Breakthrough Britain', was well received when it was published on 10 July, containing some of the most thoughtful thinking on a range of social issues that the party had produced for years. The National and International Security Group, chaired by Pauline Neville-Jones and Tom King, also presented a solid piece of work. Michael Heseltine's Cities Task Force report produced interesting proposals for revitalising civic democracy, while Ken Clarke's reports on devolution and the constitution were greeted favourably. But there were potential problems with how the other groups, particularly those concerned with the economy and the environment, would complement each other.

Oliver Letwin had overseen the policy review, liaising closely with the group chairmen throughout the process. 'Oliver's intention was that there would be creative tension,' recalls a senior aide. 'It was about showing that politics is about hard choices and being honest enough to say that there were a number of competing issues.' Zac Goldsmith's Quality of Life report was expected to recommend drastic measures to reduce carbon emissions, which might not sit easily with some of the ideas expected from John Redwood's group on economic competitiveness. Their reports were not due to be published for another month – more than enough time to showcase the work of the other groups.

But events were about to take a dangerous, if not farcical, turn. A long-planned trip by Cameron to Rwanda was intended to coincide with the publication of the global poverty and globalisation policy group report (written by Peter Lilley with the assistance of Bob Geldof and others). He would join up with dozens of Tory volunteers who had spent two weeks in the country on a regeneration project, before meeting the Rwandan president and addressing the parliament in the capital, Kigali. But just before he was to depart, the heavens opened, and parts of central and western England were soon under water. Cameron's own constituency of Witney in Oxfordshire was among the worst-affected areas. While cameras followed him around as he visited the constituency on Sunday, 22 July, most of the media's gaze was on the Prime Minister, who was swift to act in sending in troops to help alleviate the situation. Like an outbreak of Foot and Mouth disease a few weeks later, the floods presented Brown with an opportunity to show prime ministerial crisis management.

On the same day, a story appeared in the *Sunday Telegraph* which claimed that at least two, and possibly as many as half a dozen, Tory MPs had written to Sir Michael Spicer, Chairman of the 1922 Committee, asking for a vote of no confidence in the leadership. One senior backbencher was quoted as saying: 'There's a hole at the heart of the Cameron project. There is a feeling that Cameronism is exhausted ... MPs want to know what is at the heart of all this rebranding. The fear is that there is nothing at the heart of it.'[33] The rumour mill began to turn, with the press ringing MPs known to be privately critical of the leadership to see if they would go public. Another disillusioned MP recalls, 'People were desperately unhappy.' '[The report of the letters] was not true, but the lobby journalists went crazy,' claims George Eustice, Cameron's press secretary. 'The question became, would he go to Rwanda as planned [the next day], or would he be forced to abandon his plans and stay to fight for his life?'[34]

Team Cameron had an agonising conference call on the Sunday

morning. It was the first time that Andy Coulson came to the fore. He and Hilton urged Cameron to delay flying out to Kigali by one day, while Osborne and Eustice argued that that would be seen as an admission that there was indeed a crisis, and would fuel stories about discontent in the run-up to the 1922 Committee meeting that week. All agreed that they would be damned either way. A further complication was that by delaying by one day, Cameron would need to take a private flight instead of a commercial one, which would not send out the right impression. It was a close call, but Cameron finally sided with Osborne and Eustice. 'It was one of the more important decisions he made that summer, and he got it absolutely right,' recalls Andrew Mitchell, David Davis's former campaign manager and Shadow International Development Secretary since 2005, who had been in Rwanda with the group of volunteers for two weeks. 'He knew it would not be immediately popular, but he came to Rwanda because he thought it was the right thing to do.'[35]

Cameron and his entourage kept in close contact with the situation in Witney while they were in Africa. Two press conferences were held on 24 July, simultaneously in London and Kigali; Lilley presented his global poverty report at home, while Cameron took questions abroad. Inevitably, the travelling press were far more interested in why Cameron had not stayed in Witney to deal with the floods. Lilley's report had gone down well with non-governmental organisations specialising in the Third World. 'They were taking the Conservative Party seriously again,' he says.[36] This would not, however, help the embattled Tory leader, for whom it seemed that nothing could go right: even the lights went out in the middle of his address to a half-empty Rwandan Parliament. But it had been a brave decision to press ahead with the visit. International development was a subject Cameron had invested political capital in, despite the relative apathy of many in his party. There was little he could have achieved by staying at home during the floods.

Morale in the parliamentary party was very low indeed when MPs left for the summer break. Cameron's authority had diminished. 'There was no capital left in the bank,' recalled a senior member of the Shadow Cabinet. 'We knew we didn't have the goodwill to get us through the tough times.' Amid Brown's honeymoon and the open wounds of 'grammargate', the Tory leader was in a weak position. In mid-August, he headed for Brittany for some respite, and had lunch with the former Party Treasurer Lord Marland, who was staying in the seaside resort of Dinard. 'I saw him on the first day of his holiday and he looked very fatigued,' recalls Marland. 'He was mentally drained from the torrid time that he had both within and without the party, but David has great inner resolve, and I could tell from talking to him he was going to return with renewed endeavour.'[37] While the atmosphere in the party became increasingly fraught as Labour's lead in the polls grew, Cameron steeled himself for a fightback.

Desperate August

Gordon Brown had become Prime Minister without a mandate from the electorate, despite his party having won the general election only two years before. Number 10 now contemplated what had been unthinkable only a few months before: a snap election that would give Brown another four or five years in office, sealed by a fresh mandate. Although August is traditionally the silly season for the press, the talk spilling out of Labour circles was bullish – there was every chance that the party would capitalise on the new Prime Minister's honeymoon and pull the rug from under Cameron's feet. By going to the country, a historic fourth successive election victory could be in Labour's grasp. 'Brown was looking to achieve a spectacular explosion of the Tory Party,' recalls a senior Conservative MP. Brown's closest allies thought that a serious and prime ministerial Gordon Brown would make mincemeat of a callow and hapless David Cameron, and the polls seemed to support this view. By August, Labour's lead had stretched into double figures in some surveys.

The possibility of a snap election at the end of September suddenly became very real. William Hague was the most concerned among the Shadow Cabinet. In the middle of August he told Osborne that he thought Brown would ask for Parliament to be dissolved at the beginning of September for a poll at the end of the month, thereby doing away with the party conference season and denying the opposition its annual opportunity to present itself before the electorate. A short, sharp campaign would give Brown the chance to depict Cameron as out of his depth and out of control of his party.

Alarm bells began to ring at 30 Millbank, where the campaign machine had not yet fully adjusted to the changes introduced earlier in the summer. Although some of the policy groups were still publishing their proposals, Cameron asked Letwin to hastily draw up a manifesto – an enormous task given the volume of detailed proposals that had landed on his desk over the previous months – while Osborne began to prepare for a campaign. Operationally the party was far from ready for a snap poll: many constituency associations had yet to select candidates, and funds had to be raised. It was a desperate situation. 'We were sure we would lose,' recalls Andrew MacKay, Cameron's senior parliamentary aide. 'I was worried that that would mean we would lose David. I was trying to figure out what I could do to shore him up if we lost.'[38] The spectre of certain defeat loomed large.

While Letwin worked day and night to pull the manifesto together, the leadership had to maintain its poise and somehow revive its public standing. Then, in late August, the nation was shocked by the murders of Rhys Jones, an eleven-year-old Liverpool boy shot by a youth while on his way home from football practice, and Garry Newlove, who was kicked to death by vandals outside his house in Warrington. The phrase 'Britain's broken society', first adopted by Liam Fox during his leadership campaign in 2005, found a new resonance. One of Iain Duncan Smith's reports, 'Breakdown Britain', had already provided an arresting analysis about the harsh realities of family breakdown, drug abuse and youth crime. According to aides, Cameron was appalled by the Rhys Jones murder. 'He was bloody angry about it,' recalls one. 'It sparked us into getting some work done on it.' Coulson, Hilton and David Davis immediately set to work on a 'mini-manifesto' on crime.

In a speech the next day, 24 August, Cameron spoke plainly and directly. 'I promise you, unless we choose to change . . . our shock today will turn into a shrug tomorrow, just a kind of impotent ache about the state of the world. Or we can start saying to ourselves and to each other: "I've had enough of all this." ' He proposed a new 'social covenant' between parents and the state. Parents who failed to raise their children responsibly would be 'shamed', he said, while errant fathers should be treated 'like the selfish people they are'.[39] As a result of this speech, the media began to give Cameron favourable coverage for the first time in months. Tabloid editorials praised his comments, as well as his plans to introduce a cap on non-EU immigrants – immigration had barely been mentioned by senior Tories since the doomed 2005 election campaign.

The final two policy groups also provided an opportunity for the leadership to show its colours. John Redwood's economic competitiveness group recommended building more motorways and a new airport in the Thames estuary, contrasting sharply with Zac Goldsmith and John Gummer's environment report, which suggested a moratorium on airport expansion, car-parking charges for out-of-town supermarkets and taxing people who went on more than one holiday a year. This had the potential to become a public relations disaster. 'The [reports] were a stunning irrelevance, creating more problems than they solved,' one sceptical MP remarked. Party high command swiftly distanced itself from some of the more controversial Goldsmith–Gummer ideas, while endorsing some of Redwood's plans. Although the press continued to write about the 'chaotic' policy review, developing the narrative from earlier in the summer, the leadership was relieved that the media's gaze had been diverted temporarily from a resurgent Gordon Brown.

Battle Stations

While there was a small shift in the polls in the Tories' direction, Labour remained comfortably ahead. The leadership had managed to make an impact in the media in late August, and Andy Coulson's contribution to the team was making a difference. But none of this quelled the febrile mood within the party at large. Disillusioned party donors were making themselves heard. Lord Kalms, a former Party Treasurer and David Davis supporter, said that Cameron needed to do 'some rethinking', while Sir Tom Cowie, who had supported Cameron's leadership bid, vowed not to give the party any more money, complaining, 'The Tory Party seems to be run now by Old Etonians and they don't seem to understand how other people live.' Next came a direct attack from Michael Ancram, who having served under Hague, Duncan Smith and Howard in senior roles including the deputy leadership, was the most senior figure to break rank. 'Of course as Conservatives we must show we have changed, but we must beware doing so by trashing our past or appearing ashamed of our history,' he said on 4 September. 'Change for change's sake is a vacuous process, swiftly seen through by the electorate.'[40]

The representatives of the party's grassroots had also served warning on the leadership. 'David, it's not happening out there – people are not happy,' Don Porter, Deputy Chairman of the party board, told Cameron. 'I said that we had to identify with what people on the doorstep felt about crime, health and education. We also had allowed the Labour Party in the last few years to become the party of aspiration, and people didn't know what we stood for.'[41] This was a blunt summation Cameron could ill afford to ignore. He trusted Porter's candour and constructive advice, unlike the sniping from elsewhere in the party. Something had to be done to prevent a bad situation becoming even worse. In public, the leadership held the line that there would be 'no lurch to the right'. But behind closed doors, an intense debate was taking place.

What had happened to 'Vote Blue, Go Green' and the sunny optimism that had characterised Cameron's first year as leader? It was a question that the inner circle surrounding the leader – Steve Hilton, Michael Gove, George Osborne and Oliver Letwin – anxiously wrestled with. Could this be the point at which Cameron would capitulate under the pressure of events, like his predecessors? The danger of the modernising project being abandoned altogether was at the forefront of Hilton and Gove's minds. 'Michael was intensely frustrated by the feeling that we were retreating into our comfort zone,' recalls one frontbencher. 'He warned against doing a "Hague" by dipping into a basket of right-wing policies.' Ironically, it was Hague who advised Cameron to stay the course and 'ride the dip'. If ever there was advice learned from painful experience, this was it.

Some in Tory headquarters felt that by the second week of September Brown had funked his original timetable for a snap election. 'Brown's people were strangely silent during our media campaign in late August,' recalls a senior official. Yet Cameron and his advisers were taking nothing for granted. Michael Ashcroft commissioned a raft of private polls, including a daily tracker poll and polls across marginal seats, to monitor public opinion. Tory high command remained seriously worried, not least because Labour insiders began to brief the press that an election in late October or early November was under serious consideration. But a few of Cameron's aides sensed an opportunity in the making. 'When Brown didn't go when he should have done, I was among the minority of David's advisers saying, "We can make sure this election doesn't happen at all, because Brown's dithered," ' recalls Andrew MacKay. 'From that point on I said, "I don't think there'll be an election if we can turn things around." '[42] The expectation was that Brown would announce an election during Labour's conference in Bournemouth at the end of September. 'We were on a war footing,' recalls one senior MP. 'It was more like the Battle of Britain than D-Day. We knew an election was coming across the Channel – we had to send up our Spitfires to put everything in its path to stop it.'

The search for a weapon with which to frustrate Gordon Brown's election plans began in earnest. Now that the party conference would go ahead in the first week of October, Cameron and his advisers had a precious few weeks in which to devise a plan. 'We needed something big. What raw meat could you give to our conference that wouldn't go against decontaminating the brand?' recalls a senior aide. The answer was not particularly novel. Raising the threshold for inheritance tax had been floated by the party for years, but the incredible boom in property prices since the late 1990s gave the idea new currency. Even Labour's Stephen Byers, a leading Blairite and former Cabinet minister, had suggested the 40 per cent tax's abolition in August 2006. An increasing number of middle-class homeowners feared that their estates would fall prey to the tax, which began to take effect above £300,000 for married couples and civil partners. Osborne and his team considered various options for raising the threshold to £750,000. Having promised not to commit the party to unfunded tax cuts, they struck upon an innovative way of paying for the proposal. Up to 200,000 people who lived in Britain, known as 'non-domiciles' or 'non-doms', who avoided paying tax on their earnings or capital gains outside the country, would have to pay an annual charge of £25,000 to continue to enjoy their residency. The measure would show that the party would help the 'struggling' middle classes by taxing the super-rich. It was a leaf taken straight out of the New Labour playbook that would not only outflank Brown, but would also reconnect the Conservatives with a key cross-section of voters. It was decided to raise the inheritance tax threshold to the totemic figure of £1 million, so that only millionaires would be affected.

Osborne claimed that the pledge would benefit nine million families, given the rise in house prices since the mid-1990s. Rigorous focus group research conducted by the party showed that it was popular. 'What surprised us was how well it played with aspirational, working-class voters who wanted to pass something on to their children, even though they would not be affected,' says one aide. Osborne knew he would have to unveil more than one carrot at the conference, and the abolition of stamp duty for first-time buyers on homes worth up to £250,000 proved even more popular in focus groups than the inheritance tax proposal. In order to head off the charge that the party would 'slash and burn' the public services, Osborne also gave a commitment that the Tories would match Labour's spending plans over the next three years. It was a deliberate attempt to neutralise the 'Labour investment versus Tory cuts' line that Gordon Brown had used so effectively in 2001 and 2005.

There was considerable debate within the inner circle about

inheritance tax. Hilton in particular believed passionately that the test of the party's policies had to be that they helped the less well-off rather than the rich. Gove and Letwin agreed with him that cutting inheritance tax would give the wrong impression to those on low and middling incomes. But Osborne calculated that the mood in the country had changed since the 2005 general election: Ashcroft's polling research showed that inheritance tax was one of the three most unpopular taxes, along with the television licence fee and council tax. Even though levels of income tax had fallen, most recently in Brown's last budget as Chancellor, people felt overburdened by other taxes, particularly those on property. The clincher for Hilton was that the raising of the level at which inheritance tax kicked in would be paid for by the non-doms, which could be presented as a redistributive measure. In that sense it was a modernising policy rather than an uncosted tax cut designed to please traditionalists in the party. After several weeks of deliberation, the team took the final decision during Labour's conference week in Bournemouth. 'It did have a retro feel, but we weighed up the risks,' recalls a senior aide. 'We only went with it very late in the day. We all knew that the media would love it – nothing excites them more than tax and spend.' Crucially for Osborne, the proposal had had Cameron's support from the beginning. He knew then that he would override any internal opposition.

Meanwhile, the Prime Minister and his advisers were increasingly confident about their chances in a snap election. Labour's private polling showed that the government was reasonably well placed in the areas it needed to defend to win a fourth term. In the most audacious move of his short premiership so far, Brown invited his *bête noire*, Baroness Thatcher, for tea at Number 10 on 13 September. As the television cameras beamed images of Brown greeting the pink-suited former Prime Minister in Downing Street, Tory high command were taken by complete surprise. Brown's move was calculated to cause real embarrassment to Cameron, after accusations from Ancram and others that he had been 'trashing' the party's past, even though both Brown's and Thatcher's offices insisted that it was merely a courtesy invitation. But the initial panic at Tory headquarters soon subsided. 'We all thought, "Bloody hell, this is a great coup," but then we realised that he was over-reaching himself,' recalls one official. Some Labour and trade union figures were not amused. Paul Kenny, General Secretary of the GMB union, said the visit was 'a huge political mistake' which would damage Labour's credibility with its core voters. 'Mrs Thatcher was put out of Downing Street by the Tories themselves. It is unbelievable that she should be invited back by a Labour prime minister,' he said.[43] Intelligence fed back to Millbank that the confident utterances of Labour spokesmen were as much bravado as anything else. 'They were as organisationally unprepared as we were, but concentrated on spinning that an election was likely,' recalls one senior party official. 'We didn't have a sense that we were doing that badly, so we concentrated on getting the basics of our campaign in place.'

As Labour assembled in Bournemouth on 23 September for their annual conference, the Conservatives continued to plan for the expected announcement of the election at the end of the week. Surely Brown would use his first conference speech as Prime Minister to launch the campaign. Dramatic events in the financial world had presented him with another opportunity to show a firm hand at the tiller. The first signs that the credit crunch in the United States that began in the summer was affecting British banks came on 13 September, when the BBC's business editor, Robert Peston, broke a story about Northern Rock needing emergency funds from the Bank of England. It triggered the first run on a British bank since 1866. A full-blown crisis was averted when the government intervened on 17 September to guarantee all Northern Rock deposits. This turned out to be only the tip of the iceberg, but for the time being the government was commended for its response. Cameron on the other hand was roundly condemned for 'overreacting' to the crisis by blaming Brown for allowing personal indebtedness to rise to unsustainable levels since 1997. 'Though the current crisis may have had its trigger in the US, over the past decade the gun has been loaded at home,' he wrote in the *Sunday Telegraph* during the weekend of the crisis.[44] But most commentators did not lay the blame on the Treasury. The episode reinforced a narrative in the press on the eve of the party conference season that Brown was a safe pair of hands in contrast to Cameron's sniping from the sidelines. It emboldened Brown's aides even further, and as Labour's conference gathered momentum, they briefed journalists that an election was imminent. The stage was set when Brown addressed the party on Tuesday, 25 September. He lauded Labour's record in office since 1997, but strangely there was no climax to his peroration, let alone any mention of an election. 'I will not let you down,' he declared. It was hardly a battle cry.

Yet Team Cameron looked on nervously. Labour's support in some opinion polls rose to 42 per cent, while the Tories remained stuck on around 32 per cent. Ashcroft and his team were running a daily 'tracker poll' of public opinion during Labour's conference. The findings were not encouraging: Labour's lead over the Tories ranged between twelve and fourteen points. At an 'away day' of the Shadow Cabinet just after Brown's speech, the Tory leader rallied his senior team. 'David told us that we have to perform in ten days the biggest turnaround in a party's poll fortunes in modern political history – more dramatic than ever happened during the Falklands War – but we're going to do it,' recalls William Hague.[45] Some of the Shadow Cabinet were bemused, wondering how on earth this could be achieved. But Brown had once again failed to seize the moment. 'Brown's speech was just a load of calculated, tactical statements like "British jobs for British workers." But where was the big idea?' one Tory aide insisted. At the end of Labour's conference week, Cameron told staff in Millbank that there was all to play for. This certainly raised morale. In their hearts, they believed certain defeat awaited them within a matter of weeks if Brown pulled the trigger. There was no shortage of Dunkirk spirit as the party headed for Blackpool.

Bring it on in Blackpool

The primary objective of the first few days of the Blackpool conference was to seize the headlines. 'The project to modernise the party was only half done. But we were in a corner, and David had to say: "Bring it on," ' recalls one Cameron aide. 'It was all about spooking Gordon Brown into not calling the election by the end of the week.' All the leadership could do was unveil its tax proposals and pray. Labour's calculation was that the continued speculation about an autumn election would cause the Conservatives to implode, as the Cameron project would not be able to deal with the pressure given the turbulence of the last few months. Indeed, the Tories' 2003 Blackpool conference, which sounded the death knell of Iain Duncan Smith's leadership, showed just how quickly things could fall apart by the seaside. Cameron and his close advisers would have to do everything in their power to avoid a repetition of the nightmare of four years ago. The odds were stacked against them, but they felt prepared. 'Boy, we really did have a plan,' recalls Hague.[46]

Despite Cameron's upbeat and energetic performance during his interview with the BBC's Andrew Marr, there was still a quiet air of resignation among many MPs and party activists that the week would not go to plan. The atmosphere began to change when William Hague opened the conference with an ebullient speech, lambasting Brown's performance in Bournemouth and his lack of conviction. This rallied the party faithful and set the tone for the rest of the conference. The following day Osborne would drop the tax bombshell that had been the subject of so much debate over the past few weeks. 'The next Conservative government will raise the inheritance tax threshold to £1 million.' Stunned at first, the hall then burst into sustained and rapturous applause. Even Osborne was taken aback by the reaction. The party's private research and his instincts told him that the measure would go down well, but not quite as well as it did.

Little did his audience know how much preparation and discussion had gone into the contents of his speech, but it had the desired effect. The party's rolling opinion polling gave the leadership and Shadow Cabinet further encouragement. 'Even before George's speech, the daily tracker poll showed us making up ground. We were increasing by two to three points a day,' one Shadow minister recalled. Osborne's tax announcements had gone down remarkably well: the party had been served a meaty tax pledge. 'It was a real speaking-to-the-country moment,' one of his aides reflected. 'By Monday evening we were cautiously optimistic.' Tory MPs and activists had a spring in their step for the first time since Cameron's honeymoon eighteen months ago. The prospect of an imminent election began to instil a sense of unity and discipline in their ranks.

The next day brought a stroke of luck. The party and the assembled media were stunned to hear that Gordon Brown had flown to Iraq to announce the future withdrawal of British troops from Basra in the south of the country. It was unprecedented for a Prime Minister to make such a high-profile announcement during the opposition's conference week, and while the House of Commons was in recess. A greater controversy came amid confusion about the numbers that would return home, after it was revealed that some had already done so. Sir John Major launched a fierce criticism of Brown, describing the announcement as a 'shameful' political game, while in Blackpool Liam Fox, the Shadow Defence Secretary, delivered a powerful rebuke from the conference platform. The party faithful, already buoyed by Osborne's speech the previous day, were united in their condemnation of Brown's announcement. 'It turned the journalists, because they felt that they had been deceived,' Andrew MacKay recalls vividly. 'It really looked bad for Brown. Blair would not have made that mistake.'[47]

Outside the conference hall, MPs were on their best behaviour. There was not a whiff of the dissent or backbiting that had been predicted only a week earlier. The former frontbencher Graham Brady, who had resigned over the grammar school débâcle, failed to rise to the bait at a well-attended fringe meeting of the National Grammar School Association. A row of television cameras and lights had been set up in eager anticipation of an attack on the leadership. When none came, the lights went off and one by one the camera crews made a quick exit. So far, the party was holding together remarkably well. As the week approached its climax, the conference took on the appearance of a pre-election rally.

On Wednesday, 3 October, David Cameron would have to deliver the speech of a lifetime, even better than at Blackpool in 2005. His speech-writing team worked into the early hours refining the text. 'It was all about him – he accepted that the issue people were talking about was his ability to lead, and he needed to address that head-on,' one senior aide recalled. The original plan was to deliver the speech from notes, but as Cameron's confidence grew he decided to repeat the feat of two years ago by committing it to memory. The hope was that this would demonstrate his strength under fire. He spent hours with Steve Hilton rehearsing the speech, but when he woke up that morning his sense was that it could go either way: it might be an absolute disaster, and he would be finished. The sense of expectation kept the adrenalin pumping.

When Cameron walked onto the platform of the Empress Ballroom in the Winter Gardens, he appealed to the audience to bear with him. 'It may be messy, but it will be me,' he said. He need not have worried: they were willing him on to succeed. It was a courageous decision to speak from memory, given the range of subjects he would have to get through. Once or twice he peered at his notes, but he delivered his words with calm authority before mounting a defiant challenge to the Prime Minister. 'So, Mr Brown, what's it going to be? Why don't you go ahead and call that election? Let people decide who can make the changes that we really need in our country. Call that election. We will fight. Britain will win.' The audience leapt to their feet as upbeat music boomed around the hall. Cameron and Samantha waved as the cameras flashed in their faces.

They left as soon as they could. 'It was the riskiest thing I've ever had to do in my life,' Cameron remarked to an aide shortly after-wards. He and his wife, Edward Llewellyn, Andy Coulson and Steve Hilton were whisked away in their official car towards Preston, where they would catch a train to London. On the outskirts of the town they stopped at a pub, where Cameron offered his verdict: 'Well, it wasn't great, but I think it's going to be OK.' When they arrived at Euston station a few hours later, they would not be disappointed: 'Speech of a Lifetime' read the headline on the *Evening Standard* news-stands.[48]

On Tenterhooks

Cameron's speech could not have been better received. Although the party's polling showed that very few people could remember what he actually said in the speech, the manner in which he delivered it made a powerful impact. It marked a turning point in public perceptions of the Tory leader. The polls and focus group surveys were unanimous: he came across as strong, authentic and sincere. The contrast with Gordon Brown's Iraq troop announcement and hesitation over whether to call the election was clear. While Brown's personal rating began to fall, Cameron's rocketed. Still, nothing was being taken for granted by Cameron and his aides. Even before he had stepped onto the stage in the Winter Gardens, a number of staff from Campaign Headquarters had returned to London to prepare for the election campaign. During Thursday, the phones were ringing constantly with word that Number 10 was ready to go.

The next morning, Cameron assembled his team and senior members of the Shadow Cabinet at Millbank. Oliver Letwin was firmly of the view that Brown was about to call an election: he had been informed that the most senior Whitehall mandarins had been put on alert, and there was no way the Prime Minister could pull back. Andrew MacKay believed that this would not stop Brown from retracting.[49] The most encouraging news came with the daily evidence from the party's private polling, as well as two polls (one during Labour's conference and the other the week after) of the marginal seats that would determine the election. Critically, the Tories had dramatically closed the gap on key policy measures, as well as on headline voting intention.

Cameron and Hague went ahead with a planned lunch with the German Interior Minister, Wolfgang Schäuble, who was visiting London. The former Foreign Secretary, Douglas Hurd, who was also there, could not believe that the meeting had not been cancelled. 'David must have been in a heightened state of alert because of the speculation,' Hurd recalls. 'Only forty-eight hours ago he had delivered his speech in Blackpool, but here he was having a serious discussion about the defence of borders and things like that. He was completely calm, as if it was an ordinary day.'[50] Halfway through the lunch, news came through to Edward Llewellyn, Cameron's chief of staff, that the two parties were level-pegging in an opinion poll to be reported that evening on Channel 4 News. As Cameron headed for his constituency that afternoon he was on tenterhooks, regularly checking his mobile phone for any more news from Llewellyn and Coulson. The party machine was still on red alert. 'We got staff together in Campaign Headquarters and told them to go home and enjoy the weekend, because that would be it before the general election,' recalls one of Cameron's aides.

The crucial piece of information came on Saturday morning, when word leaked to Coulson from friends in the press that the *News of the World* was about to publish a poll showing the Tories six points ahead of Labour in marginal seats.[51] Not even the political editors of the main broadcasters were aware of what was happening. Cameron's aides heard that Andrew Marr was on his way to Number 10 to pre-record an interview with Brown that would be broadcast the following day, and assumed that Brown was not about to go to the country. Cameron phoned Nick Robinson, the BBC's political editor, for confirmation. Nursing a cold at home, Robinson was stunned to hear from the Leader of the Opposition that the Prime Minister was about to officially call off the election.

Sure enough, Brown used the Marr interview to rule out an election, not only for the autumn but for the following year as well. The *News of the World* poll had killed any remaining plans in Downing Street. The risks for Brown were too great. The prospect of seeing his sixty-seven-strong majority reduced or even slipping away altogether was not worth contemplating. He had let the genie out of the bottle months before, and his closest aides and ministers had succumbed to the temptation to talk up their chances to such an extent that they completely lost control of events. Idle talk cost them dearly indeed. It was a humiliating retreat for the Prime Minister, who only weeks before had been regarded by many voters as strong, decisive and straight-talking. Now the overwhelming perception was that he was indecisive and weak. Even more harmful for his reputation was his blank denial that the polls had influenced his decision, which gave the impression that he was being disingenuous. There was an immediate sense of anti-climax among senior Tory aides. 'The conference had achieved two things: providing a positive message about us as the party of aspiration and reminding people that Brown was not fit to be Prime Minister,' recalls one aide. 'By the time Gordon took the decision we were ready and up for the fight, and I think we could have won it.' Beneath the bravado, however, there was a palpable feeling of relief in Tory high command.

Once again, Blackpool's Winter Gardens had provided the setting for a captivating political drama. In October 2003 the party was on the verge of imploding, but it pulled back from the brink shortly afterwards. Two years later there was a very real risk of another disaster unfolding, albeit in different circumstances. The leadership restored its relationship with the wider party in the nick of time. The stakes could not have been higher. One false move could have tipped the scales back in Brown's favour. The Labour machine was primed for battle. A few weeks later it emerged that Labour head-quarters had already spent £1 million on buying advertising space and recruiting extra staff for an election campaign.[52]

Cameron's leadership had been on the line after a disastrous summer. The party was staring at the very real possibility of a fourth defeat. Yet it managed to unite when it most needed to. Cameron and his team had been put to the test. Ultimately, it was Gordon Brown's indecision and misjudgement that gave Cameron a precious lifeline – one he grabbed without hesitation. Osborne's tax announce-ments and Cameron's bravura performance sealed one of the greatest escapes in modern political times. In an extraordinary turnaround, Labour's 43–31 per cent lead in the polls the weekend after Brown's speech had been transformed to a 42–36 Tory lead ten days later. A 9 per cent swing represented one the largest and swiftest reversals in party fortunes in living memory.

Once the relief began to subside, Cameron's friends and supporters claimed that he had held firm throughout. 'What was important was that despite the ducking and diving with the inheritance tax proposals, fundamentally he didn't do what previous leaders had done, which was to completely shift direction,' says Nick Boles.[53] Cameron had indeed recovered from the nadir of the summer after some deft footwork. He held his nerve when many others in his party were about to give up on him only eighteen months into his leadership. 'David proved his mettle,' one sympathetic former Cabinet minister remarked shortly after the conference, before confidently adding, 'He won't be in trouble with the party again.' This turned out to be wishful thinking, but for the time being at least, the wind was back in the Tory sails.

EIGHT

Riding High
October 2007–September 2008

As the dust began to settle after a tumultuous fortnight, confidence returned inside Tory high command. 'After the anti-climax, there was a wave of elation – a feeling that we had somehow changed the political weather,' one insider recalled. The Tories accused the Prime Minister of having 'bottled it'. Yet the sense of confidence was tempered by the fact that the Parliament looked set to run a full five-year term, until spring 2010 – the last possible time a general election could be held. 'It dawned on us that we were going to go the distance, and despite all our bravado we weren't ready for government,' a senior party official recalls. But they would at least have ample time to prepare. Important lessons would be drawn from the testing summer months, and indeed from the eighteen months since Cameron became leader. There was a renewed sense of goodwill towards the leadership, but the question of whether the party had sufficiently modernised preyed on the minds of Team Cameron. It was important to avoid hubris. 'We did not think it was in the bag. Brown may have screwed up his perfect chance, but we could not take him for granted,' a former member of Cameron's team admitted. There would be two and a half years in which to present the party as a credible alternative government. Before that it would have to prove its competence as a party of opposition.

Drawing Brown's Blood

Conservative MPs returned to Westminster in confident mood after the drama of Blackpool. For the first time since he came to office,

Gordon Brown appeared vulnerable. Desperate to regain the initiative, Number 10 pinned its hopes on the forthcoming Pre-Budget Report (PBR) and the Comprehensive Spending Review (CSR). The Prime Minister and his aides calculated that by partially adopting George Osborne's inheritance tax proposals they would neutralise the Tories' new weapon.

As the Chancellor, Alistair Darling, delivered the PBR to the Commons on 9 October, Cameron and Osborne could not believe what they were hearing. To Tory cheers, Darling announced that the inheritance tax threshold for a couple's joint estate would be doubled to £600,000 (well short of Osborne's plan to raise it to £1 million). 'We were passing notes to the opposition frontbench from outside the chamber. I thought, "He can't do this – stealing one of our most successful policies!"' recalls one of Osborne's team. 'Then we realised that Labour had briefed against it so much because they were preparing to change their own policy. Ed Balls [Schools Secretary and one of Brown's closest confidants] probably thought that by adopting it, we would be left without any winnings.' Then the Chancellor announced plans to introduce a flat charge on 'non-doms', another proposal from the Blackpool conference. As soon as Darling sat down, Osborne rose to his feet to taunt the Chancellor for copying Tory ideas. The press were equally dismissive. 'Darling the Tory Tax Thief' ran the *Evening Standard*'s headline that evening, setting the tone for the next few days' coverage.[1] With typically robust humour, the *Guardian*'s cartoonist Steve Bell portrayed Darling's prominent eyebrows as two Tory oak trees.[2]

It had been charged by Conservative politicians since the mid-1990s that Blair and Brown repeatedly stole their best ideas. John Major famously complained that it felt like returning to the beach after a swim to find that all your clothes had been taken. The strategy had served New Labour well in the past, but cunning positioning looked like naked political calculation in the aftermath of the botched election decision. Newspaper editorials questioned whether the Prime Minister was taking key decisions over the public finances that had more to do with partisan manoeuvres than with the public interest.

Indeed, the PBR only reinforced the widely held opinion in the aftermath of the party conference season that the Prime Minister had suffered a damaging blow to his authority.

The day after the PBR, on Wednesday, 10 October, David Cameron gave his most effective performance at Prime Minister's Questions since Brown became Prime Minister. 'He's the first Prime Minister in history to flunk an election because he thought he was going to win it,' he declared, as Tory MPs erupted in wild laughter. Once again, Brown denied that his decision not to call an election had anything to do with the opinion polls. Cameron responded with a withering attack, reminiscent of Blair's assaults on John Major a decade before. 'For ten years the Prime Minister plotted and schemed to have this job – and for what? No conviction, just calculation; no vision, just a vacuum. Last week he lost his political authority, and this week he is losing his moral authority. How long are we going to have to wait before the past makes way for the future?'[3] Faces on the government frontbench were decidedly glum as Brown struggled to deflect Cameron's attacks.

A few weeks later, another set-piece parliamentary occasion provided Cameron with an opportunity to taunt the Prime Minister once more on the election that never was. Responding to the Queen's Speech on 6 November, he declared: 'Say what you like about Tony Blair, at least he was decisive. Isn't the only change we've had to swap a strong prime minister for a weak one?' As the Prime Minister rose to reply, his hands shook as he leant awkwardly on the dispatch box. 'It was a crystallising moment,' an aide recalls. 'You just had to look at the contrasting body language between our lot and theirs.' Brown had handed his adversary a precious political gift. By compounding earlier misjudgements, he had allowed himself to be portrayed as weak and calculating. In a matter of weeks he had ceded much of the advantage that his first three months in the premiership had achieved. The stage was now set for the Conservative leadership to exploit the government's discomfort even further.

On 20 November Alistair Darling was forced to make an emergency statement to the Commons revealing that HM Revenue and

Customs had lost two CDs containing child benefit data comprising the personal details of twenty-five million people, almost half the population. The Chancellor blamed a junior official, but the revelation did enormous damage to the government's reputation for competence. Before the announcement, Osborne was called in to the Treasury to be briefed by Darling. Like the Prime Minister's a few weeks earlier, the Chancellor's hands were trembling as he told his opposite number that he did not know where the discs were. A subsequent investigation into the lost discs raised 'serious questions of governance and accountability'.[4] Now Brown had become the subject of ridicule, deadly for any Prime Minister. Vince Cable, the Liberal Democrats' respected Treasury spokesman and caretaker leader, delivered one of the most effective one-liners about Brown. 'The House has noticed the Prime Minister's remarkable transformation in the past few weeks – from Stalin to Mr Bean.'[5]

By the end of November, Labour's average poll rating had dropped to 32 per cent, while the Tories remained steady on 40 per cent.[6] There was a sense of renewed confidence among Cameron's inner circle. 'Of course there were blunders like the lost discs, but we were in a position to capitalise on their mistakes,' one senior aide recalls. 'We had kept them in a tight space.' As party leader Hague, Duncan Smith and Howard had been unable to take advantage of the government's difficulties, from the relatively trivial débâcle over the Millennium Dome to the bloody aftermath of the war in Iraq. As long as the Conservative Party was regarded as out of touch, divided and lacking in strong leadership, it struggled to exploit Labour's weaknesses. Despite Cameron's low summer in 2007, he had managed to recover his standing and that of his party. By November, many people still doubted whether the opposition was ready for office, but they were at least prepared to listen to what it had to say.

Rolling up the Sleeves
Now that the general election was several years away, the Conservative Party would be afforded the opportunity to continue its policy-making process and sharpen up its political operation. The key lesson

from the drama of the past three months was that nothing could be taken for granted. Under the direction of James O'Shaughnessy, the young head of research at Policy Exchange who replaced George Bridges in September, the Conservative Research Department (CRD) entered a new phase. There was a feeling that the party's ability to attack and counterattack had lost focus during the first eighteen months of Cameron's leadership, while the emphasis was on decontaminating the brand. 'We were re-energising and re-politicising the CRD,' says O'Shaughnessy. 'Unless we got our message out there as aggressively as we could, it was very difficult to launch positive initiatives.'[7] Day-to-day rebuttals of government attacks and forensic analysis of government announcements should be part and parcel of an effective opposition – they were the attributes that had made New Labour such a disciplined fighting force in the mid-1990s – but they had been all too lacking since 1997, even during Howard's tenure. Although the Tory operation was still far from perfect, the attention now given to providing ammunition to fire at an embattled government began to make a difference.

The new time frame also provided an opportunity for the party to begin work on developing a serious policy platform. Oliver Letwin had hastily prepared a manifesto over the summer, taking the best ideas from the policy review. 'There was quite a long period of momentum during which we were beginning to establish a serious policy programme,' he recalls.[8] Together with the frontbench teams, the CRD took advantage of the breathing space to recruit additional policy specialists and researchers. 'The pressure of the conference and the snap election threat hugely accelerated everything, but now we had time to firm up policy,' recalls O'Shaughnessy.[9] He and Letwin hit upon the idea of publishing a series of 'Green Papers', which Cameron readily agreed to. Three themes would underpin the papers: 'the Opportunity Agenda' (shifting power from the state to individuals in areas such as schooling and housing); 'the Responsibility Agenda' (strengthening the structures of society such as marriage and welfare systems); and 'the Security Agenda' (protecting the country from external threats like terrorism and climate change).

The first of the green papers, on education, was published on 20 November. Largely the inspiration of the Shadow Schools Secretary Michael Gove, one of the intellectual powers within the Shadow Cabinet, it was a wide-ranging document that included a proposal enabling parents and other groups and charities to set up independently run state schools. Based on the successful Swedish 'Free Schools', this showed that the party was willing to learn from best practice abroad. By contrast with the criticism of some of the policy group reports during the summer months, the green papers were commended in the press and among policy experts. The third, on welfare reform, launched on 8 January 2008 and drawing heavily on successful welfare-to-work schemes in the United States and Australia, was particularly well received.

As 2007 drew to a close, there was a marked change in the way the outside world looked upon the Conservatives. Individuals and organisations were more inclined to give the party a fair hearing. 'It was a golden period,' recalls one of Cameron's aides. 'People wanted to a get a piece of David in a way that they hadn't before. I noticed a change in the calibre of people coming in to see him – from industry, the armed services, finance and charity. They were willing to be publicly associated with us, whereas before they only wanted to be in touch privately.' The policy review had already enabled Cameron to build his 'big tent', and to include within it the likes of Bob Geldof and Pauline Neville-Jones. Now the leadership invited a number of other prominent public figures from different walks of life to head *ad hoc* policy commissions to help inform party policy. They included the former Commissioner of the Metropolitan Police Sir John Stevens, who looked into border security issues, and the author Frederick Forsyth and Falklands veteran Simon Weston, who examined the Military Covenant.

In order to strengthen the policy process in the expectation that the party might take office after the next election, Cameron tasked Francis Maude with setting up an 'Implementation Unit'. Maude had been moved from the chairmanship of the party in July, which some regarded as a demotion. But as Shadow Cabinet Office minister he was given the huge task of preparing the party for office. In January 2008 he was joined by Nick Boles, the fellow moderniser he had employed to set up Policy Exchange in 2002. 'Politicians don't like to do this, because it looks like you're tempting providence, but actually the really presumptuous thing to do is not to prepare,' says Maude. Together they formed a small unit of staff and a panel of former civil servants, business leaders and other policy experts to examine the ideas being generated by the CRD and the frontbench teams. 'We started by taking a proposal from one of the policy groups or an entire green paper and just worked through it,' Maude explains.[10] Their objective was to produce practical plans for implementing policies in different scenarios, as well as feeding into the development of policy.

Underpinning the work of the unit was the belief Cameron, Osborne and Letwin shared with many commentators that Tony Blair had failed to make the most of his first term in office. They may have come to respect New Labour in some ways, but its policy preparation for office before 1997 was not one of them. 'Blair came into power with many good intentions, but for several years wandered around in the mists trying to work out how on earth to deal with things like schools and crime and hospitals and so on, and not really having very much idea,' says Letwin.[11] Only halfway through his second term, and especially after his third election victory in 2005, did Blair settle on a bold agenda for reform, and by then Gordon Brown was doing his best to obstruct it. Measures to extend choice in the public services and to reform the cumbersome welfare system chimed with Team Cameron's approach – not least because they believed they amounted to a continuation (or more accurately an adaptation) of policies that the Conservatives introduced during the 1990s. New Labour's own experience in opposition before 1997 would prove instructive: Maude and his team privately consulted a few Labour figures from that period to help inform the process. It was a sign that the party was seriously contemplating life in office for the first time in over a decade.

While the party machine was being cranked up for two more years in opposition, Cameron and his inner circle discussed strategy. Although the period of danger over the summer had passed, it posed serious questions about just how much modernisation the party as a whole could tolerate. When Osborne, Gove, Hilton and Coulson met at Cameron's house in North Kensington on Sunday evenings during the autumn, this was a recurring theme in their discussions. As a passionate advocate of modernisation, Hilton had been less inclined to tolerate the concerns of the 'backwoodsmen' in the party who resisted change. But the events of the first half of the year showed that the leadership had become dangerously detached from the wider party.

The stamp duty and inheritance tax announcements in Blackpool proved popular with the electorate, but just as important, they had the effect of reconciling the leadership with the soul of the party. 'The connection with the rank and file lasted two or three months after the conference boost, but it then began to recede,' one MP close to the leadership observed. 'We had to keep feeding them some red meat.' Much more had to be done to keep MPs and the rank and file onside. Yet some of Cameron's aides insist that he had always favoured a 'balanced approach' to modernising the party. If the leadership was to capitalise on the dramatic reversal of fortunes in October, it would have to show this far more clearly in the months to come.

The 'shock therapy' of Cameron's first few months as leader was undoubtedly too much for many Tory MPs and activists, who felt that there was not enough clear blue water with Labour. As the leadership pulled the wider party away from its comfort zone, the gasps of frustration became ever more audible by the spring of 2007. However, the 'Vote Blue, Go Green' campaign, the A-List of prospective parliamentary candidates and the focus on the NHS and social reform had begun to change the party's image in the eyes of the electorate. Any serious discussion of tax, law and order and immigration – the issues that still stirred the passions of the rank and file – could now be conducted in a measured tone, and without the charge that the party was concerned with nothing else. After the conference season, Cameron and his inner circle agreed that the 'shock therapy' phase had well and truly passed. 'There was a general willingness to move on to other things – we were all comfortable with that,' recalls one.

Some sympathetic commentators, like Matthew Parris, Michael Portillo and Daniel Finkelstein, warned against letting up on modernisation – there was still more to do to convince voters that the party had changed. However, it was not simply a question of going too slow or too fast. Opinion within Cameron's senior team, on issues from foreign affairs to social policy, was more nuanced than was often understood. It was never an identikit unit comprising only yes-men. Osborne and Gove were generally more hawkish on international issues (as demonstrated by their views on Iraq) than Cameron, whereas on the issue of supporting marriage through the tax system Cameron was the most passionate. 'There is a healthy tension between us – some of us are tacticians like George, and others are strategists like Steve. We have different views, but we talk all the time, and that's why it works,' says a senior member of the team. Cameron would invariably make a decision only after a rigorous discussion in which an idea was 'tested to destruction'. 'David sits in the chair, listens, chips in and probes the argument, while the rest of us quite often take diametrically opposed positions,' says one aide. 'Typically at the end he will go away, sleep on it and come back with a view the following morning.' Instances when this did not happen, such as the immediate aftermath of David Willett's grammar school speech (when Cameron and his inner team were unable to meet and discuss how to respond), revealed how the leadership could lose its composure and grip.

The New Year provided an opportunity for the leadership to reframe its vision for the country by showing that the party could secure 'progressive ends through Conservative means' – a phrase that James O'Shaughnessy, the head of policy, coined with Oliver Letwin. Like the speeches that had failed to catch the popular imagination in the spring and summer of 2007, this was bound to provoke reaction from the right. Lord Tebbit and Simon Heffer were among those who argued that there was nothing to distinguish this message from that of New Labour. What was the point of 'Conservative means' if they produced the same 'progressive ends' as the centre-left, such as a strong society, a green economy and a tolerance of different lifestyles? Here there was a major philosophical difference which Cameron's circle and their critics on the right would never reconcile.

Under the new slogan 'Change You Can Trust', O'Shaughnessy circulated an internal memo listing priorities for 2008. It was strikingly similar to 'Change We Can Believe In', one of the campaign slogans used by Barack Obama, the Democratic presidential candidate in the United States. The Tories would aim to win the London mayoral election in May, increase support in northern England, establish a reputation for being the party of economic competence and stretch their lead over Labour in the opinion polls to ten points or more. It was a highly ambitious list: there could be no setbacks.

From New Year Blues to Spring Optimism

The New Year was only a few weeks old when Cameron was presented with just such a setback, as a story broke which threatened to bring back memories of Tory sleaze. It was revealed that over a period of three years Derek Conway, the former whip and member of David Davis's leadership campaign, had paid his son Freddie more than £40,000 as a part-time research assistant in the Commons while he was studying for a degree at Newcastle University.[12] Cameron made no comment until the Commons Standards and Privileges Committee investigated the case. On Monday, 28 January, the Committee reprimanded Conway after 'no record' was found of Freddie Conway doing any work for him as a researcher.

The episode posed a problem for Cameron. Would he take on Conway, who still carried some influence with a number of backbenchers who remained uneasy about his leadership? Conway had a reputation as a key fixer in the parliamentary party, often to the advantage of David Davis. It was also he who had coined the disparaging phrase 'Notting Hill set'. Labour MPs pounced on the revelation: the disgrace of a Tory MP was the first piece of good news they had had in months. It was a perfect opportunity to undermine Cameron's message that the party had moved on from its sleazy past.

Having digested the Committee's findings overnight and consulted the Chief Whip, Patrick McLoughlin, the next morning Cameron decided to withdraw the whip from Conway. 'He texted us early in the morning to say that he had to go and that was it,' recalls one of Cameron's senior aides. This was the ultimate sanction a leader could deploy against an MP, casting him into parliamentary no man's land, and it was the first time Cameron had had to use such a disciplinary measure. The risks of not acting against Conway, with the damage that could have caused to the party's reputation, outweighed any other consideration. Conway duly apologised to the Commons and was suspended from Parliament for ten days.

Despite his hesitation to begin with, Cameron knew he had to show his ruthless side: the alternative would have made him look weak. A few of Conway's allies on the backbenches expressed their discontent, like Roger Gale, who decried the 'witch hunt', but Cameron had turned an awkward situation to his advantage.[13] The vast majority of the parliamentary party and the rank and file were appalled by Conway's behaviour. 'In withdrawing the whip, David succeeded in stopping the media and public thinking that this was Tory sleaze, which had been John Major's problem,' says Andrew MacKay, Cameron's senior parliamentary adviser.[14] As it turned out, the embarrassment that would be caused by the financial arrangements of MPs (from all sides) did not end with Derek Conway.

Despite the Conway affair, the Conservatives entered the spring with a sense of optimism. The next major electoral landmark was approaching: the elections for London mayor, the Greater London Assembly (GLA) and the annual round of local elections across the country. Gordon Brown and his government were showing no signs of recovery after a difficult winter. If anything, matters had turned for the worse for Labour. In his last budget as Chancellor in March 2007, Brown had lowered the basic rate of income tax by 2p, while announcing that the starter 10p rate would be abolished the following

April, at the start of the 2008–09 financial year. Brown himself had introduced the 10p tax band in 1999 so that low earners would pay less tax. Labour MPs cheered his final budget, believing that he had conjured a final act of political magic that would have little impact on the Treasury's finances. A few Labour backbenchers had spotted that lower earners would actually lose out from the abolition of the 10p rate, but any voices of dissent were kept to a minimum on the eve of Brown's succession to the premiership. At the time George Osborne called it the 'tax con' budget, for giving with one hand while taking away with the other, but his attack failed to make an impact. As the new financial year approached, respected bodies like the Institute for Fiscal Studies warned that 5.3 million families would lose out. Crucially, opinion within the Labour Party hardened. A rebellion in the Parliamentary Labour Party, led by the former Welfare Minister Frank Field, gathered pace during the spring, ahead of Alistair Darling's first budget. 'Unlike any other disquiet there has been on the backbenches, this is an issue which strikes at the core value that every Labour MP brings into politics – that is, that we are here to protect the poorest,' Field remarked.[15]

It was at this point that Labour's traditional supporters began to abandon the government, prompting a crisis of confidence in Brown's leadership within the party. By the end of April, Labour's average opinion poll rating had fallen to 31 per cent.[16] The Tory machine was already in campaigning mode for the May elections. The opposition had concentrated on 'crime mapping' (to help identify crime hotspots in local communities), and criticised 'Labour's NHS cuts' and the closure of local hospital units. However, attacking the 10p tax decision had to be handled with care – the Tories were still not associated with helping the less well-off in society. 'We chose to allow the space for people like Frank Field and the Lib Dems to attack it, because they were better at that type of attack,' explains an aide to Osborne. 'We hired actors to dress up in 10p outfits to make the point, but on the whole we were restrained.' It was a smart tactic. By the time the government acted to mollify the Labour rebellion on 13 May, through a compensation package for some of those who had lost out because of the removal of the 10p band, it was too little too late.

London Goes for Boris

Electing a Conservative Mayor of London would be no mean feat. The Conservatives had to defeat the two-term incumbent, Ken Livingstone, to show that they were firmly on the road to electoral recovery. Livingstone was hoping for a third term as mayor, despite an earlier pledge to serve only two terms. Originally standing as an independent in 2000, having fallen out with Tony Blair, he had established a powerbase in the capital. A former leader of the old Greater London Council on the left of the Labour Party, Livingstone was an experienced and plain-talking politician. By defying his leadership, he had brought about his own renaissance. By 2004 he had also made his peace with Blair, working with him on London's successful bid for the 2012 Olympics, and earning praise for his measured response to the 2005 London bombings. Despite losing some of his popular appeal during his second term after a number of controversial decisions and run-ins with the London newspaper the *Evening Standard*, Livingstone was regarded as the favourite. Cameron desperately needed to win the mayoralty to prove to commentators and the country that his party had momentum. With an electorate of 5.5 million, this would be the biggest test of opinion before the general election. Selecting the right candidate would be crucial. Steven Norris, the ebullient former Transport Minister who stood in 2000 and 2004, had failed to defeat Livingstone, and a new candidate who could personify the new Conservative Party had to be found. It would be a far from straightforward exercise.

In 2006 Cameron announced that the candidate would be chosen by an American-style open primary, with all registered London voters given a vote in the process. In the absence of high-profile names coming forward, the deadline for forming a shortlist of candidates was extended into 2007. Various campaigners and celebrities with no particular association to the party were approached – from the founder of the *Big Issue*, John Bird, to the disc jockey Mike Read and even the former Prime Minister Sir John Major. All turned the offer down, as the process descended into a farce. Even Greg Dyke, the former Director-General of the BBC, a supporter of the Liberal Democrats, was approached – he revealed in April 2007 that he had turned down an offer from the Tory leadership to run as a joint Conservative–Liberal Democrat candidate. Tory activists in the capital were furious at the idea of being deprived of the right to choose a candidate who would stand solely for the Conservatives.

One of the forty individuals to put themselves forward was Nicholas Boles, the founding director of Policy Exchange. Boles was a keen moderniser and a friend of Cameron, having narrowly missed out on becoming an MP in 2005. Openly gay, he epitomised a new generation of aspiring cosmopolitan Tories. In March 2007 he resigned as director of Policy Exchange to focus on his campaign to win the mayoral nomination, but he was forced to withdraw three months later after being diagnosed with cancer.

Until June Boles was regarded as the front-runner, and his sudden withdrawal presented the leadership with a dilemma. With the final deadline for nominations fast approaching, Boles suggested to Michael Gove and Steve Hilton the possibility of Boris Johnson. They agreed that he might have the profile to take on Livingstone. As a regular guest on satirical television programmes like *Have I Got News For You*, 'Boris' was one of the most colourful and recognisable Conservative politicians. He and Cameron went back a long way, both having gone to Eton and Oxford, where they were members of the Bullingdon Club, which infamously destroyed dining venues after bouts of raucous drinking. Boris was two years older than Cameron, and was more extrovert, but they had two things in common: unbridled self-confidence and political ambition. While Cameron chose politics, Boris went into journalism at first, and after making his name as Brussels correspondent for the *Daily Telegraph*, he became editor of the *Spectator* at just thirty-five. Only then did he make the move into politics, replacing Michael Heseltine as MP for Henley in 2001.

Boris's ascent of the greasy pole had not been as rapid as Cameron's.

They had both helped Iain Duncan Smith to prepare for Prime Minister's Questions, and Michael Howard promoted Boris to Shadow Arts Minister, but his frontbench career faltered in October 2004 after a *Spectator* editorial said Liverpool was 'wallowing in victimhood' over the execution of Iraq hostage Ken Bigley. Howard forced him to visit the city to apologise. The revelation of his affair with the journalist Petronella Wyatt the following month was the final straw for Howard, who sacked him from the frontbench. An early supporter of the Cameron campaign, Boris was made spokesman for higher education when his friend won the party leadership in December 2005. Having resigned as editor of the *Spectator*, he took to his new role with gusto. Despite his often fumbling appearance, he was an articulate politician with a growing popular appeal.

Gove, Hilton and Boles put the idea of Boris's candidacy to Cameron. They discussed the risks: how could such a gaffe-prone politician survive the glare of an intense election campaign? However, if he could combine his celebrity with discipline, he might stand a chance. It was also suggested that if Boris won, his departure from the Commons might not be a bad thing for Cameron. Some believed that his ambition knew no bounds, and that despite their friendship, a sense of rivalry between the two men had already become apparent. Despite being reluctant at first, Boris was won round to the idea. Friends suggested that running for mayor would be an attractive alternative to the long, hard slog in Parliament. After all, he had not made it into the Shadow Cabinet in July 2007, when others like Gove who had only entered the Commons in 2005 had gained promotion. Daniel Ritterband, one of Boles's campaign team (and former staffer at Campaign Headquarters) was charged with sounding Boris out at the *Spectator* summer party on a warm July evening. A few days later Boris rang Ritterband: 'Let's do it.'[17] His application was made the next day, 16 July, which happened to be the final deadline. 'I wouldn't have gone in for it if I didn't think I could win [the election],' Boris recalls. 'I always thought it would be possible even though it would be hard.'[18] At a hastily arranged press conference outside City

Hall on London's South Bank, Boris was mobbed by reporters as he arrived on his trademark bicycle. He told them that the opportunity was 'too wonderful to miss', and that he wanted to 'put the smile back on London's face'. 'It's a riot,' he told the bemused crowd before pedalling away.[19] Officials at party headquarters were far from amused, and let it be known to Boris's fledgling campaign team that the announcement was 'messy', and the candidate 'bumbling'. It was only the first of several instances when Millbank expressed their reservations about the campaign.

Boris went on to beat his lesser-known rivals on the shortlist in the 'open primary' of London voters. When the result was announced on 27 September, he had won over 75 per cent of the votes cast. Labour ministers dismissed him as a 'clown', while Ken Livingstone warned that his election could turn London's administration into a 'shambles'. Cameron, however, congratulated him, saying that he would be 'an excellent candidate, and I know the party will unite behind him to remove Ken Livingstone'.[20] Behind the scenes, though, doubts about Boris's readiness for the fight began to gather. During the autumn his team did their best to get him up to speed on the policy issues facing the Mayor of London. 'We told Cameron that we were in policy lockdown for two months, which was a mistake in hindsight because it led to tensions with his office. They wanted a no-gaffes candidate ready to campaign straight away, but we knew that if Boris made a gaffe in the first few months, the press and Livingstone would jump on us, and we would never get off the ground,' recalls one insider from the campaign. The problem was that Boris lacked an all-round team, and little in the way of help was coming from the centre. Daniel Ritterband specialised in communications, but he was not a policy specialist. James O'Shaughnessy was on the verge of fulfilling that role when he was poached from Policy Exchange to become the party's head of policy and research in September. 'By January, we still didn't have much in the way of policy – apart from promising to scrap bendy buses and help people in the outer boroughs,' says another member of Johnson's team. 'I couldn't believe the briefing that was appearing in the press about

our campaign – it was clear it was coming from party headquarters.'
Officials in Millbank were indeed worried. They feared that Boris
was gaffe-prone and invariably turned up late for events. It did not
bode well for the campaign proper, which would begin in the New
Year. 'There was a lot of nervousness – people warned that Boris
could self-destruct, and that would be damaging for us because he
had a shared background with David.'

Despite a difficult few months, the Boris campaign began to take
shape. Hard-hitting advertisements about murder rates in the capital
made a splash in the London *Evening Standard* at the beginning of
the New Year, but the campaign still suffered from a lack of experience and funds. 'Few believed that Boris could actually win, and so
we had very little cash to begin with,' recalls a campaign figure. This
changed when Lord Marland, the former Party Treasurer, became
the chief fundraiser and treasurer for the campaign. Marland was
also instrumental in recruiting Lynton Crosby, who had directed the
party's 2005 general election campaign. Having failed to tempt him
back to run Campaign Headquarters, Cameron hoped that Crosby
would seize the opportunity to direct the Boris campaign. 'If anyone
could handle Boris it was Lynton,' one of Cameron's former aides
recalls. Crosby agreed to take on the task on the condition that he
would have full operational control.

Starting in late January, Crosby had only four months in which
to turn the campaign around. Crucially, he and Boris worked well
together. 'Boris really listened to him,' recalls one of the campaign
team. 'When he gave a bad speech, Crosby would not beat around
the bush. He would say: "Do you really want to win this?" and Boris
really stepped up to it.' Relations with party headquarters also
improved. Around forty staff were seconded from Millbank to help
with the campaign, which was based at County Hall, once home to
the old GLC. Crosby had a useful ally in Steve Hilton, but when
other members of Cameron's office rang occasionally to offer advice,
he would give them short shrift. He motivated the campaign team
with three golden rules: don't take victory for granted, focus relentlessly on the outer London boroughs (where Tory support was

strongest) and concentrate solely on the campaign, not on what might happen afterwards.

As the election drew near, opinion polls conducted by YouGov for the *Evening Standard* showed Boris leading Livingstone. Boris campaigned relentlessly on tackling youth crime and improving transport. 'We were all still quite nervous that Ken was a hard man to beat, but the focus on the outer boroughs really began to work,' one campaigner recalls. The Crosby discipline was paying dividends, not least for Boris, who found his feet on the campaign trail. Livingstone and Labour ministers derided him as an inexperienced buffoon, but he had defied expectations in becoming a serious candidate without losing his popular appeal.

When Londoners turned out to vote on 1 May, Boris convincingly beat Livingstone by 53 to 47 per cent, polling over a million votes, on a turnout of 45 per cent (9 per cent higher than in the previous mayoral election, in 2004). Crosby's strategy had paid off as Conservative voters in the outer London boroughs turned out in force, overwhelming Livingstone's support, which had also increased. 'It was the first time we had won anything in a while,' recalls Marland. 'It was strange, because we had become so used to losing that when we won we couldn't quite believe it.'[21]

Defying most expectations from the start, Boris had won an impressive victory. Despite this, he felt there were greater forces at work. 'Proud though I am of what we did, we quite effectively surfed the wave that was ready to be surfed. It was a function of the changes that were taking place in the wider context of British politics. Labour had lost their great charmer in Tony Blair, and people didn't really like Brown, plus the fact that Livingstone had been there for too long.'[22] The result gave a huge boost of confidence to the Tory leadership and the wider party. 'Although Boris's ascent was not important from a modernising perspective, it showed that we could win,' recalls a party official. 'It was a fantastic leg-up.'

The elections on 1 May 2008 showed that the party was indeed riding high. Not only had the party won London (both the mayoralty and the Greater London Assembly), but it swept the board in town halls across the rest of the country, winning 44 per cent of the projected share of the vote, 4 per cent higher than the previous year. The Tories led Labour by twenty points (roughly a reversal of Labour's triumphant performance in the 1995 local elections, two years before the 1997 landslide), and exceeded all expectations by gaining over 250 councillors. No sooner had the celebrations finished than the leadership began to concentrate on the next electoral test – a by-election in the north of England.

Northern Breakthrough

The Conservatives had not won a by-election from Labour since 1982. Now the death of Gwyneth Dunwoody, the veteran Labour MP for Crewe and Nantwich in Cheshire, presented an opportunity for the party to show that it could make progress in the north as well as the south. At number 165 on the Tories' target list, it was a safe Labour seat with a majority of over 7,000. A popular local MP, Dunwoody had held the seat, which included the run-down railway town of Crewe and its rural surroundings, since 1983. The seat had not even fallen to the Conservatives in Mrs Thatcher's landslide election victory that year.

The news that Dunwoody's daughter would fight the seat for Labour did not bode well for the Conservatives. Nevertheless, Campaign Headquarters swung into action. Michael Ashcroft's team, steered by Stephen Gilbert, the party's Director of Campaigns, ensured that it was a rigorously research-led and disciplined campaign. Along with David Cameron and the entire Shadow Cabinet, scores of MPs and activists descended on the constituency to support the candidate Edward Timpson, a local solicitor and heir to the Timpson shoe-repair and key-cutting firm. Labour did their best to portray Timpson as a Tory 'toff', even hiring actors dressed in top hats and tails to follow him around on the campaign trail. Their accusations that he did not understand the problems of voters in a working-class constituency did not faze Timpson. Voters were far more concerned with the government's abolition of the 10p tax band and the rising price of petrol than with his personal background. The government's announcement on 13 May that it would compensate low earners by raising the tax-free allowance for all taxpayers came too late to boost its prospects in the by-election. Meanwhile, the Conservatives continued to invest time and resources into tailoring the party's message. 'We set ourselves up as the agents of change, while Labour looked cheap and nasty,' recalls a senior aide to the leadership.

The result on 22 May electrified the political atmosphere. 'Right up until the night itself we didn't have any idea of what would happen, but when we saw the votes piling up, it was clear that we had made a massive breakthrough,' remembers a party insider. With a huge swing of over 17 per cent, Timpson won the seat with a majority of nearly 8,000. As had happened in London, middle-class voters from outlying areas turned out to vote in large numbers for the Conservatives, and Labour's dwindling core working-class vote in Crewe was not enough to win the seat.

An exuberant David Cameron travelled to the constituency the next day to congratulate the first new Conservative MP since he became leader. Labour's charge that Cameron and his party were 'toffs' who could not win outside their traditional areas of support had suddenly lost its potency. Although he warned against complacency, Cameron hailed the 'end of New Labour here on the streets of Crewe and Nantwich'. The Conservatives were the clear beneficiaries of a major shift in public opinion against Gordon Brown's government, and had ended their notorious run of poor by-election performances. For the first time in over a decade the opposition, rather than the Liberal Democrats, had become an effective vehicle for protest against the government. Yet Crewe and Nantwich had more significance than as a mere protest vote against the government. Coming hard on the heels of the London victory, it showed that the Tories were gaining momentum across the country. By the beginning of June they began to open up double-digit leads in the polls.[23] With Labour drifting nineteen points behind the Conservatives on 26 per cent, Cameron had suddenly found uplift.

Davis's Bombshell

Events back in Westminster would soon spoil the mood of celebration. David Davis had been an effective and loyal Shadow Home Secretary since losing the 2005 leadership election. It was a role in which he had over four years' experience. By far the largest demand on him was to hold the government to account over its efforts to counter the threat of terrorism, particularly from Islamic extremists. He had led the party's opposition to Tony Blair's attempt to extend the period of detention without trial for terror suspects to ninety days as a response to the 7/7 London attacks; a Labour rebellion had forced the government to reduce the limit to twenty-eight days. Following attempted attacks in London and Glasgow in July 2007, Gordon Brown revived the argument for extending the limit, and an increase to forty-two days was agreed by the government. Davis, however, argued that this was unnecessary, and Cameron and the Shadow Cabinet agreed to oppose the measure, which was due to be voted on in the Commons on Wednesday, 11 June.

The ensuing debate was one of the hardest-fought parliamentary battles in years. The government had been defeated on the same issue in 2005, a large Labour rebellion was growing, and the Liberal Democrats and other minor parties were opposed to the measure. Despite support from some senior police officers for a forty-two-day limit, the Director of Public Prosecutions and senior figures from the legal profession weighed in against the extension. Only the nine Democratic Ulster Unionist (DUP) MPs held their counsel. As the largest party in Northern Ireland, they were less inclined to oppose tough counter-terrorism legislation.

The numbers did not look good for the government, and Davis was confident of winning until the week before the vote. In the aftermath of Crewe and Nantwich, losing such an important vote would deal a huge blow to Gordon Brown's authority. Davis and the Tory whips took nothing for granted, realising that the government had committed the Prime Minister's reputation to the measure. They were also aware that the Labour rebels were not as steadfast in their opposition as they had been over the ninety-days proposal. As the vote approached, both the government's and the opposition's negotiations with the DUP intensified. 'Even on the day we didn't know what they were going to do,' recalls one of Davis's confidants. In the event, thirty-six Labour backbenchers rebelled – enough to strip the government of its majority. Yet it scraped home by nine votes: the DUP had saved the government and prevented the opposition from inflicting a humiliating defeat.

David Davis took the result personally. He had worked night and day to defeat the government on the issue. The weekend before, he had decided that in the event of losing the vote he would resign as an MP, forcing a by-election in his Yorkshire seat of Haltemprice and Howden, which he held with a majority of just over 5,000. He anticipated that Cameron would react badly to such a step, as would the press. But he felt that only by such a high-profile announcement, live on television outside the Commons, could he 'punch through and get a positive reaction from the public and help the party', and provoke a full public debate about the defence of civil liberties against an encroaching state. 'I went through all the worst-case scenarios and still decided it was worthwhile. Having gone through all the permutations, my presumption was that my career would be over.'[24] Davis was right in that regard. Unnecessarily forcing a by-election at the public's expense was an eccentric move for a backbencher, let alone a senior member of the Shadow Cabinet.

Immediately after the key vote in the Commons on 11 June, Davis asked to see Cameron behind the Speaker's Chair. They made the short walk to the Shadow Cabinet room, where Davis dropped his bombshell. Cameron only had a few minutes to spare because he had to go to a fundraising party at his house in West London. 'Why?' he asked Davis in shock. 'This matters, David – there's no way we can stop this conventionally. If there were a cheaper way of doing it, I would have done it,' Davis insisted. 'But why?' the Tory leader repeated. 'I appreciate it's difficult for you,' Davis replied, 'and however you decide to respond to this, I quite understand, but I've got to do this.'[25] Cameron's instinctive reaction was disbelief: why was his Shadow Home Secretary resigning over something on which there was agreement within the Shadow Cabinet and the party? Within an hour of their conversation, Davis had spoken to Nick Clegg, the Liberal Democrat leader, who agreed not to put up a candidate against him. Clegg's agreement was crucial, given his party's relatively strong position in Davis's constituency.

Meanwhile, Cameron and his senior parliamentary adviser Andrew MacKay left for the fundraising party. 'We were driving from the Commons to David's house, and he then told me,' MacKay recalls. 'When we got there I was walking around like a zombie, but David was extraordinarily calm – he just carried on as if nothing had happened.'[26] Despite appearances, Cameron was deeply irritated. Later that evening he rang Davis and stressed that it would be his decision alone: the Shadow Cabinet and the party would not endorse such a move. He would appoint a new Shadow Home Secretary even if Davis returned to the Commons after the by-election.

Davis announced his resignation to the television cameras the next day. On a visit to Cornwall, Cameron described it as a 'personal decision', but pledged that he would support Davis in the by-election. He announced that the Shadow Attorney General, Dominic Grieve (Davis's number two), would be a permanent replacement as Shadow Home Secretary. The unexpected by-election was an inconvenience for the leadership just at the point when the party was gaining momentum in the face of an embattled government. Commentators questioned Davis's motives. 'If every MP were to be equally self-indulgent, democratic politics would be unworkable in Britain,' wrote Steve Richards in the *Independent*.[27] 'David Davis is a huge loss to the Tory frontbench, commented Bruce Anderson in the *Sunday Telegraph*. 'His body language is anything but wimpish. He has the ability to inspire trust among the fearful.'[28]

There was speculation that Davis had been unhappy with the direction of the party under Cameron, but Davis insists that their relationship had been amicable, as it had been during the final stages of the leadership election in 2005. 'David gave me a lot of freedom in my brief, as I had under Michael Howard, and there was no dispute over the strategy on forty-two days.'[29] However, his wide-ranging home affairs brief had shrunk following the creation of a Shadow justice portfolio to mirror changes in the government in 2007. Davis undoubtedly felt passionately about what he saw as a diminution of civil liberties by an overbearing state. As surveys of public opinion revealed in the following weeks, he was not alone in that opinion.

The by-election campaign attracted considerable media attention, as Davis had hoped. Cameron joined him on the stump for an afternoon, realising that the campaign was having a positive effect for the party (indeed the Tories' poll ratings actually went up during this period). He was also joined by Nick Clegg and a number of rebel Labour MPs, including Bob Marshall-Andrews, and received the support of celebrities and campaigners including the director of Liberty, Shami Chakrabarti, Bob Geldof and Terry Waite, the former hostage in Lebanon. After some hesitation the Labour Party refused to join the battle, dismissing it as a publicity stunt. The path was clear for Davis to win convincingly against a motley crew of single-issue candidates.

On 10 July he duly won, with 71 per cent of the vote on a 34 per cent turnout. The morning after the result, Cameron rang him. 'I can't argue with over 17,000 votes – that's a stonking result,' he told him. Davis returned to the backbenches the following week feeling vindicated. On the day he returned to the Commons he went to see Cameron for coffee in his office. 'What should we do?' Cameron asked him. Unsure whether he was referring to a possible return to the frontbench, Davis replied, 'Nothing, let it run.'[30]

Many inside and outside the party were perplexed by Davis's actions. What had he achieved? However much publicity his campaign had raised, forty-two-days' detention without trial for terrorist suspects reached the statute book five months later, and on the day Davis had resigned in June, his successor Dominic Grieve had promised that the party would repeal the measure if elected. 'We were left scratching our heads, thinking how odd the whole thing had been,' recalls a senior party official.

The Haltemprice and Howden by-election gave a senior Conservative a large amount of publicity, and most opinion polls showed that the public approved of Davis's campaign. But of all the by-elections to be held that summer, it was both the most bizarre and the least significant politically. Had Davis resigned exactly a year before, it would have had a devastating effect on party morale and raised questions about Cameron's authority. The circumstances in the summer of 2008 were very different. The party was in the ascendant in the polls. 'It was a blip – it didn't change things,' one senior member of the Shadow Cabinet recalls. Yet it was something that Cameron could well have done without. He had lost a former leadership rival who, despite his unpopularity with some around him and others in the party, was an important player in the party's frontline team. 'David believes in having the big beasts in key positions,' recalls one of Cameron's confidants, 'so it was a blow.' Indeed, the lack of 'big beasts' would become a major drawback come the autumn.

Summer High

By August, some polls showed the Tory lead extending to twenty points. The party was now hitting 45 per cent, its best performance since 1992.[31] For the first time since losing office in 1997, the Conservatives were in a commanding position. Not only was Labour struggling, but the Liberal Democrats, a perennial thorn in the side of the Tory Party since the early 1990s, had their own problems to contend with. In one of his first speeches as leader, Cameron had made a direct appeal to Liberal Democrat voters to consider switching allegiance to the Conservatives. Tory strategists were aware that at least thirty Liberal Democrat seats, particularly in the south of England, stood in the way of the party winning at the next general election.

The Liberal Democrats had performed particularly well in the 2005 election, taking advantage of Labour's unpopularity over the war in Iraq. However a succession of leadership crises after the election had damaged the party's reputation. Despite this, they could still cause the Conservatives bother in by-elections, as the result in Bromley and Chislehurst in June 2006 demonstrated. In December 2007, Nick Clegg was elected as the party's third leader in two years. In many ways, the forty-year-old Clegg was the Liberal Democrat answer to David Cameron. But while he was a polished and telegenic performer, he lacked the charisma and stature of his predecessors, Charles Kennedy, Sir Menzies Campbell and Vince Cable.

Boris Johnson's departure from the Commons after winning the London mayoralty presented Clegg with a chance to assert his leadership and prove that his party could still harm the Conservatives. Henley-on-Thames was the sort of safe Tory seat that the Liberal Democrats had form in taking. They had won similarly safe southern seats before, such as Winchester in 1997 and Romsey in 2000. Through meticulous and hard-fought campaign techniques, the party excelled in by-elections. So concerned were the Tory leadership about the threat from the Liberal Democrats in Henley that they considered calling the by-election at the earliest possible moment, to stop them from gaining any momentum. In the event, the date was set for 26 June.

As they had done at Crewe and Nantwich, the Ashcroft team rigorously researched opinion in the seat from the outset to inform the party's campaign. This paid dividends as the Conservative candidate, John Howell, held the seat with an increased share of the vote. The Henley result showed that the Liberal Democrat by-election bandwagon appeared to have been stopped in its tracks. Perhaps even more revealing was the fact that Labour's candidate came fifth.

As Gordon Brown marked his first anniversary as Prime Minister, attention turned to how long he would survive in Downing Street. On top of poor results earlier in the summer, Brown was humiliated on 24 July when Labour lost Glasgow East, its third safest seat in Scotland, to the SNP in a by-election. A number of Labour MPs, including several former ministers who had been close to Tony Blair and disgruntled backbenchers on the left of the party, concluded that Brown had become an electoral liability. Speculation reached fever pitch in late July when David Miliband, the Foreign Secretary and a former ally of Blair, wrote in the *Guardian*: 'Let's stop feeling sorry for ourselves, take a break, and then find the confidence to make our case afresh.'[32] Miliband made not one mention of Gordon Brown, which was widely interpreted as a signal that he might challenge for the leadership.

This was music to the ears of Cameron and his insiders. 'It was a really good summer,' one aide recalls. 'We were ahead by twenty points in the polls, and there was a serious expectation that Brown was going to go.' As Labour MPs returned from the summer break in September, a plot was being hatched among junior ministers and whips. On Friday, 12 September, Siobhain McDonagh, a junior whip, was the first to break cover in calling for a leadership election. Joan Ryan, the party's Vice-Chair, followed suit the next day. As the party prepared for its annual conference, the knives were out – several more MPs were about to call for the Prime Minister to make way for someone else. Twelve months before, Brown had been on the brink of going to the country in the hope of leading Labour into a fourth term. Now it appeared that his days were numbered. All this would change in the next thirty-six hours.

NINE

Crunch Time
September 2008–April 2009

In the early hours of Monday, 15 September the financial world began to shudder at the news that Lehman Brothers, one of the largest and longest-established American investment banks, was filing for bankruptcy. It was the first of a series of events that would trigger the most severe financial crisis since the Wall Street Crash of 1929, and the worst recession since the Second World War. The panic that swept from Wall Street to the Square Mile engulfed politics. But for the Prime Minister, the crisis could not have been more timely. 'It couldn't have been better designed for Gordon Brown's revival,' one senior member of the Shadow Cabinet reflects.

The fast-moving situation presented a huge challenge to the Conservatives in both ideological and practical terms. How would a party so associated with the virtues of the free market respond to such a crisis of capitalism? More immediately, how would the leadership respond as it looked helplessly on at a government taking unprecedented action to stabilise Britain's banking system? For the second time since David Cameron became leader, his leadership was tested to the core as the party struggled to find its voice during the crisis. While his right-hand man, George Osborne, got into difficulty, the question of where David Cameron was leading the party also arose. The following months would be a defining period for the party and for Cameron's leadership.

The Crash that Saved Gordon Brown
The collapse of Lehman Brothers was just the tip of the iceberg. Within hours of that news breaking, it emerged that Bank of America

had bought Merrill Lynch, another leading American investment bank facing huge losses, and the following day the largest insurance firm in the world, AIG, had to be rescued by a massive loan from the US Treasury. Although the US authorities had stepped in to save the mortgage giants Fannie Mae and Freddie Mac the previous month, they would not do the same for Lehman Brothers. Its collapse unleashed a contagion that spread rapidly throughout the global financial system. As investors panicked and markets went into free fall, governments and central banks around the world were stunned by the sheer pace of events. The FTSE lost a staggering £51 billion in value. 'Everybody got wrong exactly how catastrophic the consequences of the Lehman crash would be,' recalls Ken Clarke, the former Chancellor who was on the Tory backbenches at the time. 'If the Americans had saved the bank, it would not have put off the evil day. It merely opened everyone's eyes to the danger of an almost complete implosion.'[1]

The effects of the crash were soon felt in Britain, where the banking system was about to be brought to its knees. Banks effectively stopped lending money to other banks, while the lubricant of the global economy, the flow of US dollars, froze across the world. What had begun as a credit crunch months before was turning into a full-blown financial crisis. On Tuesday, 16 September – by sheer coincidence sixteen years to the day since Black Wednesday rocked John Major's Tory government – the Bank of England pumped £20 billion into the ailing money markets. This was not enough to prevent a collapse in the share price of Halifax Bank of Scotland (HBOS), the country's largest mortgage lender, the following day, prompting the government to waive competition rules by rapidly engineering a £12.2 billion takeover by Lloyds TSB. In the ensuing days, the US government proposed a $700 billion rescue plan to buy up the bad debts of the failing financial institutions on Wall Street. Although this temporarily buoyed the markets on both sides of the Atlantic, the extent of the malaise in Britain was becoming apparent. HBOS was highly unlikely to be the only bank affected. It was clear that the government would have to produce its own plan to rescue endangered banks. The effect of a collapse on the financial system and the wider economy would be potentially catastrophic.

While the Tory leadership did not have the same volume of information that was at the Treasury's disposal, surprisingly little was said by senior party figures in the immediate aftermath of the crash. All eyes were, however, on the Prime Minister. Even as the news of Lehman's collapse reverberated around the globe on Monday, 16 September, David Cairns, a junior minister at the Scottish Office, tendered his resignation, saying there needed to be a debate about Gordon Brown's leadership. As Labour headed to Manchester for its conference the following weekend, speculation about whether Brown would survive intensified. Several Labour MPs had publicly called on him to step down or face a leadership contest, and many more were merely biding their time. The atmosphere in Manchester was febrile. A coup was being hatched that involved more than a few junior ministers and disillusioned whips. It was known that five Cabinet ministers were seriously considering a joint resignation, which would have been fatal for the Prime Minister.

Yet as the week progressed and the full extent of the crisis in the financial world sank in, the voices of dissent gradually fell silent. Labour MPs rallied behind their leader after he delivered a well-crafted speech that captured the gravity of the moment. He sought to put an end to internal dissent by apologising for the 10p tax fiasco and promising to be on the side of hard-working families. He then took a swipe at his critics: 'The British people would not forgive us if at this time we looked inwards to the affairs of just our party when our duty is the interests of the whole country.' In his most effective attack on the opposition, he ridiculed Cameron's youth and inexperience: 'I'm all in favour of apprenticeships, but let me tell you, this is no time for a novice.'[2] He also dismissed the Conservatives' claim that Britain had a 'broken society'. 'I don't believe Britain is broken – I think it's the best country in the world. I believe in Britain.' It was a far stronger performance than his conference debut as Prime Minister the year before.

The Prime Minister had been given a helping hand by his wife

Sarah, who gave a dignified introduction to his address. Brown's statesmanlike demeanour and his wife's cameo appearance impressed party delegates and commentators. By the end of Labour's conference, Gordon Brown had recovered his poise. For the first time since his honeymoon as Prime Minister in July and August 2007, he had found his stride again.

Back in London, the mood at Tory headquarters darkened. 'There was nothing we could do. The gloomier things became, the better it was for Brown. Despite the débâcle over the 10p tax, we knew that people still saw him as the man for troubled times,' one senior party figure recalls. Gordon Brown had found safe ground in the aftermath of a crash which would call on a decade of accumulated knowledge and contacts at the Treasury. This was a moment at which the Prime Minister believed he could recover his authority, seize the political initiative, and lead the country out of a crisis.

Birmingham Ceasefire

When the Conservatives met in Birmingham the following week, the financial crisis was deepening. It was not the conference backdrop Tory high command had been hoping for. 'We had to shelve a lot of plans that we had been working on since June,' one senior party officials laments. 'The whole idea of the conference was to showcase policies about social renewal, the NHS and other areas.' 'We had a decision to make,' recalls another. 'Either we carry on, or junk our plans for the conference and talk about what was happening in the wider world.'

Events were about to take a further turn for the worse. While the US Congress prepared to vote on a massive $700 billion bail-out package for America's struggling financial industry, the entire economy of Iceland teetered on the edge of bankruptcy, and Bradford & Bingley, one of Britain's largest mortgage providers, was on the verge of collapse. By the weekend it was clear that the government had all but decided to nationalise the failing institution.

A number of commentators criticised the Tories for their inactivity in the immediate aftermath of the crash, and it now became clear that the party's leadership had not settled on a consistent response. When David Cameron appeared on the BBC's *Andrew Marr Show* on Sunday, 28 September, he expressed his scepticism about nationalisation as a solution to the crisis, on the grounds that the taxpayer bore all the risk. Little noticed was his signal that he would support the government as a 'responsible opposition' if it were to propose a rescue package for financial institutions. He was giving mixed signals on the eve of his party's annual conference.

Meanwhile, Osborne's Shadow Treasury team had been busily preparing a set of proposals to deal with the economic crisis, including an Office of Budget Responsibility to keep track of the public finances and plans to enhance the powers of the Bank of England to take over failing banks as an alternative to full-scale nationalisation, managing their affairs by recouping the costs from creditors. But the proposals were completely overshadowed by events, being announced on the day that the government stepped in to nationalise Bradford & Bingley, which dominated the headlines.

When Osborne took to the stage for his keynote address to the conference, he managed to capture the mood with greater clarity than Cameron had the day before. 'The cupboard is bare: there is no more money – tax revenues have collapsed, unemployment costs are rising, borrowing is out of control,' he told a silent audience in Birmingham. 'So it is no good us talking about the big upfront tax giveaways we might like to make, or the big spending increases it might be nice to have, but I repeat: there is no money.' He raised a small cheer in the hall with a promise that a Tory government would enable local authorities to freeze council tax for at least two years, but it was not quite the rabbit out of the hat that had left his audience gasping for breath the previous year. Interestingly, he won just as much applause for his warning to the City that taxpayers should not foot the bill for failing banks that had paid excessive bonuses, as for his attacks on Brown's management of the economy.

Osborne's measured tone had gone down well, particularly with the press, who were struck by his sober warning about the shape of the public finances. 'The cupboard is bare' was a phrase that stuck in their minds. He had also avoided looking smug, which he had been criticised for on earlier occasions. The whips had let it be known to MPs that being seen drinking champagne during the conference would be frowned upon – they were desperate to avoid the impression that the party was enjoying itself as the roof was falling in.

But once again the conference was about to be eclipsed by events from afar. Late on Monday night news came from Washington that Congress had failed to pass the huge bail-out proposed by the US Treasury, amid disputes between and within the Democrats and Republicans. It was a defining moment. If the political establishment of the world's largest economy was unable to agree a rescue package for its weakened financial sector, there was little hope for Britain or the rest of Europe. Cameron, Osborne and the inner circle conferred about how to respond to the news. 'We had to do some very fast footwork,' says one aide. 'We were clearly on display in the middle of a crisis. Obviously attention had shifted to what the government were doing, which meant that it would be difficult to cut through, but the political press were with us in Birmingham.' They agreed that the party had to rally behind the government, avoiding the partisanship and disunity on display across the Atlantic. Cameron then rang Brown to pledge the Tories' support for emergency measures to rescue any more failing institutions. 'Some people were urging us to scrap the conference altogether, but we decided that we wouldn't do that – instead David would give a short speech the next day about doing whatever necessary to make sure the banks get through this,' an aide recalls. Although Cameron's main speech was scheduled for Wednesday, his team began to draft an emergency statement. 'It was all hands to the pump,' one recalls. 'While we prepared the speech, David was tapping out a script for a party political broadcast on a laptop in a corner of the room an hour before he recorded it.'

The next day Cameron declared his party's support for the speedy passage of legislation to enable the Bank of England to rescue endangered banks, while promising not to suspend the opposition's 'critical faculties'. As the leader delivered his statement, George Osborne headed for London for emergency talks with Alistair Darling at the Treasury. Arguments about how the banks would be rescued, Cameron said, would be returned to at a later date. 'There may well need to be a marshalling of public support behind some big decisions,' he told delegates. 'Let's not allow the political wrangling and point-scoring that we've seen in America to happen here in our own country. In Britain, we are all in this together.' He also called for the government to increase the level at which savings were guaranteed from £30,000 to £50,000, to assure the public that their money was safe. The speech was an eloquent response to the national crisis, matching the Prime Minister's effort the week before. The Tories had discarded six months' preparation of their shop window to the electorate, and had seriously considered abandoning it altogether at the last minute. Cameron's impromptu speech showed that he was able to grasp a moment to directly address the country in a statesmanlike manner.

His main speech followed the next day. There was more frantic rewriting than usual as he and Hilton cloistered themselves in a hotel suite to refine the speech again and again. 'It wasn't going to be a high-wire, off-the-cuff performance like the last one, but it was going to be just as important,' recalls one of the speechwriters. With the Shadow Cabinet sitting behind him on the platform, Cameron addressed the faithful who filled the vast auditorium of Birmingham's Symphony Hall. He responded to Brown's charge a week earlier that 'this is no time for a novice' by declaring that the country needed 'character and judgement', and a change in direction was required rather than experience alone. The stridency of his attacks on Brown earlier in the year had gone, and he struck a very different tone from that of his first conference speech in 2006, when he had talked about 'optimism winning the day': 'In these difficult times we promise no new dawns . . . I'm a man with a plan, not a miracle cure.'

It was the speech which came closest to defining Cameron's interpretation of Conservatism. 'Freedom can too easily turn into the idea that we all have the right to do whatever we want, regardless of the effect on others. That is libertarian, not Conservative – and it is certainly not me. For me, the most important word is responsibility.' The passage bore the clear imprint of Steve Hilton, who believed that the party still had more to do to 'reconnect' with its values. Citing the Tories' tradition of social reform that dated back to Peel, Shaftesbury, and Disraeli, Cameron declared that Conservatism meant pursuing the 'great and noble progressive ends of fighting poverty, extending opportunity and repairing our broken society'.

This was a speech that seemed far more attuned to the heartbeat of the Tory body politic than Cameron's previous conference addresses in Bournemouth and Blackpool. It lacked the spontaneity of his hastily arranged statement the previous day, and the energy of the make-or-break performance in Blackpool exactly one year before, but the authentically Tory message and the serious tone in which it was conveyed were well received by delegates in the hall. For nearly three years David Cameron had dazzled, disappointed and perplexed them at various times. In Birmingham he stamped his authority on his party with a speech that gave them something to believe in. The Cameron project may still have been vague and ill-defined in terms of policy, but there were clear signs that the party and its leadership understood the gravity of the darkening world around them. The test now would be whether Cameron and Osborne could maintain bipartisan support while carving out a distinctive and consistent course on economic policy. It would prove to be an impossible task.

Haunted by the Rock

Cameron and his close aides returned to London buoyed by a surprisingly successful conference. However, there were reasons to be anxious. Voters were not convinced that the party was any more capable of managing the economy than the government. The run on Northern Rock in September 2007, which was a portent of things to come a year later, had damaged Labour's economic credentials, but the Conservatives had not reaped any great benefit from the public's dissatisfaction. That month, Brown and Darling had still enjoyed a healthy 38 per cent lead on the question of who was more trusted to manage the economy. Three months later, David Cameron and George Osborne had gained a meagre 6 per cent lead.[3] It was hardly a vote of confidence in the Tory alternative.

Until the autumn of 2007, Labour's reputation for competently handling the economy remained largely intact. This had been a major obstacle to the Conservative Party's electoral recovery ever since 1997. The following decade had seen huge increases in house prices, built on a credit boom on both sides of the Atlantic. Yet irresponsible lending, complicated financial instruments and naïvety on the part of home-owners and consumers had created a bubble that was bound to burst. Surprisingly, most economists failed to predict that it would lead to such a dramatic collapse. Even when the American 'sub-prime' mort-gage market ran into trouble in summer 2007, few thought that British banks like Northern Rock would suffer so spectacularly. Many people began to question how the banks had managed to over-extend them-selves to such an extent on Gordon Brown's watch, particularly as he had overhauled the framework of regulation in order to create stability. The record of Brown as the 'Iron Chancellor' who claimed to have abolished 'boom and bust' was no longer secure.

Although the government acted within days to guarantee deposits after the run on Northern Rock in September 2007, it struggled to find a private buyer for the bank. The delay in finding a medium-term solution sparked concern that the government was unsure about how to proceed without exposing the taxpayer to consider-able risks. Cameron had been quick to point to public and private indebtedness as one of the root causes of the failure of the bank, for which he was condemned as alarmist by many commentators, particularly as the economy was still growing. But after the botched snap election that autumn, Cameron's attacks on the Prime Minister's 'dithering' in securing a private buyer for Northern Rock began to hit their target. Despite offers from Richard Branson's Virgin Group to take the bank over, the government decided to take Northern Rock into 'temporary' public ownership in February 2008, with a promise to return it to private hands eventually.

The failure of Northern Rock exposed a weakness in the

Conservative position. The Liberal Democrats' Treasury spokesman Vince Cable had taken a more consistent line on the crisis, urging public ownership from the outset, and some senior Tories believed that Osborne and Cameron had missed a trick. 'Our lot went in for a knee-jerk reaction against nationalisation, which was a mistake,' recalls a senior Tory frontbencher. On 11 December 2007, Cameron said that it would be a 'monumental failure' if Northern Rock was nationalised, exposing the taxpayer to £100 billion of mortgage lending. Two months later, Osborne described nationalisation as a 'catastrophic decision'. He subsequently attacked Brown for breaking his own 'golden rules' in managing the economy and for failing to 'fix the roof when the sun was shining', which played well in the press during summer 2008, particularly as the Tories were racking up twenty-point leads in the polls. This could not disguise the fact that the leadership's original response to the failure of Northern Rock was inconsistent with its support for emergency measures sanctioned by the state to prevent any further bank collapses.

State intervention would now follow on a grand scale. On Friday, 3 October Congress passed the US bail-out on its second attempt, paving the way for the British government to produce its own plan. It would be markedly different from the American package, however. Over the ensuing weekend, Number 10, the Treasury, the Financial Services Authority (FSA) and the Bank of England held discussions with the UK's main high street banks. The crisis had revealed that the banks' balance sheets were laced with toxic debt and insufficient capital. One of the proposals being actively considered by the Treasury involved a massive government purchase of preference shares in the banks most in need of support. By injecting fresh capital, taxpayers would become the majority shareholders in the banks, which after a period of time would be restored to private ownership. It was a creative and risky solution, but in the absence of other bold ideas, it might be the only way for the banks to continue as going concerns.

The following weekend, Cameron wrote in the *Financial Times* that 'more drastic capital measures may be required', such as government injections of capital into the banks. 'Conservatives support government action when the foundations of the banking system upon which free markets depend are threatened. We will approach any proposals in a constructive and pragmatic way. Our guiding principle should be to protect the taxpayer where possible and preserve the stability of the system where necessary.'[4] George Osborne also urged Alistair Darling to contemplate a 'bigger solution' that weekend. The Chancellor, who followed Osborne on the sofa of the *Andrew Marr Show*, said he was considering all the options.[5]

In a dramatic turn of events, there was a sudden loss of confidence in the banks over the ensuing twenty-four hours. Continuing uncertainty over the government's plans was becoming a major problem. Alistair Darling failed to make a firm commitment to recapitalisation during a statement to the Commons on Monday, 6 October for fear of unsettling the markets. However, this only contributed to the climate of uncertainty and a further loss of confidence. Shares in the Royal Bank of Scotland (RBS) dropped a staggering 40 per cent at one point the next day. If investors continued to sell their shares the following day, one of the country's oldest financial institutions would go bust. The banking system was going into cardiac arrest. The banks' chief executives went to Downing Street that evening for an emergency meeting. On Wednesday evening the first details of the government's plan emerged: £37 billion would be spent on recapitalising RBS, HBOS and Lloyds. The government, through the taxpayer, would own 70 per cent of RBS and 40 per cent of the latter two. One of the reasons for the delay had been the constant communication between London and Washington about how to coordinate the plans. Indeed, the following day the US announced that it would introduce a similar plan to the UK's. The schemes brought much-needed respite to the banks. Meanwhile, the political atmosphere was about to become much more volatile.

Feeling the Heat

It was clear to Cameron and Osborne that the temporary ceasefire could not be sustained for much longer. On Tuesday, 14 October, Osborne was forced to deny that he had revealed details of a private briefing from the Governor of the Bank of England, Mervyn King, several days before the government was ready to announce the recapitalisation scheme. Senior government aides believed that Osborne had used inside knowledge to ambush Darling in his appearance on the *Andrew Marr Show* on Sunday, 5 October, passing off the Bank's advice as his own. Tory aides insist that this was not the case. 'Labour briefed hard against us, saying that we had been told by Mervyn King about the plan, which wasn't true, and that we were being totally irresponsible by talking about it. We resisted the temptation to brief back, because the whole thing would have fallen apart. We wanted to give Brown the political space to inject capital into the banks, but we knew that he would want to sever us and have a stab at every opportunity.' But sources close to the Chancellor believe that Osborne indeed broke the confidentiality of a Privy Council briefing from the Governor of the Bank.

What is undisputed is that Osborne was perceived to have been duplicitous – proclaiming support for the government on the one hand, while undermining it on the other. 'We just let it go,' admits one senior Tory aide. 'It left a feeling of a lack of sure-footedness on our part, and a lot of the press lapped it up.' There was a sense that the opposition was playing politics while the government was in the midst of taking critical decisions that would affect the solvency not only of the banks, but of the entire British economy. Recapitalisation was not the brainchild of the Shadow Treasury team; it was the Treasury's. In any event, it had been floated publicly by a number of eminent economists as a possible solution to the banking crisis. Yet under the cover of bipartisan support, the Conservative leadership pressed the government to pursue large-scale state intervention, which only months before it had considered anathema. If it was not opportunistic, the approach was at least seriously inconsistent.

In the immediate aftermath, most commentators believed that government intervention, through recapitalisation, had brought a critical situation under control. John Maynard Keynes, the twentieth-century economist who argued for state spending to stimulate floundering economies, was suddenly in vogue again, having been largely eclipsed by the champions of the free market who helped to propel Mrs Thatcher to power in 1979. 'Spend as much as you like was suddenly the media narrative,' a senior party aide grudgingly remarked. The terms of public debate changed dramatically. Market failure, which many believed to be a product of the laissez-faire capitalism that had been so associated with Thatcher's Conservative Party in the 1980s, was seen to be the root cause of the crisis. Reckless investment bankers were regarded as having exploited a deregulated financial system for their own ends, to the cost of the taxpayer. Many people identified these bankers as being the 'City friends' of the Tory Party. Indeed, as the party had called for greater deregulation of the financial services industry in the early and middle years of the decade, critics pointed out that it was in no position to blame the government for the crisis. Politicians, economists and commentators on the centre-left argued with renewed confidence that the state had a benign role to play in correcting the excesses of the free market, and saving it from self-destruction.

The government regained its nerve and sense of purpose as the Prime Minister was hailed for his swift action in defending the national interest against the greed of the bankers. 'Has Gordon Brown, the British Prime Minister, saved the world financial system?' asked the prominent American economist Paul Krugman in the *New York Times*. 'Mr Brown and Alistair Darling, the Chancellor of the Exchequer . . . have defined the character of the worldwide rescue effort, with other wealthy nations playing catch-up.'[6] The same day, Krugman was awarded the Nobel Prize for economics. Any debate about whether Brown had formerly encouraged an unsustainable boom or presided over 'light-touch' regulation of the financial industry was lost in light of the decisive action taken by the government in early October 2008.

For the first time since the previous October, the tables had turned. Gordon Brown had recovered his composure, while the opposition had been wrongfooted. A number of Tory backbenchers and front-benchers urged the leadership not to let Labour 'get away with it' by being a mirror of the government. The party was in a state of panic about what to do. Had Cameron and Osborne lost the momentum from the conference in Birmingham, where they had captured the gravity of a deepening crisis? 'We were coming under enormous pressure from all sides to be more aggressive,' recalls one party aide.

Cameron decided that the ceasefire would be abandoned on Friday, 17 October with a speech at Bloomberg in the City of London. He accused Gordon Brown of 'irresponsible capitalism and irresponsible government' which had led to borrowing on a massive scale. 'We only said that we would support them on the recapitalisation of the banks – nothing else, and David's speech was about how the government should take some responsibility for how we got into this mess. That's not how everyone else saw it,' recalls one aide. The speech was poorly received: Cameron was accused of prematurely abandoning cross-party support for his own ends at a time of crisis. 'Who knows whether there was a better way of getting out of a position where we could not criticise them at all,' recalls one aide. 'We found it very difficult.' It was about to get a lot worse.

While the press criticised the Tories for being inconsistent, internal critics asked whether Cameron and Osborne had misjudged the situation by pledging support and then withdrawing it so soon. A large number of Conservative MPs believed the leadership should not have offered Gordon Brown any cover at all, and that by doing so it had left the field clear for the Prime Minister to take the credit. Labour and the Liberal Democrats accused the Conservatives of inconsistency, pointing to the party's opposition to state intervention before the crisis. Brown labelled the Tories the 'do-nothing party', a charge they would struggle to shrug off.

Cameron and his inner circle began to discuss how to recast the party's overall strategy in light of the crisis. 'We were seriously worried that people would go for the devil you know rather than risk supporting us,' recalls a senior member of the Shadow Cabinet. 'We were in a real storm – the sails had to be changed, but we were in a real muddle about what to do,' says another. 'We could no longer talk about green politics or quality of life issues as the priorities – frankly we had to revisit them.' It was clear that the politics of plenty, the backdrop to Cameron's election as party leader in 2005, were becoming a distant memory. How could the Tory leader continue to stand by his statements early in his leadership that the 'quality of life' was a more important consideration than the 'quantity of money'? In a speech to the party's spring forum in March 2007, Cameron had declared: 'The big argument in British politics today is not about the free enterprise economy. It's about our society – because it's not economic breakdown that Britain now faces, but social breakdown.' Yet the defects of the market system were largely responsible for the worst 'economic breakdown' since the 1930s. The party's position on the economy, developed after the 2005 general election and refined during the summer of 2007, had to be reviewed. First, 'sharing the proceeds of growth' between higher public spending on public services and tax cuts was untenable given that there was unlikely to be any growth to share. Secondly, Osborne's September 2007 pledge to match Labour's spending plans now looked redundant. Thirdly, maintaining economic and financial stability above and beyond any consideration of tax cuts would need finessing. It was clear that the party had to adjust its position, and quickly.

Why was there a lack of an assured position in the immediate aftermath of the crisis? Some point to the guiding influence of Oliver Letwin in framing the leadership's original stance on the economy during benign times in the middle of 2005. 'Oliver is a brilliant man, but he's very good at convincing himself of the position he's currently in,' says a friend. 'Some of us had been warning him all along about what to say in the event of an economic problem. He couldn't accept that there would be one. Indeed, all of the key players in the party thought that the economy would be all right, and so when it went up the spout they didn't have much to say.' There may well have been an element of complacency, but Letwin cannot be held responsible for failing to foresee the worst financial crisis in over a generation. All but a few economists were taken by surprise by the extent of the crash and the malaise that overwhelmed the global economy. The Tory leadership had warned about the rising levels of private debt in 2006, and had committed itself to economic stability above promises of immediate tax cuts. Yet these messages were drowned out by a desire to shift the party's focus onto non-economic territory. It was naïve for the Tories to assume that benign economic conditions would continue, just as it had been for the government. Osborne's criticism that the government had failed to 'fix the roof while the sun was shining' was not one that had passed many Tory lips between 2005 and late 2007.

As the spectre of a recession loomed, the party's uncertain response to the crisis became a hotly contested subject for discussion within the Shadow Cabinet. Some raised the issue of how much support the party should give to the weakened banks, which had been in part responsible for the crisis. The Shadow Business Secretary, Alan Duncan, was one of those who argued that although financial institutions mattered, it was even more imperative to show that the party understood that individuals, businesses and corporations were about to go through a period of economic pain. According to those at meetings of the Shadow Cabinet, he advocated that the party should stay ahead of the government by 'suggesting something bold', such as a 2 per cent reduction in interest rates. This would demonstrate to the public that the party 'understood and owned the issue [of helping struggling businesses]'. Osborne responded that it would be unwise for the party to give a running commentary on interest rates, which fell under the Bank of England's remit. Sure enough, the Bank decided at an emergency meeting in October to cut rates by 0.5 per cent, after which Duncan and his frontbench team played much less of a public role in commenting on the economy. 'Speaking up in Shadow Cabinet to bring experience to the issue was resisted. George just didn't want to cede any territory on the economy. His team think they're in the holy enclave,' one close observer says. 'It was symptomatic of a bigger problem – selfish control, which people in the party really don't like, and it will do for them one day if they don't address it.'

The divisions within the Shadow Cabinet had indeed exposed a faultline in the Cameron project. By operating as such a tight-knit circle of a few politicians and advisers, it was easy for Cameron's team to assume that the whole Shadow Cabinet would fall in behind them. The crisis had shown that the leadership was prone to complacency.

Amid the growing tension around the top table, the leadership began to seek the opinions of experienced outsiders. Osborne asked Sir James Sassoon, a former Vice-Chairman of UBS Warburg and a senior official at the Treasury between 2002 and 2006, to review the regulation of the financial services industry. As a respected figure in Whitehall and City circles, Sassoon would give a much-needed boost to the Shadow Treasury team. Osborne and Cameron also invited former Chancellors Geoffrey Howe, Nigel Lawson, Norman Lamont, Ken Clarke and (occasionally) John Major to sit as a group of 'wise men' to discuss the ramifications of the crisis and suggest ways of adapting the party's overall policy stance. The former Permanent Secretary to the Treasury, Lord Burns, also gave advice on how to shape a new economic stance. These discussions helped to inform Cameron and Osborne about the nature of the crisis, the likelihood of a recession and the policies the party should adopt in response. Osborne also began to have regular conversations with Clarke, the last Conservative Chancellor, in the House of Commons and on the phone. 'I gave my views and advice,' says Clarke.[7] It was a portent of things to come later in the year.

One of the most important pieces of advice the ex-Chancellors gave was that the party should adopt a position of prudence – the country could ill afford to borrow too much or spend more, they argued, on unaffordable tax cuts to stimulate the economy. Although official figures were not yet available to confirm that the country was experiencing two consecutive quarters of contraction, there was enough evidence to suggest that the economy was shrinking. They told Cameron and Osborne that the party had to argue for a fiscally conservative approach to the public finances – bringing the budget back into balance after the huge government borrowing that would be required to pay for the bank rescue would have to be the priority. Allowing public debt to spiral out of control would weaken any recovery.

The gravity of the banking crisis and its knock-on effects weighed down on the Tory leadership. The government's pre-budget report was fast approaching. Brown and Darling were expected to announce some form of fiscal stimulus to revive the weakening economy, but it would also be a test of nerve and judgement for Cameron and Osborne. Just as they were preparing their response, revelations about a Russian billionaire, his yacht and Peter Mandelson would provide an unwanted, if not entirely self-inflicted, distraction.

Fighting Fire with Fire

Brown's revival was aided by the return of the man who had given the Conservatives so much grief in the past: Peter Mandelson. After Mandelson favoured Blair for the Labour leadership in 1994, Brown had been unable to forgive him, creating a feud that would consume the New Labour triumvirate for years to come. Mandelson was one of Blair's most trusted confidants and advisers, a shrewd strategist with an eye for spotting the weaknesses of his opponents. Yet he was no stranger to controversy, particularly involving wealthy business-men. His ministerial career had come to an abrupt end in 2001, when he resigned from Cabinet for the second time following claims that he had acted improperly over a passport application from an Indian billionaire, allegations which were cleared by a subsequent inquiry. He left British politics in 2004 to become European Trade Commissioner, but remained an influential figure behind the scenes while Blair remained as Prime Minister. Mandelson's rapprochement with Brown occurred over the summer of 2008. Relations began to thaw after a visit by the Prime Minister to Brussels in May, which led to the Trade Commissioner offering him advice on speeches and strategy.

Yet it came as a surprise to many – including Mandelson himself – when Brown invited him to return to government as Business Secretary with a seat in the Lords. The Prime Minister's reshuffle on 3 October was a bold move, not least because it helped to assuage Blairites who remained unsure about Brown's ability to lead the party to a fourth term in office. It reassured them that Brown was prepared to put a poisonous feud behind him and govern in the interests of the whole party. As one of the architects of New Labour, Mandelson was not prepared to see the party fall apart in government. His return was a warning shot across Tory bows: if there was one thing that united Brown and Mandelson, it was a loathing for the Conservative Party. Mandelson saw an opportunity to turn the tables on the Conservatives amid the financial crisis. 'Our initial reaction was that his return was great for us given his problems in the past,' recalls one official. 'I thought it was a masterstroke by Brown – Mandelson had caused us so much difficulty before and he could so again,' says a senior frontbencher.

The newly ennobled Lord Mandelson quickly made his presence felt across Whitehall. The press had given his latest comeback a favourable reception, and Cameron and his aides immediately noticed the effect he was having on the government. 'They became much sharper. It was clear that he was restructuring everything,' recalls one Tory aide.

Before Mandelson's return to the Cabinet, George Osborne let it be known to journalists that he had had a revealing encounter with the then European Commissioner over the summer. It was an indiscretion that he would soon come to regret. Both men had been holidaying on the Greek island of Corfu and had been invited to a birthday party for Rupert Murdoch's daughter Elisabeth hosted by the Rothschild family at their villa on 22 August. The following day Osborne and Nathaniel Rothschild, a financier and university friend, attended a dinner with Mandelson at the Agni Taverna. Mandelson reportedly 'dripped pure poison' into Osborne's ear as he gave a detailed critique of the man who would soon welcome him back to government. Mandelson did not deny that Gordon Brown had featured in their conversation, but insisted 'there was no poison being dripped', and threatened to disclose what Osborne had allegedly told him 'about his colleagues and the state of the Tory party'. Osborne commented that it was 'very surprising to hear [Mandelson] say he is joined at the hip with Gordon Brown'.[8] This was by no means the end of the tit-for-tat between the two men.

No sooner had Mandelson returned to the Cabinet than the story moved, with some encouragement from the Tory press office, from the gossip pages to the front pages. It caused considerable disquiet among some Labour MPs who believed that Mandelson's reincarnation could rebound on the government. Attention turned in particular to his links with Oleg Deripaska, the Russian billionaire who controlled Rusal, the world's largest aluminium producer. It was revealed that Mandelson was a guest on Deripaska's £80 million super-yacht, the *Queen K*, at the time he had met Osborne on Corfu. Questions were now asked about whether there had been a conflict of interest in the EU Trade Commissioner accepting Deripaska's hospitality given that he had a role in cutting aluminium tariffs, which would have benefited Rusal, a leading exporter to Europe. After a week of speculation, Mandelson appeared on television on Sunday, 19 October, and denied any conflict of interest. The press reports were nothing more than 'muck-raking' and 'innuendo', he insisted.[9]

In a further twist two days later, the Shadow Chancellor's own encounters with the Russian oligarch came to light. In a letter to *The Times*, Nathaniel Rothschild, who was an adviser to Deripaska, alleged that Osborne had visited the *Queen K* on 24 August with Andrew Feldman, the Conservative Party's Chief Executive and a prominent fundraiser, who was also on holiday nearby, in order to 'solicit a donation' of £50,000 to the party.[10] Donations to British political parties from foreign nationals are illegal, so this would have been highly damaging to the party's reputation. Rothschild also claimed that at a subsequent meeting, at which Deripaska was not present, Feldman proposed that such a donation be 'channelled' through one of Deripaska's British companies, but that Deripaska eventually decided not to make a donation. Rothschild wrote: 'it ill behoves all political parties to try and make capital at the expense of another in such circumstances. Perhaps in future it would be better if all involved accepted the age-old adage that private parties are just that.'[11] The letter electrified Westminster. Later that day Osborne confirmed that he and Feldman had met Deripaska on his yacht on two occasions, but vehemently denied soliciting any donation, telling reporters, 'We neither asked for money nor did we receive money.'[12] However, he did not deny that a discussion of a donation took place. An official party statement claimed that it was Rothschild who had in fact floated the idea of a donation during a gathering at his family villa on 23 August.[13]

The toxic issue of party funding raised by the affair had the potential to do huge damage to the Conservative leadership. As Cameron's right-hand man, Osborne was in a highly precarious position. 'George was freaked by it, and it just got worse and worse,' recalls a former aide. The flames were fanned when Gordon Brown told MPs the day after Rothschild's letter was published that he hoped the matter would be 'investigated by the authorities'. Ironically, this vague warning served to salvage Osborne's position. Within days, the Electoral Commission declared that it would not launch an inquiry, as 'soliciting a donation is not an offence'.

The affair undoubtedly weakened Osborne's position, regardless of the collateral damage inflicted on Mandelson. The impression of senior Conservatives cavorting with Russian billionaires on yachts and in villas as the world economy went into freefall was repellent to most. 'People are put off by the idea of Osborne and Mandelson sitting on a billionaire's yacht playing and colluding in some cynical political game,' says one close observer. It also showed the danger of crossing Peter Mandelson. 'It was a mistake to have attacked Mandy in the first place – it completely backfired,' admits a senior party official. Questions were asked about Nathaniel Rothschild's motives in bringing the matter to public attention, given his business links with Deripaska, but most thought he was aggrieved that his hospitality had been abused. Private conversations had entered the public domain, which was far from gentlemanly conduct.

There was huge relief in Cameron and Osborne's office when the Parliamentary Standards Commissioner announced that he would not be investigating the matter a week later. Osborne admitted that the affair 'didn't look very good', and confirmed that he would no longer carry out fundraising for the party.[14] He then kept his head down for over a week, leaving Cameron and other senior frontbenchers to take the lead on the economy. As communications chief, Andy Coulson led the damage-limitation exercise, effectively suspending Osborne's own press operation.[15] The Shadow Chancellor knew that this was the toughest test he had faced in his career to date, but while he profoundly regretted his actions, he never believed it would become a resignation issue. Crucially, Cameron stood by him. 'David said to George that we'll have to get through it. There was never any question of him jettisoning George,' says an insider. Although Osborne was, and is, indispensable to the Tory leader, the episode showed a serious lack of judgement on his part – not least because of the potential conflict between his Treasury portfolio and the demands of party fundraising.

'Yachtgate' happened at the worst possible time for the party – the faltering economy dominated the headlines, but the Tories' chief spokesman was laid low by an affair that had all sorts of unhelpful connotations. 'There was a great deal of gallows humour around,' one MP recalls, but it hardly helped – the affair had tarnished the party's image. Successive Tory leaders from Hague to Cameron had tried hard to banish any lingering impressions of the sleaze and privilege that had so damaged the party's standing in the 1990s. Embarrassingly, a photograph of Osborne as a member of the infamous Bullingdon Club at Oxford appeared in the papers at the same time, portraying him as a young man of privilege – just as an earlier image of Cameron had done. Osborne's opulent Corfu adventure seemed at odds with the fact that he had delivered a speech on poverty during the summer. His inability to resist the temptation of drawing blood from Mandelson was his principal error. Osborne had survived, but his position had been weakened. He now faced the far greater task of repositioning the party's economic policies. A strong response to the government's Pre-Budget Report (PBR) on 24 November was essential to rebuilding his reputation within the party and further afield.

Backs to the Wall

Ahead of the PBR, key decisions had to be taken that would fundamentally shift the party's stance on the economy. On 24 October came the first official confirmation that the economy had contracted for the first time in sixteen years. Two weeks later, on 6 November, central banks around the world, including the Bank of England, slashed interest rates in a coordinated move. But the reduction in interest rates to their lowest level since 1955 did not free up the credit markets, which had remained frozen since 16 September. The government began to prepare a package of measures to stimulate the economy in the hope of preventing it from slipping into a deep recession.

Brown was encouraged by polls showing a modest recovery in Labour's fortunes, as the Conservative lead shrank into single figures, and by Labour holding the Scottish seat of Glenrothes in a by-election on 6 November. He hoped that another boost would come from across the Atlantic with the election of the Democratic presidential candidate, Barack Obama, who had advocated substantial government intervention to help revive the American economy during his campaign, which Brown believed would bolster his own efforts in Britain. Shortly after Obama's election, the Prime Minister told the House of Commons that he had triumphed because he was a 'serious man for serious times', and embodied 'progressive values' shared by Labour.[16] Cameron replied: 'I read this morning that you had sent a message to the President-elect. Presumably it wasn't: "This is no time for a novice," ' turning back on Brown the line he had recently used against him. The presidential election had stirred great interest among Cameron's circle. They too hoped to capture some of the enthusiasm that Obama's 'Yes we can' campaign message had generated. The then Democratic candidate's visit to London in July had included meetings with Brown and Cameron. Obama's aides confided to his biographer that 'They preferred the energy of the up-and-coming Cameron to the dour and dreary Brown.'[17]

One of the most troubling commitments the Tory leadership had made was to match Labour's spending plans for 2010–11. Osborne had given the pledge shortly before the Blackpool conference in September 2007, when a snap election had appeared likely, in an attempt to ward off Labour's attack that the Tories were still the party of cuts. 'Labour investment versus Tory cuts' was a dividing line that Brown had effectively implanted in the public imagination during the two previous general elections. 'David and George were terrified that Gordon would repeat the two previous election campaigns accusing them of cuts,' one senior frontbencher recalls. 'The new, non-Thatcherite Conservative Party was so wedded to the virtues of good public spending that we committed to matching Labour at all costs.' Many Tory MPs had been uncomfortable with the pledge from the beginning. As pressure mounted on the leadership to abandon it, Osborne realised that it could not now be sustained either politically or economically. Labour's spending plans were considered tough by many commentators, but it was clear that the public finances were going to deteriorate sharply as the country entered recession. Falling tax receipts and rising government borrowing to fund recapitalisation of the banks made a huge budget deficit inevitable.

The 'decoupling' from Labour's spending plans, announced by Cameron on 18 November, was the easiest of the three decisions the leadership would make in November. It exposed the flank that Brown had successfully exploited in previous years, but the deteriorating state of the public finances was far more important. Some senior aides were privately anxious about the risks: 'In some ways we went back to where we were at the last general election. It is Einstein's definition of madness, doing the same thing over and over again and expecting a different result.' A far harder decision would be whether to support the government over its expected fiscal stimulus. Reducing the rate of VAT was the option the government was expected to choose.

The prospect of opposing a tax cut was not appealing to Tory MPs and commentators on the right. 'Several of us thought there would be a real rebellion within the party,' one Shadow Cabinet member recalls. 'A Labour government was pushing for a tax cut that could benefit millions of people feeling the pinch, and we were going to oppose it.' The inner circle rehearsed the arguments for opposing the cut. 'One option was to say we were in favour of a small fiscal stimulus as long as the government said how it would pay it back, but we knew that wouldn't wash, as we had said we were going to be the fiscally conservative party,' recalls one senior aide. Cameron and Osborne resolved to hold firm to the position of fiscal responsibility which the group of former Chancellors, former Treasury officials and other economists had advised them to adopt. They would oppose a short-term fiscal stimulus, which they considered to be unaffordable because of the threat of unsustainable levels of public debt. Instead, they would support monetary intervention – through interest rate cuts – and state help to facilitate lending to businesses.

As expected, when Alistair Darling delivered the PBR he announced a fiscal stimulus amounting to £20 billion, including a cut in VAT by 2.5 per cent for thirteen months only and bringing forward a government capital investment programme. It would be funded by a new 45 per cent tax rate for earnings over £150,000 and a 0.5 per cent rise in all National Insurance contributions. Critically, borrowing would double to £78 billion in 2008–09 before rising to a record £118 billion the following year. Total public sector debt would rise steadily from 41 per cent of national income in 2008 to a peak of 57 per cent by 2013, figures which did not include the effects of the bank bail-out.[18] These were 'exceptional measures' to save the economy from entering a 'deep and long-lasting recession', Darling insisted.

Osborne returned to the fray with a robust Commons performance. He lambasted the Chancellor for creating an 'unexploded tax bombshell' that would go off at the moment of economic recovery. 'It is confirmation of the time-old truth that all Labour Chancellors run out of money and all Labour governments bring this country to the verge of bankruptcy. Stability has gone out of the window, prudence is dead, Labour has done it again,' he declared to cheers from Tory MPs, who had been hoping for reassurance that their Shadow Chancellor was up to it after weeks in the doldrums. It was a nimble and spirited performance for a politician who had been on the rack for several months. Had he failed, the growing sense of his vulnerability would have been clear for all to see.

The decision to oppose the stimulus was a huge gamble. Although Osborne's confidence began to return, Brown and other ministers relentlessly reiterated their charge that the Conservatives would 'do nothing' to prevent a recession. One member of the shadow Treasury team admits that 'It felt that the whole world was against us – except the German Finance Minister' (who had described the British government's 'switch . . . to a crass Keynesianism [as] breathtaking'). Brown and Darling pointed to President-elect Obama's preparation for a much larger fiscal stimulus in the New Year as further evidence that the Tories were isolated. Osborne told his staff that he felt as if he was marching his party up a hill without knowing what was at the top of it. 'He told us that it was the hardest decision of his political life,' one aide recalls.

Or was it? Osborne was well aware that the move would prove unpopular in the short term, but he had set his sights much further ahead. For all the talk about the worsening public finances, this was a decision motivated by political expediency. He believed that the indebted state of the public finances would be the leading issue at the general election. 'The question we kept facing was, "What would you do now?" which we had to answer,' says an insider. 'But the important call we really had to get right was marking out the terrain for the election.' By the party's own admission, the £12.5 billion VAT cut would make a negligible difference in stimulating demand in the economy. The leadership's claim that it was an extraordinarily brave decision to oppose the stimulus was an overstatement. It was no more than shrewd political positioning. The party could only hope that it would pay off in the months ahead.

The third key decision the Tory leadership took in the aftermath of the PBR related to the Shadow Cabinet. Although Osborne's stock rose after his Commons fightback, he was still considered a weak link by many in the City and in the financial press, and, critically, among the wider party. A number of Tory backbenchers were painfully aware that the Liberal Democrat Treasury spokesman, Vince Cable, was outperforming their own frontbench team, and constituency activists would often draw unfavourable comparisons between Cable and the party's Treasury spokesmen, principally Osborne. 'There was no support even from our own bedrock of people. I was always asked in my local association, "Why can't we get someone like Vince Cable to come in and sort things out?" ' one backbencher complained. 'They think he has an understanding of the situation that our lot sorely lack.'

It was a weakness that Osborne and his team understood. In an effort to rebut the claim that the party would 'do nothing' to stop a recession, they worked on a flurry of policy proposals. Among those unveiled between late November 2008 and early January 2009 were a 'National Loan Guarantee Scheme', whereby a future Conservative government would underwrite billions of pounds of lending to businesses, and proposals to reduce the tax burden on savers and pensioners. These received a moderately favourable press, but a bolder gesture would be needed to respond to the perceived lack of weight in the party's frontbench line-up. Osborne struck on a solution: recalling Ken Clarke to frontline politics.

Heavyweight Return

Clarke had been an influential source of advice for the leadership since the financial crisis began. Besides his contribution to the group of 'wise men', the former Chancellor had met Osborne on a number of occasions to talk about economic policy. Although he was a three-time leadership candidate and one of the few surviving 'big beasts' from the Thatcher and Major years, Clarke had remained on the backbenches since 1997. He had declined various offers to join the Shadow Cabinet over the years, including Cameron's invitation to become Shadow Leader of the Commons in December 2005. However, he had led the party's Democracy Taskforce, producing several substantial reports on constitutional issues, and was a popular media performer, speaking forthrightly as an independently-minded backbencher with expertise on the economy. In fact he made almost as many appearances on television and radio as the frontbench Treasury spokesmen after the Lehman Brothers collapse, and Osborne valued the sixty-eight-year-old former Chancellor's candid advice.

Despite his pro-European views, which were at odds with the majority of the parliamentary party, Clarke was seen as a man of experience who could act as a counterweight to Mandelson and Cable. Osborne believed that the Shadow business portfolio was a perfect match for him, given his range of contacts in the business world. Alan Duncan would be moved elsewhere in the Shadow Cabinet to make way for Clarke's return. 'It was Osborne's idea to get Ken back in,' says one insider. 'David did not need much persuading.' Nor did Clarke himself need much convincing: 'I was enjoying being a maverick backbencher, and I wouldn't have dreamed of coming back earlier in the year, but I got to know George and David better and I became persuaded that their approach to politics was similar to mine in important respects. I thought, "These guys could be good, very good." '[19]

Clarke agreed in principle to consider returning to the frontbench over a very informal Saturday lunch at Osborne's house. A few days later, on 17 December, he met Cameron in his office. Europe was the main topic of conversation. 'We had quite a long and serious discussion about what a future Conservative government would do about Europe. Neither of us wanted me to resign before we knew where we were. We did not want the party to go ape about Europe all over again,' recalls Clarke.[20] He had previously spoken out against the party's Eurosceptic policies, which included a commitment to a referendum on the Lisbon Treaty, the successor to the stalled European Constitution, and the party's MEPs leaving the European People's Party (EPP) to form a new grouping in the European Parliament. Although he was not going to pretend that he had changed his mind on these issues, he agreed that he would be bound by collective responsibility to the 'settled policy' of the Shadow Cabinet.

The return of the Hush-Puppy-wearing Clarke would be announced in a reshuffle just after Christmas. The timing was designed to catch the media and the government by surprise, as part of a plan to regain the initiative over the Christmas–New Year period. However, there was a snag. Clarke had a long-arranged birdwatching holiday in Panama at precisely the same time. Despite the best efforts of the leadership, he refused to be talked into delaying the trip.

The Shadow Cabinet reshuffle was eventually unveiled on 19 January 2009. As a result of the delay it lost the element of surprise the leadership had hoped for: there had been reports in the press of deteriorating relations between Cameron and Alan Duncan (who had spoken out in Shadow Cabinet about the party's approach to a recession), and speculation that the ground was being prepared for Clarke's return. There was a certain amount of nervousness about whether Clarke would actually stick to the party line, but many MPs believed his appointment was a shrewd move, despite their reservations about his European views. 'Ken is back because David Cameron desperately needed heavyweights in that line-up,' one veteran former frontbencher says. 'It's not a sign of healing on Europe, but more of one that we were in dire need of competence and firepower.' Others had a different interpretation: 'It was an attempt to give our economic policies a human face,' says one member of the Shadow Cabinet.

The fact that Clarke was given a favourable welcome by the parliamentary party was an implicit recognition of the fact Europe was no longer quite the obsessive issue that had once plagued so many Tory MPs, even though it continued to excite large swathes of the press. The reshuffle also confirmed that while the relationship between Cameron and Osborne remained firmly intact, the Shadow Chancellor was not an unrivalled source of influence at the top of the party.

Besides Clarke's absence abroad, the delay to the reshuffle had also been due in part to an ongoing inquiry into claims that the Party Chairman, Caroline Spelman, had misused her parliamentary allowance to hire a nanny ten years previously. Even though the inquiry would subsequently clear her of any wrongdoing, Cameron decided to swap her with the Shadow Community Secretary, Eric Pickles. Pickles was a popular figure in the party, particularly with the rank and file, and he had impressed Cameron with his successful direction of local and by-election campaigns over the previous twelve months. The appointment of an avuncular, down-to-earth Yorkshireman as Chairman might also help to rebuff criticism that the party was run by a privileged, Old Etonian elite.

The other Yorkshireman to see his stock rise was the Shadow Foreign Secretary, William Hague. In an interview with the *Sun* a few days before the reshuffle, Cameron revealed that Hague would be his deputy 'in all but name'.[21] Hague occasionally deputised for Cameron at Prime Minister's Questions, and chaired Shadow Cabinet meetings in his absence, but this was an explicit acknowledgement that he was now a central figure in the Cameron project. The Tory leader had come to value highly the advice of one of his predecessors, which stretched well beyond his foreign affairs brief. Hague's advice to 'ride the dip' during the difficult summer of 2007 had been indispensable. 'I am one of the strictest people about not departing from the strategy that we have now adopted, and not deviating as we did when I was leader in 1999,' he says. 'Now that we are in a different position and people are listening to us, we really have to stick to our strategy of winning the centre-ground voters and pushing the themes that David has pushed. He doesn't need a lot of encouragement in that, but it is handy to have a few policemen around like me to make sure we stick to it.'[22]

Hague and others may have been around to reassure Cameron, but he was sorely missing the advice of one of his closest confidants. In the summer Steve Hilton had left for California, accompanying his now wife Rachel Whetstone, who was rising through the ranks at Google. He had flown back to London as often as he could after the conference season, but in December he realised that the operation had lost strategic focus over the autumn. The lack of confidence was striking. 'We've got to get a grip on this, but we can't do it until the New Year,' he told Cameron. Hilton had been consulted on the key decisions Cameron and Osborne took in November ahead of the PBR, but his absence on a day-to-day basis revealed how much Cameron had relied on his strategic mind. 'We had been floundering and had to find a way of turning what was seen as a credit crunch and a financial crisis into a larger economic argument,' recalls one aide. 'It had to be about the debt crisis – how could the answer to our problems be even more borrowing? We adjusted our message to attacking Labour's "debt crisis".'

Nailing the dark colours of austerity to the Tory mast could in many ways be considered an example of the deviation Hague had warned against. 'Let optimism win the day' – the phrase that summed up Cameron's first year and a half as leader – was completely out of kilter with the twin emphases on a 'broken society' and a 'broken economy'. But the team hoped that a tough and direct message would have credibility with the public during straitened times.

In the meantime, speculation mounted about the possibility of Gordon Brown going for a spring election as the opinion polls improved for Labour: one in December showed that Labour had closed the gap to within a point of the Conservatives. But while the Tories' average poll rating slipped from 42 per cent in November to 39 in December, their lead never actually disappeared.[23] The government had made up some lost ground, rising to an average rating of around 35 per cent in December. This was enough to prompt talk of an election as early as 26 February, when Brown would be in a position to take credit for his actions during the crisis. Conservative Campaign Headquarters swung into action. 'We took a fresh approach to the manifesto, rather than dusting off what was there before,' recalls James O'Shaughnessy, the party's head of policy. 'David made it very clear at the start of the year that we were in an election year. It might be a sixteen-month election year, but we would have to be geared for an election any time.'[24]

The Tide Begins to Turn

By the end of January 2009 there was a palpable change of mood within Tory headquarters. As Hilton had planned, over the New Year the party launched a concerted strategy to highlight the deterioration in the public finances. It included a hard-hitting poster of a baby that was designed to bring home the predicament the country would face for generations to come: 'Dad's nose, mum's eyes, Gordon Brown's debt – Labour debt crisis: every child in Britain is born owing £17,000. They deserve better.' In the light of the media campaign and the Shadow Cabinet reshuffle, confidence began to return. 'We got ahead of the game and worked our arses off to get the media's attention, whereas Number 10 was exhausted and their key people needed a rest,' recalls one senior official in party HQ. 'We were firing on all cylinders, and we felt that we were moving forward for the first time in months.'

By February, the Conservatives had regained a fifteen-point lead in the polls. The party's campaign may have made a difference in highlighting the mounting problem of debt, but public opinion also turned against the government because the recession was beginning to bite. Any positive effect from the small cut in VAT was completely overshadowed by the collapse of confidence among consumers, home-owners and employers. The demise of Woolworths, one of the country's oldest high street retailers, just before Christmas was one of the most visible signs of a faltering economy. 'Woolies' had survived the Great Depression of the 1930s, but it became the first high-profile British victim of the crash of 2008. Rising repossessions, bankruptcies and unemployment suggested that the country was not only entering a recession, but that it was highly likely to be the worst since the Second World War.

On 23 January official figures revealed that the economy had actually begun to contract between July and September 2008, shrinking by a further 1.5 per cent in the last three months of the year. It was the biggest fall in GDP since 1980, and it sent the pound tumbling to a twenty-four-year low against the US dollar. (Revised figures later in the year confirmed that the economy actually entered recession even earlier, during the second quarter of 2008). A deep sense of public foreboding about the nation's finances ensured that any talk within Labour circles of a spring election vanished, as did the government's short-lived opinion poll lead over the Tories on the question of which party was most trusted to manage the economy. A fearful public may well have appreciated the government's decisive response to an imploding banking system, but any hopes the Prime Minister may have pinned on being rewarded in the long term quickly disappeared.

The worsening economic climate focused the minds of senior Tories. 'It dawned upon us that if we win the election we are going to inherit the most difficult situation for decades,' Hague says. 'This is what I came into politics for. We all piled in – there was a good spirit in the Shadow Cabinet.'[25] During the spring, commentators began to revise their views about Team Cameron's decision to oppose the fiscal stimulus and highlight the problem of debt. It might not have been such an eccentric move after all, given the state of the public finances.

The budget later in the spring was expected to reveal that the deficit would be much larger than had been predicted at the PBR. Lord Mandelson had been at the forefront of the government's response, announcing initiatives to revive struggling businesses on an almost daily basis. This reinforced the impression that the government was scurrying wildly to seize headlines in the absence of a more concerted approach to recovery. 'Labour began to fall apart operationally,' recalls an aide to a senior member of the Shadow Cabinet. 'We all began to notice it. Any mistakes we made went completely unnoticed, whereas ten years ago Alastair Campbell and Peter Mandelson would have leapt on them. They used to destroy us on a daily basis. Not now.'

Gordon Brown may have had his second 'bounce' as a result of the crisis, but the energy began to sap out of the government. Cameron's circle was filled with a sense of confidence that if the Prime Minister had been unable to capitalise on the banking crisis, it was unlikely that he could ride out the economic storm unscathed before a general election, which had to be called by June 2010. Even plaudits from President Obama and other world leaders as Brown hosted a summit of the G20 in London later in the spring did little to increase his domestic standing.

Tragedy Intervenes

In the early hours of 25 February 2009, David and Samantha Cameron's six-year-old son Ivan died after being rushed to St Mary's Hospital, Paddington. Although Ivan's rare medical condition meant that he had not been expected to live a long life, his sudden death devastated the Cameron family and their friends. The weekly clash of Prime Minister's Questions was suspended that day, and Gordon Brown, whose own daughter had died at just ten days old in 2002, made a moving tribute in the Commons.

The tragic news revealed a side of David Cameron's life that had been known about by many in Westminster, but was less visible to the outside world, beyond some media coverage when he was elected as party leader in 2005. Ivan's condition, Ohtahara Syndrome, whose symptoms include epileptic fits and spasms, required around-the-clock care. The birth of Ivan in 2002 changed David Cameron's life. Describing the moment when he learned of his son's disabilities, he told the *Sunday Times* in 2005: 'The news hits you like a freight train. You are depressed for a while, because you are grieving for the difference between your hopes and the reality. But then you get over that, because he's wonderful.'[26] The Camerons would go on to have two other healthy children, but they would often meet parents with seriously ill children from other walks of life, as well as having regular contact with the NHS. 'For me it's not a question of saying the NHS is safe in my hands ... My family is so often in the hands of the NHS,' Cameron had told his party in 2006. The Camerons' loss was felt across the political divide, and attracted a wave of sympathy. Although David Cameron was out of action for the first part of March, paradoxically the country learned more about the Conservative leader in those few weeks than it had known before.

Battle is Rejoined

The spring of 2009 was an unsettling period for the Conservative leadership. Cameron's private office was still coming to terms with his tragedy, but normal political life would inevitably resume at some point. The deteriorating economic situation forced the leadership to consider casting off other spending commitments, and on 19 March Cameron pledged that the only areas of public spending that would be protected for 2010–11 and beyond would be health and inter-national development. In a wide-ranging speech, he said that if elected his administration would focus on paying off the national debt. Without giving firm details of his plans, he would save money by cutting 'quango fat cats' and abandoning government programmes such as identity cards. Controlling public spending would have to be carried out 'with a social conscience'. He also suggested that the rich would have to pay 'a fair share of the burden' in taxes. 'Let's be clear about what will now have to happen over the next few years. I am a Conservative who believes in lower taxes. But in today's fiscal circumstances, the priority must go to debt reduction,' he said. It was a daring message for a Tory leader to be ruling out tax cuts, but good housekeeping was a message the leadership hoped would resonate with party and public alike. The 'new age of austerity' was a theme Cameron returned to at the party's spring forum a few weeks later.

Some members of the Shadow Cabinet were wary of pushing an overly negative message on the economy. 'The age of austerity is important, but it has to be austerity with a purpose, and balanced with the idea that we'll emerge from the recession better and stronger,' says one. Others were worried that talking down the country's prospects laid the party open to the attack that it didn't care about the short-term pain people were enduring. 'All too often Labour now accuse us of being the Taliban who have shaved off their beards, but not changed their views,' one Shadow minister candidly admits. 'It is all very well going on about debt, but we must not forget the fact that we left parts of the country to suffer in previous recessions. We can no longer ignore the existence of growing inequalities.' Pushing the mantra of financial responsibility and prudence was all very well, but it might be a harsh message to sell when people were losing their jobs and homes. The leadership was aware that there was much more to do to convince the public that frugality had to serve a purpose. There was a danger that the 'progressive ends of fighting poverty, extending opportunity and repairing our broken society' that Cameron spoke about in his Birmingham conference speech would become lost in a threadbare Tory vision of Britain's new 'age of austerity'.

When the Chancellor unveiled his budget to the Commons on 22 April, the economic picture was revealed to be much worse than feared. Total government debt would double to 79 per cent of GDP by 2013 – the highest level since the Second World War – and Darling announced that the annual budget deficit would rise sharply to £175 billion over the next two years. The figures exceeded even the dire predictions of the Pre-Budget Report in November 2008. The 45p tax rate on higher earners (over £150,000 per year) announced at the PBR would rise to 50p, starting in April 2010, and public spending plans would have to be trimmed. It was one of the toughest budgets for years. After twelve years in office, New Labour had ditched its manifesto pledge not to raise income tax, which had long been a symbol of its desire to reassure the middle classes.

The budget received a cool reception in the City and from the CBI, which warned that it did not set out a 'credible and rigorous' path to recovery. In an impassioned response, Cameron said that the government had left an 'utter mess' of the nation's finances, which would leave a price to be paid by 'our children for decades'. Brown and Darling had hoped that raising the top rate of income tax would wrongfoot the opposition, but Cameron and Osborne had seen the trap coming after the PBR in November, and decided that to commit to reversing the 50p rate would allow Labour to portray the Conservatives as interested only in defending the rich. 'I don't like it,' Osborne said. 'I don't think in the long run higher tax rates are a great idea for an economy. However, I cannot promise to reverse it.'[27] Instead the priority would be to reverse the government's increase in National Insurance contributions, that were due to affect everyone earning more than £20,000. Some on the right of the party argued that Osborne should have made a firmer commitment to abandon the 50p rate, as it would be a disincentive to the entrepreneurs who would help create the growth necessary for any recovery, but the political imperative of closing down a potentially damaging argument with Labour prevailed.

By the end of April it was clear that the government's misfortunes were closely entangled with the bleak economic outlook. The recession had given the Conservatives fresh purpose, although this was hardly by design. The financial crisis and the onset of a deep recession provided a considerable challenge to the party. Cameron's offer to support the government in rescuing the banks allowed a spotlight to fall on his party's threadbare position on the economy. Cameron says that the period leading up to the Blackpool conference in 2007 was his most difficult time since becoming leader, yet the situation in the autumn of 2008 was just as serious. It was crunch time for the Tory leadership.

George Osborne had been instrumental in turning things around in October 2007, but twelve months later he had come to be seen as a liability. Losing Osborne would have dealt a potentially fatal blow to the Cameron project. Reinforcement in the form of Ken Clarke had given it badly-needed ballast and credibility.

It was fortuitous for the opposition that the worsening state of the public finances and the sheer gravity of the recession began to take its toll on Brown's government. The Prime Minister had regained some of the authority he had lost after his election indecision, but the expected 'Brown bounce' in the polls failed to materialise amid growing public discontent about the state of the economy. Once again the Conservatives surged ahead in the polls, while Labour faltered. By reframing the argument about the nation's finances in terms of rising debt, the Tory leadership had opened up a new front in the battle against the government. It had to act quickly to find more comfortable territory, having been isolated in the autumn. The Tory ship was still afloat, while HMS Brown was listing heavily. But just as it thought it had weathered one storm, another, more ferocious one was about to hit.

TEN

Aiming for the Summit
May–December 2009

With twelve or thirteen months remaining before the country had to go the polls, British politics had been jolted by the most severe financial crisis to hit the world in seventy years. The earthquake that took place in September and October 2008 was reshaping the contours of political debate. After a few months when it looked as though the government had regained the initiative and the Tories struggled to find a voice, a more settled pattern emerged in early 2009. Brown began to take the hit for a deepening recession, while the opposition, having positioned itself as the party of financial prudence, benefited from the public's growing dissatisfaction. The Conservatives were brimming with confidence, and the polls put them in a commanding position. But just as the dust began to settle, another crisis was about to engulf the political establishment which had the potential to undo David Cameron's efforts to present a new and changed party to the electorate. His long and uncertain climb to the summit of power was in jeopardy once again.

Politics Turns Nasty
The Easter weekend usually provides a brief respite in the political calendar. The budget was only ten days away, but all seemed quiet until news filtered out of Downing Street on Saturday, 11 April that one of the Prime Minister's most trusted advisers, Damian McBride, had resigned. Known as 'McPoison', the former Treasury official had a reputation for his tirades against journalists whose stories he disliked. Gordon Brown valued his tough approach and unswerving

loyalty, virtues which soon turned to vices when it was revealed by the political blogger Guido Fawkes that McBride was hatching a plot to smear leading Conservative politicians. When it became clear that evening that a number of Sunday newspapers were going to print the false allegations about the personal lives of Osborne and Cameron and their families, as well as a number of other Tory MPs, the following day, Cameron was incensed. 'He was absolutely furious,' recalls one of his senior aides. 'David doesn't normally lose his cool, but on this occasion he did. What infuriated him most were the fabrications about those not in the public eye, who couldn't speak up for themselves.'

Cameron asked Andy Coulson, who was on holiday, to try to prevent the details of the smears from being made public. It was to no avail, although some corrections were made and passages were removed from the newspapers' websites. McBride resigned in disgrace, and pressure mounted on Gordon Brown to dissociate himself from the affair and apologise. Only after five days of stonewalling did he reluctantly do so. In failing to respond earlier, the Prime Minister had allowed himself to be drawn into the affair, and his reputation suffered as a result. His personal poll ratings plummeted. In mid-March, 59 per cent of people were dissatisfied with his performance as Prime Minister. By mid-May, the figure had risen to 78 per cent.[1] The effect was also reflected in measures of voting intention. As Labour dropped to the mid-twenties in the polls at the beginning of May, the Tories moved into the mid-forties.[2]

The revelations about the unpleasant aspects of Brown's regime fortified the Tory leadership. 'It was one of those unifying moments for us,' recalls one of Cameron's inner circle.' The McBride affair coloured Cameron and Osborne's view of Brown. When Brown made what many considered a Freudian slip in the Commons a few months previously in reference to the banking bail-out, claiming that the government had 'saved the world', Cameron and his MPs broke out in uproarious laughter. They believed the gaffe illustrated the Prime Minister's hubris and overwhelming self-importance. The McBride affair had turned mockery into contempt – and it was not limited to the Tories; many Labour MPs felt distinctly uneasy about Brown's leadership.

Cameron says that he has a cordial relationship with Brown when they meet for official business, but although the Tory leader respects Brown's experience and drive as a politician, he dislikes his relentless desire to destroy the opposition at all costs. Those close to Cameron believe that below the professional level a deep animus exists. 'They hate each other,' says one former adviser. 'Blair and Cameron got on, but Gordon hates all of us. He loathes George in particular because he was the only Shadow Chancellor to have got under his skin when he was Chancellor. Now that he sees George and David joined at the hip, it makes him hate David even more.' The McBride affair strengthened the resolve of Cameron and his team, while reinforcing the wider party's contempt for Brown as Prime Minister. Westminster politics had turned especially nasty, rebounding on the government while putting fire into Tory bellies.

Expenses Train Hurtles in

Within weeks, the behaviour of elected politicians came under intense scrutiny, making the antics of backroom advisers pale in comparison. The scandal of MPs' expenses was one of the most damaging episodes in British politics for decades, touching all parties, including the very top of the Conservative Party. This was a political crisis waiting to happen. Ever since the Freedom of Information Act came into force in 2005, campaigners had sought publication of MPs' expenses and allowances. After a three-year battle with the Information Commissioner (who monitors the operation of the Act), the Commons was ordered in January 2008 to publish a detailed breakdown of expenses claimed by six MPs, including Gordon Brown and Tony Blair. However, in March the Commons authorities launched an appeal against the ruling. It turned out to be a costly mistake.

The first signs of trouble on the Tory side occurred the same month, when Derek Conway was found to have used his parliamentary staffing allowance to pay his younger son Freddie as a researcher, although it appeared he had carried out little or no work. It was an embarrassment for the party and the leadership, evoking memories of Tory sleaze from the 1990s. It also provided a glimpse into a flawed system of allowances and expenses that was open to abuse. Cameron removed the party whip from Conway, and in an attempt to seize the initiative announced that all Conservative frontbenchers would be required by July 2008 to set out their use of parliamentary expenses and allowances, and to declare whether they employed family members. Backbenchers would be encouraged to do the same. When the information was published, it emerged that sixty-four Tory MPs employed a family member. Cameron had turned the Conway affair to his advantage by pushing for transparency, but however much he sought to gain the initiative, the momentum towards full disclosure of all MPs' arrangements was becoming unstoppable.

In May 2008 the Commons authorities lost their legal appeal in the High Court against the publication of MPs' expenses. The authorities then began to scan four years' worth of receipts, invoices and claim forms for every MP in readiness for their publication. An illicit copy of this data found its way into the hands of the *Daily Telegraph*, and an early salvo came in February, when it was revealed that Jacqui Smith, the Home Secretary, had wrongly designated the London house belonging to her sister as her 'main home', while claiming the second home allowance to which MPs with constituencies outside London were entitled on her family home in her constituency (as well as claiming pay-per-view adult films that her husband had watched). These abuses would prove to be just the tip of the iceberg.

On Friday, 8 May, the *Telegraph* splashed details of claims made by thirteen Cabinet ministers, including Chancellor Alistair Darling, Communities Secretary Hazel Blears and Culture Secretary Andy Burnham across its front page. It also published a claim made by Gordon Brown to pay back his brother for a cleaner for his Westminster flat. Over the next two days the paper concentrated its investigation, which it called the 'Expenses Files', on government ministers. It was only a matter of time before it would turn its attention to the Conservatives. 'We saw it coming,' recalls one of Cameron's closest aides, 'but we didn't know that the *Telegraph* would splash it all. For months – no, years – people were aware of this train hurtling down the tracks. There was a lot of gallows humour around: MPs would joke that this was going to be their total nightmare.' That nightmare was about to come true.

One Tory aide urged senior figures to pre-empt the impending disaster. 'Cameron did ask frontbenchers to publish their details the previous summer after the Conway affair, but it didn't go far enough,' he says despairingly. 'I told them months beforehand, "Put everything on the party's website *and* pay back taxpayers' money before a newspaper gets hold of this stuff." It would be our genuine Clause IV moment: we would come clean, it would not look like a cover-up and we would have put Labour on the defensive. But they didn't care.' It would have been a brave move to have followed this advice and put the party above the fray, but ultimately it was one step too far for the leadership.

When Andy Coulson learned of the revelations about Labour politicians that were to appear in the following day's papers on the evening of Thursday, 7 May, he phoned Cameron at home. They knew that the *Telegraph* would turn on them shortly. Cameron agreed with Coulson that they needed to assemble as much information about individual MPs as possible, so that they would be in a position to respond. Unlike Labour they had the advantage of being prepared for the onslaught. Oliver Dowden, who had recently been appointed the party's Director of Political Operations, was given the responsibility of collating the information. The next day he set up a special unit with Douglas Smith, another senior official from Campaign Headquarters, in Cameron's and Osborne's suite of offices in the Norman Shaw South building adjacent to the Commons.[3] Charged with combing through the expenses files of every single Conservative MP, they set to work immediately, starting with the claims made by the Shadow Cabinet. Soon the team was expanded to fifteen press officers and researchers, who worked around the clock to sift through the material. Cameron and his senior aides kept a close eye on what was rapidly becoming an enormous operation.

On the morning of Sunday, 10 May, the *Telegraph* informed the party's press office that it was about to send letters to members of the Shadow Cabinet with questions about their expenses.[4] Cameron's inner circle was braced, but it did little to calm nerves throughout the party. 'There was total and utter panic when they realised these stories were all going to hit the next day,' recalls one party aide. Among the embarrassing revelations to appear in the paper on the Monday was the fact that Alan Duncan, the Shadow Leader of the Commons (whose brief included the issue of expenses and allowances) had recouped £4,000 for gardening costs, including overhauling a ride-on lawnmower. Even more bizarrely, David Willetts claimed £132 for electricians to replace twenty-five light-bulbs at his home, while Oliver Letwin claimed £2,000 to replace a leaking pipe under his tennis court. Shadow Home Secretary Chris Grayling claimed thousands of pounds to refurbish a London flat only seventeen miles from his family home. Even the pettiest of expenses were claimed, including £4.47 for dog food by the Shadow Welsh Secretary Cheryl Gillan (who said the claim had been made in error and would be repaid). Cameron himself had claimed a £680 repair bill, which included the cost of removing wisteria from the chimney of his Oxfordshire home, while Osborne had claimed £400 for the cost of a 'chauffeur' to drive him from Cheshire to London.[5] Cameron's and Osborne's expenses were relatively straightforward compared to some of their colleagues', although Cameron's substantial claims for mortgage interest payments on his constituency home raised more than a few eyebrows. The *Telegraph* did not splash his expenses on its front page, unlike those of the Prime Minister, who had received the full treatment the previous Friday.

By Sunday evening the Dowden operation had helped to prepare a coordinated response. Frontbenchers had issued short statements, mostly explaining that they had acted within the rules. However, there was a problem with one case: Michael Gove, the Shadow Schools Secretary and a key member of Cameron's inner circle. In response to the *Telegraph*'s allegation that he claimed more than £7,000 for work on a London property over five months in 2006, before claiming more than £13,000 on a Surrey property in his constituency, he strongly denied changing the designation of which was his second home, a practice that became known as 'flipping'.[6] He insisted that he had not made a profit at the taxpayer's expense, and denied any wrongdoing.

Cameron spoke to reporters outside his house on Sunday evening, and again early the next morning. 'It is another bad day for Parliament and, frankly, a bad day for the Conservative Party,' he told them. 'We have to acknowledge just how bad this is. The public are really angry, and we have to start by saying, "Look, this system that we had, that we used, that we operated, that we took part in – it was wrong, and we're sorry about it." '[7] He did not address specific allegations, but condemned the existing rules. By making a blanket apology before the Prime Minister (who apologised on behalf of all MPs later on Monday), he had seized the initiative and effectively endorsed the *Telegraph*'s investigation.

Frontbenchers from all sides of the House had played the system. Still, the potential damage to the Tory Party's reputation was clear to see. Ever since he was elected as party leader, Cameron had sought to change the public's perception of the Conservatives as the party of the rich and privileged. Memories of financial sleaze from the Major years still lingered. For Cameron and his party, events were about to take a turn for the worse.

Panic Sets in

While the media were ablaze with stories about the Shadow Cabinet's dubious expenses claims on Monday, 11 May, Cameron proceeded with a scheduled trip to Derby. Back in Norman Shaw South, Andy Coulson and the special expenses team began to sift through material from Tory backbenchers. Obtaining it was far from easy. 'They had a handle on the frontbenchers, but when it came to backbenchers, they were their own masters,' says a party aide. 'The problem was that they genuinely didn't know how bad it was, and there was no mechanism inside the party to force these guys to hand their stuff over.' By late afternoon Coulson's team was no better informed. Then at 6.30 p.m. ITN broke the news that the *Telegraph* was preparing incendiary reports for its fifth day of coverage, including the expenses claims made by a number of Tory grandees who were among the wealthiest MPs in Parliament. 'This was the point that we really began to panic,' says one insider.

As the evening wore on, more details emerged of the impending revelations. When Coulson rang Cameron, who was on the train from Derby to London, to tell him about the extravagance of the grandees, there was deathly silence on the end of the phone. In effect, they had used taxpayers' money to subsidise their country estates. Among those exposed were Douglas Hogg, the former Minister for Agriculture in the Major government; Michael Ancram, a former minister, Deputy Leader and Party Chairman; and Sir Michael Spicer, another former minister and the current Chairman of the 1922 Committee. Hogg's claims caused particular consternation. As Viscount Hailsham, he came from a landed family of Tory politicians (his father having served in successive Conservative administrations until the Thatcher era). To taxpayers, it seemed incredible that public money was allegedly being used to maintain the upkeep of his manor house in Lincolnshire. What better way to illustrate the perception that Conservative MPs live a rarefied existence, far removed from the lives of their constituents, than the revelation that one them, from esteemed aristocratic stock, was using their hard-earned money to pay to have his moat cleared?

The moat came to symbolise the excesses of the expenses system. It provoked public ridicule and contempt in equal measure. The sheer arrogance and lack of humility of the recipients was one thing, but even more damning for the Conservative Party was the evidence that a number of its MPs lived in an elite world of entitlement divorced from the reality of most voters. Cameron realised that something drastic would have to be done to stop this turning into a full-blown crisis enveloping his party and his leadership.

Asking his private office to clear the entire diary for the following day, he took soundings from senior colleagues in the Shadow Cabinet as well as talking to advisers, prominent among them his chief of staff, Edward Llewellyn, who would play a key role in helping him shape and deliver his response. The headlines on the television news bulletins later that evening were dynamite. 'It was a sudden maelstrom,' one insider recalls. '[Cameron] knew that we had to respond very quickly, and that it had to be all hands to the pump. There was a sense that the whole party could founder completely if we did not handle it properly.' It was no exaggeration: this was by far the most explosive crisis to hit the party, and Parliament as a whole, for decades. Cameron was facing the most important test of his leadership to date.

That evening he convened an urgent meeting of his close team – Osborne, Hilton, Llewellyn, Coulson and Fall – at his home to discuss how to respond to the crisis. 'There was some disagreement and a frank exchange of views, but you could tell David was fuming below the surface,' recalls one senior adviser. 'His immediate reaction was that if you lose trust as an opposition party, you really are in trouble – particularly when you are presenting yourselves as agents of change and being up-front with people about the country's problems.' Cameron was clear that not only was the fate of the Tory Party at stake, but the public's faith in the whole political system. After a few hours he stood up, thanked the others for their advice and announced that he was off to bed. He would decide what to do in the morning.

Payback Time

Early on Tuesday, 12 May Cameron rang Llewellyn with a list of instructions for the day. He would begin with one-to-one meetings with members of the Shadow Cabinet and other errant MPs, then meet the Shadow Cabinet at midday before briefing the executive of the backbench 1922 Committee. At 2 p.m. he would address the entire parliamentary party. An emergency press conference would be arranged for mid-afternoon, at which he would lay out his plan to put the Tory house in order. He agreed with Llewellyn that the special expense unit in Norman Shaw South would turn into a secretariat for a new scrutiny panel comprising the Chief Whip, his deputy John Randall, Jeremy Middleton (Chairman of the National Convention) and an outside expert. The panel would investigate every Tory MP's arrangements. At the press conference he would announce a tough new expenses regime, whereby Conservative MPs would have to publish all their claims online. 'Flipping' between homes would be banned, as would claims for furniture, household goods and food. All Tory MPs would also have to pay capital gains tax on the sale of homes against which they had made claims. He also decided that members of the Shadow Cabinet would have to pay back money they had received for certain claims and allowances in the past. 'He was very conscious that this was an occasion that he had to lead,' recalls an aide. As Cameron left his house for the Commons he gave the briefest of statements to reporters: 'I am angry about what has happened. It is out of order. Some of this is an abuse of taxpayers' money, and I am going to deal with it.'[8]

As an irate but determined Cameron sped off in his official car, television crews were primed to catch a number of Tory grandees outside their London homes. Live on camera, Douglas Hogg denounced the *Telegraph*'s reports as he briskly made his way to the Commons by foot, insisting that he had acted within 'both the letter and the spirit' of the rules.[9] By refusing to stop to answer questions, he gave the impression that he felt they were a rude interruption of his private life. 'We were watching it live, thinking, "Oh my God, this is a total fucking catastrophe," ' recalls one party aide. 'Until Monday there was resistance from frontbench people – no one wanted to stick their necks out by paying anything back, because that would have kicked off demands from everybody else. The attitude was "Let's tough it out." There was a deep-rooted feeling of not wanting to confront how bad it was, but the moat smashed everything out of the way. They realised, "This is a total disaster, and we are going to have to get our chequebooks out." '

Every member of the Shadow Cabinet who was asked to repay money did so, although one party aide claims that at least two of them were within hours of resigning. 'They had told their families and friends that they had had enough, and were ready to prepare resignation statements, but in the end they were saved by the fact that the *Telegraph* just kept throwing out more and more revelations each day.' For the next few days every Tory MP who had not yet been touched by the investigation dreaded the hours between 2 and 5 p.m., when *Telegraph* reporters would call those whose claims were to be exposed the next morning.

Tuesday, 12 May was one of the most important days in David Cameron's career as leader of the Conservative Party. Having confronted shadow ministers with the hard reality that they would have to pay money back to the Commons, he now had to deal with the grandees whose extravagance had caused him so much ire. Many of them had been ministers in the Thatcher and Major governments, and were respected elder statesmen of the party. Cameron had been a mere researcher when they were at the pinnacle of their ministerial careers. Now he was reading them the riot act. 'David saw his job to be the next Prime Minister putting the system right, rather than a shop steward for the trade union of Westminster operatives,' says a senior member of the Shadow Cabinet. 'It required tact and judgement, because some of these people had devoted their lives to public service. I didn't envy him. Some people didn't like his judgements. He was acting in the collective interest of the party and, more importantly, on the side of public opinion.' Cameron had to be ruthless. Either the grandees agreed to apologise and pay money back, or they would have to consider their positions as Tory MPs.

When Cameron confronted the parliamentary party in the Boothroyd Room of Portcullis House early that afternoon, he told them what he was about to say at the hastily arranged press conference. Far from being hostile, the mood was supportive. Among those who spoke strongly in support were two of his predecessors, Iain Duncan Smith and Michael Howard. Not one MP spoke out against Cameron's plan, but some left the room with a look of bewilderment across their faces. Only now was the sheer scale of the crisis sinking in.

Cameron was primed to deliver a stern message when he arrived at St Stephen's Club, for his press conference at 3.30 p.m. He had already apologised on Sunday evening and again the following morning, beating the Prime Minister to it. Now he would outflank him even more explicitly. 'I want to start by saying sorry,' he said. 'Sorry that it's come to this. And sorry for the actions of some Conservative MPs. People are right to be angry that some MPs have taken public money to pay for things few could afford. You've been let down. Politicians have done things that are unethical and wrong. I don't care if they were within the rules – they were wrong. I've said that a Conservative government needs to be careful, not casual, with public money. That principle of thrift should apply to Conservative MPs as well.' He named members of his Shadow Cabinet and the amounts that they had agreed to pay back, including his own maintenance bill, then outlined the measures he had decided upon that morning.

Cameron had exerted his authority at a critical moment. 'It was a high-octane day,' recalls one of his closest advisers. The party leader was unambiguous in his condemnation of his MPs' conduct and the system that encouraged such abuse. He had acted swiftly, and had spoken to the media, and the country, with a candour that few other senior politicians had so far shown. Many commentators in Fleet Street contrasted his convincing performance with the Prime Minister's.

When Cameron was asked, after he had made his statement, whether this was his Clause IV moment, he replied: 'I don't believe in these "Clause IV moments". Leading a party is about trying to make the right judgement all of the time, trying to take your party in the right direction all of the time, making it fit for power, giving it the right ethos. That is what I have tried to do over three and half years.'[10] With those words, the rumbling question about whether he needed, or had ever sought, a 'Clause IV moment' was put to one side, once and for all. What Cameron had achieved that day, which Tony Blair had managed in the mid-1990s as Labour leader, was to assert a commanding presence over a party that was in need of discipline and leadership. Like Blair, he showed that he could be ruthless if necessary in order to preserve the integrity of his modernising project. It was a defining moment for David Cameron. Two questions remained: how much more was there to come from the *Telegraph*, and would his party allow him to administer justice through the new scrutiny panel?

Cameron's new payback regime opened the floodgates for MPs on all sides. The very next day, Hazel Blears became the first Cabinet minister to follow suit. When Blears, a self-declared champion of working-class voters in her native Salford, brandished a cheque for £13,332 payable to HM Revenue and Customs (in lieu of unpaid capital gains tax) for the television cameras, the crisis turned into an even greater public relations disaster for the Labour Party. The Prime Minister was in an awkward position, seeming to be following events rather than leading them. Indeed, Labour did not set up its own investigative 'star chamber' to examine the cases of its MPs for another week. The impression soon took hold that Brown had neither a grip on his party, nor the full measure of the crisis. There was an even more damaging aspect to the expenses affair for Labour. While the behaviour of landed and wealthy Tory MPs brought back an old image of a party interested only in defending themselves, Labour politicians drew scorn as hypocrites who had used lavish amounts of public money at the expense of the working people they claimed to represent. The most serious cases, involving possible breaches of the law, centred on phantom mortgage claims by two Labour MPs, Elliot Morley and David Chaytor.

Over the following weeks the Conservative scrutiny panel trawled through almost two hundred files of material. The panel's work threw up some unpleasant surprises. On 14 May it sealed the fate of Cameron's senior parliamentary adviser, Andrew MacKay. MacKay was among the first to submit his files, confident that his expenses were clean. However, the panel discovered that he had used his second home allowance to claim more than £1,000 a month in mortgage interest payments on a flat near Westminster that he jointly owned with his wife and fellow Tory MP, Julie Kirkbride. She in turn had been claiming over £900 a month to pay the mortgage interest on their family home near her Bromsgrove constituency in Worcestershire. Having claimed public funds to pay for two 'second homes', Mackay admitted an 'error of judgement', and had no choice but to resign. Although the panel eventually cleared Kirkbride, the damage was done, and she too decided to stand down at the next election. MacKay's bruising encounter with voters at a meeting in his Berkshire constituency revealed just how angry the public were about the whole scandal.

MacKay was the first MP to lose his position over the expenses affair, and David Cameron felt his loss keenly. MacKay had been a candid and reassuring presence in the team, having served every Tory leader since Mrs Thatcher, with the exception of Duncan Smith, in some capacity. The crisis also sealed the fate of the Commons Speaker, Michael Martin. On 18 May he told MPs that he was 'profoundly sorry' that the public had been so badly let down, but this was not enough to stem the growing tide of criticism of his handling of the crisis, and he resigned the next day.

Douglas Hogg announced that he would stand down at the next election, and a large number of other MPs would follow him. Among them was the Conservative MP for Gosport, Sir Peter Viggers, whose claims included £1,645 for a five-foot high Swedish duck house for a pond at his home, which became another symbol of the tainted expenses regime. Following the *Daily Telegraph*'s disclosure that he had spent nearly £90,000 of taxpayers' money on his multi-million-pound country home over four years Sir Anthony Steen, an MP since 1974, insisted that his behaviour was 'impeccable'. 'I have done nothing criminal,' he told a reporter. 'And you know what it's about? Jealousy. I have got a very, very large house. Some people say it looks like Balmoral, but it's a merchant's house from the nineteenth century. What right does the public have to interfere with my private life? None.'[11] It was yet another intense embarrassment for the Tory leadership, who made it clear that it would be wise for Steen to retire at the next election.

On 19 May the Prime Minister announced that external regulators would be brought in to oversee MPs' pay and allowances, and ordered an audit by Sir Thomas Legg, a former civil servant, who would examine every MP's arrangements. Once again, though, the Prime Minister was to be upstaged. At Prime Minister's Questions Cameron called for an immediate general election to sweep out the old Parliament. When Brown responded that a Tory government 'would cause chaos', he presented Cameron with a priceless gift: he had effectively admitted that he would lose an election. The silence on the Labour benches was deafening.

The timing of the expenses scandal could not have been worse for the government. Local and European elections on 4 June would provide an opportunity for voters to express their discontent. As the party in power, Labour was bound to suffer heavily. The government was also struggling to contend with a relentless campaign led by the actress Joanna Lumley, whose efforts to raise the entitlements of retired Gurkhas brought about an embarrassing policy U-turn. Both Cameron and Nick Clegg had identified themselves with the campaign, and the Prime Minister had capitulated under the weight of growing public anger that former servicemen were being treated so poorly. The contrast with politicians feathering their own nests could not have been clearer.

In a speech to the Open University in Milton Keynes on 26 May, Cameron called for a 'radical redistribution of power' from the political elite to ordinary citizens. He re-announced a number of ideas that Ken Clarke's Democracy Taskforce had proposed, as well as a commitment to consider fixed-term Parliaments. The speech received a fair press: the Tory leader was trying to find ways of rebuilding public trust in the political system in the teeth of the scandal.

The Other Side Takes the Hit

There was trepidation on all sides as the local and European elections drew closer. The expectation was that the fringe parties, such as UKIP and the BNP, would benefit from discontent with politicians. Labour had most to lose. In some opinion polls it had fallen to third place behind the Liberal Democrats, whereas the Tories had fallen back only by three or four points, to an average of 38–39 per cent. Public dissatisfaction with the government was now at the same level that John Major's administration had endured in the mid-1990s.

What made matters even worse for Brown were the untimely resignations of the Home Secretary, Jacqui Smith, and Hazel Blears, the Communities Secretary, within forty-eight hours of the polls opening. The scandal had now become deeply embroiled with questions about Brown's leadership. Blears decided to quit because she felt she had been made a scapegoat. She had not impressed Brown when she ridiculed a video broadcast he had made for YouTube in April, in which he had tried to seize the initiative before the scandal broke by announcing a number of measures to reform the parliamentary expenses system. His choice of this medium, as well as his fixed smile, was derided. 'YouTube if you want to. But it's no substitute for knocking on doors,' Blears wrote in the *Observer*.[12] When he denounced her expenses claims as 'totally unacceptable', it was clear that he had lost confidence in her.

The day Blears resigned she wore a broach inscribed with the words 'Rock the boat.' She was not the only Cabinet minister to rock the boat. Just before polls closed at 10 p.m. on Thursday, 4 June, the Work and Pensions Secretary, James Purnell, a leading Blairite, resigned, telling Brown, 'I now believe your continued leadership makes a Conservative victory more, not less likely.'[13] Suddenly, the expenses crisis had turned into a question of survival for the Prime Minister.

Cameron and his team were glued to the television screens inside Campaign Headquarters in Millbank. They could not believe what was happening. 'We thought, "This was it – he's going," ' recalls one aide. 'It looked coordinated and pretty grubby – they could at least have waited for the results to come out.' In fact it was not a coordinated plot. Purnell was the only minister to resign that night, after Lord Mandelson had rung around senior members of the government suggesting that if they were to go, an early election was inevitable. David Miliband was the key figure, as he had been during Brown's previous leadership crisis in October 2008. By deciding to remain in the government, he had saved Brown's political life. If he had gone with Purnell, it would almost certainly have ended Brown's premiership. 'By 1 a.m. it was all over,' recalls a Tory insider. 'We realised that this wasn't going to be the end of Gordon Brown. Politically for us it was perfect. Gordon was wounded, but not dead – it couldn't have been better.'

They had reason to feel encouraged. By the end of the night the Conservatives had managed to take all four of Labour's remaining shire counties in northern England, while taking Devon and Somerset from the Liberal Democrats in the south-west. But despite making huge gains in local councils, the Tory share of the vote fell from its zenith of 44 per cent in 2008 to 38 per cent. The expenses scandal had hit the party's support, but by concentrating its resources on the ground the Conservatives had managed to benefit from a collapse in Labour's vote. When the European results were announced the following weekend, the picture was even more dire for Labour, which polled just 15 per cent of the vote. The Conservatives, with 28 per cent, managed only a single percentage point improvement on their 2004 performance, but the stories of the night were of the government's collapse and the election of two BNP MEPs. Labour's support had fallen so dramatically that the Conservatives came out on top even in Wales, where they led the poll for the first time in a nation-wide election since 1918.

The elections had acted like a pressure valve for the whole crisis. Voters had expressed their anger at the ballot box, and the government suffered the most as a result. The Conservatives had been braced for a backlash of their own, but it failed to materialise. While the tensions within Labour had boiled over in public, accentuating Gordon Brown's problems, the Tories had retained a strong degree of discipline. It was an exact mirror image of the circumstances before the 1997 general election, when the Conservatives fought local and European elections amid open warfare, while Labour under Blair concentrated on maximising its vote. The ideological divisions within the government may not have been present in 2009, but the complete lack of confidence in the leadership of the Prime Minister was remarkably familiar.

Cameron's deft response to the crisis proved an effective exercise in damage-limitation. Had he not acted so swiftly and decisively, the electoral situation in early June could have been more hostile. Once again, the Tories thought that Gordon Brown's misjudgements had handed them a gift. 'I thought Cameron wouldn't be able to come through the European elections unscathed, but in fact people who might have caused trouble internally kept their mouths shut and gave him a pass,' says an adviser to a senior figure in the Shadow Cabinet. The Tories had been spared the wrath of the voters, who took their revenge on the other side. While Cameron had used the crisis to go on the attack, Brown looked flat-footed. All the Tory leader could hope for was that his party remained disciplined in the months ahead, as Brown desperately tried to rebuild his authority. 'This guy is never going to give up,' Cameron confided to friends. 'He'll have another relaunch for when the next one goes wrong. He just keeps going like a steamroller.'

Topsy-Turvy Summer

Within days of the elections the Conservatives stumbled, providing what appeared to be a perfect opportunity for the Prime Minister to revive his fortunes. When Andrew Lansley, the Shadow Health Secretary, told Radio 4's *Today* programme on Wednesday, 10 June that 10 per cent cuts would have to be found in government departments apart from Health and International Development after 2011, Labour could not believe its luck. The recession and the state of the public finances had slipped off the front pages during the expenses scandal, but they now returned with the news that a senior Conservative was suggesting drastic cuts in public spending. Lansley's gaffe gave the Prime Minister ammunition for his weekly exchange with Cameron in the Commons. Brown had effectively painted the Tories as the party of spending cuts at the last two general elections. Now he could so again. Within hours Labour produced a poster with Cameron's face and the words 'Mr 10%'.

The Conservative press office immediately went into overdrive, insisting that Lansley had meant that Labour's spending plans would mean 10 per cent cuts after 2011. This did not wash with many lobby journalists, not least because of an article by the political editor of

the *Spectator*, Fraser Nelson, who asserted that the Tories were planning 10 per cent cuts.[14] Even before the budget in April, the respected
Institute for Fiscal Studies predicted that significant cuts would have
to be found in order to balance the public finances. Cameron had
already pledged that only Health and International Development
would have their budgets increased if the party won the election,
clearing the way for lower spending in other areas. But no one had
actually mentioned 'the C word' until now.

In reality, Lansley was making an argument that was already
prevalent in internal debates. 'We had a meeting, as PMQs was only
hours away,' recalls a senior aide. 'We knew we would have to have
a battle over spending at some point, but the question was, do you
try to put the genie back in the bottle, or run with it? After half an
hour, David and George just said, "Let's go for it." ' It was a brave
decision, particularly as Brown would be primed to go on the attack.
'This is the day that the Conservatives have revealed their true
manifesto for the country,' he roared. 'The choice is between a
government prepared to invest in the future, and a Tory Party which
is going to cut.' Cameron responded that the election would be
'about the mismanagement of the public finances, the appalling
deficits he has left and his plan for cuts'.[15]

Over the next five weeks, Cameron and Osborne pressed Brown
to admit that spending cuts would have to be made at some point,
but the Prime Minister refused to be drawn – against the advice of
Mandelson and his Chancellor, Alistair Darling. On 15 June, Osborne
wrote in *The Times*: 'We should have the confidence to tell the public
the truth that Britain faces a debt crisis; that real spending will have
to be cut, whoever is elected; and that the bills of rising unemployment and the huge interest costs of a soaring national debt means
that many government departments will face cuts in their budgets.'[16]

What could have been a difficult position for the opposition to
defend was turned into an attack on Brown and his ability to be
'straight with people'. Osborne's team went on the offensive, briefing
journalists with a clear breakdown of the figures, and by the middle
of June the Lansley gaffe had become a distant memory. 'The cuts

debate became a question of honesty,' says one insider. Indeed, every day that the Prime Minister refused to countenance spending restraint, his position weakened. 'What we managed to do is make a silk purse out of a sow's ear,' recalls David Willetts. 'What should have been the start of another neuralgic pre-election year when Labour attacked our spending plans, as they had before, became an advantage for us, because we were at least speaking the truth.'[17] As with the financial crisis and the expenses crisis, Brown had given the Tory leadership enough slack to find their footing. However, the pace and measure of Cameron's and Osborne's response was a world away from how their predecessors had sought to defuse potentially disastrous situations. The Cameron team believed that they had made the running on a debate which many Labour and Tory MPs believed was the only argument Gordon Brown had left in his locker. After a turbulent two months, confidence returned in Tory high command.

The fallout from the expenses crisis, however, continued to stir resentment among the parliamentary party. As the scrutiny panel continued its work, a number of backbenchers complained that they were the victims of summary justice. Why should they have to submit their records to a party body, they asked, which was using a test of 'reasonableness' to determine whether MPs should pay back money, when Sir Thomas Legg's official audit was going to do the same thing on less arbitrary grounds? 'People who were being forced to pay were inevitably going to be harmed in their constituencies,' one senior MP says. 'They didn't realise that by stoking it up they had made the likelihood of us winning the next election more uncertain, because the press would be after them,' says a former representative of the rank and file. 'There were some who were not massively happy,' recalls one of those involved with the process. 'Yet everybody agreed with the results of the scrutiny panel; we all knew that it wasn't a scientific exercise, but there was a view in each case about the appropriate repayments that had to be made.' While no Tory MP publicly defied the panel, which completed the bulk of its work by the end of June, by the end of July twenty-two of them had announced their decision to stand down at the election. They would by no means be the last.

What really caused resentment among a number of backbenchers was the charge of favouritism. 'There is a perception that those close to the leadership were being treated differently to everyone else,' says one senior party figure. Some long-serving MPs who were not close to Cameron felt they had been made pariahs, and the fact that Cameron took further pre-emptive action to improve transparency in the affairs of all his MPs, both frontbench and backbench, did little to calm nerves. On 29 June he announced that members of the Shadow Cabinet would have to give up all of their external jobs by December.

Despite this, some commentators wondered if the leadership had seized on the expenses crisis to rid the parliamentary party of backwoodsmen who were clinging onto safe seats and had no interest in the Cameron project. 'People who don't like Cameron are saying that he has used this process to ruthlessly fuck over people they don't like,' observes one party insider. Those close to Cameron insist that there was no such agenda. 'We genuinely did not think, "Here's an opportunity to get rid of our own people." What happened is that a number of MPs thought to themselves, "I don't fancy this any more," ' insists one of Cameron's aides, before adding revealingly, 'I think they made the right decision.' It was indeed convenient for the leadership that some of the more recalcitrant figures in the party were falling prey to the expenses backlash. After all, Cameron had called on local Conservative associations to de-select MPs who had been found wanting. He had also reopened the party's candidate list to give people with a record of public service, but little connection to the party, the chance to replace outgoing MPs. Those who were no longer welcome were being shown the door, and they had little choice but to walk through it.

As the summer recess drew nearer, the mood in the parliamentary party descended into melancholy. 'The Commons was a depressing, morbid place to be before the recess,' says Ken Clarke. 'It used to drive me up the wall – full of miserable people telling me that their wives were not going to put up with it any more. The ones who went out making any self-pitying or self-justifying remarks were immediately burnt in effigy by the newspapers.'[18] There was a danger that Tory MPs might turn against the leadership. One member of the Shadow Cabinet at the time observed that Cameron had become seriously isolated from the parliamentary party. 'The expenses scandal was a very serious lesson for him not to shit on his party and not to take them for granted. There's no Praetorian guard: people could have turned on him in an instant – and they very nearly did. They don't mind taking pain, but they don't like the summary justice of it, because they think it is just him being extremely nasty with a smile to satisfy the daily tabloid headline. They don't feel it's born of principle; it's done out of news management rather than principle.'

It was a criticism that failed to take account of the bar of public opinion. A number of Tory MPs were undoubtedly livid at the way they felt their careers had been dispensed with, but they had no one to blame but themselves. A large number of Conservative (and Labour and Liberal Democrat) MPs had not jumped on the gravy train, and could present themselves to the electorate with a clean conscience. But for those who had claimed extravagant amounts there was nowhere to hide. Their abuse of the system, however flawed, and their arrogance in assuming that they had done nothing wrong showed just how detached they were from public opinion. If it had not been for their leader's feel for the growing outrage among the public, the Conservative Party might well have been dragged down into the gutter, forever stained by the accusations of sleaze and selfishness that had so damaged its reputation in the 1990s.

In the eyes of many commentators and the public at large, Cameron had emerged from the crisis stronger than before. He had imposed his authority on the party, but there would be a price to pay in terms of morale. 'There is no getting around it that there is a lot of distrust around Cameron in the party,' says one party aide. 'He is not a loved character. He is loved by his gang, but outside of that there are a lot of people who don't trust him and think it's very cliquey – if you are not on the inside, then he doesn't care what you think.'

On 9 July the *Guardian* carried a story claiming that News Corp, the owners of the *News of the World*, had paid out more than £1 million to settle legal cases involving its journalists illegally hacking into the voicemail accounts of politicians and celebrities.[19] The affair surrounding the paper's royal reporter Clive Goodman had prompted Andy Coulson's resignation as editor in January 2007. Cameron immediately came to the rescue of his Director of Communications, telling reporters that it was wrong for newspapers to breach people's privacy without justification. 'That is why Andy Coulson resigned as editor of the *News of the World* two and a half years ago,' he told them. 'Of course I knew about that resignation before offering him the job. But I believe in giving people a second chance.'[20] Coulson was safe, but his alleged involvement in the scandal worried senior figures in the party. 'We would do better if Andy Coulson were not there – we would have more intellectual respectability,' says one frontbencher.

But Cameron needed Coulson. Since June 2007 he had given the party's communications a much sharper edge, and he had improved relations with parts of the media that had become seriously disillusioned with the Cameron project. Cameron had also been boosted by the return of Steve Hilton, who returned from California in May after eighteen months of travelling back and forth to London. Both Hilton and Coulson had been instrumental in shaping Cameron's immediate and longer-term response to the expenses crisis.

Fortunately for the leadership, a by-election caused by the resignation of Dr Ian Gibson, Labour MP for Norwich North, who quit the Commons after being banned by his party from standing again over his expenses claims, provided an opportunity to capitalise on Labour's continuing misfortunes. Campaign Headquarters invested vast resources in the campaign of the twenty-seven-year-old candidate Chloe Smith. Cameron himself visited the seat six times, and on 24 July the party repeated its success at Crewe and Nantwich by taking the seat from Labour with an impressive 16.5 per cent swing.

Norwich North was exactly the kind of seat the Conservatives had to win if they were to succeed at the general election. Not only did the result confirm that the party had not lost momentum, but it was an important confidence boost. Labour had raised the spectre of

Tory cuts during the campaign, but voters were determined to punish the party for forcing out a locally popular MP. 'Norwich lifted our spirits – it finished off a long year where we had made changes on all fronts and everyone was so tired,' recalls one senior party aide. Yet the by-election had an even greater significance: it confirmed the leadership's belief that Labour's attack on Tory plans for spending cuts had failed to make an impact. Important lessons would be drawn for the last party conference before the election.

It had been a topsy-turvy summer for Cameron and his party. He had been lauded for his handling of the most serious political crisis in decades, and was buoyed by average poll leads of 15–17 per cent in July and August, but he was still not held in great affection within the wider party – particularly by a large number of Tory MPs. Meanwhile, Gordon Brown continued to struggle. During August the government became embroiled in a damaging row about the release of Abdelbaset Ali al-Megrahi, the Libyan convicted for the bombing of the Pan Am flight over Lockerbie in 1988, while rising numbers of British casualties in operations in Afghanistan raised questions about the armed forces being under-equipped. When Brown announced during his speech to the TUC on 15 September that the government would have to consider cuts to public spending, he appeared to make an important concession in the debate over spending. But when he spoke to the Labour Party conference a few weeks later, he failed to mention cuts at all. Instead he delivered a list of spending promises, including a plan for a National Care Service, confounding expectations that he would emphasise prudence. The mood at Labour's conference was decidedly downbeat, with a large number of MPs failing to turn up. Lord Mandelson's tub-thumping speech lifted spirits, but reaction to the Prime Minister's speech on 29 September was completely overshadowed by news a few hours later that the *Sun* was switching its support from Labour to the Conservatives. Its headline the next day would read 'Labour's Lost It'.

The timing of the paper's endorsement was designed to cause Brown maximum damage. Ever since the *Sun* had switched sides to back Blair in 1997, the Tories had been desperate to court it. Although its impact in influencing the voting intentions of readers had declined since then, Cameron was determined to gain the support of the country's biggest selling tabloid newspaper. In supporting the Conservatives through the Thatcher years, and John Major in 1992, the paper had acclaimed a symbolic status. 'It Was the *Sun* Wot Won It' ran the famous headline after the 1992 election. The *Sun* was always keen to be seen to be supporting the winning side, so its decision to abandon its twelve-year rapprochement with Labour was not that surprising. It had been particularly critical of the government's equipping of troops in Afghanistan, but Cameron and Coulson, who had worked on the *Sun* as well as editing its sister paper the *News of the World*, had prepared the ground. In the summer of 2008 News Corp's owner, Rupert Murdoch, invited Cameron onto his yacht in the Greek islands. Just as Tony Blair had done when he flew to Australia to address a News Corp management seminar in 1995, Cameron used the opportunity to improve relations with the Australian-born media mogul.

It was not the first time they had met. During Cameron's first few months as leader, Murdoch had been unsure about the Tory leader, with reports suggesting that he felt he was a something of a lightweight.[21] Murdoch admired Margaret Thatcher and Ronald Reagan, and he had also had a high regard for Gordon Brown as Chancellor. The ice broke when Cameron laid on a dinner for Murdoch in the first half of 2007. According to one Tory source it was a success. 'There is no secret that Rupert Murdoch wondered if this youngster was really right in the eyes of an Aussie. It was only really when they spent time together that Murdoch realised David was very good at something he himself has excelled at – turning round a tired product.' Relations were significantly enhanced by the fact that Cameron and Osborne moved in the same social circles as Murdoch's son James, chairman and chief executive of News Corp, and Rebekah Brooks (previously Rebekah Wade), a former editor of the *Sun*.[22] In September 2009 the charm offensive bore fruit. 'We were delighted,' recalls a senior Cameron aide. 'It was a blow for Labour and a valuable moment for us.' The *Sun*'s backing gave the Conservatives a significant boost on the eve of their conference in Manchester. However, Cameron and Osborne would impress on the Shadow Cabinet and MPs that they should show no sign of complacency. Sobriety would be the order of the week.

Manchester Sobriety

As the last conference before the general election, Manchester would have special significance. Throughout the summer the leadership had been working on a package of announcements to reinforce the party's evolving position on the economy and the state of the public finances. The broad themes for the conference would attempt to pull together the strategic shifts that had been made since Cameron became leader. Steve Hilton suggested that the party's mission should be to fix the three 'brokens': the 'broken society' through social reform, the 'broken economy' by tackling the debt crisis, and 'broken politics' by giving people more power over their own lives, through information technology in the 'post-bureaucratic age'. His plan gave a gloss of continuity to the Cameron strategy, although in reality it had been formed in response to a combination of early ambitions and reaction to events. The social agenda had been evident from the beginning, but crafting a response to the recession required filling what was largely a blank canvas (although Cameron and Osborne had been consistent in calling for financial stability instead of unfunded tax cuts). The expenses crisis in May and June provided an opportunity to talk about democratising politics by spreading power down. 'Sure, we were responding to real crises, but we had to earn our approach,' one of Cameron's most senior advisers says. 'It did not just fall into our laps – we started to draw the battle lines. Ever since we turned around the debate on spending, Labour unravelled on tax and spend.' To an extent this is what happened, but the evolving strategy of Cameron's inner circle was essentially a blend of nurtured ideas and tactical shifts that had been forced upon them.

Along with the broad themes, the focus of the conference agenda would once again fall to Osborne's team. The Shadow Chancellor faced a far more pressing set of decisions than in the immediate aftermath of the financial crisis a year previously. Then he had been looking to the long term in opposing the stimulus and abandoning Labour's spending plans. With an election eight or nine months away at the most, he and Cameron were faced with their biggest strategic call yet. Both major parties now accepted the need for spending cuts, but the question remained of how they would be achieved. Should the Conservatives reinforce the 'age of austerity' theme Cameron had articulated in the spring, and specify how they would save money to reduce the ballooning budget deficit? Or should they keep their cards close to their chests until the last possible moment? Despite the message of 'cuts' having lost its taboo for the Tory leadership, it was risky for an opposition party to lay out its spending plans so far out from an election campaign.

'We had a huge decision to make about how much meat to put on the bones,' recalls one party aide. 'The key thing we had to convey was bringing the country with us – we had to be trusted.' Earlier in the year, Osborne and his shadow Treasury team had had discussions with former Finance Ministers from Canada and Sweden, where large-scale savings in public expenditure had been made after the recession of the early 1990s. Osborne was particularly interested in the Canadian example, where a centre-left government slashed federal budgets by 20 per cent in four years. As a result a burgeoning deficit was turned into a budget surplus, and the government was rewarded with re-election. Such significant cuts might be unpalatable in Britain, but the leadership decided that the party propose immediate cuts, in contrast to Labour, which believed that they could only be made once the economy started to recover.

The decision was reached after some of the most fraught discussions held by Cameron's inner circle since 2005. 'George was seriously stressed – I have never seen him like that before,' says one insider. 'The argument about whether they were going too far out on a limb went to and fro several times. George and David were in different places on it. They were ruling nothing out in principle.'

After months of deliberation, detailed polling and focus group research, the leadership agreed to put forward a package that would aim to save £23 billion over the first Parliament of a Conservative government. It would include freezing public sector pay for those earning above £18,000 per year, removing tax credits for well-off families, retaining the new 50 per cent tax rate on the rich and, most significantly, raising the state pension age for men to sixty-six from 2016 (ten years earlier than planned). Child benefit would be preserved as a universal benefit, and the party would not axe the winter fuel payment or free TV licences for pensioners.

Cameron and the inner circle debated the proposals throughout August and September. 'There was a nervousness about spelling out in public what we planned to do,' admits a senior Shadow Cabinet member. 'It was the classic political caution of not revealing your hand too early or in too much detail. George didn't want to commit to any further savings than the ones he proposed, but we agreed that if you aspire to govern, you needed to reassure people that you were to move quickly if elected. If we didn't lay it out, Britain's credit rating might well be downgraded on our watch.' Despite the risks of spelling out the party's plan in too much detail, Cameron decided to give the proposals a green light. Financial responsibility trumped all other considerations. 'The inner circle managed to keep the whole thing a secret – even from people in the policy unit in Campaign Headquarters,' says one party insider. 'They kept it very tightly held.'

When delegates arrived in Manchester, the talk was not about spending cuts but about Europe. After a second attempt, the Irish had voted 'Yes' in a referendum on the Lisbon Treaty – the successor treaty to the proposed European constitution which ran into the ground in 2005, when the French and the Dutch voted 'No'. Europe had steadily risen up the political agenda with the expectation that the Irish would vote to ratify the new treaty, which sought to define and expand the powers for various European institutions. Now that they had done so, only Poland and the Czech Republic had yet to ratify the treaty. This put Cameron in an awkward position on the eve of the conference, particularly as he had given a 'cast-iron' pledge to the *Sun* that he would hold a referendum on the treaty if elected.

However, this promise had been given in the expectation that the twenty-seven EU countries would not be able to ratify the treaty before the election; Cameron and Hague had made a vague commitment not to 'let matters rest' if it was indeed ratified. The most ardent Tory Eurosceptics were pressing the leadership to commit to a referendum come what may, but the leadership wanted to avoid giving any impression that the party had revived its old obsession with Europe just in time for the pre-election conference. Cameron declared the Conservatives' continuing opposition to the treaty, but said he would not want to 'prejudice' the decisions of the Czechs and Poles.

A potentially serious problem emerged when Boris Johnson, the Mayor of London, appeared to stray from the agreed line on the first day of the conference. If the treaty was in force by the time of the next general election, he said, 'You could put key parts of this treaty to the people, and you could certainly find out what people thought about it.'[23] Cameron rejected any talk of a 'split' with Boris, but the damage had been done. 'It was not helpful,' recalls one of Cameron's team. After some swift clarifications, the official party line remained in place. Boris's speech, in which he described what he had achieved so far in London, was characteristically upbeat and witty. The enthusiastic applause from the rank and file showed that he had matched or even surpassed William Hague as the darling of the conference.

Labour insiders, however, watched with interest, detecting a more profound difference between Johnson's Conservatism and that of the leadership. 'If there is one person that might help the Tories lose the next election, it's Boris,' a former Number 10 aide says. 'Tony Blair said, "I will know the New Labour project is completed when the Labour Party learns to love Peter Mandelson." The Conservative Party modernisation project will be complete only when they learn to stop loving Boris Johnson.'

Johnson's intervention did not in fact ignite a row about Lisbon. 'Look, Boris is Boris,' insists a senior party aide. 'If you ask me who would you like to cause a problem on Europe at the conference, and one of the options was Boris sounding off, then I would have chosen that one. I don't believe he arrived in Manchester to cause us grief, and the idea that there is some kind of simmering feud between him and David is nonsense.' A number of journalists have sought to tease out the differences between Cameron and Johnson. There is no doubt a degree of rivalry exists, as it does between most ambitious politicians of a similar ilk, and that tensions have arisen between Cameron's office and the Mayor's office in City Hall. But talk of intense jealousy and animosity between the two is way off the mark. 'There is no attempt by David to control Boris, and no attempt by Boris to exert his independence,' says one mutual friend. Boris himself insists that a healthy relationship exists: 'There is a constant to-ing and fro-ing of discussion. London is not a test bed or Petri dish into which the bacilli of Tory policies are being introduced, but the relationship is very good and very close.'[24] One former Cameron aide observed a more nuanced relationship: 'David knows that Boris has to be reeled in sometimes, but that's why Boris is great as Mayor, because that's who you need in that role. We wanted Boris to seem independent, so we stepped back. Sometimes Boris takes a different slant on things, and that's fine with us. We have a vested interest in Boris doing well.' The Lisbon story quickly died after Johnson departed Manchester for London. As news filtered through about the contents of Osborne's proposals the next day, attention soon turned to the central question of how the party would lay out its plans for the economy.

When Osborne delivered his package of proposals on Tuesday, 6 October with the words 'We are all in this together,' the audience in the Manchester Central Conference Centre were restrained in their applause. There were no tax goodies, unlike previous years. Instead, they were given a message of prudence. The meat of the proposals had been briefed to the press the night before, and Alistair Darling had tried his best to scupper Osborne's publicity by announcing that the government would freeze the pay of 40,000 senior civil servants in 2010–11. But Osborne's speech was measured and serious, if not doom-laden.

The proposals took the sting out of the government's attack that the opposition was bereft of policies. The press were largely sympathetic. Some seasoned observers, like Philip Stephens in the *Financial Times*, argued that the message was too pessimistic: 'Most people would agree that Britain will take some time to pay down the debts left by the bust. Many would accept that the Labour government has not removed the scars of poverty and social fracture in many parts of society. But a bankrupt and broken nation? Well, the Tory activists, lobbyists and hangers-on who packed Manchester's bars and restaurants this week seemed prosperous enough.'[25] Osborne and Cameron hoped that the party's proposals would address public concern about the state of the public finances and the economy. If Osborne had delivered a bad-cop address, Cameron would have to play the good cop at the end of the conference with something more uplifting.

Party high command were desperate not to appear triumphalist in Manchester, despite the conference slogan stating that the party was 'Ready for Change'. 'I want to see less champagne bubbles and more bubbling activity,' Party Chairman Eric Pickles told reporters.[26] The mood of sobriety was questioned by some when Cameron himself was photographed sipping a glass of champagne at a party the night before Osborne's speech.

Cameron and his aides knew that his speech on the Thursday had to present a positive reason for people to support the party. Offering spending cuts would not be enough. 'We were all clear that it had to be a blunt speech, but that it couldn't be too gloomy,' one senior aide recalls. 'It was the honesty strategy: telling it to them straight.' Unfortunately, their preparations were interrupted by the news that General Sir Richard Dannatt, who had recently stood down as Chief of the General Staff and had publicly criticised Gordon Brown's decisions on troop numbers in Afghanistan, was going to advise the party on defence matters. Cameron had planned to make the announcement in his speech, having approached Dannatt a few weeks before. Very few were aware of this, including the Shadow Home Secretary Chris Grayling, who described Dannatt's appointment as a 'political gimmick', believing it was Gordon Brown, and not Cameron, who had made it. Grayling's gaffe grabbed the headlines on the eve of Cameron's speech. Aside from the embarrassment, it showed just how tight a grip Cameron's inner circle kept on such matters.

Manchester Central was a poor setting in which to make a speech: when Cameron took the stage, his words often failed to carry. But it was a performance tailored for the television cameras. This was no time for an unscripted, off-the-cuff delivery; he stood at the lectern, speaking calmly. He talked movingly about the death of his son Ivan earlier in the year: 'It's like the world has stopped turning and the clocks have stopped ticking. And as they slowly start again, weeks later, you ask yourself all over again: "Do I really want to do this?" You think about what you really believe and what sustains you.' One passage stirred the passions of Tory delegates: 'Labour still have the arrogance to think that they are the ones who will fight poverty and deprivation. . . . Don't you dare lecture us about poverty. You have failed, and it falls to us, the modern Conservative Party, to fight for the poorest who you have let down.' The audience leapt to their feet for the longest burst of applause of the speech. It was a poignant moment. Five or ten years previously, a Tory leader would have raised the roof at conference by denouncing Labour's record on 'stealth taxes', or lampooning a European directive. It was a sign of how attitudes had changed among the grassroots that Cameron's most impassioned attack on Labour's record focused on poverty. The wider party had not changed in every way the leadership would have had liked, but the delegates' acceptance of the social agenda was significant. Cameron also announced for the first time that Iain Duncan Smith would play a leading role in shaping the social reforms of a future Tory government. This came as no surprise given Duncan Smith's influence on the leadership, but it was nevertheless a significant staging post in his rehabilitation since his downfall in 2003.

Cameron reached the climax of his speech by outlining his vision for the country. This was his moment to recapture the optimistic tone of his first eighteen months as leader. The central argument of his speech was that a Tory government would roll back 'big government' in favour of a 'stronger society'. Many interpreted this as a return to the Thatcherite rhetoric of the past, but it chimed with Hilton and Cameron's belief that individuals and organisations thrive without the constant intervention of the state. 'We can put Britain back on her feet. I know that today there aren't many reasons to be cheerful. But there are reasons to believe. Yes, it will be a steep climb. But the view from the summit will be worth it. Let me tell you what I can see.' He then described a country of 'communities governing themselves' independent of Whitehall, and of people 'pulling together' to make things happen. There were echoes of Tony Blair throughout his finale. He was trying to paint a picture of a modern, forward-looking country, as Blair sought to do in 1996, during his last conference speech before the general election.

After a turbulent year, Cameron's address gave the party something to cheer about. It was not the Cameron of Blackpool in 2005 or 2007. The theatrics of those years would have fallen flat in Manchester – both the venue and the circumstances dictated another approach. The Tory leader had conveyed his ambition to reach for the summit, but he still had a long way to go. Cameron and the rest of the leadership had added some beef to the party's spending plans, but the question remained – had they left the country with an offering that was too sour? Despite Cameron's attempt to paint a vision for the future, it somehow lacked the colour and texture to inspire. Convincing the country that it needed a change of government in May or June 2010 would require a more detailed prospectus.

Jittery Autumn

As the Conservatives prepared for the new parliamentary session, the last before the general election, a feeling of uncertainty descended upon the party. The conference had been a success – the leadership had presented its plans, and the parliamentary party had maintained its discipline. But almost as soon as MPs returned to Westminster the spectre of the expenses scandal loomed once again. Awaiting them were letters from Sir Thomas Legg following his audit of every MP's files. Cameron insisted that Tory MPs would be banned from standing at the next election if they did not accept the Legg report, and the atmosphere in the Commons returned to the mood of despair before the summer recess. 'We got straight back into the expenses saga again,' laments one Tory official. 'The conference season had given us a boost, but it felt like we were back to square one.'

Events further afield presented the leadership with another potential headache. When the Czechs finally ratified the Lisbon Treaty, it was clear that the party would have to change its European policy. This would not please the hardline Eurosceptics, but a referendum on the treaty, which would come into force on 1 December, was now academic. At a press conference on 4 November, Cameron promised that all future European treaties would be put to a public vote. He also promised a sovereignty Bill if the Tories won the next election, to 'lock in' the supremacy of UK laws, and vowed to repatriate powers on the Charter of Fundamental Rights, employment and criminal law. A few Tory MPs and MEPs expressed their discontent, but the party broadly accepted the new position. 'It has been little noticed, but organised Euroscepticism has collapsed,' says one party aide. 'There aren't loads of people spending millions on market research into people's attitudes on Europe any more.'

Inevitably, UKIP raised the ante by arguing that the Conservatives had sold out on a referendum, but even the most ardent Eurosceptics in the parliamentary party were not prepared to cause a fight over the issue. Some in the Shadow Cabinet were less sanguine, believing that at least forty MPs were priming themselves to take up the issue after the election in the event of a Tory victory. 'Oh, they haven't gone away,' says one. 'They'll start sounding off about wanting to leave the EU altogether if they get a chance.' Europe had not disappeared as an issue of importance to many in the parliamentary party and among the grassroots, but Cameron hoped that discipline ahead of the election would hold sway. He had found a practical way to settle the Conservatives' European position, which remained firmly on the side of the Eurosceptic majority in the party. In the event of the Tories forming a government, Europe will be a sensitive subject for the party, just as it was in the late 1980s and 1990s. It will require skilful diplomacy on both sides of the English Channel if Cameron is to succeed where so many of his predecessors came unstuck.

What unsettled the wider party more was the announcement in late October that from 1 January the party would impose all-women shortlists in a small number of seats, to ensure that more women candidates were selected. Twenty-nine per cent of all Tory candidates were women, an improvement on previous election years, but the fact that the latest round of selections had produced only one female candidate caused the leadership to think again. The whole debate about the A-List and interference from the centre was revived. 'It is just not OK in 2009 to have a party with more MPs called David than there are women MPs,' says one of Cameron's confidants. 'We wanted to take the party with us to the maximum extent, but we wanted to make a final push.' This raises the question of why the leadership did not countenance the idea before, instead of during the key period just before a general election. 'We were doing a lot of other things at the time of the A-List which were quite uncomfortable for some in the party, so we had to keep in mind how much of an appetite there was at the time,' says a member of Cameron's circle.

A number of figures in the party sharply criticised the move for being un-Conservative and discriminatory. The influential grassroots Conservativehome.com website denounced it as an 'unacceptable departure from Conservative concepts of meritocracy and trusting people'. The leadership also incurred the wrath of the rank and file in leafy Norfolk (who earned the sobriquet 'the Turnip Taliban') when Cameron backed Elizabeth Truss, the candidate for South West Norfolk, whose affair with a Conservative MP four years earlier was revealed in the press. Local party members claimed not to have known about the affair when she was selected, and forced a deselection meeting on 16 November. Although Truss survived, the tussle between a local association and the party machine illustrated that the tension between the leadership and the grassroots over candidate selection had not disappeared, as well as the cultural differences between the party's London elite and the rural shires. 'People are jittery – the all-women shortlists ruffled feathers among the old guard in the rank and file, and MPs in Westminster are still demoralised after the Legg and Kelly inquiries,' says one senior member of the Shadow Cabinet.

Far more troubling for the leadership was the fact that Gordon Brown had begun to find his stride in late November and early December after months in the doldrums. Although the Queen's Speech contained few pieces of legislation and the Pre-Budget Report was expected to show increasing amounts of public borrowing, the mood in Number 10 and the Parliamentary Labour Party was not as dire as it had been in the summer. The economy was still stuck in recession, but Labour believed that the Tory picture of doom and gloom overstated the seriousness of the situation. Indeed, public pessimism about the state of the economy was not as pronounced as it had been at the beginning of the year. On 2 December, Brown had his best showing at Prime Minister's Questions for over two years. Rumours abounded that the government was going to freeze, or even lower the threshold for, inheritance tax, with the intention of exposing the Tories as the party of the rich. To the cheering of Labour MPs, the Prime Minister suggested that Tory policies had been 'dreamed up on the playing fields of Eton' – a barb at Cameron's education. Number 10 felt that there was still potential to damage the Conservatives as the party of the rich elite. This was ironic, given the fact that Tory proposals to reduce inheritance tax had played a role in preventing Brown calling an early election two years previously.

On a visit to Afghanistan to meet British troops a few days later, Cameron launched a counterattack. 'If Gordon Brown and Mandelson and the rest, if they want to fight a class war, fine, go for it. It doesn't work. It's a petty, spiteful, stupid thing to do, but if that's what they want to do, you know, go ahead.'[27] Cameron's reaction showed that Brown had hit a raw nerve, and was an indication that the election campaign would become personal.

There was some evidence to suggest that Labour's sharpened attack was beginning to make an impression on the opinion polls, which showed a slight narrowing of the Tory lead. 'There is a sense of grim realism around,' says one frontbencher close to the leadership. 'It tempers everyone's confidence. We know that the election is going to be bloody.'

Muted Ambitions

The battle lines were being drawn as the New Year approached. Cameron and his team were preparing the party for a long hard slog to the finish. Despite the jitters of the autumn, the party's own research and polling was showing that it was in a far stronger position in the run-up to the general election than at any time since 1992. Relentless targeting of the 117 seats the party needed to win, which include the key marginals that determine any general election, was bearing fruit. Above all, the Conservatives sought to build support in areas outside the Tory heartlands in the south. The polls of key marginals, particularly in the Midlands and northern England, showed the party maintaining a healthy lead over Labour, while it had made inroads into Liberal Democrat territory in the south-west. Only Scotland remained a desert of support.

Lord Ashcroft's target seat operation was one of the most formidable campaigning machines the party had had for decades. The Conservatives had rebuilt an election machine from the ashes of three successive defeats, just as New Labour had achieved before 1997. On the ground, the party had come a long way from its hollowed-out and defunct presence in large parts of the country. Successive local election gains provided much-needed footsoldiers to work the streets during the campaign. But despite the progress made since 2005 in preparing the party operationally, the weight of defeat in three successive general elections weighed heavily on Cameron and his close team. For them, there was no room for complacency. 'We all feel, from the boss down, that it is a big ask to win this election – the figures are immense,' says one. 'We expect the polls to narrow, and a lot still can happen. It's not a done deal at all.'

The 2010 general election represents the best opportunity for the Conservative Party to win power for a very long time. Not since

1979, and the election of Mrs Thatcher's first government, has the party been in such a strong position to capitalise on the incumbent government's misfortunes. A sense of muted ambition pervades the party. But has it done enough to recover from its near-death experience in opposition? In October 2003, the Conservatives were teetering on the brink after two crushing defeats and a seemingly perennial crisis of leadership. On the two measures that have determined the party's success in the past – adaptability and hunger for office – great strides have been made since the nadir of 2003. The Conservatives under David Cameron have shown a capacity to adapt to fast-moving events. Whether this was by design is questionable, but in responding to a change of Prime Minister in 2007, the economic crisis of 2008–09 and the political crisis of 2009, the leadership has displayed the agility and deft touch that effective opposition requires.

That manoeuvrability was blatantly lacking in the first eight years after the party lost office in 1997. In key areas such as the economy, the new leadership has been dangerously exposed, having devised a threadbare strategy early on, but each time Cameron and Osborne managed to salvage the situation – sometimes only just in time. In good times there was a tendency for the Conservative leader to coast, revealing a flaw in his character. 'He is very good when there is trouble,' remarks a friend. 'Though he is very clever he has quite a conventional mind, and when things appear to be running along fine he just kind of sits back and thinks, "Aren't I clever?" In that way he's not anxious enough, unlike Mrs Thatcher, who was always worrying about the whole thing – she was arrogant, but unbelievably conscientious. David is not exactly lazy, but there is an element of complacency, which comes from him being too much of a well-balanced character.'

When Cameron has had his back to the wall, such as during the election that never was in October 2007 and the expenses scandal, he has been at his strongest. By turning a damaging situation to his party's advantage, reading the public mood and following his gut instincts, he and his party survived. There is no doubt that the whole Cameron project to modernise the Tory Party could have come unstuck in May 2009 if he had not acted so swiftly. If there is a lesson for Cameron from these episodes, it is that however much he thrives under pressure he can never really afford to relax, even in quiet times.

Ideologically, the party has also advanced from the narrow positions it adopted in 2001 and 2005. No longer does it obsess over Europe, tax and immigration at the expense of all other subjects. Cameron has dragged the Tories away from the margins towards the centre of British politics, which had shifted well before the party lost office in 1997. In focusing on the public services and social reform, he has earned the party a right to be listened to by the electorate – including a whole cross-section of voters who once loyally supported the party but have long since deserted it.

However, the party's journey under Cameron since 2005 has not been a carbon copy of what Labour accomplished over a longer period in the 1980s and 1990s. Labour's prolonged spell in the wilderness only came to an end when it effectively abandoned ideological fixations and moved slowly towards the new economic consensus that had been forged by Mrs Thatcher since 1979. It was the only way back for the Labour Party after four successive election defeats. The Tory journey has required an ideological shift in some areas, noticeably abandoning market-based policies in health and education, but it is not on the same scale as the transformation from old Labour to New Labour. Yet it required a change in attitudes, both social and cultural. Even in 2010, it is a process that is far from complete – the divisions that affected the party in the early 2000s have not disappeared altogether. 'There are no longer any factions,' remarks one seasoned frontbencher. 'We used to have wets and dries, Eurosceptics and Europhiles, socially liberal and socially hard. There is a remnant of social authoritarianism, but it's utterly sidelined now. It's no more than a little "Harrumph." Once the sexual agenda was complete – the age of consent for gay people, civil partnerships – and the world didn't collapse, that was that.' The preachy stance that so many senior Tory figures once held, and which so many moderate and young voters since the 1990s found so repulsive, has indeed disappeared.

Yet has the party regained its appetite for power, after so long in opposition? The expenses scandal certainly muted the ambitions of many Tory MPs. In despair, a number lost all hunger for politics, let alone office. As many as thirty-two have announced their departures at the next election, and this could easily rise above forty by polling day. Cameron is not adored by his parliamentary party; they follow him because he is the most electable leader they have had for well over a decade. Some senior figures in the Shadow Cabinet believe that the rebels will surface after the election. 'The problem is the right – there are forty or fifty of them who are annoyed that we are not proposing tax cuts, and all this wet stuff – greenery and quality of life – is nonsense, and that our man sounds like Blair. They want to go back to Thatcherism, and above all want to know why are we not about to declare that we're leaving Europe?' Yet should the party win with even a majority of one, more than half its MPs will be newly elected.[28] Their loyalty in the first instance will be to the man who got them there. There is nothing like success – at the polls, in real votes – to inspire loyalty, as successive Tory leaders since Mrs Thatcher have discovered.

David Cameron and his team are desperate to win, even though some in the party appear to be more fellow travellers than enthusiastic flag-wavers in his mission to change the party. Ken Clarke has served most Tory leaders since being elected to Parliament in 1970. He feels that the hunger for office is not quite as strong as it was in the late 1970s, not least because of weakened morale after the expenses scandal and the twenty-four-hour media appetite for personalised politics. 'The one person who exhibits the hunger all the time is David Cameron – there is a man who really is consumed by a hunger for office. He is determined and ruthless,' he observes.[29]

David Cameron embodies the prospectus of a changed Conservative Party that he hopes to offer at the general election. Gordon Brown's attack on his privileged background revealed that some in the government and the Labour Party are determined to exploit what they perceive as his weakness. Yet the Tory leader's appeal thus far has transcended old-fashioned perceptions of class that once so characterised British politics. 'It is no longer such a disadvantage in life to be an Old Etonian!' remarks a state-educated frontbencher. A more significant flaw in the party's bid for power is that it is too concentrated on Cameron himself. His team believe he is their key electoral asset as a plausible alternative Prime Minister, but voters are also being asked to choose an alternative government. If Cameron performs badly or slips up in some way during the election campaign, the effect on party morale and on the opinion polls could be marked. Indeed, the party's own focus groups reveal that while Cameron's personal 'brand' remains strong, doubts linger about the attraction of his party as a whole.[30] With the exceptions of William Hague, Ken Clarke and George Osborne (and of course Boris Johnson), most people do not recognise the leading Tories. Thirteen years in the wilderness has not helped to raise their profiles, and the leadership will have to do more to present the team as a potential Cabinet-in-waiting as polling day draws closer.

In many ways, David Cameron has emulated Tony Blair as Leader of the Opposition. The elevation of the personality and character of the leader has become a fact of life in modern politics. 'Like Harold Macmillan, David is the best presenter, although we're now in the age of mass-media politics,' reflects one senior frontbencher. 'He's not as good as Blair, but he's getting better.' The modernisation project in Cameron's first eighteen months as leader had all the hallmarks of Blair's project in the early 1990s. The single biggest tribute to Blair, however, stems from a direct acknowledgement that like Thatcher, he changed the terms of debate. 'Labour moved the centre ground of British politics, just as the Conservatives did in the eighties and nineties,' says a senior figure in Cameron's inner circle. 'Blair forced us as a party to come to terms with a number of changes, from the constitution to Bank of England independence, improving the public services for everyone and advancing socially liberal ideas, which we wouldn't dream of unwinding. That's part of his legacy – he pushed us into that by successively defeating us.' What Cameron is particularly aware of is Blair's performance as Prime Minister. 'David knows that Blair left some things too late and squandered his first term – it is a key lesson for us,' remarks one insider. 'If we win, we want to put in place a whole raft of reforms all moving in the same direction. Blair effectively refought the general election every day in his first term – we can't afford to do that.'

Tony Blair's departure from British politics gave the Conservative Party an important fillip. Although his demise and Cameron's sudden rise overlapped, it was clear that he had been the chief obstacle to the party's electoral recovery. Blair was the Viscount Palmerston of his age. Like the nineteenth-century Liberal Prime Minister, he appealed to Tory voters with charm and the good fortune of presiding over a period of prosperity. Palmerston's grip on British politics pushed the Tories to the margins for the best part of two decades, and Blair achieved similar dominance.

Boris Johnson believes that Blair's departure has made the next election an easier battle for the Conservatives. 'I don't think the Conservative Party has somehow changed its core beliefs or mutated or pupated into some beautiful new imago,' he argues. 'David Cameron has the personal qualities to embody an idea of change, and there are some very talented people who are good at creating that sizzling aroma of change and improvement which is important; but the single biggest change that has happened to the Tory Party has been the extinction of Tony Blair. Without that all of the new aroma and modernisation was undetectable as long as Blair hogged the centre ground of British politics.'[31]

This is a fair reflection on the reversal of fortunes between the two parties, although it downplays the fact that if the party had not chosen David Cameron as leader in December 2005 it might not have been in a position to benefit from Labour's unpopularity in the years that followed. Blair's exit may have aided the Tory recovery, but it began on his watch. Gordon Brown's honeymoon threatened to halt it in its tracks, but his misfortunes as Prime Minister played right into the hands of a resurgent Conservative Party. Since Brown failed to seize the opportunity to call a snap election in October

2007, his government has consistently languished in the twenties and low thirties in the opinion polls. When he recovered his standing during the financial crisis Labour closed the gap, but it was short-lived.

The rise and fall of Tony Blair and the predicament of his successor have undoubtedly shaped the recovery of the modern Conservative Party. It is an irony that the leader who presided over a party on the brink of imploding has become highly influential in its resurrection. Iain Duncan Smith's work on social justice has been central to many of the proposed reforms the party aspires to introduce. 'Iain was an unsuccessful leader,' reflects Charles Moore, 'but he launched the idea – crucial to the success of David Cameron – that the party should direct its moral and intellectual energy towards social questions. He beat the right path.'[32]

Added to the social agenda, Cameron will have to convince the country that he has what it takes to restore the country to economic health. If the party wins, it might be fortunate to inherit an economy slowly coming out of recession, but it will be lumbered with the bills. On the other hand, the economy could well deteriorate even further. Cameron's advisers are well aware of the parallels with 1979, when the economy was in difficulty. 'Mrs Thatcher's rhetoric was confrontational, and yet the reality was quite different – she didn't cut public spending; it went up. We actually do need to cut spending, but do it in a consensual and collaborative way.' It will be a tall order. Mrs Thatcher became the most unpopular Prime Minister since the war within a year of entering Downing Street as the economy worsened. 'The argument is, what are we going to do? We're going to inherit a bombed-out economy, and we're not going to have General Galtieri to save us,' worries a frontbencher, reflecting on the Falklands War as the event which helped to revive Mrs Thatcher's fortunes before the 1983 election. Cameron may well need to follow the advice of her successor, the last Conservative Prime Minister, Sir John Major. 'If he wins he'll inherit a truly hideous in-tray, not least one of the worst – if not *the* worst – economic legacy left by any government in modern history. This will seriously curb his freedom of action,' Major says. 'I believe David has the character and fortitude to be a socially sympathetic yet economically tough Prime Minister. He will need to be both, given the fragile state of the country on both fronts.'[33]

The Conservative Party has come a long way since it teetered on the brink of disaster in late 2003. It now stands on the threshold of power after thirteen years in the wilderness. Yet the summit still seems distant. 'The truth is that you can't fully convince people that you have changed in opposition, as they have only heard you say things, not do things,' a senior figure reflects.[34] 'We were elected as New Labour, and we shall govern as New Labour,' Tony Blair told the country only hours before he walked into Downing Street. Like Blair, David Cameron will only be able to prove that his party has really changed once he takes office. If the last four and a half years have been testing for Cameron's Conservative Party, the next few will be far harder, whether the party wins or loses. That decision lies, as ever, in the hands of the voters.

Acknowledgements

It has been an enormous pleasure to write this book, which would not have been completed without the kindness and help of others. I am indebted to Dalia Iskander, who spent the majority of her weekends since last spring transcribing interviews and ably assisting with research. Her enthusiasm for the project has been a source of encouragement throughout. My brother Alex generously gave up much of his time to help process a number of interviews. His assistance towards the end of the project was invaluable. Oriel Carew and Julia Harris also deserve thanks for transcribing several interviews at short notice.

I am deeply grateful to the generosity of those who read draft passages and sections of the book: Anthony Seldon, James Naughtie, Robert Shepherd, Buster Price, Amy Wygant and Laurence Norman. Their comments and advice have been invaluable. I am fortunate to have received the insight and wisdom of Malcolm Balen, Andrew Cooper and Daniel Collings, who have read the entire book, as well as numerous others who commented on particular chapters.

I am indebted to all those who agreed to be interviewed for the book since October 2008. I would especially like to express my appreciation to the following for giving up so much of their time to be interviewed on several occasions: Guy Black, Nicholas Boles, George Bridges, Ken Clarke, Lord Coe, Andrew Cooper, Dominic Cummings, Iain Duncan Smith, George Eustice, Daniel Finkelstein, Michael Gove, William Hague, Michael Howard, Danny Kruger, Mark MacGregor, Andrew MacKay, Lord Marland, Francis Maude, Charles

391

Moore, Archie Norman, Rick Nye, James O'Shaughnessy, Don Porter, Daniel Ritterband, Sir Stephen Sherbourne, Ed Vaizey and David Willetts. A special mention should also be made of the numerous private secretaries and personal assistants who have been most helpful with the arranging and rearranging of interviews.

I would like to thank the following authors whose books (all of which are cited in the bibliography) I have found particularly useful as secondary sources: Francis Elliot and James Hanning for their insightful biography of David Cameron; Michael Crick for his excellent biography of Michael Howard; Jo-Anne Nadler for her elegant life of William Hague and Simon Walters for his inside account of the Hague and the early Duncan Smith years; Anthony Seldon for his biographies of John Major and Tony Blair; Norman Fowler for his revealing account of the party in recent years; Simon Jenkins for his thought-provoking analysis of the Thatcher revolution, and finally David Butler and Dennis Kavanagh for their superb studies of countless general elections.

At the BBC, I would like to thank my former editor at *The Politics Show*, Gavin Allen, who gave valuable advice when I began the book. I am also grateful to the editor and deputy editor of the *Today* programme, Ceri Thomas and Jon Zilkha, for their support and encouragement throughout. It is a privilege to work with such a talented and interesting team of journalists. Conversations with Roger Hermiston, Andrew Hosken, James Naughtie and Evan Davis have been particularly stimulating and have provided many insights. I would like to thank Gillian Dear for her patience in considering numerous rota requests. Elsewhere in the BBC, I have had the pleasure of discussing aspects of the book with Nick Robinson, Martin Rosenbaum and Robert Shepherd (all of whom I was fortunate to work with on a Radio 4 series about British Prime Ministers and a documentary about David Cameron in 2008). Conversations with Giles Edwards, Matthew Pencharz and Michael Cockerell have also proved illuminating.

HarperCollins have been a superb publishing house to work with. My brilliant editor, Martin Redfern, has steered me through the project with great skill and patience. Robert Lacey's meticulous skills as a copy-editor are unsurpassed. I would also like to thank Helen Ellis and her team for their creative endeavours in publicising the book, and Morton Morland for illustrating the cover with such panache.

This book was conceived several months after the publication of *Blair Unbound* in November 2007. There are three people from that project whom I would like to thank expressly for encouraging me to write a book of my own. Andrew Gordon, who edited the two-volume biography at Simon & Schuster, has been instrumental in getting the book off the ground as my agent at David Higham Associates. His experience and advice have been invaluable from beginning to end. I am eternally indebted to Anthony Seldon, who has furnished me with opportunity, knowledge and encouragement for the best part of fifteen years. Were it not for his passion for contemporary history and politics, I doubt whether I would have been inspired to write this book. Finally I would like to extend my gratitude to Daniel Collings. Even from the distance of Washington, DC, his help and advice in all aspects of the book from its inception to its completion have been immense. I could not have been more fortunate in having a friend who is so thoughtful and generous, and I only hope I can repay his kindness in the years to come.

This book was completed as I looked out on the December snowfall in Montreal, far away from the hustle and bustle of Westminster politics. I cannot think of a more serene setting in which to finish a book. I am grateful to Norman and Libby McCullough for their kind hospitality during this time. My sister Briony has been a perennial source of advice and good humour, as have my longstanding friends David Farley and Andrew Trinick. Martin Blocksidge also deserves a special mention for nurturing a passion for writing, as does the late Michael Price, who encouraged a curiosity about all things current and historical. Finally, I would like to thank my parents, Patricia Price and Philip Snowdon, for their love and support throughout. They have, as ever, been a source of strength and encouragement, and I am deeply grateful.

Nothing would have been possible without my fiancée, Julia. From reading chapters to listening to my daily reports of progress or lack of it, she has endured someone who appeared to be just as engaged to the keyboard as to her over the past year. Her love, patience and support have been constant from the beginning. For this reason, I dedicate this book to her.

Sources

Interviewees who agreed to be quoted by name are referred to below, in addition to the other published sources. To avoid endlessly repeating the words 'Private interview' and 'Private information', off-the-record references are not cited individually.

Introduction

1 See Anthony Seldon and Stuart Ball (eds), *The Conservative Century* (Oxford University Press, 1994)

1 The Makings of a Landslide

1 Interview, Lord Coe, 09.03.09
2 Interview, Iain Duncan Smith, 02.06.08
3 Interview, Andrew Cooper, 20.11.08
4 Michael Portillo speaking in *Portillo on Thatcher: The Lady's Not for Spurning*, BBC2, 25.02.09
5 Interview, Andrew Cooper, 20.11.08
6 Interview, Lord Coe, 09.03.09
7 Interview, Archie Norman, 24.02.09
8 Interview, Sir John Major, 04.11.09
9 BBC Analysis and Research, monthly average of published opinion polls, 1983–2010
10 Interview, Ken Clarke, 23.09.09
11 Anthony Seldon, *Major: A Political Life* (Weidenfeld & Nicolson, 1997), p.1
12 Peter Hennessy, *The Prime Minister: The Office and its Holders Since 1945* (Penguin, 2000)
13 Interview, Ken Clarke, 11.02.08
14 Interview, Iain Duncan Smith, 02.06.08
15 Interview, Guy Black, 28.11.08
16 Interview, Rachel Whetstone, 05.11.09

17 Nigel Lawson speaking on *The Thatcher Years*, part 4, BBC1, 27.10.93
18 Nigel Lawson, *The View from No. 11* (Bantam, 1992), p.933
19 Seldon, *Major: A Political Life*, p.111
20 Interview, Sir John Major, 04.11.09
21 David Mellor speaking in *Portillo on Thatcher: The Lady's Not for Spurning*, BBC2, 25.02.09
22 Margaret Thatcher speaking in *The Thatcher Years*, part 4, BBC1, 27.10.93
23 Norman Lamont speaking in *Portillo on Thatcher: The Lady's Not for Spurning*, BBC2, 25.02.09
24 Hansard, 13.11.90, Cols. 464–5
25 Margaret Thatcher speaking in *The Thatcher Years*, part 1, BBC1, 6.10.93
26 Interview, Guy Black, 28.11.08
27 Anthony King, *Daily Telegraph*, 14.12.90
28 Interview, Sir John Major, 04.11.09
29 Ibid.
30 Seldon, *Major: A Political Life*, p.255
31 Judith Chaplin diaries serialised in the *Sunday Telegraph*, 19.09.99; *Independent*, 20.09.99
32 Interview, Sir John Major, 04.11.09
33 Interviewed by the author, *Parliamentary Brief*, February 2006

34 Interview, Sir John Major, 04.11.09
35 Seldon, *Major: A Political Life*, p.287
36 Ibid., pp.314–17
37 Norman Lamont speaking in *Portillo on Thatcher: The Lady's Not for Spurning*, BBC2, 25.02.09
38 Interview, Lord Lamont, 04.03.09
39 *What Does David Cameron Really Think?*, BBC Radio 4, 16.02.08
40 Interview, Sir John Major, 04.11.09
41 Seldon, *Major: A Political Life*, p.321
42 BBC Analysis and Research, monthly average of published opinion polls, 1983–2010
43 *The Best Future for Britain*, Conservative Party manifesto, 1992
44 BBC Analysis and Research, monthly average of published opinion polls, 1983–2010
45 Interview, Ken Clarke, 11.02.08
46 Interview, Iain Duncan Smith, 02.06.08
47 Interview, Sir John Major, 04.11.09
48 See Ivor Crewe in Anthony Seldon (ed.), *How Tory Governments Fall* (Fontana, 1996), p.427
49 Interview, Andrew MacKay, 02.07.09
50 Interview, Lord Hurd, 11.02.08
51 Interview, Sir John Major, 04.11.09
52 *What Does David Cameron Really Think?*, BBC Radio 4, 16.02.08
53 Francis Elliott and James Hanning, *Cameron: The Rise of the New Conservative* (HarperPress, 2007), p.172
54 Interview, Daniel Finkelstein, 09.02.09
55 Interview, George Bridges, 15.10.08
56 Interview, Daniel Finkelstein, 09.02.09
57 Interview, Andrew Cooper, 20.11.08
58 Ibid.
59 Interview, Boris Johnson, 05.06.09
60 Seldon, *Major: A Political Life*, p.3
61 Interview, Sir John Major, 04.11.09

2 Lost in the Wilderness: May 1997–June 2001

1 Seldon, *Major: A Political Life*, p.3
2 Norman Fowler, *A Political Suicide* (Politicos, 2008), p.189
3 Interview, Ann Widdecombe, 28.04.09
4 Interview, Dr Liam Fox, 01.04.09
5 Interview, David Willetts, 20.01.09
6 John Curtice and Michael Steed, 'The Results Analysed' (Appendix 2), in David Butler and Dennis Kavanagh, *The British General Election of 1997* (Macmillan, 1997), p.308
7 Interview, Ken Clarke, 11.02.08
8 See P. Cowley and M. Stuart, 'The Conservative Parliamentary Party', in M. Garnett and P. Lynch (eds), *The Conservatives in Crisis* (Manchester University Press, 2003)
9 Interview, Dr Liam Fox, 01.04.09
10 Interview, Ann Widdecombe, 28.04.09
11 Interview, Michael Simmonds, 18.12.08
12 Interview, Daniel Finkelstein, 10.07.01
13 Interview, William Hague, 10.03.09
14 Interview, Lord Coe, 13.05.09
15 Interview, Daniel Finkelstein, 10.07.01
16 Interview, Ken Clarke, 11.02.08
17 Interview, Lord Coe, 09.03.09
18 Interview, Archie Norman, 19.12.08
19 See M. Garnett and P. Lynch (eds), *The Conservatives in Crisis* (Manchester University Press, 2003), p.91
20 Interview, Lord Coe, 09.03.09
21 Interview, Archie Norman, 19.12.08
22 Interview, William Hague, 10.03.09
23 Interview, Archie Norman, 19.12.08
24 Interview, Lord Parkinson, 18.03.09
25 Interview, William Hague, 10.03.09
26 House of Commons Library note, 'Membership of UK Political Parties', 17.08.09; R. Kelly, 'The Party Didn't Work: Conservative Reorganisation and Electoral Failure', *Political Quarterly*, 73 (2002), p.43
27 Interview, David Willetts, 20.01.09
28 Interview, William Hague, 10.03.09
29 BBC Analysis and Research, monthly average of published opinion polls, 1983–2010
30 Interview, Francis Maude, 04.11.08
31 Interview, Andrew Cooper, 20.11.08
32 Ibid.; *Kitchen Table Conservatives: A Strategy Proposal*, October 1998
33 Interview, Andrew Cooper, 20.11.08
34 Interview, Ann Widdecombe, 28.04.09
35 Interview, Oliver Letwin, 12.03.09
36 Interview, Andrew Cooper, 20.11.08
37 Interview, William Hague, 10.03.09
38 Interview, David Willetts, 20.01.09

39 *New York Times* magazine, February 1999
40 Interview, Peter Lilley, 30.10.08
41 Interview, David Willetts, 21.11.04
42 Interview, Peter Lilley, 30.10.08
43 Interview, Lord Coe, 13.05.09
44 Interview, William Hague, 10.03.09
45 Interview Ann Widdecombe, 28.04.09
46 Interview, Lord Coe, 13.05.09
47 Interview, Michael Howard, 20.01.09
48 Interview, Peter Lilley, 30.10.08
49 Interview, David Willetts, 21.11.04
50 Interview, Daniel Finkelstein, 09.02.09
51 Interview, William Hague, 10.03.09
52 Ibid.
53 Interview, Nick Wood, 16.04.09
54 Interview, Lord Coe, 13.05.09
55 Interview, Nick Wood, 16.04.09
56 Interview, William Hague, 10.03.09
57 Interview, Peter Lilley, 30.10.08
58 *Sun*, 05.10.98
59 Interview, Lord Parkinson, 18.03.09
60 Interview, Nick Wood, 16.04.09
61 Interview, Rick Nye, 19.01.09
62 Interview Ann Widdecombe, 28.04.09
63 Interview, Nick Wood, 16.04.09
64 Simon Walters, *Tory Wars* (Politicos, 2001), pp.20–2
65 Interview, Lord Coe, 13.05.09
66 Interview, Archie Norman, 24.03.09
67 Interview Ann Widdecombe, 28.04.09
68 Ibid.
69 Interview, David Willetts, 20.01.09
70 Interview, Daniel Finkelstein, 23.03.09
71 Interview, William Hague, 10.03.09
72 Ibid.
73 Interview, Lord Coe, 13.05.09
74 Interview, Ken Clarke, 11.02.08
75 Interview, Daniel Finkelstein, 23.03.09
76 *Daily Telegraph*, 01.06.01
77 Interview, Archie Norman, 24.03.09
78 *Financial Times*, 14.05.01
79 Interview, William Hague, 10.03.09
80 Interview, Richard Stephenson, 28.05.09

3 Staring Into the Abyss: June 2001–October 2003

1 Interview, William Hague, 10.03.09
2 See David Butler and Dennis Kavanagh, *The British General Election of 2001* (Palgrave, 2001)
3 BBC News Online, 19.12.99
4 Interview, William Hague, 10.03.09
5 Interview, Iain Duncan Smith, 08.07.08
6 David Mellor speaking on *Portillo on Thatcher: The Lady's Not for Spurning*, BBC2, 25.02.09
7 Interview, Lord Strathclyde, 13.07.09
8 Interview, Dr Liam Fox, 01.04.09
9 Interview, David Willetts, 21.11.04
10 Interview, Daniel Finkelstein, 09.02.09
11 Correspondence with the author, Andrew Cooper, 11.08.09
12 Interview, Archie Norman, 19.12.08
13 *Portillo on Thatcher: The Lady's Not for Spurning*, BBC2, 25.02.09
14 Interview, Andrew Cooper, 20.11.08
15 Interview, Graham Brady, 11.03.09
16 Interview, Michael Gove, 17.12.08
17 Interview, Mark MacGregor, 12.12.08
18 Interview, Archie Norman, 24.03.09
19 Interview, Mark MacGregor, 12.12.08
20 Interview, Andrew Cooper, 20.11.08
21 Interview, Francis Maude, 04.11.08
22 Interview, Paul Goodman, 18.12.08
23 See Giles Brandreth, *Breaking the Code* (Weidenfeld & Nicolson, 1999)
24 Interview, Andrew MacKay, 11.06.09
25 Interview, Owen Paterson, 24.03.09
26 Walters, *Tory Wars*, p.207
27 Interview, David Willetts, 12.03.09
28 Interview, Oliver Letwin, 12.03.09
29 Interview, Iain Duncan Smith, 08.07.08
30 Interview, Charles Moore, 14.01.09
31 Interview, Ken Clarke, 11.02.08
32 Focus group research conducted for Iain Duncan Smith's leadership campaign, July 2001
33 *Daily Telegraph*, 21.08.01
34 Interview, Iain Duncan Smith, 08.07.08
35 Interview, Ann Widdecombe, 28.04.09
36 Interview, Ken Clarke, 11.02.08
37 Interview, Don Porter, 23.07.09
38 Interview, Iain Duncan Smith, 02.06.08
39 Interview, Nick Wood, 01.05.09
40 Interview, Iain Duncan Smith, 08.07.08
41 Interview, Ann Widdecombe, 28.04.09
42 *Independent*, 19.09.01
43 Interview, Rick Nye, 19.01.09
44 Interview, Greg Clark, 19.01.09
45 Interview, Iain Duncan Smith, 08.07.08

46 Interview, Dominic Cummings, 16.03.09
47 Memo from Dominic Cummings to the Strategy Group, 19.03.02
48 Interview, Dominic Cummings, 20.10.09
49 Interview, Greg Clark, 19.01.09
50 Interview, Dominic Cummings, 20.10.09
51 Interview, Dr Liam Fox, 01.04.09
52 Interview, Iain Duncan Smith, 08.07.08
53 Interview, Dominic Cummings, 16.03.09
54 Interview, David Davis, 18.11.09
55 Ibid.
56 *Independent*, 28.07.02
57 Interview, Mark MacGregor, 20.01.09
58 Interview, Paul Goodman, 18.12.08
59 Interview, David Davis, 18.11.09
60 Interview, Nick Wood, 01.05.09
61 *Independent*, 11.10.02
62 Interview, Michael Howard, 20.01.09
63 See Andrew Cooper, 'A Party in a Foreign Land' in Edward Vaizey, Nicholas Boles and Michael Gove (eds), *A Blue Tomorrow: New Visions for Modern Conservatives* (Politicos: 2001)
64 Interview, Mark MacGregor, 20.01.09
65 Interview, Nick Wood, 01.05.09
66 BBC Analysis and Research, monthly average of published opinion polls, 1983–2010
67 Interview, Dominic Cummings, 16.03.09
68 Interview, Lord Marland, 26.11.08
69 Interview, Francis Maude, 04.11.08
70 Vaizey, Boles and Gove (eds), *A Blue Tomorrow: New Visions for Modern Conservatives* (Politicos: 2001)
71 Andrew Cooper, 'A Party in a Foreign Land' in ibid.
72 Interview, Nicholas Boles, 22.10.08
73 Interview, Rick Nye, 19.01.09
74 Interview, Nick Gibb, 20.01.09
75 Interview, Douglas Smith, 19.02.09
76 *Daily Telegraph*, 18.06.01
77 Interview, Douglas Smith, 19.02.09
78 Ibid.
79 Interview, Paul Goodman, 18.12.08
80 Interview, Iain Duncan Smith, 08.07.08
81 Interview, Owen Paterson, 24.03.09
82 Interview, Sir John Major, 04.11.09
83 Interview, Rick Nye, 19.01.09
84 Interview, Owen Paterson, 24.03.09
85 Interview, Don Porter, 23.07.09
86 Interview, Mark MacGregor, 20.01.09
87 *Daily Telegraph*, 15.02.03
88 *The World at One*, BBC Radio 4, 21.02.03
89 Interview, Don Porter, 23.07.09
90 BBC News Online, 07.05.03
91 Ibid.
92 See Justin Fisher, 'Money Matters: the Financing of the Conservative Party' in *The Political Quarterly*, Vol. 75, No. 4, October–November 2004
93 Interview, Lord Marland, 09.10.08
94 BBC News Online, 01.05.03
95 Interview, Ken Clarke, 11.02.08
96 Interview, Iain Duncan Smith, 28.06.07
97 Ibid.
98 Interview, Iain Duncan Smith, 08.07.08
99 Interview, Nick Wood, 01.05.09
100 Interview, Iain Duncan Smith, 08.07.08
101 Interview, Don Porter, 23.07.09
102 Interview, Owen Paterson, 24.03.09
103 Interview, Danny Kruger, 19.01.09
104 Interview, Owen Paterson, 24.03.09
105 Interview, Danny Kruger, 19.01.09
106 Correspondence with the author, Andrew Cooper, 11.08.09
107 Michael Crick, *In Search of Michael Howard* (Pocket Books, 2005), p.425
108 Ibid., p.426
109 Ibid., p.427
110 Interview, Nick Wood, 01.05.09

4 False Dawn:
November 2003–May 2005

1 Interview, Oliver Letwin, 12.03.09
2 BBC Analysis and Research, monthly average of published opinion polls, 1983–2010
3 Interview, Michael Howard, 12.12.08
4 Interview, Oliver Letwin, 12.03.09
5 Interview, Dr Liam Fox, 01.04.09
6 See Michael Crick's *In Search of Michael Howard* for an excellent account of

Howard's life and, in particular, the Paxman interview in May 1997
7 *Sunday Times*, 11.05.97
8 Interview, Graham Brady, 11.03.09
9 Interview, David Davis, 18.11.09
10 Crick, *In Search of Michael Howard*, p.429
11 Interview, David Davis, 18.11.09
12 Ibid.
13 Crick, *In Search of Michael Howard*, pp.429–30
14 BBC News Online, 30.10.03
15 Correspondence with the author, 14.01.09
16 Crick, *In Search of Michael Howard*, p.433
17 BBC News Online, 30.10.03
18 Interview, Michael Howard, 12.12.08
19 Interview, Francis Maude, 04.11.08
20 Interview, Rachel Whetstone, 05.11.09
21 Interview, Michael Howard, 20.01.09
22 Interview, Sir Stephen Sherbourne, 19.11.04
23 Interview, Daniel Ritterband, 18.12.08
24 Interview, Sir Stephen Sherbourne, 19.12.08
25 Ibid.
26 Interview, Guy Black, 20.11.08
27 Interview, Matthew Taylor, 21.10.09
28 *The Times*, 02.01.04
29 Interview, Guy Black, 20.11.08
30 Interview, Ed Vaizey, 22.10.08
31 Interview, Richard Stephenson, 28.05.09
32 BBC Analysis and Research, monthly average of published opinion polls, 1983–2010
33 Interview, Sir Stephen Sherbourne, 19.12.08
34 Ibid.
35 David Butler and Dennis Kavanagh, *The British General Election of 2005* (Palgrave Macmillan, 2005), p.38
36 Iain Duncan Smith, *Briefing*, January 2004
37 Interview, George Bridges, 15.10.08
38 Interview, Guy Black, 28.11.08
39 Butler and Kavanagh, *The British General Election of 2005*, p.36
40 BBC News Online, 03.12.03

41 Interview, Sir Stephen Sherbourne, 19.12.08
42 Interview, Guy Black, 20.11.08
43 Interview, Michael Howard, 12.12.08
44 Interview, Sir Stephen Sherbourne, 19.12.08
45 *Daily Telegraph,* 29.01.04
46 Interview, Ed Vaizey, 22.10.08
47 Interview, Guy Black, 20.11.08
48 Ibid.
49 Interview, Sir Stephen Sherbourne, 19.12.08
50 Interview, Rachel Whetstone, 05.11.09
51 Interview, Guy Black, 20.11.08
52 *Sunday Times*, 18.07.04
53 Interview, Guy Black, 20.11.08
54 Interview, Rachel Whetstone, 05.11.09
55 Hansard, 20 July 2004, col. 203
56 Interview, Sir Stephen Sherbourne, 19.12.08
57 BBC Analysis and Research, monthly average of published opinion polls, 1983–2010
58 Interview, Michael Howard, 12.12.08
59 See Anthony Seldon, *Blair Unbound* (Simon & Schuster, 2007), pp.275–7
60 *Daily Telegraph*, 02.10.04
61 Interview, Guy Black, 20.11.08
62 Interview, Dr Liam Fox, 01.04.09
63 Interview, Lord Saatchi, 13.11.08
64 BBC Analysis and Research, monthly average of published opinion polls, 1983–2010
65 Interview, Lynton Crosby, 14.11.08
66 Ibid.
67 Interview, Michael Howard, 20.01.09
68 Interview, Guy Black, 28.11.08
69 Interview, Lord Saatchi, 13.11.08
70 *Daily Telegraph*, 24.07.04
71 Nick Watt's piece 'Tory Central' in the *Guardian* was one of the first group profiles to appear. *Guardian*, 28.07.04
72 *Daily Mail*, 17.08.04
73 Interview, Nicholas Boles, 22.10.08
74 Interview, Daniel Finkelstein, 23.03.09
75 Interview, Andrew Cooper, 26.11.08
76 Interview, Michael Gove, 17.12.08
77 *What Does David Cameron Really Think?*, BBC Radio 4, 16.02.08
78 Interview, Nicholas Boles, 22.10.08
79 Interview, Michael Gove, 17.12.08

80 Interview, Daniel Finkelstein, 23.03.09
81 Interview, Guy Black, 12.01.09
82 BBC Analysis and Research, monthly average of published opinion polls, 1983–2010
83 Interview, Daniel Ritterband, 18.12.08
84 Interview, Michael Howard, 20.01.09
85 Interview, Guy Black, 28.11.08
86 Ibid.
87 Interview, Sir Stephen Sherbourne, 19.12.08
88 Matthew d'Ancona, *Sunday Telegraph*, 27.03.05
89 *Sunday Times*, 24.04.05
90 Interview, Ken Clarke, 11.02.08
91 Interview, George Eustice, 06.02.09
92 *Guardian*, 19.04.05
93 Interview, Lynton Crosby, 14.11.08
94 Interview, Michael Gove, 17.12.08
95 Interview, Sir Stephen Sherbourne, 12.01.09

5 Signs of Life: May–December 2005
1 *The Times, Guardian*, 06.05.06
2 Interview, Sir Stephen Sherbourne, 12.01.09
3 Interview, Michael Howard, 20.01.09
4 Interview, Rachel Whetstone, 05.11.09
5 Interview, Michael Howard, 20.01.09
6 Interview, Sir Stephen Sherbourne, 20.11.09
7 Interview, Michael Howard, 20.01.09
8 Interview, Rachel Whetstone, 05.11.09
9 Interview, Michael Howard, 20.01.09
10 Interview, Sir Stephen Sherbourne, 12.01.09
11 Interview, Lord Marland, 09.10.08
12 See David Butler and Dennis Kavanagh, *The British General Election of 2005* (Palgrave Macmillan, 2005)
13 Michael A. Ashcroft, *Smell the Coffee: A Wake-Up Call for the Conservative Party* (Michael A. Ashcroft, 2005), pp.98–100
14 Correspondence with the author, Andrew Cooper, 11.08.09; MORI Aggregate Analysis, cited in *The Parliamentary Monitor*, May 2005, Issue 127
15 Correspondence with the author, Andrew Cooper, 11.08.09
16 Interview, David Willetts, 12.03.09
17 Interview, Ann Widdecombe, 28.04.09
18 Interview, Iain Duncan Smith, 08.07.8
19 BBC News Online, 06.05.05
20 Interview, Francis Maude, 04.11.08
21 Interview, Michael Howard, 12.12.08
22 Interview, Oliver Letwin, 12.03.09
23 Interview, Boris Johnson, 05.06.09
24 *Observer*, 08.05.05
25 BBC News Online, 11.07.08; *Daily Telegraph*, 12.06.08
26 Interview, David Davis, 19.11.09
27 Interview, Iain Dale, 27.01.09
28 Interview, David Davis, 19.11.09
29 Interview, Michael Howard, 20.01.09
30 Interview, Rachel Whetstone, 05.11.09
31 Interview, Michael Howard, 20.01.09
32 Interview, Oliver Letwin, 11.06.09
33 *Daily Telegraph*, 20.05.05
34 Interview, Oliver Letwin, 11.06.09
35 Interview, Lord Marland, 26.11.08
36 *Sunday Times*, 08.05.05
37 Interview, Ed Vaizey, 22.10.08
38 *What Does David Cameron Really Think?*, BBC Radio 4, 16.02.08
39 *Evening Standard*, 24.05.05; Interview, Nick Boles, 22.10.08
40 *What Does David Cameron Really Think?*, BBC Radio 4, 16.02.08
41 Ibid.
42 Interview, Nick Gibb, 20.01.09
43 *A 21st Century Party*, 24.05.05
44 *The Times*, 25.05.05
45 *Sunday Telegraph*, 08.05.05
46 Ashcroft, *Smell the Coffee*
47 Interview, David Willetts, 12.03.09
48 Interview, Dr Liam Fox, 01.04.09
49 David Willetts, 'What Does Modernising Conservatism Mean?', speech to the Social Market Foundation, 02.06.05
50 Dr Liam Fox, 'Let Freedom Reign', speech to Politeia, 10.05.05
51 Andrew Lansley, speech, 23.05.05
52 David Davis, 'Modern Conservatism', speech to the Centre for Policy Studies, 04.07.05
53 Edward Leigh, 'The Strange Desertion of Tory England', Cornerstone Group, July 2005
54 David Cameron, 'We're All in it Together', speech to Policy Exchange, 29.06.05

55 Interview, Andrew Cooper, 26.11.08
56 Interview, Oliver Letwin, 11.06.09
57 Interview, James Frayne, 02.04.09
58 Interview, Iain Dale, 27.01.09
59 Interview, Greg Barker, 09.10.08
60 Interview, Michael Howard, 20.01.09
61 Interview, Oliver Letwin, 11.06.09
62 Interview, George Eustice, 18.02.09
63 *The Times*, 25.02.03
64 Interview, Oliver Letwin, 11.06.09
65 Interview, David Willetts, 20.01.09
66 Interview, Daniel Ritterband, 18.12.08
67 Interview, George Eustice, 18.02.09
68 Interview, David Willetts, 12.03.09
69 *Sunday Times*, 04.09.05
70 Interview, George Eustice, 18.02.09
71 Interview, Michael Gove, 26.10.09
72 Interview, George Eustice, 18.02.09
73 Interview, Oliver Letwin, 11.06.09
74 Interview, Paul Goodman, 18.12.08
75 BBC News Online, 03.10.05
76 Interview, Lord Marland, 09.10.08
77 *What Does David Cameron Really Think?*, BBC Radio 4, 16.02.08
78 Interview, George Eustice, 18.02.09
79 Interview, Andrew Mitchell, 12.05.09
80 Interview, Paul Goodman, 18.12.08
81 Interview, Andrew Cooper, 26.11.08
82 Interview, Greg Barker, 09.10.08
83 Interview, Paul Goodman, 18.12.08
84 Ibid.
85 Interview, Andrew Mitchell, 12.05.09
86 Interview, Peter Kellner, 18.09.08
87 Interview, Greg Barker, 09.10.08
88 Ibid.
89 Interview, Andrew Mitchell, 12.05.09
90 Interview, Iain Dale, 27.01.09
91 Interview, Greg Barker, 09.10.08
92 Interview, Dr Liam Fox, 01.04.09
93 Interview, Andrew Mitchell, 12.05.09
94 Ibid.
95 Interview, Andrew MacKay, 11.06.09
96 Interview, Greg Barker, 09.10.08
97 Interview, Lord Hurd, 12.02.08
98 Interview, George Eustice, 23.02.09

6 Leaving the Comfort Zone: December 2005–December 2006
1 Interview, Ed Vaizey, 28.11.05
2 Hansard, 07.12.05, Col. 861
3 Seldon, *Blair Unbound*, p.418

4 Letter to the *Guardian*, 11.11.09 from Bryan Criddle, co-author, *The Almanac of British Politics*
5 Interview, David Davis, 18.11.09
6 Interview, William Hague, 10.03.09
7 Iain Duncan Smith and Danny Kruger, *Good for Me, Good for My Neighbour* (Centre for Social Justice, May 2005)
8 Interview, Iain Duncan Smith, 08.07.08
9 *Observer*, 18.12.05
10 Interview, Oliver Letwin, 11.06.09
11 Ibid.
12 *Daily Telegraph*, 23.12.05
13 *Guardian*, 16.01.06
14 Interview, George Bridges, 27.01.09
15 Interview, George Eustice, 23.02.09
16 Interview, George Bridges, 27.01.09
17 Interview, Andrew Cooper, 26.11.08
18 BBC Analysis and Research, monthly average of published opinion polls, 1983–2010
19 Interview, George Bridges, 27.01.09
20 Ibid.
21 Interview, Daniel Ritterband, 09.02.09
22 Interview, George Bridges, 27.01.09
23 *Built to Last*, The Conservative Party, February 2006
24 *Daily Telegraph*, 01.03.06
25 BBC News, 12.12.05
26 Interview, Francis Maude, 04.11.08
27 Interview, Michael Gove, 26.10.09
28 Interview, George Bridges, 09.02.09
29 Interview, George Bridges, 27.01.09
30 Interview, Nick Boles, 17.03.09
31 Interview, Andrew MacKay, 11.06.09
32 Interview, George Bridges, 27.01.09
33 *Observer*, 02.09.07
34 *Daily Telegraph*, 11.07.06
35 Interview, Danny Kruger, 19.01.09
36 See Seldon, *Blair Unbound*, pp.479–99
37 Interview, Danny Kruger, 19.01.09
38 Ibid.

7 The Great Escape: January–October 2007
1 An ICM poll for the *Guardian* on 20 February 2007 put Cameron thirteen points ahead of Brown. *Guardian*, 20.02.07
2 Interview, David Willetts, 13.07.09
3 *Daily Telegraph*, 02.12.06

4 Interview, Don Porter, 23.07.09
5 Interview, Francis Maude, 04.11.08
6 Interview, George Bridges, 09.02.09
7 Ibid.
8 BBC Analysis and Research, monthly average of published opinion polls, 1983–2010
9 Interview, David Willetts, 13.07.09
10 *Guardian*, 09.01.06
11 Interview, Andrew MacKay, 02.07.09
12 Conservative Party manifesto 1997; *Conservative Campaign Guide 2005*
13 YouGov poll, *Daily Telegraph*, 18.05.07
14 Interview, Graham Brady, 11.03.09
15 Conservative Party website, 21.05.07
16 Interview, Graham Brady, 11.03.09
17 *Evening Standard*, 31.05.07
18 Interview, David Willetts, 13.07.09
19 BBC News Online, 25.09.05
20 *Sunday Telegraph*, 27.05.07
21 Interview, Andrew MacKay, 02.07.09
22 Interview, Andrew Cooper, 20.11.08
23 *Guardian*, 16.11.06
24 BBC News, 27.06.07
25 *Daily Telegraph*, 18.06.07
26 In conversation with the author, 01.07.07. See Seldon, *Blair Unbound*, p.xiv
27 *Daily Telegraph*, 13.06.07
28 *Independent*, 19.11.06
29 BBC Analysis and Research, monthly average of published opinion polls, 1983–2010
30 Interview, Francis Maude, 02.07.09
31 BBC Analysis and Research, monthly average of published opinion polls, 1983–2010
32 *Sunday Telegraph*, 20.05.07
33 *Sunday Telegraph*, 22.07.07
34 Interview, George Eustice, 23.02.09
35 Interview, Andrew Mitchell, 12.05.09
36 Interview, Peter Lilley, 30.10.08
37 Interview, Lord Marland, 26.11.08
38 Interview, Andrew MacKay, 11.06.09
39 *Guardian*, 24.08.09
40 *Daily Telegraph*, 04.09.07
41 Interview, Don Porter, 23.07.09
42 Interview, Andrew MacKay, 11.06.09
43 BBC News Online, 13.09.07
44 *Sunday Telegraph*, 16.09.07
45 Interview, William Hague, 10.03.07

46 Ibid.
47 Interview, Andrew MacKay, 11.06.09
48 *Evening Standard*, 03.10.07
49 Interview, Andrew MacKay, 11.06.09
50 Interview, Lord Hurd, 12.02.08
51 *News of the World*, 07.10.07
52 *Guardian*, 22.10.07
53 Interview, Nick Boles, 17.03.09

**8 Riding High:
October 2007–September 2008**
1 *Evening Standard*, 09.10.07
2 *Guardian*, 10.10.07
3 Hansard, 10.10.07, Col. 289
4 The Poynter Report, 25.06.08
5 *Guardian*, 29.11.07
6 BBC Analysis and Research, monthly average of published opinion polls, 1983–2010
7 Interview, James O'Shaughnessy, 06.04.09
8 Interview, Oliver Letwin, 11.06.09
9 Interview, James O'Shaughnessy, 20.01.09
10 Interview, Francis Maude, 04.11.08
11 BBC News Online, 18.09.09
12 BBC News Online, 29.01.08
13 *Today* programme, BBC Radio 4, 29.01.08
14 Interview, Andrew MacKay, 02.07.09
15 *Independent*, 21.04.08
16 BBC Analysis and Research, monthly average of published opinion polls, 1983–2010
17 Interview, Daniel Ritterband, 09.02.09
18 Interview, Boris Johnson, 05.06.09
19 *Daily Telegraph*, 16.07.07
20 BBC News Online, 27.09.07
21 Interview, Lord Marland, 26.11.08
22 Interview, Boris Johnson, 05.06.09
23 BBC Analysis and Research, monthly average of published opinion polls, 1983–2010
24 Interview, David Davis, 18.11.09
25 Ibid.
26 Interview, Andrew MacKay, 02.07.09
27 *Independent*, 17.06.08
28 *Sunday Telegraph*, 16.06.08
29 Interview, David Davis, 18.11.09
30 Ibid.
31 BBC Analysis and Research, monthly

average of published opinion polls, 1983–2010

32 *Guardian*, 30.07.08

9 Crunch Time:
September 2008–April 2009

1 Interview, Ken Clarke, 23.09.09
2 BBC News Online, 23.09.08
3 Populus time series on the economy, September 2007–June 2008
4 *Financial Times*, 05.10.08
5 *Andrew Marr Show*, BBC 1, 05.10.08
6 *New York Times*, 13.10.08
7 Interview, Ken Clarke, 23.09.09
8 *Daily Telegraph*, 05.10.08
9 BBC News Online, 19.10.08
10 *The Times*, 21.10.08
11 Ibid.
12 BBC News Online, 19.10.08
13 Conservative Party statement on BBC News Online, 19.10.08
14 *The World at One*, BBC Radio 4, 27.10.09
15 Elliott and Hanning, *Cameron*, p.357
16 BBC News Online, 05.11.08
17 Richard Wolffe, *The Making of Barack Obama* (Virgin Books, 2009) p.268
18 BBC News Online, 24.11.08
19 Interview, Ken Clarke, 23.09.09
20 Ibid.
21 *Sun*, 14.01.09
22 Interview, William Hague, 10.03.09
23 BBC Analysis and Research, monthly average of published opinion polls, 1983–2010
24 Interview, James O'Shaughnessy, 21.01.09
25 Interview, William Hague, 10.03.09
26 *Sunday Times* cited on BBC News Online, 27.02.09
27 *Independent*, 24.04.09

10 Aiming for the Summit:
May–December 2009

1 YouGov surveys, 14.03.09 and 16.05.09
2 BBC Analysis and Research, monthly average of published opinion polls, 1983–2010
3 Robert Winnett and Gordon Rayner,

No Expenses Spared (Bantam Press, 2009), p.169
4 Ibid., p.168
5 BBC News Online, 11.05.09
6 Ibid.; Winnett and Rayner, *No Expenses Spared*, pp.173–4
7 BBC News Online, 11.05.09
8 BBC News Online, 12.05.09
9 Hogg argued that he had not specifically claimed for the £2,200 bill for clearing the moat, and would repeat this defence to the television cameras the following morning, before changing his position by lunchtime, when he accepted that the moat claim had not been 'positively excluded' from paperwork he submitted to the Commons fees office in support of his allowances claim for the upkeep of his estate. He later agreed to pay back the money. *Daily Telegraph*, 12.05.09, BBC News Online, 12.05.09
10 *Guardian*, 12.05.09
11 *The World at One*, BBC Radio 4, 21.05.09
12 *Observer*, 03.05.09
13 *Guardian*, 04.06.09
14 Fraser Nelson, *Spectator* (Coffee House blog), 27.05.09
15 BBC News Online, 10.06.09
16 *The Times*, 15.06.09
17 Interview, David Willetts, 13.07.09
18 Interview, Ken Clarke, 23.09.09
19 *Guardian*, 09.07.09
20 *The Times*, 09.07.09
21 *Guardian*, 30.09.09
22 *Independent*, 01.10.09
23 BBC News Online, 05.10.09
24 Interview, Boris Johnson, 05.06.09
25 *Financial Times*, 08.10.09
26 *Scotsman*, 07.10.09
27 BBC News Online, 06.12.09
28 *The Times*, 03.12.09
29 Interview, Ken Clarke, 23.09.09
30 *Observer*, 06.12.09
31 Interview, Boris Johnson, 05.06.09
32 Interview, Charles Moore, 14.01.09
33 Interview, Sir John Major, 04.11.09
34 Interview, David Willetts, 13.07.09

Bibliography

Ashcroft, Michael A., *Smell the Coffee: A Wake-Up Call for the Conservative Party*, (London: Michael A. Ashcroft, 2005)

Ball, Stuart and Seldon, Anthony, *Recovering Power: The Conservatives in Opposition Since 1867* (London: Palgrave Macmillan, 2005)

Blake, Robert, *The Conservative Party from Peel to Major* (London: Heinemann, 1997)

Brandreth, Gyles, *Breaking the Code: Westminster Diaries* (London: Weidenfeld & Nicolson, 1999)

Butler, David and Butler, Gareth, *Twentieth-Century British Political Facts 1900–2000* (London: Macmillan, 2000)

Butler, David and Kavanagh, Dennis, *The British General Election of 1992* (London: Macmillan, 1992)

Butler, David and Kavanagh, Dennis, *The British General Election of 1997* (London: Macmillan, 2001)

Butler, David and Kavanagh, Dennis, *The British General Election of 2001* (London: Palgrave Macmillan, 2001)

Butler, David and Kavanagh, Dennis, *The British General Election of 2005* (London: Palgrave Macmillan, 2005)

Clark, Alan, *Diaries* (London: Weidenfeld & Nicolson, 1993)

Clark, Alan, *The Tories: Conservatives and the Nation State 1922–1997* (London: Weidenfeld & Nicolson, 1998)

Clark, Alan, *The Last Diaries* (London: Weidenfeld & Nicolson, 2002)

Crick, Michael, *In Search of Michael Howard* (London: Pocket Books, 2005)

Crowson, N.J., *The Longman Companion to the Conservative Party Since 1830* (London: Longman, 2001)

Elliot, Francis and Hanning, James, *Cameron: The Rise of the New Conservative* (London: Harper Perennial, 2009)

Fowler, Norman, *A Political Suicide* (London: Politicos, 2008)

Garnett, Mark and Lynch, Philip (eds), *The Conservatives in Crisis* (Manchester: Manchester University Press, 2003)

Gould, Philip, *The Unfinished Revolution* (London: Abacus, 2001)

Hennessy, Peter, *The Prime Minister: The Office and its Holders Since 1945* (London: Penguin, 2000)

Jenkins, Simon, *Thatcher & Sons: A Revolution in Three Acts* (London: Penguin, 2006)

Jones, Dylan, *Cameron on Cameron: Conversations with Dylan Jones* (London: Fourth Estate, 2008)

Lawson, Nigel, *The View from No. 11* (London: Bantam, 1992)

Lee, Simon and Beech, Matt (eds), *The Conservatives Under David Cameron* (London: Palgrave Macmillan, 2009)

Major, John, *The Autobiography* (London: HarperCollins, 2000)

Nadler, Jo-Anne, *William Hague: In His Own Right* (London: Politicos, 2000)

O'Hara, Kieron, *After Blair* (London: Icon Books, 2007)

Ramsden, John, *An Appetite for Power* (London: HarperCollins, 1998)

Rawnsley, Andrew, *Servants of the People* (London: Hamish Hamilton, 2000)

Seldon, Anthony (ed.), *How Tory Governments Fall* (London: Fontana, 1996)

Seldon, Anthony, *Major: A Political Life* (London: Weidenfeld & Nicolson, 1997)

Seldon, Anthony, *Blair* (London: Simon & Schuster, 2004)

Seldon, Anthony and Ball, Stuart (eds), *Conservative Century: The Conservative Party Since 1900* (Oxford: Oxford University Press, 1994)

Seldon, Anthony and Collings, Daniel, *Britain Under Thatcher* (Harlow: Longman, 2000)

Seldon, Anthony and Snowdon, Peter, *The Conservative Party: An Illustrated History* (Stroud: Sutton, 2004)

Seldon, Anthony with Snowdon, Peter and Collings, Daniel, *Blair Unbound* (London: Simon & Schuster, 2007)

Shepherd, Robert, *The Power-Brokers: The Tory Party and its Leaders* (London: Hutchinson, 1991)

Sorkin, Andrew Ross, *Too Big to Fail: Inside the Battle to Save Wall Street* (London: Allen Lane, 2009)

Thatcher, Margaret, *The Downing Street Years* (London: HarperCollins, 1995)

Trewin, Ion, *Alan Clark: The Biography* (London: Weidenfeld & Nicolson, 2009)

Vaizey, Edward, Boles, Nicholas and Gove, Michael (eds), *A Blue Tomorrow: New Visions for Modern Conservatives* (London: Politicos, 2001)

Walters, Simon, *Tory Wars* (London: Politicos, 2001)

Wheatcroft, Geoffrey, *The Strange Death of Tory England* (London: Penguin, 2005)

Winnett, Robert and Rayner, Gordon, *No Expenses Spared* (London: Bantam, 2009)

Wolffe, Richard, *The Making of Barack Obama* (London: Virgin Books, 2009)

Young, Hugo, *One of Us: A Biography of Margaret Thatcher* (London: Macmillan, 1991)

Index